Still Sovereign

Still Sovereign

Contemporary Perspectives on Election, Foreknowledge, & Grace

Edited by Thomas R. Schreiner
and Bruce A. Ware

Baker Books
A Division of Baker Book House Co
Grand Rapids, Michigan 49516

Published by Baker Books
a division of Baker Book House Company
P.O. Box 6287, Grand Rapids, MI 49516-6287

Fourth printing, December 2004

Printed in the United States of America

Published 1995 in two volumes titled
The Grace of God, the Bondage of the Will: Volume 1,
    Biblical and Practical Perspectives on Calvinism
The Grace of God, the Bondage of the Will: Volume 2,
    Historical and Theological Perspectives on Calvinism

Library of Congress Cataloging-in-Publication Data

Schreiner, Thomas R. and Ware, Bruce A.
    Still Sovereign / edited by Thomas R. Schreiner and Bruce A. Ware.
      p.   cm.
    Includes bibliographical references.
    ISBN 0-8010-2232-0
    1. Grace (theology) 2. Calvinism. 3. Arminianism. 4. Predestination—Biblical teaching. I. Schreiner, Thomas R. II. Ware, Bruce A.
    BT761.2.G694   1995
    234´.9—dc20   95-6821

For information about academic books, resources for Christian leaders, and all new releases available from Baker Book House, visit our web site:
                        http://www.bakerbooks.com

Contents

Part 3   Pastoral Reflections

Abbreviations

AB	Anchor Bible
Am Pres	American Presbyterians
BAGD	W. Bauer, W. F. Arndt, F. W. Gingrich, and F. W. Danker, Greek-English Lexicon of the New Testament
BASOR	Bulletin of the American Schools of Oriental Research
BDF	F. Blass, A. Debrunner, and R. W. Funk, A Greek Grammar of the New Testament and Other Early Christian Literature
Bib	Biblica
BibSac	Bibliotheca Sacra
CBQ	Catholic Biblical Quarterly
CH	Church History
CTJ	Calvin Theological Journal
EQ	Evangelical Quarterly
HTR	Harvard Theological Review
ICC	International Critical Commentary
Int J Ph Rel	International Journal for the Philosophy of Religion
JBL	Journal of Biblical Literature
JCS	Journal of Cuneiform Studies
JETS	Journal of the Evangelical Theological Society
J Pres H	Journal of Presbyterian History
JSNT	Journal for the Study of the New Testament
JSNTSup	Journal for the Study of the New Testament—Supplement Series
KJV	King James Version
LCC	Library of Christian Classics
LCL	Loeb Classical Library
LSJ	Liddell-Scott-Jones, Greek-English Lexicon
LXX	Septuagint
mg	margin
NASB	New American Standard Bible
NCB	New Century Bible
NEB	New English Bible
NIBC	New International Biblical Commentary
NICNT	New International Commentary on the New Testament

NICOT	New International Commentary on the Old Testament
NIDNTT	*New International Dictionary of New Testament Theology*
NIGTC	New International Greek Testament Commentary
NIV	New International Version
NKJV	New King James Version
NovT	*Novum Testamentum*
n. s.	new series
NTS	*New Testament Studies*
Perkins J	*Perkins Journal*
Ref J	*Reformed Journal*
Ref R	*Reformed Review*
Ref Th R	*Reformed Theological Review*
RSV	Revised Standard Version
SJT	*Scottish Journal of Theology*
TDNT	*Theological Dictionary of the New Testament*
TDOT	*Theological Dictionary of the Old Testament*
TNTC	Tyndale New Testament Commentaries
ThZ	*Theologische Zeitschrift*
Trinity J	*Trinity Journal*
TToday	*Theology Today*
TynBul	*Tyndale Bulletin*
USQR	*Union Seminary Quarterly Review*
WEC	Wycliffe Exegetical Commentary
Wesley Th J	*Wesleyan Theological Journal*
WTJ	*Westminster Theological Journal*
WUNT	Wissenschaftliche Untersuchungen zum Neuen Testament
ZTK	*Zeitschrift für Theologie und Kirche*

Contributors

S. M. Baugh. Ph.D., University of California, Irvine. Assistant Professor of New Testament, Westminster Theological Seminary in California.

Jerry Bridges. Staff member, The Navigators Community Ministries Group. Author and lecturer.

D. A. Carson. Ph.D., University of Cambridge. Research Professor of New Testament, Trinity Evangelical Divinity School.

Edmund P. Clowney. D.D., Wheaton College. Adjunct Professor of Practical Theology, Westminster Theological Seminary in California.

Wayne Grudem. Ph.D., University of Cambridge. Professor and Chairman of Biblical and Systematic Theology, Trinity Evangelical Divinity School.

Raymond C. Ortlund, Jr. Ph.D., The University of Aberdeen. Senior Minister, First Presbyterian Church, Augusta, Georgia.

J. I. Packer. D. Phil., Oxford. Board of Governors' Professor of Theology, Regent College.

John Piper. D. Theol., University of Munich. Senior Pastor, Bethlehem Baptist Church, Minneapolis.

Thomas R. Schreiner. Ph.D., Fuller Theological Seminary. Professor of New Testament Interpretation, Southern Baptist Theological Seminary.

C. Samuel Storms. Ph.D., University of Texas, Dallas. President, Grace Training Center, Metro Vineyard Fellowship, Kansas City, Missouri.

Bruce A. Ware. Ph.D., Fuller Theological Seminary. Associate Dean of the School of Theology and Director of Professional Studies, Southern Baptist Theological Seminary.

Donald J. Westblade. Ph.D. candidate, Yale University. Assistant Professor of Religion, Hillsdale College.

Robert W. Yarbrough. Ph.D., University of Aberdeen, Scotland. Resident Research Scholar, The Scriptorium.

Preface

We are pleased to offer a reprinting of these fourteen chapters from the original two-volume *The Grace of God, the Bondage of the Will.* We are sorry that, for reasons of space, some chapters had to be omitted. Yet, we believe that these essays continue to contribute much needed argumentation for a view of God that displays his majesty, glory, and sovereignty most fully and most faithfully.

Ours is a culture in which the tendency is to exalt what is human and diminish what is divine. Even in evangelical circles, we find increasingly attractive a view of God in which God is one of us, as it were, a partner in the unfolding drama of life. But lost in much of this contemporary evangelical theology is the full omniscience, omnipotence, splendor, greatness, supremacy, rulership, and unqualified lordship of God. In contrast, the vision of God affirmed in these pages is of One who reigns supreme over all, whose purposes are accomplished without fail, and who directs the course of human affairs, including the central drama of saving a people for the honor of his name, all with perfect holiness and matchless grace.

The essays here also speak of the responsibility humans bear before this sovereign Lord and King. While many think that a strong view of God's comprehensive sovereignty rules out human responsibility, we believe the Scriptures make clear that both truths must be held. The bondage of the will (as used by Luther, and noted in the opening sentence of our original introduction) does not mean that fallen humans possess no will or are incapable in any absolute sense to exercise that will. Rather, it means that whenever and wherever they do use their will, they are bound to use it for sinful purposes. They are, then, "bound" to sin, though the choice of which sin is theirs to make. And herein lies the basis for responsibility. While God sovereignly regulates all that occurs in history, including the choices and actions of human beings, all humans use their volition to choose what they fully intend to carry out. They intend. They choose. They act. Yet, in and through all this, God's will is performed, not frustrated. As Joseph states so clearly in Genesis 50:20 regarding the responsible actions of his brothers, "You meant it for evil, but God meant it for good." God is sovereign in and through the free actions we perform and for which we bear responsibility. The Bible everywhere affirms this, and so we believe.

We hope and pray these essays will shed some light on several facets of this complex but beautiful doctrinal gem. We wish for God to be exalted. That his glory matters most must be reaffirmed today when we are told in so many ways it is we who are most valuable. We pray that self-esteem will give way to God-esteem, that human elevation will be transformed into divine glory, and that our joy will be found, as God intends, in him alone. We hope and pray that God will be pleased with the meager efforts of these pages to extol his greatness. He is, indeed, still sovereign.

Thomas R. Schreiner
Bruce A. Ware

Introduction

The discerning reader will note that the original title of this work is dependent upon Martin Luther's famous response to Erasmus, *The Bondage of the Will*.[1] We are convinced that Luther was correct in his understanding of sinful human inability to know, please, or seek after the true God. Prior to the provision of God's effectually drawing grace, the human will is in bondage to sin. All people as descendants of Adam are born with a sin nature (Rom. 5:12–19). As descendants of Adam they are destined to die (Rom. 5:15, 17), condemned before God (Rom. 5:16, 18), and constituted as sinners (Rom. 5:19). What is the extent of sin's hold upon unbelievers? Scripture clearly teaches that before salvation we are in bondage to sin. Paul says in Romans 6:15–23 that unbelievers are "slaves of sin." Slaves to sin cannot do what is right, nor do they want to do what is right. Being a slave to sin involves a willing captivity to its power. "The sinful mind is hostile to God. It does not submit to God's law, nor can it do so. Those controlled by the sinful nature cannot please God" (Rom. 8:7–8). Notice that Paul does not merely say that unbelievers do not obey God's law. He specifically says that they cannot obey it. The motivation of their heart is to carry out the desires of the flesh (cf. Eph. 2:1–3).

In this doctrine of sinful depravity and moral inability, Paul reflects Jesus' previous teaching. In John 3, for example, Jesus makes clear that those who are morally corrupt and so engaged in evil deeds both love the darkness of their evil (3:19) while they correspondingly hate the light of God's revelation and truth (3:20). This leads them, on their own, to flee from the light (3:20). In contrast, those in whom God's grace has been at work (3:21b) come to the light and carry out deeds fitting to that light. Apart from grace, sinful humans persist in their love affair with evil and their hatred of God's glorious truth.

How can the bondage of the human will be broken? Only by the liberating and enlivening grace of God. That is why we initially titled our work *The Grace of God, the Bondage of the Will*. Human beings do not have the ability or the desire to break the power of sin.

All evangelicals would agree that grace breaks the power of sin. This agreement goes only so far, however, for we have very different conceptions

---

1. In *Luther and Erasmus: Free Will and Salvation*, LCC (Philadelphia: Westminster, 1969). *The Bondage of the Will* was translated and edited by P. S. Watson.

13

of grace. Calvinists do not understand grace as merely providing the opportunity to choose what is right. We understand the Bible to present this grace, rather, as a power that transforms the desires of the heart, so that people turn from sin and begin instead to delight in God as their highest treasure. In the descriptive language of Jesus, they are transformed from those who love evil and hate the truth into people who love and practice the truth (John 3:19–21). God's grace, then, does not merely make personal saving faith possible; it effects and guarantees it. Augustine was profoundly right when he said, "Give what you command, and command what you will." His point in saying this was to stress that we cannot obey God's commands unless he grants us the power to keep them. Apart from the power of transforming grace we will always choose to sin.

The differing conceptions of grace are apparent when a reader compares our previous title to two books, *Grace Unlimited* and *The Grace of God, the Will of Man,* edited by Clark Pinnock.[2] The understanding of grace in these works is that grace is distributed equally to all people, and that is why it is unlimited. The "will of man" chooses whether to submit to grace given. In this scheme the human will plays the ultimate and decisive role in personal salvation.

Our understanding of God's saving grace is very different. We contend that Scripture does not teach that all people receive grace in equal measure, even though such a democratic notion is attractive today. What Scripture teaches is that God's saving grace is set only upon some, namely, those whom, in his great love, he elected long ago to save, and that this grace is necessarily effective in turning them to belief.

This latter understanding of grace is found, for example, throughout John 6.[3] Take John 6:37, "All that the Father gives me will come to me; and whoever comes to me I will never drive away." The "coming" of John 6:37 is synonymous with "believing." That the words *coming* and *believing* are different ways of describing the same reality is confirmed by what Jesus says in John 6:35, "I am the bread of life. He who comes to me will never go hungry, and he who believes in me will never be thirsty." To come to Jesus is to satisfy one's hunger and to believe in him is to quench one's thirst. It is easy to see from this verse that "coming" and "believing" are synonyms, just as the metaphors of satisfying one's hunger and quenching one's thirst are parallel ways of saying that Jesus meets our every need. Two verses later Jesus says "all that the Father gives me will come to me." We would not, therefore, do

2. *Grace Unlimited*, ed. Clark H. Pinnock (Minneapolis: Bethany Fellowship, 1975); *The Grace of God, the Will of Man: A Case for Arminianism*, ed. Clark H. Pinnock (Grand Rapids: Zondervan, 1989).
3. For a fuller discussion of effectual calling and grace in John 6 and other texts, consult Bruce A. Ware, chapter 8 of this work.

any violence to the meaning of this verse in wording it as follows: "All that the Father gives to me shall believe in me." Of course, not all people "come to" or "believe in" Jesus. The verse says that this will be true only of those whom the Father has given to Jesus. In other words, only some have been given by the Father to the Son, and they will come, and they will never be cast out, and they will be raised up on the last day (John 6:39–40).

Or, consider John 6:44, "No one can come to me unless the Father who sent me draws him; and I will raise him up at the last day." The first half of this verse indicates, as Arminians gladly acknowledge also, that God's grace (i.e., the drawing of the Father) is necessary for personal salvation. But the question before us is what kind of grace this is. Is it unlimited or common grace, given to all? Or is it a particular grace, an efficacious grace given only to some? The second half of verse 44 answers our question, for there we find that the one who is drawn is also raised up on the last day. In other words, the one who is given grace (who is drawn by the Father) is actually saved (raised up). The drawing of the Father, then, is not general, but particular, for it accomplishes the final salvation of those who are drawn. God's grace, without which no one can be saved, is therefore an efficacious grace, resulting in the sure salvation of those to whom it is given.

The point we have been making is that the grace of God is given effectively and savingly only to some. This is what theologians have meant when they spoke of irresistible grace. This does not mean that people do not or cannot resist the Holy Spirit. Stephen accuses his hearers of this very fault (Acts 7:51). And Paul warns believers who possess the Spirit not to grieve (Eph. 4:30) or quench (1 Thess. 5:19) the Spirit of God. What it does mean is that God overcomes the resistance of those whom he has chosen and brings them savingly to himself. Pinnock and like-minded persons would decry this position as a limitation of grace and exalt their view as "grace unlimited." What is limited or unlimited depends upon one's perspective. We find the view of grace espoused by Pinnock and others to be quite limited because it does not necessarily effect anything. It only makes personal salvation possible. In our understanding grace in fact is unlimited in its power because it actually and necessarily effects salvation; it accomplishes what God has purposed. Human beings do choose to believe, but they make that choice only because divine grace opens otherwise blind eyes to see the beauty of the glory of Christ (2 Cor. 4:6).

Unity and Controversy

Perhaps we should say something about theological writing that engages in controversy. Is it edifying and useful to argue about such matters? Why cannot we as Christians celebrate what we agree upon instead of criticizing each other? We heartily agree that unity is to be cherished. Contrary to the opinion of some, heaven will be more interesting and delightful because we will all agree theologically. Our hearts are in danger of being captivated by a negative spirit if we find ourselves drawn toward attacking the views of others. Let us say at the outset, therefore, that controversy for the sake of controversy is no virtue. We respect those with whom we disagree. We want to acknowledge that thoughtful and intelligent Christian people have raised numerous hard questions for the position we advance as the Bible's own teaching. Their questions have provoked us to examine afresh the view we hold and to see if these things are really taught in Scripture (Acts 17:11). We know that God can work powerfully in those who are of a different theological persuasion, as the life of John Wesley so wonderfully illustrates. We believe with all our hearts that it is possible to disagree passionately with people, even to see their views as wrong and harmful, and still love them.

Unity is something to be cherished, but not at all costs. There is also a place for "contend[ing] for the faith that was once for all entrusted to the saints" (Jude 3). Elders are to exhort in "sound doctrine and refute those who oppose it" (Tit. 1:9). It is appropriate "to correct with gentleness those who are in opposition" (2 Tim. 2:25, authors' translation). Our motivation is to speak "the truth in love" (Eph. 4:15).

Motives for This Work

We hope that the preceding comments illumine the spirit with which this work is written. But it should also be said that we believe that the teaching espoused by Arminians is incorrect and will, to the degree it is accepted, work to weaken the church of Jesus Christ. Our motive, then, in producing this work is not at all to engage in academic jousting. Rather our motives are several.

First, we love the doctrines of grace, for these doctrines are at the center of the glory of God. We believe that these doctrines, rightly understood, are the foundation for a God-glorifying, Christ-centered, Spirit-saturated, Scripture-based theology. They keep us radically God-centered instead of human-centered. God deserves all the praise, glory, and honor for our salvation. He saved us "to the praise of his glorious grace" (Eph. 1:6, 12, 14). We would never have chosen him on our own, and thus we bow down before our sovereign God with joy and holy fear. We believe what Yahweh said about Israel long ago is true of the church of Jesus Christ as well:

> For my own name's sake I delay my wrath;
>   for the sake of my praise I hold it back from you,
>   so as not to cut you off.

> See, I have refined you, though not as silver;
>   I have tested you in the furnace of affliction.
> For my own sake, for my own sake, I do this.
>   How can I let myself be defamed?
>   I will not yield my glory to another. (Isa. 48:9–11)

We fear that denial of the doctrines of grace involves a reduction of the supremacy of God in the minds and hearts of God's people. The God-centered vision of Scripture is foreign to all of us, and we need the corrective glasses of Scripture to see it.

Second, the doctrines of grace provide for a strong, faithful, confident, and joy-filled church. When people catch a vision of the undeserved, freely bestowed, and life-transforming power of the grace of God that broke through their hardness of heart and enlivened their wills to respond in joyous faith to God in Christ; when they see that God's plan from eternity past was to provide a Savior and the sure work of the Spirit to ensure their salvation; when they understand the glory of God manifest in God's free choice to secure those whom he alone can effectively save; and when they revel in the confidence that it is to holiness and Christlikeness that they have been called, and that God will not fail to fulfill his purposes—the result is a joy and a longing for faithfulness that flows out of a deeply-informed realization of the surpassing greatness of God's love for his people, unto his matchless glory. Strength of character, faithfulness in conduct, courage of conviction, humility of spirit, and hope for the future all stem from these glorious doctrines of grace. With these, the church is strengthened; without them, the church is hindered.

Third, these doctrines also fill us with faith and hope that the cause of God will triumph in the world. His "purpose will stand" and he will "do all that [he] please[s]" (Isa. 46:10). God's electing work does not diminish missions but provides the motivation to engage in it. Despite all the obstacles involved in the missionary task, we know that he has purchased some persons for God "from every tribe and language and people and nation" (Rev. 5:9). Jesus assures us, "I have other sheep that are not of this sheep pen. I must bring them also. They too will listen to my voice, and there shall be one flock and one shepherd" (John 10:16). Notice that Jesus says that he will bring in the other sheep that have not yet come. He will bring them in; they shall hear his voice; and they shall become one flock with those previously saved, following their common Good Shepherd. The cause of the gospel will triumph; it will succeed! Those who are brought in will hear Jesus' voice through his disciples, for they will come to believe in him "through their [the disciples'] message" (John 17:20). Many mission fields are exceedingly difficult, but Jesus has promised that there are those who will respond. Such confidence in the power of the gospel (Rom. 1:16) and the certainty that Christ will not fail to build his church (Matt. 16:18) can only serve to encourage and to empower the missionary to press on.

Fourth, the doctrines of grace motivate us to pray. We do not simply pray that God will move on people so that it is possible for their wills to respond. Such prayers are characterized by hesitancy since their outcome is dependent ultimately on the human will. We pray rather that God will invade their lives and turn the desires of their heart around so that they will be saved. We do not ask God simply to make salvation possible; we pray that God will save them, all the while knowing that God's perfect will, from all eternity, is alone wise and right.

Fifth, the doctrines of grace and divine providence are a bulwark for suffering. The world is a frightening place, and horrible sufferings occur. The Book of Job teaches us that no suffering occurs, even that which Satan brings, apart from God's will. Not a sparrow falls apart from God's will, and God has numbered the hairs of our heads (Matt. 10:29–30). The inference is that nothing happens to us that does not pass through God's loving hands. We are not saying that suffering will not be agonizingly painful, nor are we suggesting that there will be no process of questioning or grief. But we are saying that we can live in the confidence that no action or event—not one!— can ever occur outside of God's all-encompassing and wise plan. Even though life is not always easy, "God works for the good of those who love him, who have been called according to his purpose" (Rom. 8:28). We can trust our lives to a loving Father who shelters us under his wings and works everything out so that we will be more like Jesus (Rom. 8:29). The world is not spinning out of his control. He is guiding it according to his own wise plan, which is beyond our understanding.

Having said this, we are convinced that the central reason that the doctrines of grace are questioned is not because of scriptural exegesis, although we grant that those who disagree with us would interpret many Scriptures differently. But their fundamental objections are certain logical problems that are provoked by the Augustinian-Calvinist theology we affirm. It should be granted that the logical difficulties raised pose legitimate and difficult questions for those who embrace Calvinism. The objections go something like this: If God chooses only some, then how can he be loving? If God's grace is irresistible, then what happens to human free will? If God saves those he has chosen, why pray or get involved in missions? If God is in control of the world, then why do anything at all? If God is sovereign, then why is there suffering in the world? If God governs all events, then why is evil our responsibility, not his?

Calvinists would not answer all of these questions in the same way. In fact, as careful readers will surely observe, there are differing opinions even among the contributors to this work as to the most satisfying answers to these questions. Nonetheless, there would be agreement among Calvinists that God is sovereign, and that his free election of individuals to receive his efficacious grace alone accounts for personal salvation. God's unconditional election and irresistible grace cause all who believe to put their faith in Christ to be saved. We suggest that the answers to the preceding questions are often complex because the reality of life as portrayed by the Scriptures is complex. God is completely sovereign, and yet human choices and responsibility are not a charade. God ordains all that comes to pass and is good; and yet evil exists, and it is really evil. God chooses only some to be saved, and yet there is also a true sense in which he desires the salvation of all. Those who are elect will never lose their salvation, and yet those who do not persevere to the end will not inherit the kingdom of God. All Calvinists we have ever read acknowledge that the full and final resolution of divine sovereignty and human responsibility is a mystery. People do not become Calvinists because Calvinism solves all such logical problems. Rather, the fundamental reason people should embrace the Calvinist doctrines of grace is because they believe these doctrines are taught in Scripture. Our attempt to solve the problems posed by our theology, then, is an example of "faith seeking understanding."

Structure of This Work

In this work we hope to demonstrate that Calvinist theology is still the most satisfying approach, both biblically and theologically, to the doctrines of grace. We are grateful to the contributors, among whom are a number of well-known authors who have powerfully supported Augustinian theology for years. Others are scholars and pastors who will, Lord willing, continue to have an influence in the church of Christ in the coming years. The chapters are divided into three sections, the first two of which contain essays devoted to biblical exegesis and theological issues. The last section presents the practical concerns of God's sovereignty.

We want to give readers a taste of what is in store for them. One's theology should be based on careful and thorough biblical exegesis. It is conventional to say this, but Scott Hafemann has prophetically warned evangelicals that a return to biblical exegesis is the crying need of the hour.[4] The first four chapters, by Ray Ortlund, Robert Yarbrough, Don Westblade, and Tom Schreiner, are foundational, in that they demonstrate that the Calvinist understanding of divine sovereignty and unconditional election is rooted in the biblical text. The Arminian view founders because it cannot adequately explain the teaching of divine election found in the Old Testament, John, and Paul (not to mention other New Testament authors who could have been

---

4. Scott Hafemann, "Seminary, Subjectivity, and the Centrality of Scripture: Reflections on the Current Crisis in Evangelical Seminary Education," *JETS* 31 (1988): 129–43.

covered). These chapters convincingly demonstrate that the Calvinist ideas of election and divine sovereignty flow from the most natural and responsible reading of Scripture.

This is not to say that there are not hard texts for Calvinists. The theology that should be accepted must provide a plausible explanation of all the scriptural data. Thus, John Piper tackles the difficult issue of whether or not there are two wills in God. Some texts say that God chooses only some to be saved, while others say that God desires all to be saved. How do these two fit together? The virtue of Piper's essay is that he considers both sides of the biblical evidence, explaining in what sense both assertions are true. In addition, his answer is clearly based on biblical exegesis, and he does not conveniently appeal to an outside standard to solve the problem. Too many biblical scholars today, even among evangelicals, reject any attempt to discern how Scripture fits together theologically. Such a course is exceedingly dangerous because it is a tacit admission that Scripture does not speak a unified word, and thus each person chooses his or her preference.

Another difficult area is represented by the texts in Scripture that threaten judgment on those who fall away. Many different texts could have been examined, but most scholars agree that the warnings in Hebrews raise the most difficult questions for Calvinists who believe in the perseverance of the saints. An analysis of the warning passages in Hebrews, then, would be representative of how such texts should be handled. Wayne Grudem in a careful and innovative exegetical analysis takes seriously the warnings given in Hebrews, and also shows that they do not yield the conclusion that believers can apostasize.

The biblical meaning of "foreknowledge" has been a perennial debate between Calvinists and Arminians. The nub of the controversy focuses particularly on what the word means in texts that speak of God's foreknowledge. S. M. Baugh demonstrates that the term refers to God's foreordination of future events and includes the idea of God's covenantal commitment. He also shows that those who deny God's exhaustive foreknowlege have become subbiblical and have fallen prey to the same errors as the Socinians.

Section 2 examines several crucial theological issues. Bruce Ware analyzes the role that the twin doctrines of effectual calling and irresistible grace play in a Calvinistic soteriology. He demonstrates that these doctrines are firmly established by Scripture's teaching; and as such, they provide necessary support for Calvinism while rendering an Arminian-Wesleyan soteriology impossible.

Arminians, especially from the Wesleyan tradition, have defended the idea that all people have the ability to choose salvation because God has shed his prevenient grace upon all. The chapter by Tom Schreiner explores the biblical support for prevenient grace in the Wesleyan sense. He concludes that the

Wesleyan conception of prevenient grace cannot be found in Scripture, and thus one of the key and necessary pillars of Wesleyan theology falls away.

A complicated theological issue relates to the assurance of the saints. Calvinists stress that one must obey God in order to persevere, but if this is true then how can one have assurance of salvation, for how does one know that one will persevere? D. A. Carson, who is well known for his exegetical and theological work, steers a sophisticated and biblically grounded course in his chapter, deftly balancing the various biblical and theological issues. He explains how believers can be assured that God will finish the good work he has begun; at the same time, the warnings given in Scripture to wavering believers are to be taken seriously.

Equilibrium is also needed in order to understand the scriptural teaching on God's love. There is a sense in which God loves all people, and another sense in which his love is particularly set upon those whom he has chosen to be his people. One of the foremost evangelical theologians, J. I. Packer, demonstrates how these different strands of biblical teaching relate.

Divine sovereignty is important because it makes a difference in everyday life. Randall G. Basinger thinks that Calvinist theology does not make any difference because the Calvinist and Arminian will do the same things, despite their theology.[5] Basinger operates with a reductionistic view of human beings, so that what ends up counting is external human behavior. He does not take into account the role that beliefs, hopes, motivations, and convictions take in human behavior. Arminians and Calvinists may both get involved in evangelism and use the same material, but with different theologies of evangelism. Jerry Bridges is well known for his immensely practical but theologically rooted books on Christian living. He has written a powerful book on the difference divine sovereignty makes in suffering.[6] In this essay he provides further sensible help, explaining the practical benefits of believing in divine sovereignty.

One of the most common objections raised against divine sovereignty is that it takes away the motivation to pray and to evangelize. Samuel Storms is a pastor-theologian who has written on both prayer and divine election.[7] As a pastor he is committed to seeing biblical truth become a reality in the lives of his people. He explains why divine sovereignty is a boon to prayer and evangelism.

5. Randall G. Basinger, "Exhaustive Divine Sovereignty: A Practical Critique," in *The Grace of God, the Will of Man: A Case for Arminianism,* ed. Clark H. Pinnock (Grand Rapids: Zondervan, 1989), 191–205.

6. Jerry Bridges, *Trusting God* (Colorado Springs: NavPress, 1988); see also his *Transforming Grace: Living Confidently in God's Unfailing Love* (Colorado Springs: NavPress, 1991).

7. C. Samuel Storms, *Chosen for Life: An Introductory Guide to the Doctrine of Divine Election* (Grand Rapids: Baker, 1987) and *Reaching God's Ear* (Wheaton: Tyndale, 1988).

Some pastors believe in divine sovereignty but do not think that the doctrine should be preached, since it is controversial. This is a tragic mistake, for it provides strength to the people of God and was revealed for our good. Edmund Clowney has made a notable impact in his preaching and writing. He shows how divine sovereignty undergirds the preaching task.

Our prayer is that God may be pleased to use this volume to strengthen his people in the conviction that the doctrines of grace are both true and God-glorifying. As this occurs we trust that people will be built up in their faith and hope in the invincibility of God's purposes. And furthermore, we earnestly desire this conviction and confidence to have a fortifying effect in bold, holy, and sacrificial Christian living, preaching, prayer, and mission. May God's matchless name be proclaimed and glorified to the ends of the earth!

Part 1
Biblical Analyses

1

The Sovereignty of God:
Case Studies in the Old Testament

RAYMOND C. ORTLUND JR.

Does the Old Testament teach the sovereign freedom of God in his dealings with man, as classical Calvinism affirms?[1] The purpose of this chapter is to argue afresh that the Old Testament does indeed contain such teaching. It is not the purpose of this chapter to explore the profound mystery of divine sovereignty interfacing with human responsibility.[2] I aim rather to demonstrate that passages in the Old Testament can be shown to be agreeable with the confidence of Calvinism that, from his position of absolute supremacy, God rules over all things in a way which necessarily precludes his being limited by creaturely factors.

In pursuing this aim I am in no way insinuating a denial of the reality of human responsibility. Rather, I wish to follow Holy Scripture in its strong

---

1. "God from all eternity did, by the most wise and holy counsel of his own will, freely and unchangeably ordain whatsoever comes to pass; yet so, as thereby neither is God the author of sin, nor is violence offered to the will of the creatures, nor is the liberty or contingency of second causes taken away, but rather established," according to the Westminster Confession of Faith, 3.1.

2. I prefer "responsibility" to "free will," since human agency is limited in many immutable ways, whether one is a Calvinist or an Arminian or a Hindu. Every one of us lives within the circle of a God-ordained existence, for his glory and our own joy, and we are morally accountable to respond to our limitations and possibilities, as set for us by God's decrees and providences, with reverent trust. Moreover, the words *free will* often carry the connotative baggage of "autonomous and undetermined" will (to quote John Murray, *Collected Writings* [Edinburgh: Banner of Truth Trust, 1977], 2:60), which concept I deny most emphatically. If we are created beings, then in what meaningful sense can we boast autonomy without pushing God away to some sort of deistical remoteness?

affirmation of the ultimacy of God over and in all things, including authentic human responsibility. I will leave to others the further question as to how divine sovereignty and human responsibility dovetail in such a way that the moral significance of human agency is safeguarded while, at the same time and in a deeper sense, human agency in no way whatever limits the freedom and efficacious power of God or renders uncertain the fulfillment of his eternal decrees. I believe that reality does indeed disclose the infallibly effectual unfolding of God's will through responsible human agency, and I have a few thoughts on how such a wonder might make sense; but here I intend only to ground the doctrine of God's sovereignty in the bedrock of several specific Old Testament passages. For all who accept the biblical text as their major premise in theological thought, any other questions subsequently raised must be considered in the clear and glorious light of the doctrine of God's unfrustrated sovereignty, once it is established exegetically.

The collections of essays entitled *Grace Unlimited* and *The Grace of God, the Will of Man* together devote only one chapter to the Old Testament.[3] Regrettably, this chapter overlooks conspicuous Old Testament declarations of God's sovereignty. For example, no mention is made of God's decision to bypass Esau in favor of Jacob or of the hardening of Pharaoh's heart, both of which are important in Paul's New Testament exposition of the sovereign ways of God. Reading this essay, one would never know that the Old Testament declares:

"Who gave man his mouth? Who makes him deaf or mute? Who gives him sight or makes him blind? Is it not I, the LORD?" (Exod. 4:11)

"I form the light and create darkness,
I bring prosperity and create disaster;
I, the LORD, do all these things." (Isa. 45:7)

Why, O LORD, do you make us wander from your ways
and harden our hearts so that we do not revere you? . . .
No one calls on your name
or strives to lay hold of you;
for you have hidden your face from us
and made us waste away because of our sins.
Yet, O LORD, you are our Father.
We are the clay, you are the potter;
we are all the work of your hand. (Isa. 63:17; 64:7–8)

3. David J. A. Clines, "Predestination in the Old Testament," in *Grace Unlimited*, ed. Clark H. Pinnock (Minneapolis: Bethany House, 1975), 110–26. Pinnock surveys the primeval history from creation to Abraham on pages 95–109 of the same volume, but his purpose seems less to expound the narrative than to use it as illustrative of the authenticity of human free will.

> Who can speak and have it happen,
>   if the Lord has not decreed it?
> Is it not from the mouth of the Most High
>   that both calamities and good things come? (Lam. 3:37–38)
>
> His dominion is an everlasting dominion;
>   his kingdom endures from generation to generation.
> All the peoples of the earth are regarded as nothing.
> He does as he pleases
>   with the powers of heaven
>   and the peoples of the earth.
> No one can hold back his hand
>   or say to him: "What have you done?" (Dan. 4:34–35)

Such striking testimonies to God's supremacy over us, which not only invite theological exploration but also demand bowed heads and humbled hearts, are disregarded in the Arminian presentation. Moreover, the discussion that is offered lacks the exegetical demonstration necessary to give the argument persuasive force. My point in making this critical observation is simply to explain why this chapter will not respond directly to the Old Testament argumentation put forward in *Grace Unlimited* and *The Grace of God, the Will of Man*. There is little to respond to.

I intend to show that the Old Testament contains passages which must, by any reasonable interpretative standard, be accepted as teaching a divine sovereignty operative in human life that is *individual* (rather than merely corporate), *salvific* (rather than merely historical), and *effectual* (rather than contingent).[4] Let us consider three such texts.[5]

---

4. As one observes in the pattern of argumentation in *Grace Unlimited* and *The Grace of God, the Will of Man: A Case for Arminianism*, ed. Clark H. Pinnock (Grand Rapids: Zondervan, 1989), these points are central to the difference between the Arminian and the Calvinistic readings of Scripture. Arminianism gravitates toward a diffused, corporate election of a people of God to play a special role in history, a calling which they may frustrate and perhaps even defeat. Calvinism gravitates toward an election of individuals to constitute the people of God, who are destined, far beyond their appointed historic mission, to their true inheritance in heaven, their sinful resistance to which is anticipated, compensated for, made to be useful, and effectually overcome by sovereign grace. The particular line of argument I have taken does not permit me to address the important question of the election of the nation of Israel. Paul's commentary on God's choice of Israel in Romans 9 is discussed, however, by Thomas R. Schreiner in chapter 4 of this work. (Please note that the word *salvific*, as used in this text, is not intended to mean "converting" sovereignty only but, more largely, "ministering" sovereignty in the fullest sense, including aspects of the whole of God's gracious care for the believer.)

5. Rather than survey broadly the Old Testament vision of God's sovereignty, I prefer to open up a few select passages, since, at the end of the day, the argument will stand or fall at the exegetical level. For a more sweeping summary of this Old Testament doctrine, see D. A. Carson, "Broad Motifs in the Old Testament," in *Divine Sovereignty and Human Responsibility* (Atlanta: John Knox, 1981), 18–38—although the purpose of Carson's work is to set forth the wholesome tension which exists between divine sovereignty and human responsibility in the Bible rather than to respond critically to Arminianism as such.

Psalm 139

Psalm 139 is divided into four paragraphs of six verses each. In verses 1–6, David affirms God's intimate knowledge of him. In verses 7–12, he affirms God's ubiquitous presence with him. In verses 13–18, he affirms God's sovereign creation of him. And in verses 19–24, David responds to God's love with open-hearted consecration. It is important to bear in mind that, as David composes this psalm, his life is at risk. He has taken a stand for God, but powerful and villainous people are opposing him for it. Their hatred of God leads them to hate David and threaten his very life, as may be surmised from verses 19–22. He does not yet know what will become of him, but his response is to flee by faith to God. There, in God's presence, David takes stock of his life. "What do I have going for me? What can I count on right now?" And he finds assurance in the truths that God knows him searchingly, that God is with him universally, and that God created him sovereignly. Rather than feel threatened by such a God, David draws strength from his loving care and is renewed within to fight on.

Our interest here lies in the first and third paragraphs. Firstly then, in verses 1–6, David prays, "God, you know me."

> O LORD, you have searched me
> and you know me. (v. 1)

In Job 28:3 the verb translated "search" is used of miners digging down into the earth. In Judges 18:2 it is used of explorers spying out a land. In Proverbs 25:2 it is used of kings inquiring into the depths of an intellectual problem. In an analogous sense, God has searched through David with the result that he knows him thoroughly. It is evident from verse 23, moreover, that David is not threatened by this all-knowing God. He gladly opens his heart to and finds reassurance in God's penetrating scrutiny of his soul.

When the risen Lord appeared to the apostle John to address the seven churches of Asia Minor, he revealed himself as one "whose eyes are like blazing fire . . . who searches hearts and minds" (Rev. 2:18, 23). He began his message to each of the seven churches with the words, "I know." And in the Book of Acts God is twice described as the "Heartknower" (Acts 1:24; 15:8).[6] In the letter to the Hebrews we read that "nothing in all creation is hidden from God's sight. Everything is uncovered and laid bare before the eyes of him to whom we must give account" (Heb. 4:13). Therefore, what David affirms with regard to himself in Psalm 139 is no less true for all of God's people. The psalm is paradigmatic of the ways of God.

---

6. I owe this observation to John R. W. Stott, *What Christ Thinks of the Church* (Grand Rapids: Eerdmans, 1972), 75.

You know when I sit and when I rise;
you perceive my thoughts from afar. (v. 2)

Before a word is on my tongue
you know it completely, O LORD. (v. 4)

In verse 2a David acknowledges that his outward behavior lies exposed before God, while in 2b David extends the divine knowledge even to his inner life, his secret thoughts, motives, and desires. God knows it all "from afar." In verses 7–12 David makes the point that God is always present with him. The distance in view in verse 2, then, must be not spatial but temporal, as this word is also used in Isaiah 22:11, 25:1, and 37:26. Long before any impulse wells up from within David's psyche, long before David himself knows what his next mood or feeling will be, long before he knows where his train of thought will eventually lead, God perceives it all.

Verse 4 makes the same point, only reinforcing it with respect to the very words coming out of David's mouth. Before David said "Before," God knew it. Before he said "a," God knew it. Before he said "word," and so on. God is never caught by surprise or thrown off balance by David. God also knows what David's enemies are going to plot against him before they themselves know. No one gets a step ahead of this omniscient God, and David drinks this truth in as his theological fountain of youth.

You hem me in—behind and before;
you have laid your hand upon me. (v. 5)

In the first line of this verse David uses a strong word, weakly rendered "hem in" by the New International Version. This verb is frequently used in the Old Testament of an army laying siege to a city, as when Joab besieged Rabbah (1 Chron. 20:1). David is confessing his vivid awareness of God's unrelenting attentions bombarding the fortress of his soul from all sides. Wherever he turns, David is confronted by the all-seeing eyes of God. As a result, God has David under his control, as the second line implies. All David can do is yield. And neither may David's enemies touch him, unless God allows it.

Such knowledge is too wonderful for me,
too lofty for me to attain. (v. 6)

Now David concludes, with relief and joy, that he is no match for this all-knowing God. Is it not interesting how David presses his theology to the limit, seeking reassurance that no conceivable extremity of distress could possibly push him out beyond the range of God's watchful care? David's whole point in verses 5–6 is that he cannot surprise God, he cannot anticipate

God, he cannot move ahead of God. And so he collapses in a sort of glad defeat, overwhelmed by this inescapable and loving God. Everywhere he turns, every thought he thinks, every fear he dreads, David encounters God, and he joyfully surrenders.

How then can God be thought of as one who responds to man, in an Arminian sense?[7] If God exercises such foreknowledge of us as we see in Psalm 139, then in what ultimate sense is God in a position of responding to us? How can we limit God's choices or impose conditions upon him? And more to the point exegetically, for what purpose is David reviewing the truth of God's intimately personal omniscience? To draw strength from this God who never loses sight of him, who understands what he is thinking and how he is feeling right now and who is always far out ahead of David's current situation. Divine foreknowledge, one of the very things some Arminians seem anxious to minimize by qualifications, David glories in. There is more at variance between Arminianism and Calvinism than theological formulation. These systems also represent two disparate sets of values and affections. Arminianism rejoices in human autonomy and divine limitation, while Calvinism rejoices in human dependence and divine all-sufficiency.

Then, in verses 13–18, David prays, "God, you made me."

> For you created my inmost being;
> you knit me together in my mother's womb.
> I praise you because I am fearfully and wonderfully made;
> your works are wonderful,
> I know that full well. (vv. 13–14)

The emphatic word in the first line of verse 13 is "you." Behind, in, and through the natural process of fetal development, God himself was at work on David: "*You* made me."[8] To separate the work of God from the secondary causes and processes he employs to accomplish his will is highly artificial biblically and quite unnecessary logically. However events emerge and transpire, they are "your works," according to verse 14. The Arminian impulse, so quick to distinguish the human from the divine in the unfolding of

7. Cf. Jack W. Cottrell, "Conditional Election," in *Grace Unlimited*, 64: "This is the very essence of Christianity: because man has sinned, God has provided redemption. Virtually every action of God recorded in the Bible after Gen. 3:1 is a *response* to human sin. The Abrahamic covenant, the establishment of Israel, the incarnation of Jesus Christ, the death and resurrection of Christ, the establishment of the church, the Bible itself—all are part of the divine reaction to man's sin." To identify God's responsiveness to human sin as the essence of the gospel, rather than God's own intention to glorify himself through our redemption, marks a significant difference in basic orientation between Arminianism and Calvinism.

8. J. A. Motyer writes, "The Bible does not exercise itself to deny chains of causation, but equally it is not accustomed to clog up its reasoning by giving them undue prominence. It leaps back directly to the divine Agent from whom come all things and by whose will they happen." Quoted in Carson, *Divine Sovereignty*, 27.

events—to guard the autonomy of human agency, presumably—seems a curiously misplaced concern. David feels no such urgency in his interpretation of reality, as one can see here. Indeed, it is the very presence of God within events which David finds reassuring.

David also confesses that God created his "inmost being." The usage of this word (e.g., Prov. 23:16, "my *inmost being* will rejoice"; Ps. 73:21, "my *spirit* was embittered") suggests that this is David's psyche, his inner man responding freely to the realities of his experience. And David is saying that God created and shaped this very capacity for perceiving, thinking, and feeling. The only instrument David has for connecting with reality is David, and God crafted even that. Although his inner reflexes are authentic and morally significant—as their appearance in the psalm implies, to say nothing of biblical teaching generally—they cannot be thought of as functioning autonomously, for God made them by his own sovereign act to begin with. God and David, then, cannot be equal players in the operation of reality, however divine sovereignty and human responsibility interact.

> My frame was not hidden from you
>   when I was made in the secret place.
> When I was woven together in the depths of the earth,
>   your eyes saw my unformed body.
> All the days ordained for me
>   were written in your book
>   before one of them came to be. (vv. 15–16)

The New International Version's rendering of verse 16 obscures the force of the text, as if it were declaring that the total number of days in David's life were recorded in God's book.[9] But that is not what the Hebrew suggests, nor is it as relevant to David's controlling purpose in the psalm. That God has ordained the number of days David will live is not unimportant, but David's actual point is more profound. The Revised Standard Version interprets the Hebrew text more plainly:

> . . . in thy book were written, every one of them,
>   the days that were formed for me,
>   when as yet there was none of them.[10]

9. One notes with interest the interpretative footnote in *The NIV Study Bible* at this point: "The span of life sovereignly determined."

10. I say that the Revised Standard Version interprets the Hebrew text "more plainly" than the New International Version does, in that the New International Version intrudes more interpretation into its English rendering while the Revised Standard Version allows the Hebrew to speak for itself. Translated very woodenly, the Hebrew text reads, "And upon your book all of them were written, days were formed, and (there was) not one of them." The Revised Standard Version, as one can see, smooths over the Hebrew text with minor embellishments necessary for

David is affirming that God wrote the script of his life in the great book of God's intentions before the actual events began to unfold, indeed, before David was even born. And, mixing his metaphors, David also says that the days of his life were formed or shaped, suggesting the action of a potter shaping clay. He means that his life, considered not only as a whole but also right down to his daily experience, was determined (what other word fits?) ahead of time.[11] And why does David make this point? Because it assures him that he is not here in this present danger by chance. He is living out God's will and plan for his life, and this faith gives David godly poise in the face of danger.

This deserves a moment's reflection. David is thinking his way down to the bedrock of his existence, where his faith can find rest. The distressing hostilities around him threaten both body and soul. Everything around him swirls in uncertainty. He could lose his nerve. So what does he need right now? *Certainty.* It would not make sense for David to appeal to a *contingency* as he searches for a place to stand. It does make sense that David is reaching out to hold fast to that which stands immovable. And in his soul's quest, where does David land? On God's sovereignty, shaping the events of his personal life day by day and foreordaining even his present emergency. That puts it into a completely new, theocentric perspective, so that David can stand, serene, confident, and ready to face anything. This strong doctrine of a strong Sovereign has the power to make a strong believer out of otherwise frightened David.[12]

---

elegance of English expression, but it retains the essential structure and sense of the Hebrew. The New International Version, by contrast, goes so far as to rearrange the elements of the unusual Hebrew syntactical equation in the interests of simplified English, and the net result misrepresents the precise sense intended by David. It is that sense, lost in the New International Version, which one must apprehend clearly to appreciate the force of David's assertion.

11. In *Grace Unlimited,* 18, Pinnock writes, "The idea that God's will is something which is always and infallibly accomplished does not derive from biblical teaching. God's purpose according to Scripture is not a blueprint encompassing all future contingencies. It is a dynamic program for the world, the outworking of which depends in part upon man." But does not David's affirmation cast doubt on Pinnock's assertion? David would have no incentive for clasping to his heart the thought of a "dynamic [whatever that means] program for the world" but only an infallibly operative and salvific divine plan for his own life.

12. B. B. Warfield, *Selected Shorter Writings* (Phillipsburg, N. J.: Presbyterian and Reformed, 1973), 1:383–84, illustrates the strengthening power of Calvinism with the following anecdote: What is "the indelible mark of the [Westminster] Shorter Catechism"? We have the following bit of personal experience from a general officer of the United States army. He was in a great western city at a time of intense excitement and violent rioting. The streets were overrun daily by a dangerous crowd. One day he observed approaching him a man of singularly combined calmness and firmness of mien, whose very demeanor inspired confidence. So impressed was he with his bearing amid the surrounding uproar that when he had passed he turned to look back at him, only to find that the stranger had done the same. On observing his turning the stranger at once came back to him, and touching his chest with his forefinger, demanded without preface: "What is the chief end of man?" On receiving the countersign, "Man's chief end is to glorify God and to enjoy him forever"—"Ah!" said he, "I knew you were a Shorter Catechism boy by your looks!" "Why, that was just what I was thinking of you," was the rejoinder.

> How precious to me are your thoughts, O God!
> How vast is the sum of them!
> Were I to count them,
>   they would outnumber the grains of sand. (vv. 17–18a)

David feels overwhelmed by God's detailed, constant, watchful care. The loving attention of God, hovering over his child, is so minute, so comprehensive, that David cannot fully grasp it. He sees by faith an invisible and powerful Presence with him, enveloping him, caring for him, orchestrating each day of his life, and he rejoices.

In this light, it seems odd that anyone would refer to Calvinism as "the determinist kind of theology, the type that subordinates God's love to the ideal of absolute power."[13] Why must one create a dichotomy between God's love and his absolute, determining power? Psalm 139 does not do that. One can see here in the text that God's power over David's daily life draws from him a response of deep gladness and wonder, precisely because God exercises his power in love. Reflecting upon God's sovereignty over him, David feels loved. He understands that the almighty Determiner is no less the solicitous Lover. That is the very reason why David reminds himself of this truth at this time. David has his back against the wall. Violent men are moving in on him. He does not know whether he will live out the day. How does David fortify himself within? With the exhilarating truth that a sovereign God loves him, has always loved him, and will not therefore let him fall by chance into the abyss of human cruelty.[14]

If Arminianism were true, then evil would exercise autonomous power.[15] In that case, not only David but we as well would have something to worry

13. To quote Pinnock, *The Grace of God, the Will of Man,* xi. On page ix Pinnock articulates the question which *The Grace of God, the Will of Man* was written to answer, namely, "Is God the absolute Monarch who always gets his way, or is God rather the loving Parent who is sensitive to our needs even when we disappoint him and frustrate some of his plans?" Notice the language. Pinnock envisions an absolute Monarch "who always gets his way." Such language implies a pettiness in the divine Monarch. Notice also that, according to Pinnock, this Monarch cannot at the same time be a loving Parent sensitive to our needs. On page x Pinnock states that "God is love, and therefore expresses his power, not by having to control everything like an oriental despot. . . ." But is it not possible for the God who is love to express his controlling power in some way more worthy of our worship than an oriental despot's Machiavellianism? For what reason must controlling power and loving mercy work at cross purposes or be mutually exclusive of one another? Their harmonious union may be morally improbable for any one of us, but is God incapable of such largeness and complexity?

14. Cf. Calvin, *Institutes,* 1.17.7, where he states that God's providential care inspires "gratitude in prosperity, patience in adversity, and a wonderful security respecting the future."

15. On page xii of *The Grace of God, the Will of Man,* one reads that God decided to create a world "possessing relative autonomy, . . . in order to give it room to be." Overlooking for now "*relative* autonomy"—a problematic concept, in my view— it is noteworthy that Arminianism even feels the need for the world to have its own "room to be." One thinks of Calvin on Hebrews 1:3, which says that the Son "sustains all things by his powerful word." There Calvin

about. Evil would operate outside the controlling love of God. It *is* at work. It *is* on the move. Its malice takes aim between our eyes. And God is not in full control of it? Dreadful thought, in this world of child molesters and drunk drivers and drive-by shootings! But Arminianism is not true. How could David have written Psalm 139, if his theology had been the equivalent to Arminianism? David's reasoning in this psalm is premised upon the conviction that evil is fully subservient to God's sovereign love. Without this virile theology, Psalm 139 would never have arisen out of David's soul.

Jeremiah 1

The call of the prophet Jeremiah also illustrates the operation of God's sovereign grace effectually energizing, lifting, and strengthening an individual, to the greater glory of God. Upon some unspecified occasion, the Lord confronted Jeremiah by revealing to him the divinely chosen mission for which he had been born:

> The word of the LORD came to me, saying,
> "Before I formed you in the womb I knew you,
>   before you were born I set you apart;
>   I appointed you as a prophet to the nations." (vv. 4–5)

God explains to Jeremiah that his life has a larger significance than he had ever known before. God has appointed him to lift a prophetic voice to the nations, for which mission Jeremiah has long been prepared. God formed him in the womb, shaping and equipping him in a way suited to the divine purpose. And even before his conception in the womb, God "knew" Jeremiah. In one sense, of course, God foreknew Jeremiah no more or less than God in his omniscience and eternality foreknows every human being. But that cannot be the point here, because mere foresight is no guarantee of special favor, which is the very thing timid Jeremiah needs assurance of at this moment. This divine foreknowledge must entail something special personally, or else God's claim carries no force. The verb translated "know" (yd^c) is used elsewhere of more than mere cognition:

> "Abraham will surely become a great and powerful nation, and all nations on earth will be blessed through him. For I have chosen him [lit., known him] so

---

comments, "To 'sustain' is used in the sense of to care for and to keep all creation in its proper state. He sees that everything will quickly disintegrate if it is not upheld by his goodness" (*The Epistle of Paul the Apostle to the Hebrews*, trans. William B. Johnston [Grand Rapids: Eerdmans, 1980], 9). Such "room to be" as Arminianism desiderates would expose us to quick disintegration if it were not for the moment-by-moment sustaining grace of our sovereign Lord. "In him we live and move and have our being" (Acts 17:28). Realizing this, who would want his own "room to be," beyond the range of his powerful love?

that he will direct his children and his household after him to keep the way of the LORD. . . ." (Gen. 18:18–19)

For the LORD watches over [lit., knows] the way of the righteous,
but the way of the wicked will perish. (Ps. 1:6)

> "But I am the LORD your God,
>   who brought you out of Egypt.
> You shall acknowledge no God but me,
>   no Savior except me.
> I cared for you [lit., knew you] in the desert,
>   in the land of burning heat." (Hos. 13:4–5)

> "You only have I chosen [lit., known]
>   of all the families of the earth;
> therefore I will punish you
>   for all your sins." (Amos 3:2)

Such relational knowledge must be intended in Jeremiah 1:5, because only that kind of sense functions meaningfully as the follow-up announcement to "Before I formed you in the womb." There seems to be a heightening in the progress of thought, moving from the lesser to the greater, so that "Before I formed you in the womb" followed by "I foresaw your existence" falls flat. By contrast, to complement "Before I formed you in the womb" with "I chose you" is rhetorically meaningful and personally powerful. The parallel ideas ("I set you apart" and "I appointed you") corroborate the interpretation of "I knew you" as a sovereignly operative foreknowledge. And more principially, divine foreknowledge must entail divine purpose:[16]

> "I am God, and there is none like me,
> declaring the end from the beginning
>   and from ancient times things not yet done,
> saying, 'My counsel shall stand,
>   and I will accomplish all my purpose.'" (Isa. 46:9b–10 RSV)

God does not foreknow events with bare prescience, so that he must look on as events unfold in history out of his control. He foreknows all things, actual and potential, "the end from the beginning," including authentic human choices, precisely because "My *counsel* shall stand, and I will accomplish all

---

16. Cf. Geoffrey W. Bromiley, "Foreknowledge," in *Evangelical Dictionary of Theology*, ed. Walter A. Elwell (Grand Rapids: Baker, 1984), 420. See also chapter 7 by S. M. Baugh in this work.

my *purpose.*"[17] The import of God's word to Jeremiah, therefore, amplified and paraphrased, is something like this:

> I discerned which peculiar traits and characteristics, which special graces and virtues, would be ideal for the fulfilling of my purpose for your life mission. You now have them, for I devoted my personal attention to your conception and development in the womb, so that all the variables would concur for the actualization of my will. And that special care itself was only the implementation of my prior choice of you to play this part in the drama of redemptive history. I singled you out and set my affection on you before you even existed. You are, and always have been, surrounded by my personal care and purposeful guidance.

One wonders, therefore, why Calvinism is caricatured in the following manner: "Divine election [according to Arminianism] functions more like a love affair between persons than a preprogrammed computer operation [as in Calvinism]."[18] This misrepresents the Calvinism that I, along with millions of others, believe in and cherish. Of course, the Calvinistic understanding of election is a love affair and not a Reader's Digest Sweepstakes computer selection! The glory of sovereign election is that the One choosing us loves us with a love that will never let us go, unlike the helplessly pleading divine love of Arminianism which can offer no promise of consummation.

In reply to Jeremiah's astonished and pained cry of reluctance, God does not deny the prophet's inadequacy; but he does insist that human inadequacy cannot defeat the divine purpose:

> "Ah, Sovereign LORD," I said, "I do not know how to speak; I am only a child."
> But the LORD said to me, "Do not say, 'I am only a child.' You must go to everyone I send you to and say whatever I command you. Do not be afraid of them, for I am with you and will rescue you," declares the LORD. (vv. 6–8)

The New International Version misrepresents the sense at one point. We read that Jeremiah "must go" to everyone God sends him to and "[must] say"

17. Richard Rice, "Divine Foreknowledge and Free-Will Theism," in *The Grace of God, the Will of Man,* 134, frankly argues that God does not know some aspects of the future: "God knows a great deal about what will happen. . . . All that God does not know is the content of future free decisions, and this is because decisions are not there to know until they occur." But does not history consist in large part of human decisions? And would that not, therefore, block out much of the future from God's foreknowledge? This vision of God fails to reckon with his eternality, which requires that he be equally present to all points of time at once. We peer fearfully into the darkness of the future, but God is already there now. This vision of God fails to reckon with his wisdom, by which he is able to implement his sovereign will through human choices without violating their authenticity or jeopardizing the certainty of his intended outcomes. But most devastatingly, this vision of God fails to reckon with the biblical texts which affirm his foreknowledge of all things, including human decisions.

18. John E. Sanders, "God as Personal," in *The Grace of God, the Will of Man,* 177.

whatever God commands him. This interpretation of the prefixed Hebrew verbs is not impossible, but neither is it the most apposite. How does it encourage fearful Jeremiah for God to insist all the more sharply upon what the prophet *must* go and do? Such an approach to this needy man is psychologically improbable. Another sense must be intended.

Consider the logic of the verses. Jeremiah is paralyzed with insecurity. His perspective and emotions are so thoroughly anthropocentric that he is defeated already. But God, in his wisdom, understands which spiritual remedy to apply to Jeremiah's condition. The man needs a strong dose of security in God's sovereignty. That is why an indicative construction of these verbs is more convincing:

> "Do not say, 'I am only a child.' You will go to everyone I send you to and say whatever I command you."

Now Jeremiah has a satisfying reason to look beyond his own limitations. By the sovereign grace of God, he *will* go to whomever God sends him and he *will* speak whatever God commands him. Note the ambiguity in Jeremiah's charge. God does not tell him where he will be sent or what he will say. Why? Because these words are not a command. They are assurance. "I will send you, and you will go. I will command you, and you will speak. It will happen, Jeremiah, even though you are no match for the task. All my intentions for you will be realized. This really is going to work out. So do not be afraid." And, in fact, God kept his word. Jeremiah went on to live a life of rugged, persistent obedience "against wind and tide,"[19] when any man without the support of sovereign grace would have shaved the radical edge off of God's word and prudently adapted his message to the times.

> Then the LORD reached out his hand and touched my mouth and said to me, "Now, I have put my words in your mouth. See, today I appoint you over nations and kingdoms to uproot and tear down, to destroy and overthrow, to build and to plant." (vv. 9–10)

God's instructions to Jeremiah remain general in nature. No particular message is imparted. No particular nations and kingdoms are identified. God does not command Jeremiah to do anything in particular. God simply tells him what to expect in general, namely, that he will use Jeremiah's inspired words to overthrow and to restore nations. God only shows him how effectually powerful his ministry will prove to be, in the sovereign purpose of God.

It is striking that no response from Jeremiah is recorded, in contrast with Isaiah's response to his call in Isaiah 6:8. There is a seam in the text between

---

19. Derek Kidner, *The Message of Jeremiah* (Downers Grove, Ill.: InterVarsity, 1987), 7.

verses 10 and 11, creating the presumption that this episode concludes at the end of verse 10. We hear no more from Jeremiah at this time. The fact that the Book of Jeremiah exists at all witnesses, in a way, to Jeremiah's affirmative reply to the call of God. Nevertheless, the passage concludes at verse 10 without any further registration of Jeremiah's response. Why? Because the theological center of gravity in this passage is not Jeremiah but God—the sovereign initiative, providential care and effectual grace of God in Jeremiah's life and ministry. The prophet's personal response, while important, is not the point of the text. God is all.

Compare God's role in the drama with Jeremiah's role. According to the text, God initiated his revelatory word to Jeremiah. God formed him in the womb. God "knew" him. God set him apart. God appointed him as a prophet to the nations. God will send him so that he will go to everyone to whom he is sent. God will command him so that he will say everything he is to say. God will be with him. God will rescue him. God reaches out and touches his mouth, putting inspired words there. God appoints him over nations and kingdoms to herald as certain their destruction or construction. That is God's role, according to the text. And Jeremiah's part? He is to stop saying he is only a child and stop being afraid. Is this not suggestive? In this light, it is interesting to observe what one significant evangelical commentary argues concerning verse 5:

> Although the verse may imply some form of theological determinism or predestination, that is hardly its purpose. From one perspective, the initial divine words to Jeremiah seem to present him with a *fait accompli:* he was set aside before he was born. Yet, in the dynamics of the dialogue, the opening words present Jeremiah with an overwhelming sense of God's purpose, but they still require a response from him and subsequent acts of obedience. In fact, despite the deterministic tone of the opening statement, the undertones throughout the narrative are those of human freedom and the capacity to respond to the divine call.[20]

This is eisegesis. I would not deny the vital importance of a proper response to the divine call, but is that the point of this text? The commentators' theological predispositions are interfering with the burden of the passage. They deny that its purpose is "some form of theological determinism or predestination." But does not the logic of the text, the weight of it, argue the other way by exploiting to full effect that very point? Jeremiah is frozen in fear. The whole purpose of the deterministic flavor of the passage is to lift him up out of himself into the fullness of God. What these commentators wish to mini-

20. Peter C. Craigie, Page H. Kelley, and Joel F. Drinkard Jr., *Jeremiah 1–25* (Dallas: Word, 1991), 10.

mize is the very thing God wants Jeremiah most to feel. And as for the subsequent narrative of the book, only God's sovereign grace can explain how Jeremiah was enabled to keep on against all the odds.

And neither would I deny Jeremiah's "freedom and capacity to respond to the divine call"—in a certain, duly qualified sense. Human passivity is neither required logically nor evident factually. Neither would I argue that Jeremiah does not matter in the unfolding of subsequent events. But the text does imply that God matters more, for he is the effective cause in all things. This passage is not a case of divine and human cooperation working together to effect a certain result, much less the divine will being frustrated by human opposition or even incompetence. It is a case of God's sovereign all-sufficiency overwhelming Jeremiah's natural timidity in *the* defining moment of his life, which marked him forever:

> O LORD, you deceived me, and I was deceived;
>   you overpowered me and prevailed.
> I am ridiculed all day long;
>   everyone mocks me.
> Whenever I speak, I cry out
>   proclaiming violence and destruction.
> So the word of the LORD has brought me
>   insult and reproach all day long.
> But if I say, "I will not mention him
>   or speak any more in his name,"
> his word is in my heart like a fire,
>   a fire shut up in my bones.
> I am weary of holding it in;
>   indeed, I cannot. (20:7–9)

Jeremiah's confession should sober both the Calvinist and the Arminian, lest we trivialize the doctrine of God's sovereignty as a mere debating point. The one who has been gripped by it will pay a price for such holy possession, especially as our age becomes increasingly hostile to biblical principle.

One sees in Jeremiah a man whose sensitive temperament was formed by God for the purpose that God's strength might be made perfect in Jeremiah's weakness. I am not arguing that Jeremiah's case holds for all believers in general or even for ministers in particular, although I could do so.[21] My point is simply to show another clear illustration of the effectual operation of God's sovereign grace in an individual life in the Old Testament.

---

21. In *The Grace of God, the Will of Man,* 113 and 291, it is asserted that such passages as we are considering should not be construed as paradigmatic for all believers. Interestingly, however, the biblical passages which might be interpreted as favoring Arminianism *are* accepted as normative for all.

Jonah

The Book of Jonah provides an even more provocative illustration of divine sovereignty in the life of an individual, because the prophet displays a consistent failure to appreciate God's will. If the purpose of God is accomplished here, it will be no thanks to the uncooperative instrument of "human cooperation." The book is a case study in sovereign grace triumphing over human defiance.

Rather than recount the well-known story, I wish only to point out some of the features in it which display the sovereignty of God. In addition, two questions invite special attention. One concerns how Jonah's disobedience figures into the larger equation of God's work, and the other concerns the meaning of God's repentance in 3:10 and 4:2.

But first, the book's presentation of God's sovereignty may be divided into two categories: explicit affirmations of divine sovereignty at work, and reasonable inferences of the same. The explicit affirmations of God's sovereignty include the following:

The Lord initiates his word to Jonah (1:1)

He hurls a great wind upon the sea (1:4)[22]

In the words of the ship's captain and the Ninevite king, God is one who cannot be forced by the will of man, but man must wait upon God (1:6; 3:9)

In the words of the ship's crew, the Lord has acted in these events just as he pleased (1:14)

The Lord appoints[23] a great fish to rescue Jonah (1:17)

The Lord throws Jonah into the deep, even though it is done by the hands of the sailors, and it is his waves and his breakers[24] that sweep over Jonah (2:3)

Jonah declares that "salvation comes from the Lord" (2:9), meaning that it is entirely his to give or to withhold

---

22. The New International Version, rather weakly, renders, "Then the Lord sent a great wind on the sea." The Revised Standard Version shows the more accurate, and the more robust, "The Lord hurled a great wind upon the sea." Cf. usage of this verb (Hiphil of √*ṭwl*) in Jonah 1:4, 12, 15.

23. The New International Version reads "provide," but the Revised Standard Version's "appoint" is more apt. The Piel of √*mnh* is also used in Daniel 1:11 in the sense of appoint or assign (to office or role). This is the sense of the Pual in 1 Chronicles 9:29 as well. The Qal is found in Isaiah 65:12 for destining (to destruction), in a clever play with "Destiny" in verse 11. Cf. also Jonah 4:6, 7, 8.

24. The New International Version reads, "all your waves and breakers swept over me," but the Revised Standard Version is careful to include both Hebrew possessive pronouns with its "all *thy* waves and *thy* billows passed over me" (italics added).

The fish obeys the command of the Lord (2:10)
The Lord initiates his word to Jonah a second time (3:1)
He appoints a plant and makes it grow up over Jonah (4:6)
He appoints a worm to ruin the plant (4:7)
He appoints a scorching east wind to blast Jonah (4:8)

The text also includes events which are clearly providential in their occurrence, even though they are not explicitly attributed to God. The author whispers to us of divine intervention when God confronts the fleeing prophet through the words of the pagan captain of the ship (1:6),[25] when the lot falls on Jonah (1:7), when Jonah bears witness to his faith before the sailors on board ship, even though a witness to the pagan world is the very thing he is trying to evade (1:9), when the severity of the storm prevents the valiant sailors from rowing safely to land and thus sparing Jonah (1:13), and when the sea becomes calm immediately after Jonah has been thrown overboard (1:15). Both explicitly and implicitly, the book demonstrates that God has more ways of confronting Jonah than Jonah has ways of eluding God.[26] Jonah has met his match.

The Book of Jonah teaches the compassion of God's sovereignty. He takes no pleasure in the death of the wicked—even though Jonah relishes the prospect—and is able to draw them to himself. The book teaches the detail of God's sovereignty. From the great fish of 1:17 to the little worm of 4:7, the whole of creation stands ready to do his bidding—unlike stubborn Jonah, who refuses to bow to God if doing so crosses his petty self-concern. The book teaches the effectiveness of God's sovereignty. He controls the destiny of every soul on board that ship sailing out of Joppa harbor. He is able to put the ship in such danger that it is on the verge of breaking up, but only to separate one man out for redemptive recovery while sparing—indeed, saving—the rest. God not only confronts Jonah, but also adds to his redeemed community one ship's crew of heretofore pagan sailors, in addition to the repentant people of Nineveh.

One wonders, therefore, how anyone could argue that "those who attempt to act on the position that God is in sovereign control of the events in their lives run into grave problems. At its best, this approach is unlivable."[27]

---

25. Cf. Alexander's observation in David W. Baker, T. Desmond Alexander, and Bruce K. Waltke, *Obadiah, Jonah, Micah* (Downers Grove, Ill.: InterVarsity, 1988), 103: "The irony of the [captain's] request can hardly have escaped Jonah: *Get up and call on your god!* After all, Jonah's sole reason for being on board the vessel was to flee from the presence of his God. Moreover, by repeating the imperatives *qum*, 'arise,' and *qᵉrāʾ* 'call,' the captain parodies closely Jonah's initial summons from God (v. 2). Each word mocks him."

26. I thank my colleague, Dr. Dennis Magary, for articulating this for me.

27. Randall G. Basinger, "Exhaustive Divine Sovereignty: A Practical Critique," in *The Grace of God, the Will of Man*, 195.

I would not claim that Calvinism, as sometimes formulated, is problem-free, either principially or practically. But the Book of Jonah insists that the divine control of the events of our lives is our only hope. If any approach to life is unlivable, Jonah demonstrates it for us, namely, in trying to wrest the control of his life from the gracious Sovereign who cannot be outmaneuvered by Jonah's grasping after autonomy.

One wonders no less how anyone could argue that a consistent Calvinism "cuts the nerve of moral endeavor and leads the Christian into a passive life of moral resignation."[28] The only passive character in the Calvinistic Book of Jonah is the nasty, sulky prophet, and clearly he is the bad example we are not to follow. By contrast, the Lord shows a pattern of ineluctable initiative drawing sinners to his mercy with transforming power, and clearly he is the hero we are to admire. That point is forcefully insinuated by the concluding speech in 4:10–11. The sovereign God is our model of caring action.

But two questions still press themselves upon us. One, how is Jonah's disobedience related to God's sovereign will? Does Jonah frustrate the fulfillment of the decrees of God? Or is he only living out those very decrees, even in his recalcitrance? And if the latter, then how does his disobedience serve the holy will of God? The text itself does not answer the question. The answer must be drawn out of our larger theological understanding of how reality works. The Bible does affirm that God retains ultimacy in all things. In addition to the passages quoted near the beginning of this chapter, the following may also be cited:

> "To God belong wisdom and power;
>   counsel and understanding are his.
> What he tears down cannot be rebuilt;
>   the man he imprisons cannot be released.
> If he holds back the waters, there is drought;
>   if he lets them loose, they devastate the land.
> To him belong strength and victory;
>   both deceived and deceiver are his." (Job 12:13–16)

> There is no wisdom, no insight, no plan
>   that can succeed against the LORD. (Prov. 21:30)

> The LORD Almighty has sworn,
> "Surely, as I have planned, so it will be,
>   and as I have purposed, so it will stand." . . .
> For the LORD Almighty has purposed, and who can thwart him?
>   His hand is stretched out, and who can turn it back? (Isa. 14:24, 27)

28. Ibid.

Significantly, the Bible does not contain statements which reverse this theology. We do not read anything like, "There is no wisdom, no insight, no plan of God's that can succeed against man."[29] The Bible does affirm the reality and authenticity of human participation in the purposes of God, but not on a par with God. We are subordinate to his finality. Grand statements such as are previously quoted provide the overall framework within which one makes sense of the more situation-specific perspectives of Scripture. The Bible does not trouble itself constantly to explain everything in terms of the ultimate. Very often it limits its horizon to that which is more immediate, leaving the larger questions up to our own biblically informed powers of systemization.

How then does Jonah's disobedience serve the will of God? One may propose at least this. Jonah is a marked man. God is after him. God loves him and intends to win him. The drama of the book consists primarily in God's saving pursuit of Jonah. And Jonah must first experience his own disobedience and God's salvation, in chapters 1–2, to give the Lord's actions and arguments in chapters 3–4, especially his gracious persistence with Jonah, morally persuasive force. If Jonah has been saved from the consequences of *his* disobedience, how can he begrudge the Ninevites' being saved from the consequences of *their* disobedience? The power of the events—and the power of the book's message to us—would be crippled without Jonah's resistance to God. This becomes clearly evident if one edits the book to omit all the material relevant to Jonah's hard-heartedness and includes only the remaining material concerned with his first call, his journey to Nineveh, his message to the city, and its repentant response. The entire book would then consist of 1:1–2 and 3:3–10 only. As such, it would accomplish so little as to be innocuous, and the person of Jonah would be incidental to the plot. As it stands, however, most of the narrative concerns Jonah's struggle with God, while the remainder supports and enhances that central theme. Jonah's disobedience, therefore, serves God's purpose no less than his obedience. It is necessary to the drama of the book, which in turn is an inspired reflection of reality. And what is God's purpose? To display his sovereign mercy toward sinners—most notably toward Jonah himself. Jonah's own need for grace is at the heart of the drama, because underlying the events of the story is God's determination to reveal the extent his mercy toward people like Jonah will go. We readers conclude chapter 4 marveling at the patience of this gracious God,

---

29. Cf. Augustine *The Enchiridion* 32, who observes that one could not take Paul's statement, "So it depends not upon man's will or exertion, but upon God's mercy," and reverse it to say, "So it depends not upon God's mercy, but upon man's will and exertion," as if the divine and human factors in the equation of reality were equally significant and capable of cancelling each other out.

43

whose longsuffering puts up not only with Jonah but also with us. And so we are humbled, and God is glorified.

The other question demanding attention is this. How does God's repentance in 3:10, along with its theological confirmation in 4:2, cohere with his sovereignty?[30] Certainly, human overtures cannot cause change in God. But still, how is one to understand the declaration that God "repented of the evil which he had said he would do to them"? Once again, the text is not intended to provide the answer. One may explore the question only in connection with the deeper theological substructure of the text, which one surmises from Scripture as a whole. That substructure insists that God is unchangeable:

> "God is not a man, that he should lie,
> nor a son of man, that he should change his mind.
> Does he speak and then not act?
> Does he promise and not fulfill?" (Num. 23:19)

> "He who is the Glory of Israel does not lie or change his mind; for he is not a man, that he should change his mind." (1 Sam. 15:29)[31]

> "I the LORD do not change. So you, O descendants of Jacob, are not destroyed." (Mal. 3:6)

God cannot be shown to have erred so that he must make a mid-course correction. He cannot be more fully informed or emotionally manipulated so that he alters his will. God knows the end from the beginning.

Still, the portrayal of God in Jonah 3:10 and 4:2 is no less truthful than other biblical disclosures of his nature—less profound, perhaps,[32] but no less truth-

30. The New International Version obscures the force of 3:10 at the crucial point: "When God saw what they did and how they turned from their evil ways, he had compassion and did not bring upon them the destruction he had threatened." The Revised Standard Version represents the Hebrew more clearly: "When God saw what they did, how they turned from their evil way, God repented of the evil which he had said he would do to them; and he did not do it."

31. Robert P. Gordon, *I & II Samuel: A Commentary* (Grand Rapids: Zondervan, 1986), 146: "Too much can be made of the surface tension between the statements, in verses 11 and 29, concerning the possibility or impossibility of God's repenting. When God issues a decree that is plainly intended as irrevocable, as in the rejection of Saul, then, says our text, there is no possibility of that decree being rescinded (cf. Nu. 23:19)."

32. With "less profound," I have in mind the Latin *profundus*, "deep, vast." And I mean this. Every passage in the Bible reveals something true about God, but some passages take us further down into the mysteries of his being and works. No passage takes us all the way to the very depths of God, but some take us deeper than others. Those passages which point beyond immediate circumstances to final causation in God and which go beyond appearances to the inner reality and deeper meaning of things, I call "more profound." I wonder whether Arminians may at times fail to make such a distinction, with the result that they try to explain the more profound in the light of the less profound, rather than the reverse.

ful.[33] What then might be the positive exegetical function of God's repentance in the Book of Jonah? It highlights this important point. In the course of the book, one observes significant changes in most of the characters. The pagan sailors convert to the God of Israel. The Ninevites turn from their sins in repentance before God. The Lord relents concerning the disaster he had threatened. All the characters of the book are presented with a measure of morally appropriate responsiveness—except Jonah.[34] His complaint in 4:2 reveals that his deep antipathy for the Ninevites has not changed at all in the course of events. In fact, the book's abrupt conclusion leaves unresolved the moral dissonance racking Jonah's soul.[35] And that is deliberate. The book is designed to shock us with the headstrong obstinacy of the human heart, including the heart steeped in biblical truth and rich with covenant privilege. It is designed to search us with its concluding question at 4:11, as a sovereign God full of pity shines his light on our hearts to discover traces of Jonah's whimpering, whining meanness concealed under our own doctrinal correctness and impeccable evangelical credentials. And the book hints to us that, if we will repent, we will find God to be no less responsive to us than he was to the Ninevites. "Draw near to God, and he will draw near to you" (James 4:8 RSV). That is the burden of the Book of Jonah, and one must always use a text according to its discrete purpose. This book is energized by a practical pastoral aim and is not meant to address more profound questions concerning God's nature ultimately considered. Understood in this sense, the repentance of God in Jonah is no more or less problematic than the free gospel invitation in Scripture generally and requires no more or less vindication than that does.[36] In view of God's sublime immutability, therefore, one must presume that divine repentance in the Bible is meant to describe not some sort of existential reaction in God but rather his perfectly just moral reciprocity.

At the end of the day, however, one cannot fully explain, but can only adore, the mysteries of God's sovereignty encompassing and employing human sin and of God's mercy truly offering and freely giving grace to the penitent.

---

33. Hugh Martin, *The Prophet Jonah* (London: Banner of Truth Trust, 1966), 292, makes this wise point: "For it lies at the foundation of all intercourse between God and man that God should Himself address us, and permit us to address Him, in expressions suited to our weak capacities and conceptions, rather than dictated by what were suitable to His infinite glory and searchless being. Does it then follow that in thus condescending unto the weakness of our nature, He does injustice to His own, or misrepresents it? That does not follow. God can speak of Himself after the manner of man, and what He thus speaks may yet be worthy of God."

34. Thanks are due again to Dr. Dennis Magary for his insight on this point.

35. One can only guess, but it seems probable that God's grace eventually won Jonah's heart. God is still in control of the situation at the end of the story. He appoints a plant, a worm, a hot wind. What is next? Anything God wants to use to get through to Jonah, he may. The whole universe is at his disposal. Jonah, therefore, is cornered. How can he resist a God whose resources are as inexhaustible as his patience?

36. Cf. J. I. Packer, *Evangelism and the Sovereignty of God* (Downers Grove, Ill.: InterVarsity, 1971), 100–104, on the free and universal offer of the gospel within a Reformed theological framework.

45

Oh, the depth of the riches of the wisdom and knowledge of God!
How *unsearchable* his judgments,
and his paths *beyond tracing out!* (Rom. 11:33, italics added)

Calvin describes the sovereignty of God as "a secret so much excelling the insight of the human mind that I am not ashamed to confess ignorance. Far be it from any of the faithful to be ashamed of ignorance of what the Lord withdraws into the glory of his inaccessible light."[37]

The narrative of Jonah urges upon us, then, a vision of God as both sovereign and compassionate. These two dimensions of God's infinite and unknowable majesty do not work at cross purposes, according to the Book of Jonah. They mingle together for his glory and our salvation.

Conclusion

We have good reasons in the Old Testament to lay Arminianism aside as a wrong-headed and limiting system of biblical interpretation. And we also have good reasons in the Old Testament to rejoice in the strong, Calvinistic doctrine of a gracious God reigning without limitation over all things, ourselves included. We have a reason in Psalm 139 for moral courage in the face of opposition. We have a reason in Jeremiah 1 for bold truthtelling in hard times. We have a reason in Jonah for confidence that even our sins cannot defeat the gracious purposes of God. And in each case that reason is the individual (not merely corporate), salvific (not merely historical), effectual (not contingent) working of God's sweet sovereignty in our lives. *Soli Deo gloria!*

---

37. John Calvin, *Concerning the Eternal Predestination of God*, trans. J. K. S. Reid (London: James Clarke and Co., Limited, 1961), 124.

2

Divine Election in the Gospel of John

ROBERT W. YARBROUGH

Divine election in this chapter refers to God's determinative initiative in human salvation. The Old Testament uses the verb *bāḥar* (to choose, elect, decide) some ninety-two times to refer "to God's sovereign action, the normative divine initiative which is accountable to none."[1] *Bāḥar* "is used to express that choosing which has ultimate and eternal significance."[2] The word "indicates God's prerogative in deciding what shall happen, independently of human choice."[3] It has a variety of uses, ranging from the choice of a place to worship, to the choice of persons for particular offices or tasks, to the choice of a people to be participants in covenantal relationship with God by faith. Whether referring directly to covenant blessing, or more indirectly to the religious or social infrastructure God established to mediate the benefits of his gracious choices, "divine election" refers to God's voluntary and sovereign activity by which he implements and furthers his saving purposes.

The fourth Gospel, as we shall see, builds on and expands this Old Testament conception. In its three major divisions—the prologue (1:1–18); the narrative leading up to the night Christ was betrayed (1:19–12:50); and the denouement consisting of the upper room discourse, the crucifixion, and the resurrection with its aftermath—John's Gospel implicitly and explicitly as-

1. G. Quell, "*eklegomai*," in *TDNT*, 4:150. On the Old Testament's view of divine election more generally see the preceding chapter.
2. J. N. Oswalt, in *Theological Wordbook of the Old Testament*, ed. R. Harris, Gleason Archer, and Bruce Waltke (Chicago: Moody, 1980), 1:100.
3. I. Howard Marshall, "Elect, Election," in *Baker Encyclopedia of the Bible*, ed. Walter A. Elwell (Grand Rapids: Baker, 1988), 1:682.

serts God's choosing, his election, of lost sinners to eternal life. In the same vein, and no less significantly, it points to numerous broader ways in which God exercised his elective prerogative so as to ensure the execution of the redemptive strategy that he conceived in gracious love and carried out in human history.

Divine Election in John's Prologue

Books often begin with an introduction that outlines their contents. Many scholars agree that John 1:1–18 is such an introduction. These verses are a prologue, or foreword. They lay the foundation for the treatise that follows, and they contain several clues that point to the author's conception of divine election.

Election is implicit in John's opening words, "In the beginning . . ." (1:1), a clear echo of Genesis 1:1. Creation (cf. John 1:1 with 1:3), which the flow of John's prologue, like the flow of Genesis, links inexorably to redemption, is rooted in divinity's eternal being expressed through the free decision to establish the material world. Creation, and accordingly also redemption, can have no other explanation than that God is, and that he willed to create and to save.[4]

Subsequent to creation sin, and with it the need for redemption, entered the world; this is the "darkness" of which John 1:5 speaks. Into that darkness "there came a man who was sent from God," John the Baptist (John 1:6). The opening chapters of Luke give details of John's conception and birth, which from one point of view were quite normal. But the words *from God* in John 1:6 underscore the divine initiative and agency lying behind his appearance.

Into the darkness came not only the Baptist but also the light (John 1:7). The light was Jesus Christ. His coming into the world sheds light on the spiritual need and hope of every person (John 1:9).[5] Neither mankind generally nor the Jewish people in particular attached the same importance to him that God did (John 1:5, 10–11). The Messiah's[6] mission and achievement were not the product of either Jewish religious industry or Gentile ratiocination. God

---

4. Oswalt, *Theological Wordbook of the Old Testament,* 1:100, rightly stresses that in the Old Testament, "The scriptural doctrine of divine capacity for choice demonstrates that purpose and personality, not blind mechanism, are at the heart of the universe." It is no less true for the New Testament, and John's Gospel, that God's will, though in important respects ultimately inscrutable, is not impersonal or hostile. Of the same awesome God who mysteriously created the universe John can elsewhere say with relaxed and reflective personal confidence, "God is love" (1 John 4:16).

5. For further discussion of this verse see chapter 9 by Thomas R. Schreiner in this work. In the context of John's Gospel it can certainly not be taken to refer to universal salvation. Schreiner shows that it is also unlikely to refer to prevenient grace as Wesleyans understand it.

6. The word *Messiah* as such occurs in the New Testament only in John 1:41, 4:25. John explicitly presents the "light" of the prologue as God's anointed, the "Christ" of God's special choosing.

chose to send the light, not because but in spite of human desire and readiness for it.

Divine election receives sharp emphasis in John 1:13, which sheds light on the identity of "all who received him" in 1:12. That is, those who savingly received the Messiah for who he truly was (1:12) did so because they were "born of God" (1:13)—and not vice versa. More specifically, they cannot ultimately attribute their saved status, if they possess it, to "natural descent," their Jewishness or descent from Abraham (cf. John 8:33). They cannot ultimately attribute it to "human decision," their own act of belief alone, or their parents' decision to have a child who would eventually declare belief in Christ. Nor is saving faith analogous to a husband's decision to father a child; their belief is not like being "born . . . of a husband's will." Although human response is required to appropriate the redemption Christ brings (John 1:12), that response has a more primal origin than the will of humans who hear and respond, John insists.

With John 1:12–13 underscoring the particular focus and result of God's elective will, the remainder of the prologue stresses the divine initiative in human salvation in two broader yet equally fundamental ways. First, it points to the incarnation (1:14). This too is God's doing, not man's. God "made his dwelling among us" and showed "his glory" through one sent "from the Father." None of these realities originated in human agency or was dependent on human initiative. John 1:18 clinches the point. No person "has ever seen God"; the Lord is known only as "God the One and Only, who is at the Father's side, has made him known." If, as John 1:13 taken with 1:18 implies, saving knowledge of God in Christ is concealed from mankind apart from God's deliberate free move to reveal himself to particular individuals through Christ, then the individual's role in choosing salvation is subsidiary to the divine will electing him or her. How could someone be anything like an equal partner in choosing that which, apart from God's independent, sovereign, and particular self-revelation, he cannot even glimpse?

Second, John mentions grace (1:14, 17). Grace can be understood, as Arminians understand it, as no more than the opportunity to choose the redemption God offers in Christ. But this surely falls short of capturing what John means by the word[7] if we view "grace" in the light of passages like John 1:13 and John 3 (see the next section), and if we view human competence in the light of verses like John 2:24–25: "Jesus would not entrust himself to them, for he knew all men. He did not need man's testimony about man, for

---

7. It occurs in John's Gospel only four times, all in the prologue. Its meaning is so akin to that found in Paul's writings that Hans-Helmut Esser suggests John has been "perhaps influenced by Pauline thought" (*NIDNTT*, 2:119). Esser continues, "In the teaching of [John] as a whole, the gifts which the Revealer brings such as 'life' and 'light' are identified with Jesus Christ himself, and can only be understood as gifts of his grace."

he knew what was in man."[8] As a series of verses will show, grace for John can hardly refer to autonomous human competence to perform that which God will bless with his favor. But unless it does, then its mention in the prologue calls attention to God's initiative in making certain the salvation of particular individuals. It calls attention to divine election.

Divine Election in John's Central Narrative Section

John 1:19–12:50 covers a period of some three years. It narrates aspects of Jesus' life and teaching from the time he was baptized by John[9] to the night Jesus was betrayed. In this section as in the prologue, divine election holds a prominent place as the drama of redemption unfolds.

Divine Election Affirmed in Nine Key Verses

At least nine separate verses contain language that explicitly points to divine initiative, whether of the Father or the Son, in individual salvation. First, John 5:21 states, "For just as the Father raises the dead and gives them life, even so the Son gives life to whom he is pleased to give it." Here is a powerful analogy: As corpses depend on God's vivifying voice to resurrect them, so recipients of "life," or salvation, depend on the Son's good pleasure to give it.

In the famous discourse in which Jesus calls himself "the bread of life" (John 6), three more verses bespeak divine election. One is 6:37: "All that the Father gives me will come to me, and whoever comes to me I will never drive away." Jesus indicates that those who respond to his call somehow do so at the Father's bidding. The Father "gives" to the Son whoever responds. A second verse is 6:44: "No one can come to me unless the Father who sent me draws him, and I will raise him up at the last day." "No one" is unequivocal; whoever comes to the Son does so as the result of the Father's forceful attraction.[10] The individual who is drawn comes and will most assuredly be raised

8. Cf. John 5:34, where Jesus states even of the Baptist's message, "Not that I accept human testimony; but I mention it that you may be saved."

9. The fourth Gospel alludes to but does not explicitly describe Jesus' baptism. Cf. John 1:32–33 and the Synoptic parallels (Matt. 3:16; Mark 1:10; Luke 3:22), all of which speak of the dove that appeared when Jesus was baptized.

10. "Draw" in 6:44 translates the Greek *helkuō*. Outside of John it appears in the New Testament only at Acts 16:19: "they seized Paul and Silas and dragged them into the marketplace. . . ." John's Gospel uses the word to speak of persons being drawn to Christ (12:32), a sword being drawn (18:10), and a net full of fish being hauled or dragged to shore (21:6, 11). The related form *helkō* appears in Acts 21:30 ("they dragged him from the temple") and James 2:6 ("Are they not the ones who are dragging you into court?"). It is hard to avoid the impression that John 6:44 refers to a "forceful attraction" in bringing sinners to the Son.

on the last day. It is hard to imagine a more explicit description of the Lord's selective and effectual drawing activity. A third verse is 6:65, in which Jesus reiterates, "This is why I told you that no one can come to me unless the Father has enabled him." God's enabling activity, which involves the exercise of his elective prerogative, conditions—one could even say triggers—the human decision to come to the Son.

A fifth relevant passage in John 1:19–12:50 is 6:70: "Then Jesus replied, 'Have I not chosen you, the Twelve?'" Later Jesus elaborates on this: "You did not choose me, but I chose you and appointed you to go and bear fruit—fruit that will last" (15:16). These verses speak primarily of Jesus' selection of twelve men to be a core group and to receive special training, responsibility, and ministerial empowerment under his tutelage. One of the twelve, Judas Iscariot, fell away; in his case the "choice" of which Jesus speaks is a step removed from sovereign election to actual salvation in the full sense.[11] Still, for the remaining eleven Jesus' choice of them for service proved to be of a piece with their election to salvation. Is Judas possibly among those of whom Jesus speaks in the difficult saying, "For many are invited, but few are chosen" (Matt. 22:14)?

Sixth, in dealing with Jews who cling to their Abrahamic descent as sufficient merit to lay claim to divine acceptance, Jesus counters, "He who belongs to God hears what God says. The reason you do not hear is that you do not belong to God" (John 8:47). From a standpoint that stresses the autonomy of human will this logic is backward; Jesus should have said: The reason you do not belong to God is that you do not hear and believe. But Jesus furthers the motif, by now well established in John's Gospel, that human response to God owes its ultimate origin to God's elective grace.

Seventh, in John 10:26 and 28 Jesus says to those who reject the implications of his miracles, "You do not believe because you are not my sheep. . . . I give them [i.e., his sheep] eternal life. . . ." This is the same logic just encountered in John 8:47. (It will be seen again at 14:17: "The world cannot accept him, because it neither sees him nor knows him.") The sequence of thought in John 10:26 bears emphasis. Notice that Jesus does not say, "You are not my sheep because you do not believe." That is no doubt true, but it is not what Jesus says. He speaks instead at a level deeper than the surface one of apparent cause and effect, where visible human faith in Christ results in ostensible membership in the body of Christ. Jesus deals with the issue of why certain listeners fail to believe in the first place, not with why they are not his sheep. The answer: They fail to believe because they are not members of his flock.

---

11. Perhaps Jesus' choosing of the Twelve was carried out at the Father's prompting but without Jesus' specific knowledge at that time that not all those he "chose" in a general sense would prove to be savingly "chosen" in the strong sense.

Robert W. Yarbrough

In any case, in John 10:26–27 Jesus again points to the gift of being incorporated by God into Christian community. Without this gift one remains outside the redemptive fold and impervious to the redemptive message. One even attacks that message. Why? Jesus associates this tragic behavior with failure to believe—but he attributes it more fundamentally to not being recipients of the gift that engenders belief.

Eighth, in the same context Jesus refers to the Father as the one "who has given them [his sheep] to me" (John 10:29). This pointer to the divine initiative lying behind the response of those who come to Christ is by now familiar.

Ninth, near the onset of passion week Jesus exclaims, "But I, when I am lifted up from the earth, will draw[12] all men to myself" (John 12:32). Now some contend that to understand *draw* in John as implying irresistible grace results in universalism, since John 12:32 speaks of "all men."[13] But this contention fails on at least two counts. First, it requires that the word *draw* have exactly the same meaning wherever it appears. Such insensitivity to specific context is a linguistic mistake; "draw" can in principle refer to the work of irresistible grace in some passages and to a more general attraction that, say, renders persons accountable but not yet regenerate in others. Second, it overlooks the likelihood that "all men" in John 12:32 refers to all—both Jew and Gentile—that the Father has given to the Son. The fourth Gospel's ubiquitous stress on salvation as something given by God (occurrences of *didōmi* [I give] referring to either Father or Son total more than forty) requires that this possibility receive serious attention. And more particularly, the immediate context, in which Jesus pronounces the climactic fulfillment to his ministry as Gentiles seek him out (John 12:20, 23), suggests that "all" here refers to the elect of both Jewish and Gentile origin, not to the general benevolent effects of the atonement on the human race as a whole.

We are accordingly compelled to understand John 12:32 as a ninth verse teaching that all who come to Christ do so because of his initiative. His lifting up, his crucifixion (John 12:33), is the necessary condition for the possibility of salvation to all who will believe. That crucifixion, though it involved mundane contrivance by both Gentile and Jew at one level, was at a higher level God's own express will in both history[14] and eternity.[15] It owes its occur-

12. See note 10 for other uses of this word in the New Testament.
13. See, e.g., Grant R. Osborne, "Soteriology in the Gospel of John," in *The Grace of God, the Will of Man: A Case for Arminianism*, ed. Clark H. Pinnock (Grand Rapids: Zondervan, 1989), 249.
14. See Old Testament prophecies of the Messiah's atoning death; also, possibly, John 1:29 as well as John 2:19, 3:14.
15. The Father loved the Son "before the creation of the world" (John 17:24) and "sent" him (passim in John's Gospel) from his eternal dwelling place of essential unity within the Godhead (John 1:1) to win salvation in accordance with the divine intention.

52

rence and efficacy to the God who conceived it and arranged for it to take place—and who himself furnished the sacrifice that gives it regenerative power.

Divine Election and the Infrastructure of Salvation History

John's central narrative section (1:19–12:50) contains a number of additional features that call attention to the reality and activity of divine election. The nine key verses are set within a redemptive framework, a salvific infrastructure, that mediates God's saving work in history. This infrastructure is not merely incidental to John's explicit statements regarding divine saving initiative but was rather integral to their actualization in antiquity. And it remains essential to their proper interpretation today.

First, Jesus himself is the product of God's choice, his election. This is seen in John 1:29, when Jesus is identified by John as God's chosen instrument for bearing "the sin of the world." A variant reading of 1:34 calls Jesus "the elect one of God." John 3:35 declares God's unique love for the Son; the Father "has placed everything in his hands." John 5:20 sounds a similar note: "For the Father loves the Son and shows him all he does." Clearly the Son has been singled out by the Father's elective choice. John 6:27 states, "On [Christ] God the Father has placed his seal of approval." In John 6:46 the reader is reminded, "No one has seen the Father except the one who is from God; only he has seen the Father." Jesus is the one "whom the Father set apart as his very own and sent into the world" (10:36). Jesus' ministry, indeed his very presence as bearer of good news, is not due to natural historical process, perceptive human strategizing, or efficacious human belief. It is rather a function of God's own choice in loving and sending his unique elect Son.

Predictive prophecy points to a second facet of the salvation-historical infrastructure chosen and implemented by God. God's knowledge of and control over future events are seen in the Baptist's pronouncements concerning his mission and Jesus' identity (1:23, 33), in Jesus' prediction of his present and coming descent and ascent (1:51; cf. 6:62), in Jesus' perfected embodiment of Davidic zeal (2:17; cf. Ps. 69:9), in Jesus' prediction of his bodily resurrection (2:22), in Jesus' pronouncement to and about the Samaritan woman and her lovers (4:18–19), in Jesus' prediction of recovery for the royal official's son (4:50), in Jesus' prediction that certain of his hearers would die in their sins (8:21), and in Jesus' prediction that Lazarus's death would in a few days result in God's glory (11:4). All these statements—and John's Gospel contains others like them—point to God's elective prerogative in bringing about his redemptive ends.

Third, a cluster of verses in John's central narrative section deserves mention as pointers toward divine election.[16] Given the Old Testament precedent of God's elective activity, the nine verses cited in the previous section, and the salvation-historical infrastructure of Jesus' own election and predictive prophecy, these verses are best understood as confirming that the credit for human redemption is to be reckoned most fundamentally to the account of divine election. Three groups of verses bear this out.

1. Of the Holy Spirit's saving activity Jesus says, "The wind blows wherever it pleases. . . . So it is with everyone born of the Spirit" (3:8). Those who accept Christ's truth and live by his light do so "that it may be seen plainly that what he has done has been done through God" (3:21).
2. A number of passages use a form of the word *give* or *gift* in such a way as to underscore election. John the Baptist, a man of great faith, nevertheless testifies, "A man can receive only what is given him from heaven" (3:27). Jesus calls the eternal life he offers "the gift of God" (4:10). Jesus speaks of "the water I give" twice in the same verse (4:14). Jesus' Jewish listeners claim that their manna-giving deliverer of old had been Moses (6:31), but Jesus insists it was rather God "who gives you the true bread from heaven" (6:32).
3. Finally, Jesus draws a direct analogy between his dependence on the Father's gracious sending and sustaining of his chosen Son, on the one hand, and the Son's gracious feeding of those who come to him, on the other: "Just as the living Father sent me and I live because of the Father, so the one who feeds on me will live because of me" (6:57). If the elective will of the Father sends and sustains the Son, the elective will of the Son works likewise in those who believe.

Divine Election in the Upper Room Discourse and Beyond

The final section of John's Gospel (13:1–21:25) reiterates and in some ways deepens the conception of divine election already established in earlier chapters.

First, there is extensive explicit reference to the election of believers. This is concentrated in John 17, where Jesus speaks of all those whom the Father gave to him (17:2), again stressing the Father's active volition as a causative

16. Out of space considerations we leave aside what we may term God's "semiotic" elective initiative, that is, his expressed will in working miraculous signs *(sēmeia)* to engender faith. See, e.g. , 2:11, 23; 3:2; 4:53–54; 6:2, 14; 9:16; 10:42; 11:45; 12:11. John's entire central section is held together in part by this string of sovereignly effected acts. Their intent is to ground faith. It would be curious if faith in them were to ground its existence in itself.

factor in persons receiving eternal life. Jesus confirms this a few verses later: "I have revealed you to those whom you gave me out of the world. They were yours; you gave them to me . . ." (17:6). In 17:18 the elect Son draws a direct analogy with elect believers as he prays to the Father, "As you sent me into the world, I have sent them into the world." In 17:24 Jesus again speaks of believers as "those you have given me." Through all of John 17 the overarching context, in which Jesus draws a dichotomy between his own and "the world," should be noted: Disciples will see Jesus but "the world" will not (14:19; cf. 14:22); Jesus prays to the Father, "I am not praying for the world, but for those you have given me, for they are yours" (17:9); Jesus likewise prays, "Righteous Father, though the world does not know you, I know you, and they [i.e., disciples] know that you have sent me" (17:25). It would be a mistake for believers, then or now, to fancy that God's prerogative working in their behalf is a reflection of their intrinsic merit—this was the error of some strands of Judaism in Jesus' day[17]—but it cannot be denied that Jesus betrays awareness of a distinctive relationship that obtains between those given by the Father to the Son, on the one hand, and the nonelect "world," on the other.

Second, John 13–21 is replete with more general, but no less telling, rhetoric of ultimate dependence of believers on Christ's (or the Father's) saving initiative. John 13:3 divulges Jesus' awareness that "the Father had put all things under his power." "All things" must include the grace to save and keep his own (cf. John 10:28–29). Conversely, unless Jesus' followers submit to the explicit means he furnishes for their deliverance, they have no part with him (13:8).

Similar rhetoric of ultimate dependence is present in other contexts: Jesus knows those whom he has "chosen" (13:18). His followers are branches on a vine, not the vine itself (15:1). They are clean because of Jesus' word (15:5). Jesus tells the Eleven, "I chose you" (15:16) and "I have chosen you out of the world" (15:19). In various ways and to various degrees, the language of these verses comports with a general understanding that behind knowledge of, or relation to, Christ stands divine election. Believers are ultimately dependent on a gracious working that is deeper and more powerful than human resolve or response could, or should, hope to be.

Third, the final section of John appears to presuppose the same salvation-historical infrastructure that we saw earlier in the central section. An impressive series of verses speaks of the divine superintending will that is active in effecting what the Scripture foretells (17:12; 18:9, 32; 19:24, 36, 37). An even longer string of verses underscores Jesus' foreknowledge of events in

17. See, e.g., Everett Ferguson, *Backgrounds of Early Christianity* (Grand Rapids: Eerdmans, 1990), 427. Romans 11 gives evidence that Gentile Christians were not immune from similar misguided self-importance.

both the near and more distant future (13:33, 38; 14:2–3, 16, 29; 16:2, 4, 8, 20, 32; 18:4; 19:28; 21:19). With Augustine we may rightly insist that such predictions do not imply that human "wills are in the grip of any physical or metaphysical determinism";[18] G. Quell rightly states:

> in the N[ew] T[estament] we never find the danger against which the history of dogma has continually to fight, namely, that of bringing the concept of election into too close proximity to a view which is to be described as enslavement to . . . fate. [Election] is never separated from responsibility and decision. It is never remote from living history. If anchored in eternity, it is also functional in history.[19]

But while predictive prophecy and divine foreknowledge in no way deny human freedom and responsibility, they do limn its parameters. John's closing chapters are of a piece with earlier ones in attributing the divine life at work in believers to divine election.

Divine Election: Cause or Effect of Faith?

John's Gospel lays great stress on divine initiative in salvation. This naturally raises the question: What is the role and importance of human faith? After all, the verb or participle of *pisteuo* (to trust, exercise faith, believe) appears some one hundred times in the fourth Gospel. It is likely that the Gospel's purpose is evangelistic (John 20:31)—it seeks to elicit saving faith. How do divine election and human belief relate?

Grant R. Osborne[20] argues that in John's Gospel "sovereignty and responsibility exist side by side" (245). He suggests that divine election works "with one's faith decision." Election does not produce faith. He terms this solution to the election-belief issue "a modified Arminian theology that balances sovereignty and responsibility" to provide "a better explanation of all the data regarding soteriology in the Gospel of John" (258).

Clearly Osborne's reading of John's Gospel is at variance with the one offered in this chapter. In the remainder of this chapter we will attempt to gauge the contributions and liabilities of Osborne's study, first as a means of appreciating it in its own right, and ultimately for the purpose of arriving at the understanding of divine election in John's Gospel that most adequately reflects what John writes.

---

18. J. N. D. Kelley, *Early Christian Doctrines*, rev. ed. (San Francisco: Harper and Row, 1978), 365.
19. Quell, in *TDNT*, 4:192.
20. "Soteriology in the Gospel of John," in *The Grace of God, the Will of Man*, 243–60. Parenthetical page numbers refer to this essay.

Contributions

A first contribution of Osborne's essay, given the sometimes controversial nature of the topic, is its irenic tone. It is warm with conviction, but exudes no rancor. The author is to be commended for argumentation that is respectful and substantial rather than cutting and merely rhetorical.

Second, the essay is tacitly critical of much contemporary Johannine criticism. Many modern scholars trace John's accounts to traditions or literary processes with little necessary connection to actual history or fact. Or it is claimed that John's content reflects the polemics of one or more early Christian faction against other factions or against the Jews. Osborne calmly and wisely declines to take such theories as seriously as they take themselves. He rightly treats the text as furnishing reliable information regarding actual words of Jesus. Although he makes positive use of modern criticism's real insights, he maintains independent judgment and does not succumb to the authority of a current fashionable school of thought. His exegesis is both contemporary, in terms of critical awareness, and classic, in terms of attempted humble fidelity to revealed biblical truth.

Third, the essay attempts to deal with the full range of the data. It does not flinch at full disclosure of the numerous passages that stress divine sovereignty in human faith. Osborne concedes that John's Gospel explicitly "center[s] more on the sovereignty of God" when compared with some other biblical writings (245). He cites a stress on sovereignty in John 3:1–15 (246). Of John 5:21 ("For just as the Father raises the dead and gives them life, even so the Son gives life to whom he is pleased to give it") he writes, "There is no denying the strong predestinarian thrust of this verse" (247). Of John 6:35–40 he writes, "Here the sovereign control of salvation by God is given greater stress than anywhere else in John . . ." (ibid.). In John 9 and 10 there is "stress" and "emphasis on sovereignty" (250). Sovereignty is likewise "especially strong in 15:16, 19" (252), although Osborne interprets it as referring exclusively to discipleship rather than predestination as well. "Chapter 17 provides major material for the priority of divine sovereignty" (254). Also, "the major theme of John's passion story centers on Jesus' sovereign control of his destiny" (255). Osborne concludes, "For John election is a reality; those who are Jesus' followers have been chosen and given to Christ" (256). In short, Osborne is forthright about the mass of material pointing to the determinative role of divine election in human salvation. It is helpful to see such material discussed rather than passed off as insignificant or ignored.

A fourth contribution is the essay's clarity in terms of its unambiguous dogmatic stance. John's Gospel, Osborne thinks, straddles a theological fault line, a basic unresolved tension between the "conflicting realities" of divine election and human choice (257). How can these two apparent opposites be reconciled?

God is an "equal opportunity" convicter who, in drawing all to himself, makes it possible to make a true decision to accept or reject Jesus. Those who accept are "chosen" and "given" to Christ. That decision is not possible without God's drawing power but it is a free moral decision without irresistible coercion. Election is still theologically true but is not absolute, i.e., apart from man's decision. (257)

As Osborne goes on to explain, election is based on God's foreknowledge (257–58). He sees in advance who will and who will not accept. Those who do are elect. Thus, "election is still theologically true. . . ." But man retains veto power over God's saving choice.

It is helpful that Osborne has left no doubt as to how, in his view, election functions in John's Gospel. The question, however, is whether his view most adequately reflects what John writes.

Difficulties

Despite the merits of Osborne's study, several considerations caution against embracing the conclusion at which he arrives.

First, from a purely logical point of view, divine election and human free will cannot stand on exactly the same level, as Osborne claims they do, unless we are content to find either antinomy (apparent but not necessarily real contradiction) or material discrepancy (contradiction both apparent and real) at the center of John's Gospel. But Osborne opts for neither of these two positions. Thus, while he does maintain that divine election and human choice have equal formal status, the latter is ultimately determinative for the former.[21] Osborne's practical recourse to the primacy of human will demonstrates the logical difficulty of his formal claim and undercuts the viability of his overall argument.

Second, it is doubtful whether John's heavy stress on divine election, which Osborne concedes is found nearly everywhere in the fourth Gospel, can be harmonized with the dogmatic view that sinful humans have an ultimately autonomous capacity to choose Christ and be saved. In other words, Osborne's implicit theological anthropology, one that grants sinners the real potential to elect their present spiritual loyalties and eternal destiny by their own free will, is so sparsely attested in John's Gospel that we doubt its presence can be documented at all. Osborne admits this in conceding that a key

21. A useful analogy is the relationship of Scripture and tradition in Roman Catholic theology. In formal terms they have historically been accorded equal weight. In practice, however, it is the latter that tends to be determinative when the two appear to conflict. The Reformers, themselves steeped in Catholicism, understood this and rightly insisted on the authority of Scripture alone. A similar Gordian knot must, we suspect, inevitably be cut in the question of how divine and human will interrelate. Osborne cuts it to semi-Pelagian proportions.

element in his understanding of election in John—divine foreknowledge as we described it in the previous section—is not found in John (257–58). He admits that he must go to Paul to find words that furnish support. But this is surely a damaging admission, especially since the verses he cites (Rom. 8:29, allegedly confirmed by 1 Pet. 1:2) do not necessarily uphold the view of foreknowledge and election he advocates. Is it not preferable to abide by John's own stated stress in determining what his Gospel means by divine election?

Third, Osborne's presentation yields an unsatisfactory answer to the pressing question of just why recalcitrant first-century sinners, who as a whole neither understood nor received their Creator and Redeemer (John 1:5, 11),[22] ever chose to turn to Christ in penitent personal trust. John's answer, we have suggested, is grounded in the mystery of God's eternal goodness, love, and grace, and mediated in history through what theologians have come to call "election." Salvation is of the Lord. This neither denies nor minimizes human responsibility. But it does indicate who is to be praised for human faith when it arises. Sinners came to Christ because God showed them mercy. Their faith was real, required, and saving—but secondary in causative import when compared with the primary redemptive catalyst of God's free grace. As Donald G. Bloesch explains, "God is the sole source and mainspring of all redemptive action," although "not the sole actor. He is the sole efficient cause of salvation" although "not the only causal factor in salvation. There are also secondary or instrumental causes that have to be taken into account."[23] Osborne's solution is unsatisfactory, then, because it fails to comport with the overwhelming thrust of John's Gospel, in which human faith is a necessary condition for salvation but not a sufficient one.[24] He elevates "secondary or instrumental causes" to such a degree that they supplant the sole sufficiency of divine grace.

Even Osborne admits that in spite of human competency to choose "there is still sovereignty; it is not the act of faith-decision but Jesus' sacrifice that removes sin" (245). We would affirm and expand on this insight as founda-

---

22. Surprisingly, Osborne looks to these verses as evidence of the prologue's stress on human responsibility (244). If so, they show humanity's blind impotence to see the light apart from enabling grace.

23. Donald G. Bloesch, *Essentials of Evangelical Theology* (San Francisco: Harper and Row, 1982), 1:201.

24. The keen observations of a seasoned exegete, premier interpreter of John, and overlooked theologian bear mention here: "If faith bends back upon its own worth and effectual power, then the idea of election arouses only doubt and fear. For the question of when our faith is steady and large enough to make our fellowship with God eternal is just as misguided as the question: When is faith large and strong enough that it is our righteousness . . ." (Adolf Schlatter, *Das christliche Dogma* [Stuttgart: Calwer, [3]1977 (=[2]1923)], 604 n. 297). Schlatter explains: "Because faith is not our own work, but our being grasped [*unsere Ergriffenheit*] by God's work; because it does not stem from self-cultivation but is given to us; faith carries with it no claim that we could enforce as our right before God" (ibid., 446). See also note 26.

tional for grasping John's view of the matter at hand. God's prior act, however it be delimited and named, is the basis for human redemption, in both objective and subjective (experiential) terms. John's Gospel is, overall, adamant on this point. Osborne's study labors, valiantly but unsuccessfully, under the onus of giving a free-will reading to a divine-sovereignty manifesto.

Conclusion

Divine election, foreknowledge, predestination—these are all weighty and complex doctrines. No student of the Bible, church history, or theology should suppose that any one interpreter or theological system has yet managed to grasp and present their nature and function in full scope. Nor should it be supposed that any single biblical document alone can provide all the information needed to ground and expound such doctrines, redolent as they are of themes, events, persons, and truths that cut across the entirety of biblical revelation.

Yet where biblical revelation speaks clearly regarding divine election, as we believe it does in John's Gospel, thoughtful interpreters will consider the normative insights that are present. We have attempted to do that in the first three sections of this chapter, in which we canvassed the whole of the fourth Gospel for its input on the issue of divine election. Our conclusion was that as John presents things, and as the Old Testament seems to support, divine election grounds and gives rise to saving faith, not vice versa. We find ample exegetical support in John's Gospel for the double-edged caveat voiced by Bloesch:

> One must be careful not to convert man into an automaton or robot. He must be recognized as a free agent, though the power and motivation by which he exercises his freedom come wholly from God. To give all the glory to God in the accomplishing of our salvation is not to reduce man to nothing. Yet we must also not say that man gets some of the credit for his salvation, that man can help in the procuring of his salvation. On the one hand is the peril of a divine determinism or fatalism which makes a mockery of human freedom; this is more Stoic than Christian. On the other hand is an egalitarian voluntarism that makes salvation wholly conditional on man's free response. Christ then becomes only half a Savior, and it is no longer possible to speak of the sovereignty of grace.[25]

Thoughtful interpreters will also try to determine the parameters outside of which Scripture's stated truths are no longer adequately recognized or heeded. In the previous section we examined one recent reading of John's

25. Bloesch, *Essentials of Evangelical Theology,* 1:201.

Gospel and suggested points at which it fails to do justice to the full range of what John seems to assert on the question of election.

The claim that faith ultimately precedes, attracts, and in that sense justifies the bestowal of election falls short of grasping the fourth Gospel's combined emphasis on abject human need and sovereign divine grace.[26] The same holds true for the claim that divine election and human choice are suspended in a mutually conditioning, symbiotic state, or that they coexist paradoxically.[27] John's Gospel makes it clear that one is basic to the other, although both are quite real.

Yet even if this chapter's central contention—that John's Gospel affirms the primacy of divine election in human redemption—proves correct, a possible area of significant overlap between it and the position held by Osborne should not be overlooked. Clark H. Pinnock has rightly observed, "There is a spectrum of Calvinisms all the way from supralapsarian to sublapsarian, and a spectrum of Arminianisms from evangelical to rationalistic."[28] Osborne's "modified Arminianism," with its stated intention of giving due weight to biblical statements about divine sovereignty, concurs substantially with more Reformed understandings at those points where its analysis and synthesis lend support to a monergistic rather than starkly synergistic reading of Scripture.

In an age where liberal modernisms and post-modernisms compete with each other in saturating human consciousness everywhere they can with the myth of radical human autonomy, and thus a synergistic understanding of religion where God and religion are taken seriously at all, those who cling to the sole sufficiency of grace in Christ can ill afford to expend their short lives in internecine feuding.[29] This is not to say that issues like divine election in John are not worth careful, even sharp, in-house discussion. It is also not to deny that some of Osborne's language does lend support to a synergistic understanding of justification. But his recourse to the paradoxical coexistence of sovereign grace and human choice at least attempts to leave God free to do his sovereign bidding. We conclude, accordingly, that in an important

26. Schlatter, *Das christliche Dogma*, 604 n. 298, makes a similar observation concerning moves to define election purely in terms of the purpose for which persons are chosen: "The same danger attaches to the attempt to interpret the divine will teleologically as it does to grounding it in our faith: In both cases we prize our work as that which procures for us the divine grace, thereby elevating ourselves over God."

27. But see Bloesch, *Essentials of Evangelical Theology*, 1:201, who defends an understanding of the grace-faith relationship as paradoxical. Yet unlike Osborne he does so without making autonomous free will the final arbiter of who will receive divine grace.

28. "Introduction," in *The Grace of God, the Will of Man*, x.

29. A similar call for cooperation on a wider range of issues, not between Reformed and modified Arminians but between evangelical Protestants and Catholics, is the basis for William Bentley Ball, ed., *In Search of a National Morality* (Grand Rapids: Baker; San Francisco: Ignatius, 1992).

sense Osborne and those of like persuasion are among those who still man the battle line drawn by Scripture, and for that matter by the Reformation, between those who believe that humanity is ultimately its own savior, on the one hand, and those who by the Spirit defer to the Bible's consistent prophetic (and unflattering) insistence that the Lord alone saves, on the other. John's stress on sovereignty, backed, for example, by Paul's epistle to the Galatians, insists that the difference between the two views is by no means insignificant, and certainly not negotiable.

Divine election as sketched in John's Gospel may, then, as Osborne urges, be taken as a salutary reminder to the Reformed believer that human responsibility is a real factor in salvation. It should likewise remind the Arminian-leaning believer that salvation is ultimately God's doing and that both humility and healthy fear of God warn against a doctrine of human sufficiency that would in any way make man equal partners with God in what the Lord in Christ alone can accomplish. It would be tragic if theological differences, real though they be, resulted in neglect of that significant aspect of John's message on which all agree and which both church and world desperately need to hear.

For given the current social, intellectual, and theological climate in North America, Britain, western Europe, and not a few points beyond, it seems likely that divine initiative is in rather more danger of neglect than the fact of human responsibility to choose and the optimism that man can secure his own future by doing so. Thus John's stress on sovereignty, far from requiring fundamental modification or radical reinterpretation along anti-Augustinian lines, calls rather for renewed recognition of the God who inspired John's testimony and of the true nature of his gracious dealings with mankind in Christ.

3

Divine Election in the Pauline Literature

Donald J. Westblade

The apostle Paul taught that God predestines an elect people to be conformed to Christ, to live for the praise of his glory, and ultimately to be glorified in Christ. This much is subject to little dispute. Paul speaks in nearly these words in well-known passages at Romans 8:28–30 and Ephesians 1:3–14.[1] Attempts to understand exactly what Paul meant to affirm in teaching about God's predestining work have sparked differences among Christians of good will across the centuries, differences that persist in the dialogue that this volume engages. It will be the work of this chapter to consider anew the relevant texts in order to see what resolution they can bring to these differing perspectives on Paul's teaching about questions that press at the heart of our moral life: If God is utterly sovereign, are we his creatures robbed of respon-

---

1. Paul's direct authorship of Ephesians, like that of Colossians, the three pastoral epistles, and even 2 Thessalonians, although it is affirmed in the salutation of each letter, is challenged by many contemporary scholars. By far the greater number of those who have declared themselves party to the present discussion of Paul's understanding of election and the human will have also declared themselves as unconvinced as I by the proffered evidence of these letters' sure inauthenticity. They have therefore been ready to align the boundaries of what contributes to a Pauline view to conform with what the church has traditionally confessed by its canon to be Pauline. We must aim to let every text speak for itself, but if I speak of the disputed letters as Paul's my intent is to share the canonical view of what belongs in the domain of this chapter's title, not to dismiss arguments about authorship that call for due consideration in other contexts.

sibility and left to his whim and caprice? If we creatures enjoy some degree of moral autonomy, is God sufficiently in control of the future to keep his promises?

Paul's Overriding Concern

We do not understand Paul well when we remove our questions of him from the larger context of the only answers he makes available to us: his letters to the people and the churches of his mission. Isolated from the aims of the letters, word studies and topical summaries yield abstractions shaped more by our modern interests than by Paul's own stated objectives.[2] It will not suffice to know what terms like "election" or "predestination" mean. Even to Paul they might have signified a range of possible things. We want rather to hear Paul telling us what he understood himself to be doing in distinguishing an "elect" people from another people, whom he usually called "the world." Like everyone else, Paul makes sense of what he does and says by stringing a sequence of purposes together. From those sequences we can gain an understanding of how he ordered his own priorities.

Suppose someone were to ask what I am doing in putting pen to paper. Merely to answer, "writing words," does not address the question sufficiently. I would normally be expected to answer in terms of my purposes: I put ink to paper to compose an argument to contribute to a discussion of grace and election. My intent is to come to clearer resolution of divergent perspectives on a topic of serious moral relevance to the life of the church. One could press me further: And why would you want to do that? I might reply with another objective: I think truth cannot stand in two contradictory places at once and I want to help and be helped to pursue what is true; or with a more subjective purpose: theology and exegesis are my delight. I love to dig deeper into God's Word. I describe my actions in terms of an ordering of my desires and my aims and priorities.

Paul displays a noteworthy consistency when he describes his own actions and those of his churches in terms of the purposes that he aimed for them to serve:

- Paul represents his calls to generosity as calls for the grace of God himself to be extended to more and more people. That in turn becomes a

---

2. See, for example, Krister Stendahl's critical description and reformulation of the earlier Biblical Theology movement in his well-known entry in *The Interpreter's Dictionary of the Bible* (Nashville: Abingdon, 1962), 1:418–32. See likewise James Barr's critique of the *Theological Dictionary* project in *The Semantics of Biblical Language* (1961; Philadelphia: Trinity Press International, 1991), 206–62.

call for increased thanksgiving to God and thus a call to glorify God (2 Cor. 4:15, 9:12–13; Phil. 4:18). Givers do not just give. They worship.

- In opposing judgmental one-upmanship in his churches, Paul acts not only to deter social offenses but also to build harmony in the church, and that not merely for its own sake but for the sake of a united voice to glorify God (Rom. 15:5–6; 1 Cor. 10:27–31).

- To shun immorality, Paul teaches, is to regard one's body as a temple of the Holy Spirit, and that is in turn to glorify God in one's body (1 Cor. 6:18–20; Rom. 6:12–13).

- To sin, by contrast, is not just to break a rule; it is to fall short of the glory of God (Rom. 3:23).

- Paul calls every person to be subject to governing authorities not as a mere act of civil cooperation but because the authorities are ministers of God. In paying them the respect they are due, one pays respect to God himself (Rom. 13:1–7).

- While in prison, Paul refrains from criticizing partisan preachers because he was able to view the restraint not as endorsement of the pretense but instead as support for the proclamation of Christ (Phil. 1:17–18).

- Paul's determination to be released from prison arises from a conviction that his continuing ministry among the Philippians would nurture their progress and joy in the faith, and that in turn is to provide them cause to glory in Christ Jesus (Phil. 1:25–26; cf. 2 Tim. 2:10).

- Even Paul's sufferings (Rom. 5:3–5) and weaknesses (2 Cor. 12:9–10) become occasions for boasting in God because they open up channels for God's love and strength to be displayed.

- In short, Paul believes that whatever one does, even eating and drinking, can and should be conceived of as acts of glorifying God (1 Cor. 10:31).

It was no departure from Paul, therefore, when the Westminster Catechism declared that our chief end as humans is to glorify God and to enjoy him forever. This, I believe we may say without caricature, absorbed Paul as his overriding concern. What he exclaims, quoting Psalm 51:4 in Romans 3:4–5, of the faithlessness of some of his own fellow Jews, "let God be true, though every man be false!" (RSV throughout, unless noted), he might equally say of the narrow scope of every system of value that would honor anything short of God.

The Sovereignty of God: Human Security

Paul's appeals to God's predestining work in the course of history, electing some, hardening others, directing everything without exception toward the good of those who love him (Rom. 8:28) and toward the praise of his own glory (Eph. 1:6, 12, 14), contribute clearly to Paul's overriding concern. The full mastery of God over the present, his complete freedom from challenges that could ever thwart his own will, is the necessary condition of God's deserving full credit for every event in creation. The complete supremacy of God over the future, his complete freedom from the vagaries of contingency, is the necessary condition for God's absolute guarantee to keep his promises. All things, Paul exults in benediction, must ultimately be "from him and through him and to him" if "to him [is to] be glory forever" (Rom. 11:36).

In the context of defending that unobstructible command God enjoys over creation's course toward redemption, to the encouragement of a people groaning inwardly and longing eagerly for what we do not yet see, Paul introduces the reassuring news in Romans 8:29–30 that those who now have the first fruits of the Spirit (8:23) are already "predestined to be conformed to the image of his Son." The revealing of the children of God is already evident, despite the obstacles that tribulation, distress, persecution, famine, nakedness, peril, and sword erect, because nothing shall separate us from the love of Christ (8:35, 38–39). God is supreme.

The sovereignty of God in Romans 8:29–30 supplies the emphasis and the security to the promise Paul holds out to men and women who have grown conscious of the death to which sin had consigned them: "if the Spirit of him who raised Jesus from the dead dwells in you, he who raised Christ from the dead will give life to your mortal bodies also through his Spirit which dwells in you" (8:11). That in turn brings Paul to his conclusion that we are therefore "debtors not to the flesh" (8:12). Our debt is to God, who deserves all the glory.[3]

Paul underlines the completeness of God's sovereignty by making it clear at the outset that the human condition apart from a movement of God's Spirit is death. Apart from God, sin reigns in our lives, so runs the message of Romans 7, and its effect is to leave us no more able to choose what is good than a corpse can. The mind without God is set on the flesh and hostile to God; "it does not submit to God's law, indeed it cannot; and those who are in the flesh cannot please God" (8:7–8). The death of which Paul speaks is first of all a spiritual death, albeit with eventual consequences for the body as well (8:10). In this death, the body still performs its deeds (7:15–20; 8:13); it still lives, even if it walks according to the flesh (8:4–5) and suffers decay (8:21). The rigor mortis has set in on the spirit and mind. "Flesh" is a moral term in this context. What cannot submit and cannot please God is the will. No physical impediment hinders that such a person could set the mind on the

3. Observe how consistently Paul offers all of his thanks, even for benefits obtained through his friends and churches, to God alone. Paul never expresses direct thanks to a human being anywhere in his extant correspondence.

Spirit if he would. The death of the will means he will not submit. The Spirit alone gives it life.[4]

As if death and decay were not sufficient to stress the helplessness of our condition in the absence of the Spirit of life, Paul underscores the point with metaphors of captivity (7:23; 8:21; cf. 6:16, 20). In the absence of the Spirit, Paul recognizes no freedom of the will; only imprisonment and a cry for deliverance (7:24; 8:2, 21). Paul then names the condition upon which escape into the security of freedom and life depends: "you are not in the flesh, you are in the Spirit, if in fact the Spirit of God dwells in you" (8:9), "if Christ is in you" (8:10), "if the Spirit of him who raised Jesus from the dead dwells in you" (8:11). Security may be found only in God. Likewise, freedom consists not in self-determination, for that is bondage, but in rescue from the malevolent destiny of sin into the glorious destiny promised by God.

This promise of security evidently does not apply to all people, however. If it did, Paul would be misleading his readers by appending to his reassurance that God will work all things together for good[5] a restriction of it solely to those "who love him, who are called according to God's purpose"[6] (8:28). If everyone is now or will finally be called in this sense, he could have broadened the expectation of security among his readers by locating it everywhere, albeit at the expense of inviting everyone to take it for granted or to assume that its source is in ourselves. Moreover, readers who prefer an existence for which there is a purpose, and a beneficial one at that, to a world in which

4. Compare 1 Corinthians 2:14. The unspiritual *(psychikos)* person fails not in any physical ability to receive the gifts of the Spirit. The *psychikos* fails to welcome *(dechesthai)* or take delight in those gifts. The gifts do not suffer from inaccessibility but from an appearance of foolishness *(mōria)*. The inability *(ou dynasthai)* to understand them derives therefore not from any physical incapacity (that would render us without responsibility) but from an absence of spiritual discernment *(pneumatikōs anakrinesthai)*, a moral inability (that leaves us without excuse).

5. Both textual variations and ambiguities in translation render the precise wording of this phrase less than fully certain. Still, although commentators divide between the alternatives, "he [God] works all things together" and "all things work together," even Cranfield, who opts with the King James Version for the latter, concludes that "what is expressed is a truly biblical confidence in the sovereignty of God." (C. E. B. Cranfield, *A Critical and Exegetical Commentary on the Epistle to the Romans*, ICC [Edinburgh: T. and T. Clark, 1975], 1:427).

6. The Greek text reads literally, "according to purpose." The phrase is open to interpretation to the effect that God called them "according as they purposed." Early Greek commentators tended thus to see the human act of choice as the basis for God's call in this context, and Forster's and Marston's study of predestination cites their early authority in support of their view of the self-determining power of the human will (Roger T. Forster and V. Paul Marston, *God's Strategy in Human History* [Minneapolis: Bethany House, 1973], 178). But, as Sanday and Headlam note, the Greek fathers adopted this reading of the text chiefly as a counter reaction against their Gnostic opponents (William Sanday and Arthur C. Headlam, *A Critical and Exegetical Commentary on the Epistle to the Romans* [Edinburgh: T. and T. Clark, [5]1975], 216–17). Exegetical considerations (especially the context of the "call" in v. 30; and cf. Rom. 9:11; Eph. 1:11; 3:11; 2 Tim. 1:9) make it unlikely—in Cranfield's view, "decisive," in fact (*Romans*, 430)—that any other purpose than God's is in view here.

outcomes are indiscriminate are bound to welcome the news that the blessings of God's promise in Romans 8:28 are limited according to a principle that is just. No one will be pleased to meet an unrepentant serial killer in the kingdom of God as a result of God's indiscriminately extending his promises of mercy everywhere.

Some would wish to find God's principle of selectivity in a choice that belongs to "those who love him." This is certainly one expression of the restrictive principle, but if it lies ultimately and independently there then the source of our security remains still in ourselves, an unreliable source indeed, and an utterly powerless one at that, Paul would add. This solution by its nature furthermore excludes any purpose for human existence beyond a simple mission to exercise our choice, since the very reason for preferring human choice as a final principle is to reject the controlling influence of any purpose outside the individual's own will.

Yet there, in the purpose of God, is precisely where Paul's restriction explicitly locates our security. Those who love him do so because they have been "called according to his purpose *(prothesis)*." As a principle of selection, his formulation comes as a strong guarantee to readers who know that the purpose of God never changes. It allows, moreover, that individuals do not merely achieve their human purpose in the act of choosing but that history itself has a purpose that gives meaning to every individual's choice. Like the calling of 1 Corinthians 1:23–24, the call to which Paul refers in this verse is a discriminating call. It discriminates on the basis of God's purpose.

Unless the word changes its sense altogether in the verses immediately following, we may also conclude that the calling is, as the systematicians say, "effectual."[7] It always succeeds in setting those to whom it comes onto the path toward glory. The logic of 8:29–30 fails to deliver the full security of the Spirit's first fruits' blossoming into glorification with Christ, upon which Paul's argument depends, if it is not the case that all "those whom God called he also justified." All those whom God calls in this sense must therefore possess saving faith. The call, as Paul uses it here and in every other context where God is its subject,[8] differs, in other words, both in scope and in effect from that general exhortation to faith that Paul issues to all people wherever he preaches. Like the minister's pronouncement that a man and a

---

7. See chapter 8 by Bruce A. Ware in this work and also Calvin, *Institutes*, 3.24.17; Canons of Dort, 2:8; Leon Morris, *The Epistle to the Romans* (Grand Rapids: Eerdmans, 1988), 332–33; or opposing the concept, Robert Shank, *Elect in the Son* (Minneapolis: Bethany House, 1989), 166ff.

8. The only occurrence of the root that falls outside this category in Paul's letters appears in 1 Corinthians 10:27. The calling of 1 Corinthians 1:26 and of 1 Corinthians 7:17–24 are open to interpretation as calls to vocations other than salvation, but in neither case does the summons from God suggest the optional response of a mere invitation. First Corinthians 7:15, Galatians 5:13, Colossians 3:15, 1 Thessalonians 4:7, and 1 Timothy 6:12 represent interesting cases in which the certainty of the call's effect seem to be in question in view of the exhortation

woman are now husband and wife, or a person's shout to a sleeper to "wake up!" this call is a performative utterance. It accomplishes, in the saying, what it says.[9]

Not infrequently, one encounters the protest that God is unworthily pictured as entertaining these same two conflicting wills about the salvation of the world.[10] That God "desires all men to be saved and to come to the knowledge of the truth" (1 Tim. 2:4; cf. 2 Pet. 3:9) is understood to preclude a call from God that discriminates, and discriminates effectually, for any purpose. The objection, however, does not square with common experience. Good parents who are not willing that their children should suffer injuries prefer a world in which their children do suffer some scrapes and falls in order to learn sturdiness and responsibility as they explore the limits of their abilities, to a world in which their children never experience the discipline of a misstep. An important official charged with law enforcement might be similarly of two minds if a close relative were taken hostage: she might be willing for personal reasons to pay any ransom or negotiate any concessions in order to obtain the loved one's freedom; at the same time she understands that her obligations to the public trust demand of her a steadfast will to refuse any concessions to the captors, lest their success encourage others to seek advantages by means of kidnapping.[11]

To attribute two wills in a similar manner to God is no less consistent, no more an affront to his character, and no more anthropomorphic than to attribute one will to him. Even those who displace the point of effectuality

---

to put into practice what is not yet a reality. These cases will be taken up in the context of our human responsibility in the face of divine sovereignty.

9. Further discussion of the performative utterance may be found in J. L. Austin, *How to Do Things with Words* (Cambridge: Harvard University Press, 1962); Donald Evans, *The Logic of Self-Involvement* (London: SCM, 1963); and David H. Kelsey, *The Uses of Scripture in Recent Theology* (Philadelphia: Fortress, 1975), 78–85.

10. To illustrate but one instance, Shank, having cited Calvin as affirming both that God's good pleasure is to doom many (*Institutes,* 3.21.7) and that our desire as evangelists ought to be that all may be saved (*Institutes,* 3.23.14), objects: "What inconsistency! It is tragic, especially in view of the baneful effects on the Church and the cause of the Gospel through four centuries and more, that Calvin's theology prevented him from acknowledging that God desires what Calvin himself desired: the salvation of all men." *Elect in the Son,* 165 n. 2. Even I. Howard Marshall's balanced appraisal of the biblical evidence concludes that the competition Calvinists find between God's preceptive will and his decretal will yields an "intolerable self-contradiction." ("Predestination in the New Testament," in *Grace Unlimited,* ed. Clark H. Pinnock [Minneapolis: Bethany House, 1975], 137). On the question of there being two wills in God, see chapter 5 by John Piper in this work.

11. Recall the analogous and credible, if fictitious, dilemma of a U.S. president in *Fail-Safe,* Eugene Burdick and Harvey Wheeler (New York: McGraw-Hill, 1962). Despite his will that his wife should live, his will that millions be protected from nuclear war prompts him to invite the nuclear destruction of a single city, a city in which he knows his own wife happens to be visiting.

from God's call to an alleged free will in the human agree (unless they are prepared to affirm an eventual universalism) that God elevates a will that the world should include people who in their freedom do perish over his will that not any should perish. This they can do only by assuming that Paul's view of God's overriding concern makes human freedom paramount. Yet Paul consistently awards pride of place instead to God's purpose to glorify himself.

Just as Jesus can weep over the death of Lazarus and the unbelief of his survivors in Bethany, knowing that he has and will employ the power to overcome both, just as parents can be upset that a lazy child has received a failing grade in school and in the same moment be glad that the school has shown integrity by awakening their child to the consequences of laziness, so also God is capable, without contradiction, of understanding the same event from varying angles and with varying contexts in view. Therefore, no need remains on the strength of this objection to disregard the exegetical observation that Paul speaks of a call of God that is extended to some and not to others, a call that ensures the justification and the glorification of those to whom God directs it.

Paul goes on in the following two verses to enlarge upon the call of God in two directions. The results of the call are assurances of justification and glorification. The bases for the call are God's foreknowledge and predestination. Questions about the absolute sovereignty of God over the election of his people arise primarily at the root of foreknowledge from which Paul affirms the blossom of glorification assuredly springs. Many of the early church fathers, for example, understood Paul's reference to foreknowledge in this verse as an endorsement of the view that God's work of foreordination depended upon God's advance knowledge of a human faith and a fitness that people would display wholly apart from his initiation.[12] In this view, human self-determination takes the first step. God, who has voluntarily limited his sovereignty in this respect in order to preserve human freedom, opts to wait, to cajole, and to react.

Several curious results emerge from this initially plausible perspective.[13] First, God's reaction to human faith apparently and remarkably precedes the waiting and the pleading that eventually do elicit faith in some hearers. But if God possesses infallible foreknowledge that some will have faith, he has as little and as much reason as any strong predestinarian to wait, to plead, or to send missionaries to these foreseen believers. Second, if God knows reliably that some are not going to choose to put their faith in him in response to the means of persuasion that he also knows will carry the gospel message in each case, why does he not also experimentally alter those means until he hits

---

12. See, for example, Theodoret and Origen; Cyril of Alexandria supplies with "foreknew" the words "that they would be conformed to the image of his son."

13. See chapter 7 by S. M. Baugh in this work for a detailed study.

upon the means that he sees in advance do succeed in persuading? Is there not, on the premises of this view, some possible world in which everyone chooses freely to exercise faith and so fulfill God's desire that all should be saved and come to a knowledge of the truth? The point of mentioning such curiosities is to underline what Jonathan Edwards once made so clear: infallible foreknowledge of an event presupposes the necessity of that event and therefore precludes its real freedom.[14] If it can be foreknown with certainty that I shall leave this room in half an hour, I have no freedom to do otherwise than certainly leave this room in half an hour. No attempt to carve a realm of freedom (to do otherwise) out of the wholly foreknown future can ever yield coherent results.

Most modern commentators, having recognized this logic, have come close in varying degrees to identifying foreknowledge with election itself.[15] But even if we were to concede Roger T. Forster's and V. Paul Marston's insistence that the Bible nowhere uses the words *know* or *foreknow* to mean "choose" or "elect" and only at best connotes the idea with these words,[16] we must still conclude that foreknowledge in Romans 8:29 and elsewhere implies the certainty of future events. That certainty and the security it holds out to those who believe God's promises are all the weight that Paul requires the word to bear in this context. And any attempt to smuggle in an ultimate role for the human will on the vessel of Paul's word, foreknowledge, only diminishes Paul's capacity to affirm his message of certainty.[17]

14. Jonathan Edwards, *Freedom of the Will*, ed. Paul Ramsey (New Haven: Yale University Press, 1957), 2, sect. 12, 257–69. The same is acknowledged in a careful essay by Richard Rice ("God's Foreknowledge and Free-Will Theism," in *The Grace of God, the Will of Man: A Case for Arminianism*, ed. Clark H. Pinnock [Grand Rapids: Zondervan, 1989], 127–28), who therefore goes on to defend an Arminian view in which the foreknowledge of God must be limited from any awareness of "the content of future free decisions" (134). That limitation then precludes the use to which the early fathers put God's foreknowledge in Romans 8:29–30 as a way of resting God's predestination upon a prior human faith. It also, however, exposes God to the genuine risk that the future may yet turn out contrary to his deepest intentions.

15. Ernest Käsemann, *Commentary on Romans*, ed. and trans. Geoffery W. Bromiley, 4th ed. (Tübingen, 1980; Grand Rapids: Eerdmans, 1980), 244: "προγινώσκειν refers to eternal election"; Morris, *Romans*, 332: so close are they that "we must be on our guard against making the two say the same thing"; F. F. Bruce, *The Epistle of Paul to the Romans: An Introduction and Commentary*, TNTC, vol. 6 (Grand Rapids: Eerdmans, 1963), 177: to foreknow has "that connotation of electing grace which is frequently implied by the verb 'to know' in the Old Testament"; James R. Edwards, *Romans*, NIBC (Peabody, Mass.: Hendrickson, 1992), 219: "Foreknow refers to God's eternal purpose"; Cranfield, *Romans*, 431: "it denotes that special taking knowledge of a person which is God's electing grace"; J. Zeisler, *Romans* (Philadelphia: Trinity Press International, 1989), 226: "'Foreknew' amounts to the same thing as elected."

16. Forster and Marston, *God's Strategy*, 178–208. See similarly William W. Klein, *The New Chosen People: A Corporate View of Election* (Grand Rapids: Zondervan, 1990), 163–64.

17. In Morris's words, summarizing his reading of this verse, "We are not to think that God can take action only when we graciously give him permission. Paul is saying that God initiates the whole process" (*Romans*, 332).

We see that Paul's overriding concern to ascribe sovereign glory to God forever by depending upon all things from him, apprehending all things through him, and attributing all things to him comes to consistent expression throughout the epistle to the Romans as he offers an extended defense of his joyous lack of shame in the gospel (1:16; 11:36). In most of his other letters the same perspective on election is more presupposed than brought into the foreground; but one letter, the circular letter addressed in most manuscripts to the Ephesians, may rival Romans for forthright and elevated statement of God's sovereignty over the destiny of his creatures.[18]

Three times the opening chapter of Ephesians draws up the work of God in electing *(eklegesthai)* the saints before the foundation of the world to be fellow heirs with Christ into God's grander purpose to magnify the praise of his glory (1:6, 11, 14).[19] All things that have been created (1:10) and all things that occur (1:11) accord with the good pleasure (1:5, 9, *eudokia;* RSV: purpose) of God's will, a purpose that he set forth beforehand in Christ as a plan *(oikonomia)* for the fullness of time. Those who have now heard the word of truth in the gospel and have put their faith in Christ have therefore been sealed *(sphragizesthai)* with the promised Holy Spirit who, as in Paul's argument to the Romans, is thus the security (1:13, *arrabōn;* see also 2 Cor. 1:22; 5:5) of the saints' inheritance. In order that the grace of God receive all the praise, Paul leaves no room for human boasting that our hope for the future may be found in anything that is true about ourselves (2:8–9). Salvation is a gift of God and depends wholly upon God's call (1:18; 2:8).

Paul also diagnoses the human condition apart from God in terms nearly identical to those in the epistle to the Romans. Without God we are dead (2:1, 5). Sin, marching to orders from "the spirit that is now at work in the sons of disobedience" (2:2), has killed the human capacity for passion toward anything but the flesh, those desires of body and mind (2:3). The incapacitation is a moral one that does not hinder us physically but clouds "the eyes of the heart" (1:18). In that state we may look for no hope in ourselves

18. As what Samuel Taylor Coleridge called "the divinest composition of man" (*Table Talk* [Princeton: Princeton University Press, 1990], cited by F. F. Bruce, *The Epistle to the Ephesians* [Old Tappan, N.J.: Revell, 1961], 11), Ephesians may well rival any literature for sublimity. The address to the Ephesians in the letter's superscription is missing in the earliest manuscripts. Marcion's copy (ca. 150) was apparently addressed "to the Laodiceans." But the specific provenance of the letter does not affect the present discussion. In accepting the traditional name, Ephesians, we remind ourselves that the letter, as a probable circular letter, was intended for a larger audience than the Ephesian church, an audience that reasonably includes ourselves.

19. It is worth noting how regularly the term *to elect (eklegesthai)* serves as a synonym for God's gracious love *(agapan)* both in Paul and elsewhere in the New Testament. Luke substitutes "elect" for "beloved" in God's baptismal designation for his Son in the formula of the other Synoptics. And Paul, as he does in Ephesians 1:4–5 and 2:4–6, also directly associates the two terms in Romans 11:28 and 1 Thessalonians 1:4. It is fitting that Paul, who considers God's merciful love the pinnacle of the glory that God gives his saints to praise (Eph. 1:6; cf. 1 Cor. 13), should equate God's call and its divine purpose with the exercise of that glory.

(2:12). Moral corpses that we are, the only hope we have for a will that turns its passion toward God lies in the call of God, sounding effectually into the grave where we lie helpless. By that merciful call God makes "us alive together with Christ (by grace you have been saved!)" (2:5). It is not our doing, Paul declares (2:8).

We stand secure only because God has brought his hostility against our rebellion to an end (2:16). He accomplished that reconciliation through the death of Christ, Paul explains (2:13–16). And the sovereignty of God over that human event ordained its occurrence with such certainty that Christ could come confidently preaching its peace for a lifetime before it actually took place (2:17). That is the same security that Paul wants the recipients of this letter to seize for themselves in their anticipation of the life of praise that is the saints' glorious inheritance, thanks to the resurrection of Christ from the dead (1:19–20). Paul's employment of the vocabulary of election and predestination consistently serves his aim to build confidence that God reigns in sovereign control over human affairs.

Clearest evidence of Paul's own confidence in the sovereignty of God over the human heart and will may be found in the manner in which he prays. Nowhere does Paul pray that God should withhold his hand from human wills and respond only at the prompting of human faith. Rather he prays

> that God would enlarge the love of the Philippians more and more (Phil. 1:9)
>
> that the Lord would make the Thessalonians increase and abound in love to one another (1 Thess. 3:12)
>
> that the Lord would give the Thessalonians peace, eternal comfort, and good hope (2 Thess. 2:16; 3:16)
>
> that God would make the Thessalonians worthy of his call and fulfill every good resolve and work of faith by his power so that—by grace!—the name of the Lord Jesus would be glorified in them (2 Thess. 1:11–12)
>
> that God would prevent wicked people from hindering the progress of the gospel toward triumph (2 Thess. 3:1)
>
> that God would direct the hearts of the Thessalonians to the love of God and the steadfastness of Christ (2 Thess. 3:5)
>
> that God would bring his Jewish kinspeople to salvation (Rom. 10:1)
>
> that God would overcome the unbelief of people in Judea to the end that they would welcome and not reject the offering Paul was bringing to them from Gentiles (Rom. 15:31)
>
> that God would ensure that the effect of evangelism would be to promote knowledge of the good that is ours in Christ (Philem. 6)

that God would give the Ephesians a spirit of wisdom and revelation by enlightening the eyes of their hearts (Eph. 1:17–18)

that God would give him boldness for preaching (Eph. 6:19–20)

that God would so fill the Colossians with the knowledge of his will that they would lead a worthy life that pleases him (Col. 1:9–10)

that God would strengthen the Colossians with the sort of power that makes endurance and patience joyful[20] (Col. 1:11–12)

And he asks others to pray

that God would overrule in the circumstances of his imprisonment in order that Paul could be freed to minister further to the Philippians (Phil. 1:19–20)

that God would overcome their anxieties with his peace that passes understanding and that keeps hearts and minds in Christ (Phil. 4:6–7)

that God would provide Paul with receptive opportunities (an "open door") for his preaching and that he would make the gospel as clear as he ought when those opportunities occur (Col. 4:3–4)

that God would prompt kings and rulers to make decisions that ensure a quiet and peaceable life for Christians (1 Tim. 2:1–2)

And he says that Epaphras prays

that God would enable the Colossians to stand mature and fully assured in all the will of God (Col. 4:12).

Paul's persistent prayers of thanksgiving, we have already noted, express all gratitude to God for every activity of faith, hope, and love that he knows his congregations have performed. The thanks are due to God because the attitude has come as a gift from God (e.g., 1 Thess. 1:2–3; 2 Cor. 8:16).

Forster and Marston maintain that "God leaves man with free choice. He does not 'force' repentance on a man who chooses a path that does not delight him. If it has been our practice to pray that God will do the latter, then our practice should change, not our theology. Our theology should be the same on our knees as in a Bible study."[21] The evidence just cited betrays no sign that Paul expects God to "force" a person to do anything. No one who understands even the strictest Calvinist aright could conclude that Calvinism

---

20. Regardless of whether the sentence is punctuated so that the phrase *with joy* modifies "being strengthened" or "giving thanks" (NASB), this attitude of the will remains part of what Paul prays that God would impart.

21. Forster and Marston, *God's Strategy*, 39.

itself expects this of God, if by "force" one means that God causes persons to act contrary to their will. In praying that God would cause a person's will to be in harmony with God's own will, one prays that in obeying God the person's will would be in wholehearted agreement.[22] Paul does pray in expectation that God would sovereignly and irresistibly motivate repentance in persons who now walk a path that does not delight him. He displays no reluctance to call upon God to extend the reach of his sovereign power as far as the human will. Whose practice is otherwise? If our theology elevates the human will to a status that requires us to pray any differently than Paul, then our theology should change, not our practice.

Paul's theology, both in deed and in word, leaves the human in the rôle of proposer and God always in the role of disposer (cf. Prov. 16:33; Job 34:13). Paul's vigorous defense of the sovereignty of God aims in turn always at the same two-sided goal: that God should receive the glory for all things that are and occur, including the choice of whom he shall call and the response of these elect in faith; and that the elect should recognize the unshakability of their security in the unwavering resolve of God himself to be glorified for his faithfulness to his own purposes. Because his own glory is at stake in them and he is sovereignly in control, the promises of God are absolutely certain.

The Image of God: Human Responsibility

Paul seems to have succeeded only too well in establishing the security of God's elect people within God's sovereign direction over history. But at what cost? some may protest. Prisoners in solitary confinement are secure. Children of overly protective parents are secure. Many people stagnate in stultifyingly tedious jobs because those jobs and their benefits are secure. If the security that Paul promises the Romans and the Ephesians therefore proves to leave no room for creative and responsible expression of our individual wills, then the gospel he preaches is upon closer inspection not such "good news" after all.

---

22. The suggestion that the "will" can be "forced" is already incoherent. A person might be forced against his will, in which case our judicial sentiments transfer responsibility to the one doing the forcing. But if an act of motivation changes the will itself, then this is the opposite of what we mean by "force." We now say that the person acts voluntarily or willfully, and our judicial sentiments assign responsibility to the one whose will was changed.

A corollary to this observation is that certain senses of the term *free* when applied to the will result equally in incoherence. If by the attribution of freedom we mean only that a person in the exercise of her will encounters no physical hindrances, then there is no incoherence but only an application of the term strictly to the will's being exercised. But if by the attribution of freedom we refer to the will's determination and allege it to be uncaused or self-determined apart from external causes (including God), then we commit ourselves to an infinite regression of the will's determining the will and forfeit coherence.

But nothing Paul says implies that under the sovereign direction of God the human will, of sinner and saint alike, suffers any loss of responsibility. He considers the evidence that God deserves the praise of all people for the splendor of his glory and the trust of all people for the faithfulness of his promises to be so fully evident that no one escapes accountability to it (Rom. 1:20–21). Paul finds God's moral expectations so sufficiently clear that finally "every mouth may be stopped and the whole world may be held accountable to God" (Rom. 3:19).

Paul likewise anticipates great creativity from and ascribes great significance to the endeavor of human wills. Corinthian zeal to participate in Paul's collection stirs up Macedonian eagerness to give, and their liberality becomes a spur to greater Corinthian generosity, all of which overflows in supplying human needs in many places and in prompting many thanksgivings to God (2 Cor. 8–9). Paul himself, moved by the conviction that no one can call upon him in whom they have not believed nor believe in him of whom they have never heard nor hear without a preacher (Rom. 10:14), labored under great obstacles to spread the gospel across the Mediterranean world. These are not the activities of robots nor of those who think they have to do with robots.

Behind these human responsibilities stood Paul's conviction that God's human creatures, having been made in his image, have a capacity to imitate God's nature. God sets forth purposes (*prothesin protithesthai*, Eph. 1:9); so too does Paul (Rom. 1:13; 2 Tim. 3:10). God makes judgments (Rom. 2:16; 3:6; 1 Cor. 5:13); so also are the readers of Paul's letters to do (1 Cor. 5:12; 6:2–3).

Christ provides Paul his perfect example of humanity in the image of God's character (Phil. 2:6; Col. 1:15, with 2:9). But perfect fidelity to the original is not the decisive feature of an image. However imperfect the image might grow through its successive reflections, Paul takes a sanguine view of the possibility that he may in a strong and meaningful sense imitate Christ and that his congregations may further imitate him as he does so (Phil. 2:5; 1 Cor. 11:1; Eph. 5:1; 2 Thess. 3:7–9).

Above all, the imitation is moral. As God has a will, so his creatures are given a will with which to purpose and to choose. And Paul unmistakably summons those human wills into action in all his letters and preaching. The actions to which he summons them are, moreover, no mere rôle assignments to actors or optional suggestions for passing the time. Paul presents them as indispensable conditions for his readers' eternal salvation. "To set the mind on the flesh is death, but to set the mind on the Spirit is life and peace" (Rom. 8:6 RSV). "If you live according to the flesh you will die, but if by the Spirit you put to death the deeds of the body you will live" (Rom. 8:13). The Spirit bears witness that if we are children of God then we are heirs of God and fellow heirs with Christ, "provided we suffer with him in order that we may also be glorified with him" (Rom. 8:16–17). If anyone preaches a gospel contrary to the one he preached, Paul declares, he is subject to anathema (Gal. 1:8–9). As curious as it initially appears, we find throughout Paul's letters that the certain future God sovereignly guarantees to his chosen saints depends upon their fulfilling moral conditions, yet at no expense to the certainty of that guaranteed future.

There is thus in Paul's writings none of the fatalistic or mechanical determinism of which predestinarian positions are sometimes accused.[23] Rather one finds an emphatic both/and. God is absolutely sovereign, and his human creatures are possessed of full responsibility. Similarly, as I. Howard Marshall has argued, "there is evidence that the Pauline doctrine of salvation emphasizes both the believer's assurance of salvation and the possibility of falling into grievous sin and even of loss of salvation."[24] Marshall refers to it as a paradox.[25] We are here up against what New Testament ethicists have long referred to as "the tension between the indicative and the imperative." Paul proclaims the accomplished fact, for example, in Colossians 3:3, that "you have died, and your life is hid with Christ in God." He then proceeds in nearly the next breath to exhort the Colossians to "put to death therefore what is earthly in you" (3:5) as though they had not already died. On several occasions Paul follows up a declaration of the accomplished and effectual call of God itself with admonitions to put the call into practice (Gal. 5:13; Col. 3:15; 1 Tim. 6:12).

One sees a distinct family resemblance between this apparent conflict and Jesus' language of the kingdom of God in the Gospels. There Jesus refers at times to the kingdom as having already arrived and at times to its having not yet arrived. The resolution that George E. Ladd and others have succeeded in bringing to that tension raises hopes that the similar "paradox" in Paul may also not lie beyond resolution. Like the interim between an election and an inauguration or the one between D-Day and V-E Day, Ladd argued, there is a sense in which the dawning promise of the future already works as a present reality, and another sense in which one awaits its full consummation. Both are true at once.[26]

An analogous resolution presents itself in the case of the tension in Paul's language of ethics and will, because both cases hinge upon the way in which promises work in our human experience. Consider two patients suffering identical subjective symptoms from identically alarming and painful tumors. At the

---

23. E. g., Shank, *Elect in the Son*, 163, 224–26; Forster and Marston, *God's Strategy*, 34–35, 81; note I. Howard Marshall's similar caution against pressing biblical predestination into the mold of mechanical causation ("Predestination in the New Testament," 138).

24. I. Howard Marshall, *Kept by the Power of God: A Study of Perseverance and Falling Away* (Minneapolis: Bethany, 1969), 122.

25. Ibid., 75.

26. See George E. Ladd, "The Solution to the Problem of the Future and Present Kingdom," in *Crucial Questions about the Kingdom of God* (Grand Rapids: Eerdmans, 1952), 77–98.

moment, their levels of physical suffering are completely comparable. Yet, while one is still awaiting word of his condition, the other has received news that her tumor is benign and operable; she is assured that her prognosis is for a speedy recovery. Despite the outwardly identical state of their suffering now, the certainty of the latter patient's happy prognosis has interposed a world of difference between these two patients. The one describes her condition with confidence, the other with looming despair. What resides wholly in the future as a promise has already begun to transform the reality of the present.

Does the certainty of future health relieve our hopeful patient from the responsibilities of submitting to active and frequently painful therapies along the route to recovery? By no means. On the contrary, it motivates her to undergo them. She finds the incentive of renewed health irresistible. Those therapies, she knows, are the indispensable condition of her regaining her health, and the certainty of the promise that she will attain to good health through them furnishes her the will to endure whatever temporary suffering they may entail.

So it is with Paul's evident understanding of our route to spiritual health. The certain future God sovereignly guarantees to his elect saints can depend without contradiction upon their fulfilling moral conditions if the promise of the certain future itself can be counted upon irresistibly to furnish sufficient incentive for fulfilling the moral conditions. That incentive will prove irresistible, Paul indicates, wherever God is pleased in his merciful purpose to give his Spirit of life and freedom (Rom. 8:5, 9, 11, 14; 1 Cor. 2:12, 14) to deliver a person from the distorting and fatal influence of sin (Rom. 7:9–25). The promises of God may be both certain and conditional, because God sovereignly supplies the condition. Both are true at once.[27]

In our analogy we must therefore suppose that the doctor now arrives not with bad news for our first patient, but with good news. The difference is that this patient, despite every good reason to do so, cannot find it within himself

---

27. This compatibilist conclusion enjoys a strong consensus of those who focus their study on the biblical evidence, despite their contrasting perspectives in other regards. Compare, for example, Marshall's critiques of Calvinism (*Kept by the Power of God,* 210) with D. A. Carson's more sympathetic view of Calvinism in *Divine Sovereignty and Human Responsibility: Biblical Perspectives in Tension* [Atlanta: John Knox, 1981], 220.

Historically strict Calvinists themselves championed the same compatibility, even if modern stereotypes often paint a one-sided picture of their stress on divine sovereignty. The thesis Jonathan Edwards set out to prove in his monumental *Freedom of the Will* (152) asserted that "necessity is not inconsistent with liberty." A century earlier John Owen (*A Display of Arminianism* [1642; Edmonton: Still Waters Revival Books, 1989], 36) argued similarly: "though some agents, as the wills of men, are causes most free and indefinite, or unlimited lords of their own actions, in respect of their internal principle of operation (that is, their own nature), [they] are yet all, in respect of his decree, and by his powerful working, determined to this or that effect in particular; not that they are compelled to do this, or hindered from doing that, but are inclined and disposed to do this or that, according to their proper manner of working, that is, most freely."

See also the references to evidence of the compatibility in Jewish sources given by Zeisler, *Romans,* 226 note q.

to believe this good news and so lapses even further into despair. His failure to believe disinclines him from all surgery and therapy. Despite the assurances of new health if he would only undergo treatment, he in his refusal succumbs to death.

So again it is with Paul's understanding of the path to spiritual death. But here the inevitable objection must be met: Those under the fatal influence of sin should not be held responsible in the same way as the despondent patient for their failure to fulfill the conditions of spiritual health, because the analogy has broken down. Unlike the patient's doctor, God himself gives and withholds the ability to trust. God, not the sinner, should therefore be held responsible. Once again, however, as plausible as it appears in abstraction, the objection does not square with our own human experience.

Let us first of all note that the ability the patient cannot find within himself, or by analogy the ability Paul affirms that God gives, an ability to trust or to have a will that is favorably disposed, is a moral ability, one that we commonly distinguish in practice from our natural or physical abilities. My natural inability, as a human, to fly and my physical inability, as an untrained amateur, to run a four-minute mile differ demonstrably from my inability to bring myself to inflict injury on someone I love. Naturally and physically I may be equipped with the necessary strength and skill to abuse a loved one. I can do it. But I still speak conventional, moral sense when I also say I cannot do such a thing or, perhaps more idiomatically, that I cannot bring myself to do such a thing.

The ambiguity in our language is important to observe, because responsibility depends upon the freedom of my physical and natural abilities, and not upon the freedom of my moral ability. I cannot be held responsible for failing to take flight on command. I cannot be held responsible, at least without months or years of preparation, for failing to run a mile in four minutes, even if someone's life depended on it. But I can be held responsible if I could not bring myself away from my easy chair to prepare an afternoon's lecture or if I could not restrain myself from overindulging in pastries since we moved next door to that bakery.

To the degree that our patient's inability to believe his optimistic diagnosis may be traced to chemical and hormonal imbalances, he and we would tend to excuse his abandonment of hope and try to correct its physical causes. But to the degree that he knows the inability arises from a sheer failure of nerve or resignation to despair (the illustration is far from hypothetical!), the patient himself will experience guilt. He will hold himself responsible.

In these examples of moral inability, ones that philosophers call cases of the weak will, I know what I am doing is wrong and contrary to my better interests, even as I lounge and overindulge, just as the patient in the latter case knows his resignation is both ungrounded and counterproductive. Therefore we can agree that, if I and he were free, in a morally important

79

sense of that term, namely, free from any hindrance to attain what is in our best interest, we would do what we knew was to the greatest advantage instead of allowing our short-sightedness to get the better of us.

In admitting to ourselves the irrationality and the self-destructiveness of our behavior, we acknowledge that something apparently restricts our freedom. The restriction confronts us as a given and not a product of our deliberations about what is best. This is what we find our wills now desiring. All the same, in my experience (and in the professed experience of classrooms full of students who have acknowledged finding the same weakness of will in themselves), an awareness that we lack this moral freedom never relieves our own conscience of an ounce of its feeling of guilt. If anything, it arouses it. In just the same way Paul, having concluded that "if I do what I do not want, it is no longer I that do it, but sin which dwells within me" (Rom. 7:20), nevertheless displays no sign of absolving himself of the least bit of responsibility for his failure. If our conscience then raises no objection against our responsibility when it knows the will to be driven by the malevolent taskmaster of sin, even less objection should arise from the knowledge that God's benevolent sovereignty determines its bent instead.

We find confirmation therefore in our own experience that Paul need be charged with no inconsistency in setting statements of our moral inability and our lack of moral freedom side by side with robust reminders of our responsibility as though there were no question of their compatibility. When we inquire far enough after the purposes for the actions we feel we do voluntarily, we invariably run up against a certain givenness about why we do what we do.[28] As much as we will ourselves to be who we are, there remains as strong a sense that we also cannot help but be who we discover ourselves to be.

Champions of the will's self-determination preclude themselves by their premises from arriving at any ultimate answer to why we find ourselves disposed to will in the way that we do. Proponents of God's absolute sovereignty over the will, conversely, are prepared to attribute our malign dispositions to sin, and even those, like our better dispositions, ultimately to God. That God and a righteous purpose should be found at the origin of our ability or inability to trust ought finally to be preferable to the poor patient's coming upon no identifiable reason at all for his inability to trust his doctor's news, or to my being at a loss to explain why I relax in the easy chair while urgent work calls to me in vain from my desk.

If the illustration from experience succeeds in resolving the alleged conflict between God's sovereignty and human responsibility and its expression in the conditionality Paul attributes to promises that he also assures are certain, the

---

28. No less an authority than Aristotle observed and stated the same long ago: "[everyone] takes some end for granted"; what we deliberate about is "how and by what means it can be achieved" (*Nichomachean Ethics* 3.3.11 [1112b.15]).

resolution has not, we must hasten to add, dispelled any of the divine mystery that continues to characterize Paul's perspective on God's work of election. It does, however, relocate the mystery from these conflicts where systematicians tend to find it into the practical sphere of human behavior where Paul himself locates it. To Paul, the mystery is not that we retain responsibility in the face of God's sovereign control over us. To Paul the mystery is the presence of sin and lawlessness in the world (2 Thess. 2:7)—that faced with the desirability of the promises God holds out before us we (and he; Rom. 7) would ever consent to sell the birthright we have in them for a mess of pottage.[29] Sin, to Paul, is no mere violation of a rule. Sin is inexplicable foolishness.

There is no question for Paul that the image of God in which the human creature is made imparts to us a responsible, creative will. But an image implies two things at once. We are in the image of God, but we are only the image of God. Our wills are responsible like God's, but we are at the same time wholly dependent upon God for the exercise of our responsibility.

As a preoccupation with subjective enjoyment in our recreation, rather than with the skiing, the boating, or the music itself, spoils the attainment of joy, so, too, the moment we remove our eyes from the security and motivation of the promises by which God calls us, to focus instead upon our own willing and walking, we sink like Peter on the water. Nowhere in Paul is there a suggestion that God deals with us coercively, but everywhere there is the conviction that he deals irresistibly with those who find his promises irresistible. He appeals to all people as responsible humans, not as marionettes, holding out his promises as motives to the will. And whosoever has a will that has been made alive by the Spirit and rescued from the bondage of sin to will freely, not only may but will come.[30]

The Justice of God: Human Exultation

Again Paul may have succeeded in establishing the avenue of responsibility by which God sovereignly guarantees his elect people their share in the inher-

---

29. Marshall's studies of the New Testament evidence arrive at the same conclusion: *Kept by the Power of God,* 196; "Predestination in the New Testament," 138; "Universal Grace and Atonement in the Pastoral Epistles," in *The Grace of God, the Will of Man,* 69.

Paul's other major use of the term *mystery* applies it to the long-awaited gospel that has now been revealed in Christ. These references occur almost entirely within the context of correspondence to cities in proximity to a major center of the Greek mystery religions (Corinth, Ephesus, Colosse), where the word enables Paul to supplant the focus of local religious attention with the gospel, showing the gospel's superiority on the mysteries' own terms.

30. To those who may object with a wishful lament that they desire to be among these elect but fear that God may be excluding them, Paul would therefore admonish them that they take heart from their very desire that God has indeed begun to enliven them and that they should lay hold of these promises as their own. But the guarantee that they are elect resides always in the promise of God, not in the evidence of their desire.

itance of Christ. But at what cost? some will protest. Whosoever will may come, but if the ultimate determination of who it is that does will lies in God and not the voluntary individual, then God, it would appear, is not just. He is arbitrary. Marshall, for instance, demurs: "I cannot see how it can be just arbitrarily to save one guilty sinner and not another; and there can be no doubt that any human judge (for it is the pattern of the judge which provides the model) who behaved in this way, and a fortiori any human father who treated his sons in this way, would be regarded as falling below the standards of Christian justice."[31]

Paul is by no means oblivious to the objection. He deliberately angles his argument in Romans 9 to address it. "Is there injustice on God's part?" (9:14). And "why does [God] still find fault? For who can resist his will?" (9:19). Because in Paul's logic the promise of a sure and glorious future depends utterly upon God's faithfulness in keeping his word, this argument to which he turns in Romans 9–11 is essential to and scarcely separable from the conclusion he has defended in Romans 8:1, 11, 21, 28, and 37–39. God has made similar promises to his elect people in Israel, and yet (Paul can barely bring himself to state the problem directly; one has to return to 2:17–24 or 3:3, 9 for even an oblique formulation of it) some of those in Israel, to whom the very oracles (promises)[32] of God had been entrusted, have proven to be unfaithful and under the power of sin. Their very law that taught them to discern what is excellent (Rom. 2:18; cf. Phil. 1:10) had become twisted into an invitation to its own violation. The commandment that promised life was instead breeding death (Rom. 7:10–11). Despite God's sovereignty, some even in Israel were apparently excluded from among God's elect.

As Robert Shank and others have stressed, throughout Paul's letters "election is Christocentric."[33] Yet even that statement turns out, in the divine economy Paul describes, to be penultimate. Ultimately, in Paul's argument to the Romans and his Ephesian doxology, as everywhere in Paul, election is theocentric. We must consider then that Paul's concern about the charge of injustice on God's part represents but a piece of a larger and even more distressing concern that his assurances of security appear to stand upon a promise from God that now may have failed. And we must therefore widen the lens at first to review this larger picture before focusing again upon the question of God's evenhandedness.

Space does not permit a full and detailed exegesis of these three important

31. Marshall, "Predestination in the New Testament," 136.
32. The Greek word *logia*, which can refer to any sort of sayings or oracles, is applied in the standard BAGD lexicon of New Testament Greek (476) at Romans 3:2 in particular to "God's promises to the Jews."
33. Shank, *Elect in the Son*, 27.

chapters.[34] For the course of Paul's argument let us content ourselves to observe that Paul means to attest most emphatically that the word of God has in no way whatsoever failed. All that has transpired across the span of Israel's history, from the prospering of Jacob and the hardening *(sklērunein)* of Pharaoh's heart to the insensibility *(pōrōsis)* that has come upon part of Israel[35] and the spiritual riches that have come to the Gentiles, has happened according to plan, in conformity with and in pursuit of God's purpose of election (9:11). No hint of a notion occurs here or anywhere in Paul's letters that God may be rolling dice. The case could not be put more plainly than Paul does it himself: God's determination to extend compassion to whomever he will "is not [a matter] of [human] willing or running but of the mercy of God" (9:16, author's translation). The objections of 9:14 and 19 carry their force precisely because God's absolute sovereignty to elect whom he will according to his own divine purpose is the point Paul wants to stress. The good news Paul proclaims is that God has limited himself neither in knowledge nor in power from fulfilling his promises to glorify those who love him, those who are called according to his purpose.

We may also observe in the context of Romans 9–11 Paul's most concentrated use of the term *election*. Six of his letters make but a single reference to the elect, to election, or to God's electing (Eph. 1:4; Col. 3:12; 1 Thess. 1:4; 1 Tim. 5:21; 2 Tim. 2:10; Tit. 1:1). In 1 Corinthians 1:27–28 we find also a clustered contrasting of God's choices with worldly, human choices. But in these three chapters of Romans Paul speaks of election *(eklogē)* four distinct times (9:11; 11:5, 7, 28); in addition, he has already spoken in 8:33 of "God's elect" *(eklektoi)*.

Of the four occurrences of "election" three play their usual rôle as the principle according to which God enacts his purpose. As 9:11 puts it, it is an

---

34. Exegesis of the most controverted portion of these chapters relevant to questions of divine sovereignty in election (Rom. 9:1–24) has, in any case, been convincingly argued already in John Piper's *Justification of God: An Exegetical and Theological Study of Romans 9:1–23* (Grand Rapids: Baker, [1]1983, [2]1993). In addition, see chapter 4 by Thomas R. Schreiner in this work.

35. It is worth remarking at least in passing that the solution Paul offers to the problem at hand entails a rejection of the premise that election is strictly national. The allegation that God had broken his word to Israel rested upon the premise that descent from Jacob, which defined the nation, also defined the range of God's mercy. This Paul denies, declaring that "not all who are descended from Israel belong to Israel" (9:6). Individual branches of this family tree were broken off because of their unbelief (11:20). Recently Klein has argued well that Paul has the election of corporate entities in view throughout the argument of Romans 9–11 (*The New Chosen People*, 173–76). The argument is in my view persuasive but not exclusive. If God can single out a body of people as heirs to his promises without objection, then no new objection should arise against his singling out the individuals who compose that body, as he has evidently done in distinguishing the "children of the promise" from the "children of the flesh" (9:8) or in dividing corporate Israel into "the election" that obtained the promise and "the rest" who were hardened (11:7). See further chapter 4 by Thomas R. Schreiner in this work.

"according-to-election purpose" that God is carrying out in history. God's determination to choose a particular people through whom to display his faithfulness to his promises, Paul reiterates, explains why one cannot conclude that God has abandoned Israel despite all distressing appearances (11:1, 28). The evidence amid the distress lies in the persistence of a remnant, individual members of Israel like Paul, and like the seven thousand in Elijah's day (11:4; cf. 1 Kings 19), whose life of faith God also ensures "according to the election of grace" (11:5, author's translation).

Immediately after the appearance of the term in 11:5, where he has exemplified the security of God's faithfulness to the chosen nation by providing present evidence for it in a set of its individuals, Paul abruptly shifts the use of "election" in the fourth instance from the abstract principle to its concrete embodiment in the remnant chosen by that principle (11:7). Here the election is set into contrast not with a principle of works (9:11; 11:5) nor with a gospel that the Jews reject (11:28) but with those Israelites themselves who "were hardened."[36] Here also Paul becomes most explicit about the manner and the purpose with which he understands God carries out his work of election.

As to the manner, two points receive emphasis. First, in an adamant echo of 9:16, Paul insists that the presence of a faithful, elect remnant has nothing to do with its human deeds or distinctives and has solely to do with the mercy of God (11:6). Those who belong to this number could do so only because God has taken the initiative effectually to call them into it. Second, the presence of a hardened remainder is equally the work of God. The passive expression, "were hardened," in 11:7 could only refer to God's action, in view of the scriptural text that Paul immediately cites in its elaboration.[37] "God gave them a spirit of stupor" (11:8 = Isa. 29:10). Although Scripture is understandably reticent to dwell upon God's ultimate will that some of his creatures be consigned to destruction, one can only with difficulty deny that Scripture expressly ascribes actions of hardening, blinding, rejection, and even destruction to God; they are not merely acts of response. Indeed, that God should single some out for election to life and freedom already entails the necessity of his rejecting all others in the process.[38] Paul's point is that the rejection is purposeful.

36. Sanday and Headlam (*Romans*, 313) suggest that the use of the abstract term for these clearly physical individuals indicates a concern on Paul's part to stress that the reason for their success in obtaining what the rest did not lay in God's action rather than in their identity as the elect.

37. Edwards (*Romans*, 262) calls it "clearly a 'divine passive,' meaning God's hardening of Israel."

38. In Paul Jewett's words, "Election obviously implies rejection. . . . If the scriptural language of election sounds unfamiliar to our ears, surely the language of rejection sounds even more so. Yet such language is too prominent and persistent in Scripture to be simply edited out of the vocabulary of contemporary theological discourse" (*Election and Predestination* [Grand Rapids: Eerdmans, 1985], 26).

As to the purpose, Paul is concerned in this context with God's unexpected severity in hardening this large portion of Israel. He allays that concern with the ensuing argument of 11:11–32. In verse 11 he asks the purpose of Israel's current disobedience.[39] Is this late stumbling of so many destined to bring their long heritage as the chosen people to nothing but ruin? It is a more specific way of posing his major question of 9:6: Has the word of God itself failed? The point of the extended diatribe in these chapters is to answer both with a resounding no. In giving to part of Israel "a spirit of stupor" God is not in the act of dooming his chosen people; he is in the act of expanding his work of reconciliation abroad to the entire world (vv. 12, 15). He is in the act of magnifying his merciful character for all to see (v. 32).

Some do stumble. Many of those who stumble do fall to ruin. Only the universalist will argue otherwise. Those whose overriding concern is human self-determination and a preservation of human standards of fairness must argue that the ruin of those who fall is a declaration of the value of humanity and of human freedom. Paul, on the other hand, argues that God "endure[s] with much patience the vessels of wrath made for destruction, in order to make known the riches of *his* glory," a glory that includes not only his mercy to those "prepared beforehand for glory" but also his power and wrath (9:22–23; italics added). If it were the case that none at all fell, the full force of the wrath of God in opposition to sin and the full strength of his dedication to preserving the integrity of his glory as a perfect gift to those who desire it would never become known or displayed. There, in Paul's scheme of values, lies the greater potential injustice.

The justice *(dikaiosynē),* or righteousness, of God, Paul has made clear earlier in 3:1–26 among other places,[40] consists not merely in his loyalty to his covenants of mercy, nor merely in his commitment to honor the just requirements of the law, nor merely an evenhanded fairness in his treatment of

---

39. Commentators dispute whether verse 11 in fact raises the question of purpose, despite the formal purpose clause *(hina pesōsin).* As Sanday and Headlam note (*Romans*, 321), the stricter grammarians of nineteenth-century German philology contended for consistent application of the classical (purposive) sense of *hina* even in the New Testament Koine. English interpreters, on the other hand (to which Sanday and Headlam proceed to join themselves), "admit the laxer use." Israel is the one doing the stumbling, those who dispute the purposive *hina* would argue, and a deliberate intent to fall cannot sensibly be ascribed to Israel. Yet in the second half of the verse, Israel is also the one committing the trespass, and it would be just as senseless there that Israel should be deliberately disobeying the gospel in order to contribute to the salvation of Gentiles. Clearly in this second half, Paul's focus lies upon the purpose God is working out through the vehicle of Israel's behavior. There is therefore no reason that should not be the case, and every presumption that it should, similarly in the first half.

40. See the arguments by John Piper in "The Righteousness of God in Romans 3, 1–8," *ThZ* 36 (1980): 3–16, and "The Demonstration of the Righteousness of God in Romans 3:25, 26," *JSNT* 7 (1980): 2–32.

humanity, but foremost, at the root of each of these consequent commitments, an uncompromising dedication to honor himself. This is but the universal application of the most ordinary definition we give to justice in the human sphere: God is unswervingly resolved that all credit should go where credit is due. That is, without exception, to himself.

There can be no objection, Paul concludes, least of all on the grounds of justice, if God's purpose for his actions is to ensure the full display of his wrath and power together with his mercy, as a complete expression of his glory (9:22). If he feels constrained to hide some aspect of his glory, he falsely implies that something about him is shameful. If he does not magnify the full extent of his glory, he fails to be completely loving to those for whom his glory is their highest delight, for he withholds from them something of himself that is grand. If friends are deeply chagrined to receive a gift that has been cheapened by exposure to belittling ridicule on the way to being given, how much more Paul expects God at all times resolutely and fiercely to defend his glory against the offenses of sinful rebellion. That he so protects and defends this most precious gift he has to give to them is not simply an act of justice. It is finally an act of love in which the elect exult.

Far from a random act of capricious choice, God's work of election is guided by the highest of all purposes. For God to act according to any lesser standard would in the end prove intolerable to us.[41] The same judicial sentiment that would respect a human judge for his evenhandedness would vilify him for setting a paramount value upon a wooden evenhandedness if it came at the genuine expense of national security or massive, unnecessary loss of human life.

Paul indicates by his own exultation in the doxology at the close of Romans 9–11 that he believes his argument has vindicated the justice of God from charges of unfaithfulness and caprice. God sets the cause of absolute justice before him in every decision he makes. It comes to expression in his fulfilling the just requirements of the law (Rom. 8:4). It comes to expression in his keeping his promises of mercy in the covenants (11:27). And it comes to expression in the evenhanded fairness he shows in appealing to every individual through the avenue of the will. God offers his glory to everyone who, having been given a taste for it, desires it. Paul seems to anticipate that no one will go to destruction shaking a fist at God for unfair or undeserved treatment. Therefore all those who do recognize the justice of God in his dealings with the world will find in it great cause to exult.

41. In C. K. Barrett's words, cited by Morris (*Romans*, 332): "The history and personal make-up of the Church are not due to chance or to arbitrary human choices, but represent the working out of God's plan. . . . Our own intentions, like our own virtues, are far too insecure to stand the tests of time and judgement."

Conclusion

The apostle Paul affirms without hesitation that God elects individuals in the world to become heirs of his promises in Christ. His anthropology requires such a view of election, for he believes a person apart from the life-giving Spirit of God lies spiritually, helplessly dead, with a will hopelessly in the clutches of sin. His theology requires this view of election, for he believes God is and must be acknowledged as the source and spring of all that is and occurs in creation. But election for Paul is an evangelical message, a declaration of good news. And his missiology takes inspiration from his view of election, for it is finally an evangelical conviction, a declaration of good news. The sovereignty of God promises security to his people, even as the image of God imparts creative responsibility to each one. Election proves as pivotal to Paul's theology as it was to his Israelite ancestors, for the God who announced to Moses, "I will be what I will be," still sets at the heart of the revelation of his just purpose to Paul the proclamation that "I will have mercy on whom I have mercy. . . so that my name may be proclaimed in all the earth."

4

Does Romans 9 Teach Individual
Election unto Salvation?

THOMAS R. SCHREINER

Calvinists typically appeal to Romans 9 to support their theology of divine election.[1] In particular, they assert that Romans 9 teaches that God unconditionally elects individuals to be saved.[2] By "unconditionally" they mean that God, in eternity past, freely chooses specific individuals whom he will save (Eph. 1:4) and that his choice is not based on their foreseen faith or effort (Rom. 9:16). God does not simply foresee, say Calvinists, that certain people will put their faith in him, for apart from his work of grace to overcome their resistance to him no one would or could desire to come. Rather, he foreordains and determines that those who have been chosen will exercise faith.

The Calvinist exegesis of Romans 9, however, is increasingly questioned today.[3] Many scholars believe that the doctrine of individual election unto salvation is read into the text by Calvinists and cannot be defended by an examination of the entire context of Romans 9–11. In this chapter I want to

From Thomas R. Schreiner, "Does Romans 9 Teach Individual Election unto Salvation? Some Exegetical and Theological Reflections," *JETS* 36, 1 (March 1993): 25–40. Reprinted by permission. This chapter includes some minor changes from the original.

1. I am particularly grateful to Craig Blomberg, who carefully read this chapter, pointed out some weaknesses, and helped me sharpen my argument at some points. It will become evident that Blomberg and I still disagree on some interpretive issues.
2. For the best recent defense of this viewpoint see John Piper, *The Justification of God: An Exegetical and Theological Study of Romans 9:1–23* (Grand Rapids: Baker, [1]1983; [2]1993).
3. Romans 9:1–29 is specifically in mind, but for convenience I shall often label the text as Romans 9 in this chapter.

explain two of the objections to the Calvinist reading of Romans 9, and then to examine whether the objections are compelling and persuasive.

The two most common objections to the Calvinist interpretation of Romans 9 are as follows: (1) Romans 9 is wrongly explained if one understands it to refer to salvation. Paul is not referring to salvation in this text. Instead, the historical destiny of different nations (especially Israel) is being narrated. (2) Even if Romans 9 does relate to salvation in some sense, it does not refer to the salvation of individuals. The section relates to the salvation of groups, of corporate entities, and not of individuals.

Each of the two objections will be explained and examined more closely.

Historical Destiny or Salvation?

The first objection is that the text does not necessarily relate to salvation. Rather, Paul is describing the historical destiny of nations.[4] For example, while discussing Romans 9:14–18, Roger T. Forster and V. Paul Marston say, "The question at issue is not the eternal destiny of anyone, but the history of Israel and their significance as the chosen nation."[5] This same understanding is reflected in a comment of C. E. B. Cranfield on Romans 9:14–18:

> It is important to stress that neither as they occur in Genesis nor as they are used by Paul do these words refer to the eternal destinies either of the two persons [Jacob and Esau] or of the individual members of the nations sprung from them; the reference is rather to the mutual relations of the two nations in history. What is here in question is not eschatological salvation or damnation, but the historical functions of those concerned and their relations to the development of the salvation-history.[6]

Others argue similarly that the temporal destinies of both Esau and Jacob are in view in both the Old Testament citations (Gen. 25:12; Mal. 3:1) and in Romans 9:11–13.[7] To understand that salvation is in view in the reference to

4. J. D. Strauss, "God's Promise and Universal History: The Theology of Romans 9," *Grace Unlimited*, ed. Clark H. Pinnock (Minneapolis: Bethany Fellowship, 1975), 195; Leon Morris, *The Epistle to the Romans* (Grand Rapids: Eerdmans, 1988), 356.

5. Roger T. Forster and V. Paul Marston, *God's Strategy in Human History* (Wheaton: Tyndale, 1973), 67. They go on to say, "Neither Moses' nor Pharaoh's eternal destiny is in question. It is the bearing of Moses and Pharaoh on the earthly function and destiny of Israel that is at issue" (75). And the choice of Isaac rather than Ishmael is described in similar terms (53–54). They assert that the choice of Isaac rather than Ishmael was related not to salvation but to God's overall strategy in history.

6. C. E. B. Cranfield, *A Critical and Exegetical Commentary on the Epistle to the Romans* (Edinburgh: T. and T. Clark, 1979), 479.

7. Cf. Craig L. Blomberg, "Elijah, Election, and the Use of Malachi in the Old Testament," *Criswell Theological Review* 2 (1987): 109–16; W. S. Campbell, "The Freedom and Faithfulness of God in Relation to Israel," *JSNT* 13 (1981): 29.

Esau and Jacob in Romans is very unlikely, according to Craig Blomberg, because there is no doubt that the Old Testament contexts refer to the temporal and historical destiny of peoples rather than to salvation.[8]

Despite the apparent plausibility and increasing popularity of the view that Paul is referring to historical destiny rather than salvation in Romans 9, such an interpretation is mistaken. (It should be noted, however, that Blomberg believes that single predestination to salvation is present in Romans 9:21–23 but should not be read into the earlier part of the chapter.)[9] It is erroneous because it fails to account for both the specific context of Romans 9 and the wider context of Romans 9–11. In other words, what concerns Paul in Romans 9–11 is not merely that Israel has lost temporal blessings, or that its historical destiny has not evolved the way he anticipated. Paul agonizes over the place of Israel in Romans 9–11 because too many in his nation were not saved. The evidence to support that salvation is the issue in view is as follows.

When Paul speaks of the anguish in his heart and his desire to be accursed because of his fellow Israelites (Rom. 9:1–3), he feels this way not because Israel is merely losing out on temporal blessings. Distress torments his heart because his kinsmen from Israel were not saved. Paul is almost willing "to be cut off from Christ" (9:3) because his fellow Israelites are separated from Christ.

The thesis of Romans 9–11 in 9:6 to the effect that "the word of God has not failed"[10] *refers to God's promises to save his people Israel.*[11] The assertion that God's word has not failed in verse 6 should be linked to what Paul has just suggested in verses 1–5 about his kinsmen being separated from Christ. He is not merely speaking of the temporal blessings of Israel in history, nor is he making a general statement about God's strategy in history. The particular question in his mind in verses 1–5 relates to the salvation of Israel, and thus the claim that God's word has not failed (9:6) must be interpreted in relationship to the issue that is at the forefront of Paul's mind—namely, the salvation of Israel.[12]

8. Blomberg, "Election," 109–11.
9. Ibid., 112–13.
10. So Cranfield, *Romans*, 473; Campbell, "Freedom," 28.
11. R. Badenas rightly sees the intimate connection between God's faithfulness to his promises and the salvation of Israel in 9:6 (*Christ the End of the Law: Romans 10:4 in Pauline Perspective*, JSNTSup 10 [Sheffield: JSOT, 1985], 85). Nonetheless, he still asserts that the subsequent verses do not relate to salvation.
12. S. Williams questions such an interpretation in his review of Piper, *Justification*, because Romans 9:6 speaks of the faithfulness of God's word to Israel in relation to the promise that Gentiles would be included in the people of God (*JBL* 104 [1985]: 549–50). Williams also affirms that the separation of Israel from Christ in 9:3 is only temporary. God will eventually have mercy on all (11:32). Williams's first point can be affirmed without affecting the main point being argued for here. One reason Paul brought up the salvation of Israel was precisely because if God's promises to Israel could not be trusted, then how could Gentile believers be sure that the one who predestined them to salvation would bring about their promised glorification (8:28–

Those interpreters who assert that Paul is referring merely to the historical destiny of Israel and not to salvation do not account plausibly for the relationship of verses 1–5 to the rest of the chapter, for verses 1–5 make it eminently clear that the reason Paul brings up the question of the faithfulness of God in verse 6 is that a great portion of Israel is not saved. Indeed, in the rest of Romans 9–11 Paul tries to unfold how God's word has not failed, even though a large portion of ethnic Israel does not now believe in Christ. The succeeding verses (9:6b–11:36), therefore, are best understood as dealing with the specific issue that Paul raised in verses 1–6a—namely, God's faithfulness to Israel, even though many Jews fail to believe in Christ.[13] Interpreters who think Paul is describing the historical destiny of the nation apart from any reference to salvation are forced to say that Paul departs from the very issue that he brought up in 9:1–6a.

The subsequent context in Romans 9:6b–29 also demonstrates that salvation is in view. For example, Paul argues that mere ethnic descent from Abraham does not make anyone a child of God (9:6b–9). It is the children of the promise who are truly the children of God. The phrases *children of God* (*tekna tou theou,* 9:8) and *children of the promise* (*tekna tēs epangelias,* 9:8) always refer in Paul's writings to those who are the saved children of God (cf. 8:16, 21; Phil. 2:15; Gal. 4:28).[14]

---

30)? If God's promises to Israel are left unfulfilled, then the church can have no assurance that nothing will separate her from the love of Christ (8:35–39). Nevertheless this does not negate the fact that Paul is still referring to the salvation of ethnic Israel in these verses. That ethnic Israel is in view is rightly argued by B. W. Longenecker ("Different Answers to Different Issues: Israel, the Gentiles and Salvation History in Romans 9–11," *JSNT* 36 [1989]: 96–97). What Paul says about Israel has implications for the Gentiles, but it is not entailed that Paul is speaking about Gentile Christians in 9:6b–9. Williams's second point cannot be examined in detail here, but it seems to suggest that Paul believed that all people would be saved and that the divine hardening will ultimately be lifted for all. In fact, Piper has elsewhere shown that universalism cannot plausibly be read out of Romans 11 ("Universalism in Romans 9–11? Testing the Exegesis of Thomas Talbott," *Ref J* 33 [1983]: 12–13).

13. So Longenecker, "Different Answers," 96.

14. Blomberg's objection ("Election," 114) that "this proves too much" since Paul's goal is "to point out the perennial existence of a remnant *within Judaism*" does not seem convincing. I agree with Blomberg that Paul is probably speaking only of Jews in Romans 9:6–9, but such an admission hardly damages the point that when Paul says "children of God" (9:8) or "children of the promise" he is thinking of people who are saved. In this particular case he has in mind Jewish believers. All Blomberg's objection proves is that Paul is not referring to all Christians, but his comment hardly proves that Paul now uses the phrase *children of God* or *children of the promise* to refer merely to the reception of earthly promises. Paul typically uses these phrases to describe those who are part of the redeemed community, and the specific context of Romans 9 represents a narrowing of the term in the sense that Jewish Christians can also be designated as "children of God" and "children of the promise." Paul restricts himself to describing Jews who are "children of God" and "children of the promise" because of the specific issue that he is examining—namely, the failure of many in Israel to believe (9:1–5). To put it another way: The larger set of "children of God" and "children of the promise" includes all those who believe, both Jews and Gentiles. But here in 9:8, because of the specific issue on his mind, Paul refers to a subset of "children of God" within the larger set. The fact that he refers to a subset

In addition, Romans 9:11–12 confirms that the topic is salvation and not merely the reception of earthly promises, for Paul says that God's election is not "by works but by him who one calls." Elsewhere when Paul speaks of works he refers again and again to the thesis that no one can be justified by "observing the law" or by doing any works at all (cf. Rom. 3:20, 27–28; 4:2, 6; 9:32; 11:6; Gal. 2:16; 3:2, 5, 10; Eph. 2:9; 2 Tim. 1:9; Tit. 3:5). Since Paul typically claims that salvation is not by works, the burden of proof is on those who see him employing this terminology in a nonsalvific way in Romans 9:11–12. The specific context of Romans 9 confirms that salvation is in Paul's mind since his concern in 9:1–5 is that Israel is not saved.

Second Timothy 1:9 supports the idea that salvation is in view in Romans 9:11–12, for the subject matter of the verses is remarkably similar. Second Timothy 1:9 says God "saved us and called us to a holy life—not because of anything we have done but because of his own purpose and grace. This grace was given us in Christ Jesus before the beginning of time." This is remarkably parallel to Romans 9:11–12. The parallels between the texts are at least fourfold: Both speak of God's "call" *(kaleō)*; both stress that the call was not based on "works" *(erga)*; both refer to God's saving "purpose" *(prothesis)*; both say that this salvation was decided before human history began. It should also be noted that in 2 Timothy 1:9 the calling is expressly defined as a saving one. Indeed, "calling" in Paul (Rom. 9:7, 24, 25, 26; 1 Cor. 1:9; Gal. 1:6, 15; 5:8; Eph. 4:1, 4; 1 Thess. 2:12; 4:7; 5:24; 2 Thess. 2:14; 1 Tim. 6:12; 2 Tim. 1:9) is most often associated with a call to salvation. And Romans 9:24–26 in the near context clearly refers to the call of both Jews and Gentiles to salvation.

Romans 9:22–23 also suggests that Paul is speaking of salvation and eternal destruction, for he contrasts the "objects of wrath—prepared for destruction" with the "objects of mercy, whom he prepared in advance for glory." The word for "destruction" *(apoleia;* Phil. 1:28; 3:19; 2 Thess. 2:3; 1 Tim. 6:9) Paul often uses for eternal destruction, while "glory" *(doxa;* Rom. 2:10; 8:18; 1 Thess. 2:12; 2 Tim. 2:10; cf. Col. 3:4) is sometimes utilized to describe eternal life. And we should note again that all of this fits with the main issue that troubled Paul when he wrote this chapter—namely, that Israel was not saved. He has not left this issue when he comes to the end of the chapter, for he cites Isaiah to the effect that "the remnant will be saved" (Rom. 9:27).[15]

---

within the larger set of those who are designated the children of God does not logically prove Blomberg's point that "children of God" does not refer to salvation here. In fact both the narrower context of Romans 9–11 and the Pauline usage of the phrase indicate that salvation is in Paul's mind.

15. Another argument in favor of the idea that Paul has salvation in mind in Romans 9 is the connection between 8:28–39 and 9–11. In 8:28–39 Paul asserts that those who have been predestined to salvation will be glorified, that God will give them all good things, that no charge will stand against them in God's court, and that nothing will separate them from the love of Christ. But how can believers count on these great saving promises in 8:28–39 if God's promises

A compelling argument against the view that Paul is merely discussing the historical destiny of nations is the wider context of Romans 9–11. It is generally agreed upon by New Testament scholars that these chapters are a unit and should be interpreted as such.[16] If this is so, then it is unlikely that Paul treats one issue in 9:1–29 and then moves to an entirely separate question in 9:30–11:36. The point I am making is that if the subsequent context of Romans relates to the salvation of Israel (and Gentiles), it is probable that the previous context (9:1–29) does as well. The argument goes as follows:

When Paul says in 9:30–33 that Israel failed to attain righteousness by law because she pursued the law "not by faith but as if it were by works," it is clear that he is referring to Israel's failure to attain right standing with God. I know of no scholar who maintains that Paul is speaking merely of the earthly promises that Israel failed to obtain.

The issue of Israel's salvation or the lack thereof continues in chapter 10, for Paul informs the reader that his prayer to God is for Israel's salvation (10:1). The expression of Paul's desire for Israel in 10:1 is parallel to his anguish for Israel in 9:1–3, and in both texts the concern of Paul's heart is that Israel is not saved, that she is separated from Christ (cf. 9:3). In other words, since chapters 9 and 10 both begin with the same concern (many in Israel are not saved), it is very improbable that chapter 9 relates merely to earthly promises for Israel while chapter 10 speaks of her failure to obtain salvation. Both chapters should be taken together (along with chapter 11) as an answer as to why many in Israel are not presently saved.

Israel's failure to obtain salvation and the inclusion of Gentiles into the people of God continue in the subsequent verses. Israel tried to establish her own righteousness (10:3), and thus she did not experience the righteousness that comes from God. Paul is referring to the fact that Israel has not been saved because she tried to establish her righteousness by works (10:4–8). And that Paul has salvation in mind is confirmed by 10:9–19, for verse 9 says

---

to Israel have not been fulfilled? If the saving promises made to Israel came to nought, then the saving promises made to the church may as well. By affirming that God will fulfill his promises to Israel, Paul also assures the church that the promises made in 8:28–39 will come to fruition. The link between 8:28–39 and 9–11 suggests that the saving promises of God are what Paul has in mind. For this same point see W. D. Davies, "Paul and the People of Israel," *NTS* 24 (1977–78): 13.

16. The unity of Romans 9–11 is a given in New Testament scholarship. Most recent New Testament scholarship on these chapters does not examine the theological issues being investigated in this chapter. Issues such as the relationship between Jews and Gentiles in Paul's theology, the consistency of the chapters, the light they cast on the Roman situation, and his view of ethnic Israel are at the forefront of New Testament scholarship today. For some representative examples see Longenecker, "Different Answers," 95–123; Campbell, "Freedom," 27–45; Badenas, *Christ the End*, 81–96; M. A. Getty, "Paul and the Salvation of Israel: A Perspective on Romans 9–11," *CBQ* 50 (1988): 456–69; E. J. Epp, "Jewish-Gentile Continuity in Paul: Torah and/or Faith? (Romans 9:1–5)," *HTR* 79 (1986): 80–90; N. Walter, "Zur Interpretation von Römer 9–11," *ZTK* 81 (1984): 172–95.

that those who confess and believe in Jesus "will be saved." Indeed, Paul affirms that "everyone who calls on the name of the Lord will be saved" (10:13). Israel's problem is that she has not "accepted the good news" (10:16), and thus the Gentiles have become recipients of salvation to provoke Israel to jealousy (10:19).

Romans 11 confirms the idea that all of Romans 9–11 should be understood as answering the question about the fulfillment of God's promises regarding the salvation of Israel, since Paul introduces himself as an illustration of a saved remnant (11:1–10). Paul does not introduce the concept of the remnant in order to say that the earthly promises given to Israel are coming to fruition in the remnant. His point is clearly that God has not forsaken his people Israel, because he is saving a portion of them.

It should be pointed out that some of the themes unfolded in 11:1–10 remind the reader of what Paul said in 9:6b–29. Both passages refer to God selecting a remnant out of ethnic Israel (9:6b–13, 27–29; 11:2–5), to the election of some (9:11–13, 24–26; 11:5–7), and to the hardening of others (9:17–18; 11:7–10). Presumably both passages speak to the same issue—namely, the salvation of Israel.

And Paul is not merely speaking of earthly promises or the temporal destiny of Israel in 11:11–32. The whole point of the olive-tree illustration is that God can graft back onto the tree those Jews who have disbelieved (11:23).[17] The ingrafting of the Gentiles onto the olive tree demonstrates that salvation is in view, for they were not made partakers of the earthly promises given to Israel but were savingly made part of the people of God. Moreover the passage climaxes with the revelation of the mystery that "all Israel will be saved" (11:26). The specific meaning of this verse is debated, but there is no doubt that Paul is here describing Israel's salvation from sin.

It seems clear that 9:30–11:36 relates to Israel's salvation (or lack thereof), but it seems that the implications of this fact need to be related to 9:1–29. Given the fact that Romans 9–11 is a unit, that there is no reason to think his major concern changes, and that there is specific evidence that Paul's concern is with Israel's salvation in 9:1–29, it is not surprising that Paul would describe in 9:30–11:36 why Israel fails to obtain salvation. It is quite improba-

---

17. Some scholars have recently said that Paul conceives of the salvation of Israel without requiring them to believe in Jesus as Messiah (cf. K. Stendahl, *Paul Among Jews and Gentiles and Other Essays* [Philadelphia: Fortress, 1976], 4; F. Mussner, "'Ganz Israel wird gerettet werden' (Röm. 11:26)," *Kairos* 18 [1976]: 241–55; L. Gaston, "Israel's Misstep in the Eyes of Paul," *Paul and the Torah* [Vancouver: University of British Columbia, 1987], 135–50). But this interpretation has rightly been refuted (E. P. Sanders, "Paul's Attitude Toward the Jewish People," *USQR* 33 [1978]: 175–87; F. Hahn, "Zum Verständnis von Römer 11.26a: '. . . und so wird ganz Israel gerettet werden,'" in *Paul and Paulinism: Essays in Honour of C. K. Barrett*, ed. M. D. Hooker and S. G. Wilson [London: SPCK, 1982], 221–36; R. Hvalvik, "A 'Sonderweg' for Israel: A Critical Examination of a Current Interpretation of Romans 11.25–27," *JSNT* 38 [1990]: 87–107).

ble that in one context Paul is merely discussing the temporal destiny of Israel (9:6b–29) and that then in the succeeding passage he suddenly begins to explain why Israel failed to attain salvation (9:30–11:36). The unity of the text is such that all of Romans 9–11 constitutes Paul's answer as to how God's word has not failed with reference to the promises of salvation for Israel, even though many in Israel have not believed in Jesus as Messiah.

The four arguments I have described suggest that the salvation of Israel is in view throughout Romans 9–11, but the strongest objection to this interpretation is that the use of the Old Testament text shows that individual salvation is not in view in 9:6–21.[18] The Old Testament texts that Paul cites do not, according to some scholars, refer in their historical contexts to the damnation of individuals. So, it is claimed, there is no clear evidence that Ishmael, Esau, and Pharaoh were damned. In fact it is pointed out that Esau was reconciled with his brother, showing he was saved (Gen. 33).

Blomberg asserts that there is no doubt that Genesis 25:23 and Malachi 1:2 refer only to temporal blessings for nations and not salvation.[19] Without going into detail I would like to register my hesitation in thinking that Genesis and Malachi concern merely temporal matters. Temporal and salvific blessings cannot be separated so easily in the Old Testament.[20] The permanent indignation of the Lord against wicked Edom in Malachi 1:4 suggests that Edom is not part of the saved people of God.[21] The promise of the inheritance probably refers to both salvation and temporal blessing.

But even if these scholars are right in saying that the Old Testament texts refer only to temporal blessings, it does not necessarily follow that these texts refer only to historical destiny when they are employed by Paul. The key question is how the texts are used in the specific context of Romans 9–11. The issue in Paul's mind is not the earthly promises given to Israel. He is almost willing to be cursed and separated from Christ because his brothers are not saved (9:3; 10:1). It is the issue of the salvation of Israel that concerns Paul throughout all of Romans 9–11.

But if the Old Testament texts employed in Romans 9 refer to the historical destiny of nations in the Old Testament, how can we explain Paul using these same texts in a context that relates to salvation? Does he not contradict the meaning of the Old Testament texts in their historical contexts? Not nec-

---

18. See Blomberg, "Election," 109–16.

19. Ibid., 109, 111.

20. Blomberg's objection ("Election," 114–15) that this does not work since so many Old Testament Jews rebelled is not compelling. The fact that not all ethnic Jews are children of the promise is precisely the point Paul is making in Romans 9:6–13. Not all ethnic Jews are recipients of the promise of salvation merely because they are ethnic Jews. There has always been a winnowing process.

21. In making this statement I am not asserting that every individual Edomite was doomed. The point is that the majority of Edomites were unsaved, and thus a general statement regarding their destiny can be made.

essarily. When New Testament writers use the Old Testament, they often do not intend to provide the meaning of the Old Testament text in its historical context. The significance of the Old Testament may be applied to new situations in the life of the church. For example, Paul uses Isaac and Ishmael in another text (Gal. 4:21–31) to illustrate that the sons of the free woman, not the sons of the slave woman, are heirs. Virtually all scholars agree that Paul is departing from the historical meaning of the Old Testament in this text, and that he is using Isaac and Ishmael to depict those who are saved and unsaved. This example is particularly illuminating because Isaac and Ishmael are also in view in Romans 9:6–9. Since they are used to illustrate issues pertaining to salvation in Galatians 4, such a usage is also possible in Romans 9.

But one could object that Galatians 4:24 specifically says that the Old Testament text is being used allegorically. And Blomberg claims: "If a N[ew] T[estament] text can make sense in light of the plain meaning of the O[ld] T[estament] passages it cites, then one should not complicate matters by introducing new interpretations."[22] This interpretive principle, however, is not adequate. Almost every use of an Old Testament text in the New Testament can make sense by interpreting it in accord with the Old Testament meaning.[23] The question is whether such interpretations yield the most plausible sense. Such a principle probably straitjackets too much the use of the Old Testament in the New Testament. A better principle is to determine first what makes best sense in the context in which the Old Testament citation is used, for New Testament writers often apply Old Testament texts to new situations.

In any case it would not be surprising if Paul used Esau as an illustration of an unsaved person (Rom. 9:11–13) since the writer of Hebrews seems to use him as an example of a person (Heb. 12:16) who was unsaved. And even if Esau were saved, the author of Hebrews is using his renunciation of the birthright as an illustration to warn the church about the danger of apostasy from salvation. In other words, if for the sake of argument we grant that Esau was

---

22. Blomberg, "Election," 111.

23. Witness Walter C. Kaiser's valiant attempt to show that virtually every Old Testament citation in the New Testament fits with the original meaning of the Old Testament text (*The Uses of the Old Testament in the New Testament* [Chicago: Moody, 1985]). The problem with Kaiser's view is not that his specific proposals do not make sense. The issue is whether his solutions are plausible. They are, but it seems that a more complex understanding of the relationship between the Testaments should be adopted. For a solution that is more satisfactory than Kaiser's see Douglas J. Moo, "The Problem of *Sensus Plenior*," in *Hermeneutics, Authority, and Canon*, ed. D. A. Carson and John D. Woodbridge (Grand Rapids: Zondervan, 1986), 179–211. On the use of the Old Testament in Romans 9–11 see J. W. Aageson, "Scripture and Structure in the Development of the Argument in Romans 9–11," *CBQ* 48 (1986): 265–89; "Typology, Correspondence, and the Application of Scripture in Romans 9–11," *JSNT* 31 (1987): 51–72; C. A. Evans, "Paul and the Hermeneutics of 'True Prophecy': A Study of Rom. 9–11," *Bib* 65 (1984): 560–70; O. Hofius, "Das Evangelium und Israel. Erwägungen zu Römer 9–11," *ZTK* 83 (1986): 297–324.

saved, then the author of Hebrews employs his rejection of temporal blessings as an illustration of the danger of forsaking eternal salvation.[24] The way Hebrews uses the example of Esau is extremely important as a principial argument. For if Hebrews is saying that Esau is unsaved, then it would not be at all surprising if Paul draws the same conclusion in Romans 9. If he were saved, then Hebrews is not citing the Old Testament text in accord with its historical meaning but uses Esau to make a point regarding the salvation of the readers. Now if Hebrews uses Esau in such an illustrative fashion, then there is at least a precedent for Paul using the Old Testament in the same way.[25]

To conclude, the first objection to the Calvinist reading of Romans 9 is not persuasive, for the issue in Paul's mind in Romans 9–11 is not merely the historical destiny of Israel. What is at the forefront of his mind is the question of Israel's salvation.

Corporate or Individual Salvation?

The second objection (linked to the first for many scholars) to a Calvinist reading of Romans 9 is that even if the chapter refers to salvation, it describes the salvation of groups, not the salvation of individuals.[26] Thus William Klein says that "Paul's concern is the elect people of God, a corporate entity."[27] Leon Morris says, "It seems clear that Paul intends a reference to nations rather than individuals."[28] This interpretation is supported by showing that Paul is thinking of the nation of the Edomites in contrast to Israel (Gen. 25:13). Thus Cranfield says, "There is no doubt that the concern of Mal[achi] I.2–5 is with the nations of Israel and Edom, and it is natural to suppose that by 'Jacob' and 'Esau' Paul also understands not only the twin sons of Isaac but also the peoples descended from them."[29] Those who em-

---

24. For a defense of the idea that the author of Hebrews is warning the readers about apostasy in Hebrews 12:14–17 see Philip Edgcumbe Hughes, *A Commentary on the Epistle to the Hebrews* (Grand Rapids: Eerdmans, 1977), 536–41; Donald A. Hagner, *Hebrews* (New York: Harper, 1983), 205–8; F. F. Bruce, *The Epistle to the Hebrews*, NICNT (Grand Rapids: Eerdmans, 1964), 364–68.

25. Of course the connection between the use of Esau in Hebrews and Romans stands only if the context of Romans 9 also refers to salvation. But I have provided a number of specific reasons why it does.

26. Badenas, *Christ the End*, 85; Clark H. Pinnock, "From Augustine to Arminius: A Pilgrimage in Theology," in *The Grace of God, the Will of Man: A Case for Arminianism*, ed. Clark H. Pinnock (Grand Rapids: Zondervan, 1989), 20.

27. William W. Klein, *The New Chosen People: A Corporate View of Election* (Grand Rapids: Zondervan, 1990), 166; see also 173–75.

28. Morris, *Romans*, 356; see also his comments on 345, 354, 363. Forster and Marston say, "People often fail to understand that in this whole section the apostle is talking about nations and not about individuals" (*God's Strategy*, 59).

29. Cranfield, *Romans*, 479–80; see also 450, 489.

phasize that election is corporate rather than individual contend that this distinction helps one to see that God does not elect some individuals to salvation and reject others.

This second objection to a Calvinist reading of Romans 9 has persuaded many scholars. Nevertheless I will argue that the election Paul describes in this passage is both corporate and individual and that a reference to the former does not rule out the latter. Four lines of argument converge to support this thesis.

Evidence that individual election is also in Paul's mind is found in Romans 9:15, where he cites Exodus 33:19: "I will have mercy on whom I have mercy, and I will have compassion on whom I have compassion." The word *whom (hon)* is singular, indicating that specific individuals upon whom God has mercy are in view. The singular is also present in the inference Paul draws from Romans 9:15 in 9:16. God's mercy does not depend on "the one who wills, nor the one who runs." The conclusion to all of 9:14–17 in 9:18 utilizes the singular once again: "God has mercy on whom he wants to have mercy, and he hardens whom he wants to harden." In the same vein 9:19 continues the thought: "Who *(tis)* resists his will?" And Paul also uses the singular when he speaks of one vessel being made for honor and another for dishonor (9:21). Those who say that Paul is referring only to corporate groups do not have an adequate explanation as to why Paul uses the singular again and again in Romans 9.

The selection of a remnant out of Israel (Rom. 9:6–9; 11:1–6) also involves the selecting out of certain individuals from a larger group. Of course the remnant is a smaller group within a larger group. One should not conclude, however, that since the remnant is made up of a group of people that individuals are not in view. Paul uses himself as an example of one who is part of the remnant (11:1). Clearly Paul is an individual who has been saved, and yet he is part of the remnant. The election of the remnant to salvation and the election of individuals who make up that remnant are not mutually exclusive. They belong together.

Romans 9:30–10:21 calls sharply into question the thesis that Paul is speaking only of groups in Romans 9–11 and is not referring to individuals. Calvinists have sometimes been criticized for not considering all of Romans 9–11 in formulating their doctrine of election.[30] But those who espouse the view that Paul is speaking only about corporate realities in Romans 9–11 are inconsistent with their own position in 9:30–10:21. We have already seen that all agree that Romans 9–11 is a unit and that it is a sustained attempt to demonstrate that God's word with reference to Israel has not fallen. But if the reference to Israel in Romans 9–11 is only corporate, then Israel's failure to pursue the law from faith, and her attempt to be righteous by works (9:30–

---

30. Klein, *Chosen People*, 174 n. 43, sees this as "one of the major flaws in Piper's book."

10:8), must be exclusively a corporate problem and not an individual one. But no interpreter that I know of has ever said that Israel's attempt to be righteous by works was only a corporate problem. Specific individuals within Israel are condemned because they have sought to establish their righteousness on the basis of works instead of submitting to the righteousness that comes from God, while other individuals—that is, those constituting the remnant—are saved by faith.

Now Paul does say that "Israel" (9:31; 10:19) as a whole or as a corporate entity has failed to attain the righteousness of God. Of course he is not intending to say that this is the case with every individual within ethnic Israel, for elsewhere we are told that there is a remnant from ethnic Israel that is saved (9:6–9; 11:1–6). His point is that the majority of ethnic Israel has stumbled on the stumbling stone and has failed to believe in Christ (9:32–33). We can conclude, then, that Paul is speaking of corporate Israel in 9:30–10:21, but what he says about Israel corporately is also true of individual Israelites. One cannot legitimately say that Paul is merely describing corporate Israel but not individual Israelites.

The rest of Romans 10 proves that one cannot separate corporate Israel from individual Israelites. Again and again Paul emphasizes that one must exercise faith to be saved (10:4, 5, 6, 8, 9, 10, 11, 14, 17). Obviously Paul can speak of Israel as a whole of falling short because so many within the nation have not exercised faith (10:19). But no one would assert that the failure to exercise faith was only a group problem and not an individual problem. One cannot sunder the connection between individuals and groups.

The conclusion I want to draw is this: If it is inappropriate to draw a distinction between individuals and groups in Romans 9:30–10:21, then there seems to be no exegetical basis for drawing such a distinction in 9:1–29 or 11:1–36. The three chapters are a unit, and the reference to Israel does not lurch between a reference only to corporate Israel in chapters 9 and 11 and then refer to both individuals and groups in chapter 10. The reference to Israel must be interpreted consistently in the three chapters. Paul is describing Israel corporately, but the group also involves individuals.[31] Thus Romans 9 and 11 do describe the election of corporate Israel to salvation, but this election of corporate Israel by definition also includes the election of some individuals from within Israel.

31. Someone might object that this opens the door up to universalism since Romans 11:32 says, "For God has bound all men over to disobedience so that he may have mercy on them all." One might conclude that if "all" refers to both groups and individuals, then every individual will be saved. But we have already seen in 9:30–10:21 that Paul depicts Israel as a whole as disbelieving in the gospel without suggesting that every single individual Israelite is unsaved. Thus the "all" in 11:32 surely refers to a group made up of individuals, but it is unwarranted (given what Paul says elsewhere in Romans 9–11) to understand this "all" to refer to every individual.

To say that election involves the selection of one group rather than another raises another problem that warrants an extended explanation. Most scholars who claim election is corporate argue that personal faith is the ultimate and decisive reason why some people are saved rather than others. Calvinists, on the other hand, assert that faith is the result of God's predestining work. But those who opt for corporate election think that they have a better conception of election than do Calvinists, and at the same time they can maintain that faith ultimately determines one's salvation. A flaw in this reasoning is fatal to those who espouse corporate election. If God corporately elects some people to salvation, and the election of one group rather than another was decided before any group came into existence (9:11), and it was not based on any works that this group did or any act of their will (9:11–12, 16), then it would seem to follow that the faith of the saved group would be God's gift given before time began. But if the faith of any corporate entity depends upon God's predestining work, then individual faith is not decisive for salvation. What is decisive would be God's election of that group. In other words, the group elected would necessarily exercise faith since God elected this corporate entity.

But if what I have said is correct, then one of the great attractions of the corporate view of election vanishes. Many find corporate election appealing because God does not appear as arbitrary in electing some to salvation and bypassing others. But if corporate election is election unto salvation, and if that election determines who will be saved, then God is no less arbitrary. It hardly satisfies to say that God chose some individuals to be saved and passed by others but that it is true that he chose one group to be saved and bypassed another group.

Those who champion corporate election, however, would object, and the reason is that they do not actually hold to corporate election of a group or of people. When those who advocate corporate election say that God chose "the Church," "a group," or a "corporate entity," they are not really saying that God chose any individuals who make up a group at all.[32] The church group is an abstract entity or a concept that God chose. Those who become part of that entity are those who exercise faith.[33] God simply chose that there be a "thing" called the church, and then he decided that all who would put their faith in Christ would become part of the church. In other words, the choosing of a people or a group does not mean that God chose one group of people rather than another, according to those who support corporate election. God chose to permit the existence of the entity called "the church," which corporate whole would be populated by those who put their faith in Christ and so become part of that entity.

32. I think this is a fair deduction from Klein's discussion (*Chosen People*, 176–84) of election.
33. Klein, *Chosen People*, 182.

If corporate election involves the selection of an abstract entity like the church, and then people decide whether or not to exercise faith and thereby become part of the church, it seems to follow that the selection of the church does not involve the selection of any individuals or group at all. Instead God determined before time that there would be a "thing," called the church and that those who exercise faith would be part of it. The problem with this view, however, is that the church is not an abstract entity or a concept. It is made up of people. Indeed the biblical text makes it clear again and again that election involves the selection of people, not of a concept. For example: "He chose us in him before the foundation of the world" (Eph. 1:4); "God chose the foolish . . . God chose the weak . . . he chose the lowly" (1 Cor. 1:27–28); "God chose you as the firstfruits for salvation" (2 Thess. 2:13; also Rom. 9:23–25; 11:2; 2 Tim. 1:9). The point I am trying to make is that those who advocate corporate election do not stress adequately enough that God chose a group of people, and if he chose one group of people (and not just a concept or an abstract entity) rather than another group, then the corporate view of election does not make God any less arbitrary than the view of those who say God chose certain individuals.

An analogy may help here.[34] Suppose you say, "I am going to choose to buy a professional baseball team." This makes sense if you then buy the Minnesota Twins or the Los Angeles Dodgers. But if you do this, you choose the members of that specific team over other individual players on other teams. It makes no sense to say "I am going to buy a professional baseball team" that has no members, no players, and then permit whoever desires to come to play on the team. In the latter case you have not chosen a team. You have chosen that there be a team, the makeup of which is totally out of your control. So to choose a team requires that you choose one team among others along with the individuals who make it up. To choose that there be a team entails no choosing of one group over another but only that individuals may form into a team if they want to. The point of the analogy is that if there really is such a thing as the choosing of a specific group, then individual election is entailed in corporate election.

Those who espouse corporate election could counter, by stressing that election is in Christ (Eph. 1:4).[35] The idea then is that Jesus Christ is the one whom God elected, and he has elected a corporate group, the church, to be in Christ.[36] Forster and Marston say, "We are chosen in Christ. This does not mean that we were chosen *to be put into Christ*. . . . It means that as we re-

---

34. This analogy was suggested to me by Bruce A. Ware.

35. Klein, *Chosen People*, 179–80; Forster and Marston, *God's Strategy*, 97, 131–32.

36. I am distinguishing this view from that of Karl Barth (*Church Dogmatics* 2.2.1–506), for Barth's view seems to lead to universalism. Cranfield's exegesis (*Romans*, 448–50) has been decisively influenced by Barth. Paul K. Jewett effectively critiques the Barthian view (*Election and Predestination* [Grand Rapids: Eerdmans, 1985], 47–56).

pented and were born again into the body of Christ, we partake of his cho-senness."[37] A few things should be said in response to this interpretation. First, the text does not specifically say that Christ was elected. The object of the verb *chose* is "us" in Ephesians 1:4. It is incorrect to see the emphasis on the election of Christ inasmuch as the verse stresses the election of people.[38] And since Ephesians 1:4 says that we were chosen "before the foundation of the world," there is no evidence that the choice was based on our foreseen faith. To claim (as Forster and Marston do) that the faith of people is decisive reverses the emphasis of the text, for Ephesians 1:4 (and all of 1:3–14) fo-cuses on the work of God, and thus to insert faith into the verse is to smuggle in an idea that is not stated. Moreover, Romans 9:11–13 confirms what we have suggested from Ephesians 1:4—namely, that faith is the result of being chosen.

Second, when the text says "he chose us in him" it probably means that God chose that the church would experience salvation "through Jesus Christ." He is the agent and person through whom the electing work of God would come to fruition. When God planned to save some, he intended from the beginning that their salvation would be effected through the work of Christ. Third, thus it seems to me that those who stress that election is in Christ end up denying that God chose a group in any significant sense. All God's choice of a group means is that God chose that all who put their faith in Christ would be saved. Those who put their faith in Christ would be des-ignated the church.

Those who defend corporate election are conscious of the fact that it is hard to separate corporate from individual election, for logic would seem to require that the individuals who make up a group cannot be separated from the group itself. Klein responds by saying that this amounts to an imposition of modern western categories upon biblical writers.[39] He goes on to say that it requires a "logic that is foreign to their thinking."[40] Clark H. Pinnock also says that the Arminian view is more attractive because he is "in the process of learning to read the Bible from a new point of view, one that I believe is more truly evangelical and less rationalistic."[41] Those who cannot see how election is corporate without also involving individuals have fallen prey to imposing western logic upon the Bible.

This objection strikes me as highly ironic. For example, Klein also says that it makes no sense for God to plead for Israel to be saved (Rom. 10:21)

---

37. Forster and Marston, *God's Strategy*, 97.
38. Contra Marcus Barth, *Ephesians*, AB (Garden City, N.Y.: Doubleday, 1974), 1:107–8.
39. Klein, *Chosen People*, 264; see also 260.
40. Ibid., 264.
41. Pinnock, "Augustine," 21. He goes on to say, "Of course, there will be some nostalgia when we leave behind the *logically* and beautifully tight system of determinist theology" (28, italics added).

if he has elected only some to be saved.[42] But this objection surely seems to be based on so-called western logic. Klein cannot seem to make sense logically of how both of these can be true, and so he concludes that individual election is not credible. Has he ever considered that he might be forcing western logic upon the text and that both might be true in a way we do not fully comprehend? Indeed, one could assert that the focus upon individual choice as ultimately determinative in salvation is based on "western" logic inasmuch as it concentrates upon the individual and his or her individual choice. And on the same page that Pinnock says he is escaping from rationalism, he says he cannot believe "that God determines all things and that creaturely freedom is real" because this view is contradictory and incoherent. He goes on to say, "The *logic* of consistent Calvinism makes God the author of evil and casts serious doubt on his goodness."[43] These kinds of statements from Pinnock certainly seem to reflect a dependence on western logic.

Most Calvinists would affirm that logic should not be jettisoned, but they would also claim that the relationship between divine sovereignty and human responsibility is finally a mystery. The admission of mystery demonstrates that Calvinists are not dominated by western logic. In fact, those who insist that human freedom and individual faith must rule out divine determination of all things are those who end up subscribing to western logical categories.

My own view of the role of logic needs to be clarified so that what I have just said will not be misunderstood. The law of noncontradiction was not invented by Aristotle. It was articulated and defended by him and is characteristic of all meaningful human thought and speech. That which is contradictory cannot be true. Thus it is legitimate to ask if a particular theological position is contradictory or illogical. The law of noncontradiction cannot be dismissed as western, for all people intuitively sense that what is contradictory cannot be true. This explains why Klein and Pinnock revert to the law of noncontradiction even while claiming that they are freeing themselves from western logic.

Nevertheless, to subscribe to the law of noncontradiction does not mean that logic can resolve every problem in theology. There are times when Scripture strongly affirms two realities that cannot finally be resolved logically by us. For example, the doctrines of the Trinity and of the two natures of Christ in one person are theological constructs that are rightly derived from the Bible, and yet we cannot ultimately explain how there can be three persons and yet only one God. This does not mean that the doctrine of the Trinity is irrational. It means only that it is above our present rational capacities. Such

42. Klein, *Chosen People*, 267.
43. Pinnock, "Augustine," 21 (italics added).

mysteries should be adopted only if that is where the biblical evidence leads. I believe the biblical evidence compels us to see such a mystery in the case of divine election and human responsibility. A mystery is not required, however, in the case of corporate election, and so there is no need to postulate a discontinuity between corporate and individual election. In fact individual election cannot be dismissed, since it is taught in too many texts (John 6:37, 44–45, 64–65; 10:26; Acts 13:48; 16:14; etc.).

Biblical exegesis requires us, then, to see a mystery in the case of divine election and human responsibility. Romans 9 teaches that God does elect individuals and groups unto salvation, and he determines who will exercise faith. Nevertheless, Romans 9:30–10:21 teaches us that those who do not exercise faith are responsible and should have done so. How can both of these be logically true? We cannot fully grasp the answer to this question, for as with other mysteries in Scripture we affirm that our human minds cannot adequately grasp the full import of divine revelation.

Conclusion

In this chapter I have explored whether two of the main objections to a Calvinist exegesis of Romans 9 are persuasive. These objections are that Romans 9 does not relate to salvation at all but to the historical destiny of Israel and its role in temporal history and that the election described in Romans 9 is not an individual election unto salvation but is corporate. I have argued that neither of these objections works. The first one fails because the entire context of Romans 9–11 relates to the salvation of Israel. When Paul introduces the chapters in 9:1–5 he makes it plain that he would almost wish to be cursed because his kinsmen from Israel are not saved. It is this question of Israel's salvation (or the lack thereof) that informs all three chapters. Since the specific issue that introduces Romans 9–11 relates to salvation, it is quite improbable that Paul would insert a discussion in chapter 9 about the earthly promises given to Israel and then suddenly revert to the main issue of salvation in 9:30–11:36.

The second objection to the Calvinist reading of Romans 9 also fails to convince because corporate and individual election are inseparable. The recipients of God's electing work are often referred to in the singular in chapter 9, and the selection of a remnant implies that some individuals were chosen out of a larger group. In addition, those who advocate corporate election claim chapters 9 and 11 refer to corporate Israel, whereas Paul speaks of individual Israelites in chapter 10. There is no exegetical justification for such a shift. It seems to be due to a philosophical bias that cannot see how individuals can still be held responsible if divine election is true. Moreover, those who advocate corporate election are vague in their own description of what corporate election involves. The way corporate election is defined makes it doubtful that they are describing election of a group at all. I conclude, then, that the Calvinist view that God chose individuals to be saved is persuasive both exegetically and theologically.

5

Are There Two Wills in God?

JOHN PIPER

My aim in this chapter is to show from Scripture that the simultaneous existence of God's will for "all persons to be saved" (1 Tim. 2:4) and his will to elect unconditionally those who will actually be saved[1] is not a sign of divine schizophrenia or exegetical confusion. A corresponding aim is to show that unconditional election therefore does not contradict biblical expressions of God's compassion for all people, and does not nullify sincere offers of salvation to everyone who is lost among all the peoples of the world.

First Timothy 2:4, 2 Peter 3:9, and Ezekiel 18:23 might be called the Arminian pillar texts concerning the universal saving will of God.[2] In 1 Timothy 2:1–4 Paul says that the reason we should pray for kings and all in high positions is that this may bring about a quiet and peaceable life which "is good, and acceptable in the sight of God our Savior, who wills *(thelei)* all persons to be saved and to come to the knowledge of the truth." In 2 Peter 3:8–9 the apostle says that the delay of the second coming of Christ is owing to the fact that with the Lord one day is as a thousand years and a thousand years is as a day. "The Lord is not slow about his promise as some count slowness, but is forbearing toward you, not willing *(boulomenos)* that any

---

1. Matt. 22:14; John 6:37, 44, 65; 8:47; 10:26–29; Rom. 8:29–30; 9:6–23; 11:5–10; 1 Cor. 1:26–30; Eph. 1:4–5; 1 Thess. 1:4; 2 Thess. 2:13; James 2:5. Unless otherwise indicated, Scripture references are the author's own translation.

2. In numerous other texts God expresses his will for the salvation of those who finally turn away from him. For example, "O Jerusalem, Jerusalem, killing the prophets and stoning those who are sent to you! How often would I have gathered your children together as a hen gathers her brood under her wings, and you would not!" (Matt. 23:37).

should perish, but that all should reach repentance." And in Ezekiel 18:23 and 32 the Lord speaks about his heart for the perishing: "Do I indeed delight[3] in the death of the wicked, says the Lord GOD, and not rather in his turning from his way that he might live? . . . I do not delight *('eh^ephoz)* in the death of the one who dies, says the Lord; so turn and live" (cf. 33:11).

It is possible that careful exegesis of 1 Timothy 2:4 would lead us to believe that "God's willing all persons to be saved" does not refer to every individual person in the world, but rather to all *sorts* of persons, since the "all persons" in verse 1 may well mean groups like "kings and all in high positions" (v. 2).[4] It is also possible that the "you" in 2 Peter 3:9 ("the Lord is longsuffering toward you, not wishing any to perish") refers not to every person in the world but to "you" professing Christians among whom, as Adolf Schlatter says, "are people who only through repentance can attain to the grace of God and to the promised inheritance."[5]

Nevertheless the case for this limitation on God's universal saving will has never been convincing to Arminians and likely will not become convincing, especially since Ezekiel 18:23, 32 and 33:11 are even less tolerant of restriction. Therefore as a hearty believer in unconditional, individual election I rejoice to affirm that God does not delight in the perishing of the impenitent, and that he has compassion on all people. My aim is to show that this is not double talk.

The assignment in this chapter is not to defend the doctrine that God chooses unconditionally whom he will save. I have tried to do that elsewhere[6] and others do it in this work.[7] Nevertheless I will try to make a credible case that while the Arminian pillar texts may indeed be pillars for universal love, nevertheless they are not weapons against unconditional election. If I succeed

---

3. The emphatic doubling of the infinitive absolute with the finite verb for "delight" is another way of expressing the oath in Ezekiel 33:11, "As I live, says the Lord God, I do not delight in the death of the wicked." The King James Version of Ezekiel 18:23, "Have I *any pleasure at all* that the wicked should die," is not necessarily implied in the wording. The intensification of God's denial of delight is to stress that he absolutely means what he says, not that the absence of delight is absolute, as we will see.

4. John Gill, *The Cause of God and Truth* (1735–38; London: W. H. Collingridge, 1855), 49–52.

5. Adolf Schlatter, *Die Briefe des Petrus, Judas, Jakobus, der Brief en die Hebräer, Erläuterungen zum Neuen Testament,* vol. 9 (Stuttgart: Calver Verlag, 1964), 126. This is especially true in view of verse 15, which urges the readers themselves to "count the forbearance of God as salvation"; and in view of the fact that the delay of the second coming seems to result not in more individuals being saved worldwide, but in more being lost as the love of many grows cold (Matt. 24:12).

6. See especially *The Justification of God: An Exegetical and Theological Study of Romans 9:1–23* (Grand Rapids: Baker, [1]1983, [2]1993); *The Pleasures of God: Meditations on God's Delight in Being God* (Portland, Ore.: Multnomah, 1991), 47–78, 123–59; "How Does a Sovereign God Love?" *Ref J* 33, 4 (April 1983): 9–13; "Universalism in Romans 9–11? Testing the Exegesis of Thomas Talbott," *Ref J* 33, 7 (July 1983): 11–14.

7. See especially chapters 1–3 in this work.

then there will be an indirect confirmation for the thesis of this book. In fact Arminians have erred in trying to take pillars of universal love and make them into weapons against electing grace.

Affirming the will of God to save all, while also affirming the unconditional election of some, implies that there are at least "two wills" in God, or two ways of willing. It implies that God decrees one state of affairs while also willing and teaching that a different state of affairs should come to pass. This distinction in the way God wills has been expressed in various ways throughout the centuries. It is not a new contrivance. For example, theologians have spoken of sovereign will and moral will, efficient will and permissive will, secret will and revealed will, will of decree and will of command, decretive will and preceptive will, *voluntas signi* (will of sign) and *voluntas beneplaciti* (will of good pleasure).[8]

Clark H. Pinnock refers disapprovingly to "the exceedingly paradoxical notion of two divine wills regarding salvation."[9] In Pinnock's more recent volume *(A Case for Arminianism)* Randall G. Basinger argues that "if God has decreed all events, then it must be that things *cannot* and *should not* be any different from what they are."[10] He rejects the notion that God could decree that a thing be one way and yet teach that we should act to make it another way. He says that it is too hard "to coherently conceive of a God in which this distinction really exists."[11]

In the same volume Fritz Guy argues that the revelation of God in Christ has brought about a "paradigm shift" in the way we should think about the love of God—namely, as "more fundamental than, and prior to, justice and power." This shift, he says, makes it possible to think about the "will of God" as "delighting more than deciding." God's will is not his sovereign purpose which he infallibly establishes, but rather "the desire of the lover for the beloved." The will of God is his general intention and longing, not his effective purpose. Guy goes so far as to say, "Apart from a predestinarian presupposition, it becomes apparent that God's 'will' is always to be understood in terms of intention and desire [as opposed to efficacious, sovereign purpose]."[12]

These criticisms are not new. Jonathan Edwards wrote 250 years ago, "The Arminians ridicule the distinction between the secret and revealed will

---

8. See Heinrich Heppe, *Reformed Dogmatics* (1860; Grand Rapids: Baker, 1978), 143–49, for the way the sixteenth- and seventeenth-century Reformed theologians talked about the relationship between God's decrees and his moral law.

9. Clark H. Pinnock, *Grace Unlimited* (Minneapolis: Bethany Fellowship, 1975), 13.

10. Randall G. Basinger, "Exhaustive Divine Sovereignty: A Practical Critique," in *The Grace of God, the Will of Man: A Case for Arminianism* (Grand Rapids: Zondervan, 1989), 196.

11. Ibid., 203.

12. Fritz Guy, "The Universality of God's Love," in *The Grace of God, the Will of Man*, 35.

of God, or, more properly expressed, the distinction between the decree and the law of God; because we say he may decree one thing, and command another. And so, they argue, we hold a contrariety in God, as if one will of his contradicted another."[13]

But in spite of these criticisms the distinction stands, not because of a logical or theological deduction, but because it is inescapable in the Scriptures. The most careful exegete writing in Pinnock's *Case for Arminianism* concedes the existence of two wills in God. I. Howard Marshall applies his exegetical gift to the Pastoral Epistles. Concerning 1 Timothy 2:4 he says,

> To avoid all misconceptions it should be made clear at the outset that the fact that God wishes or wills that all people should be saved does not necessarily imply that all will respond to the gospel and be saved. *We must certainly distinguish between what God would like to see happen and what he actually does will to happen, and both of these things can be spoken of as God's will.* The question at issue is not whether all will be saved but whether God has made provision in Christ for the salvation of all, provided that they believe, and without limiting the potential scope of the death of Christ merely to those whom God knows will believe.[14]

In this chapter I would like to undergird Marshall's point that "we must certainly distinguish between what God would like to see happen and what he actually does will to happen, and [that] both of these things can be spoken of as God's will." Perhaps the most effective way to do this is to begin by drawing attention to the way Scripture portrays God's willing something in one sense that he disapproves in another sense. Then, after seeing some of the

13. Jonathan Edwards, "Concerning the Decrees in General, and Election in Particular," in *The Works of Jonathan Edwards*, vol. 2 (Edinburgh: The Banner of Truth Trust, 1974), 526. And of course the theological distinction between two kinds of willing in God goes back much further. In the fourth part of *The Cause of God and Truth* (see n. 4) Gill gives one hundred double-column pages of references from the early Fathers (from Clement to Jerome) concerning this and other "Calvinistic" distinctives.

14. I. Howard Marshall, "Universal Grace and Atonement in the Pastoral Epistles," in *The Grace of God, the Will of Man*, 56 (italics added). One of the things that seriously weakens the argument of Marshall's article is the omission of any discussion or even mention of 2 Timothy 2:24–26, which says, "The Lord's servant must not be quarrelsome but kindly to every one, an apt teacher, forbearing, correcting his opponents with gentleness. *God may perhaps grant that they will repent and come to know the truth,* and they may escape from the snare of the devil, after being captured by him to do his will." Marshall poses the question whether any text in the Pastorals would lead us to believe that "faith and repentance are the gifts of God, who gives them only to the previously chosen group of the elect" (66). He concludes that there is not, even though the text that comes closest to saying this very thing is passed over. The text is even more significant because its wording is used in 1 Timothy 2:4. Compare the desire of God for people to "be saved and come to a knowledge of the truth" (in 1 Tim. 2:4) with the gift of God that people repent "to a knowledge of the truth" (in 2 Tim. 2:25). These two texts alone probably teach that there are "two wills" in God: the will that all be saved, and the will to give repentance to some.

biblical evidence, we can step back and ponder how to understand this in relation to God's saving purposes.

Illustrations of Two Wills in God

The Death of Christ

The most compelling example of God's willing for sin to come to pass while at the same time disapproving the sin is his willing the death of his perfect, divine Son. The betrayal of Jesus by Judas was a morally evil act inspired immediately by Satan (Luke 22:3). Yet in Acts 2:23 Luke says, "This Jesus [was] delivered up according to the definite plan *(boule)* and foreknowledge of God." The betrayal was sin, and it involved the instrumentality of Satan; but it was part of God's ordained plan. That is, there is a sense in which God willed the delivering up of his Son, even though the act was sin.

Herod's contempt for Jesus (Luke 23:11), Pilate's spineless expediency (Luke 23:24), the Jews' "Crucify! Crucify him!" (Luke 23:21), and the Gentile soldiers' mockery (Luke 23:36) were also sinful attitudes and deeds. Yet in Acts 4:27–28 Luke expresses his understanding of the sovereignty of God in these acts by recording the prayer of the Jerusalem saints:

> Truly in this city there were gathered together against thy holy servant Jesus, whom thou didst anoint both Herod and Pontius Pilate, with the Gentiles and the peoples of Israel to do whatever thy hand and thy plan *(boule)* had predestined to take place.

Herod, Pilate, the soldiers, and Jewish crowds lifted their hand to rebel against the Most High only to find that their rebellion was unwitting (sinful) service in the inscrutable designs of God.

The appalling death of Christ was the will and work of God the Father. Isaiah wrote, "We esteemed him stricken, *smitten by God . . . It was the will of the* LORD *to bruise him; he has put him to grief*" (Isa. 53:4, 10). God's will was very much engaged in the events that brought his Son to death on the cross. God considered it "fitting to perfect the author of their salvation through sufferings" (Heb. 2:10). Yet, as Edwards points out, Christ's suffering "could not come to pass but by sin. For contempt and disgrace was one thing he was to suffer."[15]

It goes almost without saying that God wills obedience to his moral law, and that he wills this in a way that can be rejected by many. This is evident from numerous texts: "Not everyone who says to me Lord, Lord, will enter

---

15. Edwards, "Concerning the Decrees in General, and Election in Particular," 534.

into the kingdom of heaven, but he who does the will *(thelema)* of my Father who is in heaven" (Matt. 7:21). "Whoever does the will of my Father in heaven, he is my brother and sister and mother" (Matt. 12:50). "The one who does the will of God abides forever" (1 John 2:17). The "will of God" in these texts is the revealed, moral instruction of the Old and New Testaments, which proscribes sin. Therefore we know it was not the "will of God" that Judas and Pilate and Herod and the Gentile soldiers and the Jewish crowds disobey the moral law of God by sinning in delivering Jesus up to be crucified. But we also know that it was the will of God that this come to pass. Therefore we know that God in some sense wills what he does not will in another sense. Marshall's statement is confirmed by the death of Jesus: "We must certainly distinguish between what God would like to see happen and what he actually does will to happen."

The War against the Lamb

There are two reasons that we turn next to Revelation 17:16–17. One is that the war against the Son of God, which reached its sinful climax at the cross, comes to final consummation in a way that confirms what we have seen about the will of God. The other reason is that this text reveals John's understanding of God's active involvement in fulfilling prophecies whose fulfillment involves sinning. John sees a vision of some final events of history:

> And the ten horns that you saw, they and the beast will hate the harlot; they will make her desolate and naked, and devour her flesh and burn her up with fire, for God has put it into their hearts to carry out his purpose by being of one mind and giving over their royal power to the beast, until the words of God shall be fulfilled. (Rev. 17:16–17)

Without going into all the details of this passage, the relevant matter is clear. The beast "comes out of the abyss" (Rev. 17:8). He is the personification of evil and rebellion against God. The ten horns are ten kings (v. 12) and they "wage war against the Lamb" (v. 14).

Waging war against the Lamb is sin and sin is contrary to the will of God. Nevertheless the angel says (literally), "God gave into their [the ten kings'] hearts to do his will, and to perform one will, and to give their kingdom to the beast, until the words of God shall be fulfilled" (v. 17). Therefore God willed (in one sense) to influence the hearts of the ten kings so that they would do what is against his will (in another sense).

Moreover God did this in fulfillment of prophetic words. The ten kings will collaborate with the beast "until the words of God shall be fulfilled" (v. 17). This implies something crucial about John's understanding of the fulfillment of "the prophesies leading up to the overthrow of Anti-christ."[16] It implies that (at least in John's view) God's prophecies are not mere predictions that God knows will happen, but rather are divine intentions that he makes sure will happen. We know this because verse 17 says that God is acting to see to it that the ten kings make league with the beast "until the words of God shall be fulfilled." John is exulting not in the marvelous foreknowledge of God to predict a bad event. Rather he is exulting in the marvelous sovereignty of God to make sure that the bad event comes about. Fulfilled prophecy, in John's mind, is not only prediction, but also promised performance. This is what God meant in Jeremiah 1:12 when he said, "I am watching over my word to perform it."

This is important because John tells us in his Gospel that there are Old Testament prophecies of events surrounding the death of Christ that involve sin. This means that God intends to bring about events that involve things he forbids. These events include Judas' betrayal of Jesus (John 13:18; Ps. 41:9), the hatred Jesus received from his enemies (John 15:25; Ps. 69:4; 35:19), the casting of lots for Jesus' clothing (John 19:24; Ps. 22:18), and the piercing of Jesus' side (John 19:36–37; Exod. 12:46; Ps. 34:20; Zech. 12:10). John expresses his theology of God's sovereignty with the words, "These things happened in order that the scripture be fulfilled." The events were not a coincidence that God merely foresaw, but a plan that God purposed to bring about.[17] Thus again we find the words of Marshall confirmed: "We must certainly distinguish between what God would like to see happen and what he actually does will to happen."

The Hardening Work of God

Another evidence to demonstrate God's willing a state of affairs in one sense that he disapproves in another sense is the testimony of Scripture that God wills to harden some men's hearts so that they become obstinate in sinful behavior that God disapproves.

The most well known example is the hardening of Pharaoh's heart.[18] In Exodus 8:1 the Lord says to Moses, "Go in to Pharaoh and say to him, 'Thus says the LORD, "Let my people go, that they may serve me."'" In other words God's command, that is, his will, is that Pharaoh let the Israelites go. Never-

16. Robert H. Mounce, *The Book of Revelation* (Grand Rapids: Eerdmans, 1977), 320. Mounce is following Isbon Beckwith, *The Apocalypse of John* (1919; Grand Rapids: Baker, 1967), 703.

17. "Characteristically John sees a fulfillment of Scripture in these happenings. The purpose of God had to be fulfilled . . . Note the significance of the *hina*." Leon Morris, *The Gospel According to John* (Grand Rapids: Eerdmans, 1971), 822.

18. For a detailed study of the hardening texts in Exodus see Piper, *Justification of God,* 139–62. The relevant texts are Exodus 4:21; 7:3, 13, 14, 22; 8:15, 19, 32; 9:7, 12, 34, 35; 10:1, 20, 27; 11:10; 13:15; 14:4, 8, 17. See also G. K. Beale, "An Exegetical and Theological Consideration of the Hardening of Pharaoh's Heart in Exodus 4–14 and Romans 9," *Trinity J* 5 (1984): 129–54.

theless from the start he also willed that Pharaoh not let the Israelites go. In Exodus 4:21 God says to Moses, "When you go back to Egypt, see that you do all those wonders before Pharaoh, which I have put in your hand; but I will harden his heart, so that he will not let the people go." At one point Pharaoh himself acknowledges that his unwillingness to let the people go is sin: "Now therefore forgive, I pray, my sin" (Exod. 10:17). Thus what we see is that God commands that Pharaoh do a thing that God himself wills not to allow. The good thing that God commands he prevents. And the thing he brings about involves sin.[19]

Some scholars have tried to avoid this implication by pointing out that during the first five plagues the text does not say explicitly that God hardened Pharaoh's heart but that it "was hardened" (Exod. 7:22; 8:19; 9:7) or that Pharaoh hardened his own heart (Exod. 8:15, 32), and that only in the sixth plague does it say explicitly "the LORD hardened Pharaoh's heart" (9:12; 10:20, 27; 11:10; 14:4). For example, Roger T. Forster and V. Paul Marston say that only from the sixth plague on God gave Pharaoh "supernatural strength to continue with his evil path of rebellion."[20]

But this observation does not succeed in avoiding the evidence of two wills in God. Even if Forster and Marston are right that God was not willing for Pharaoh's heart to be hardened during the first five plagues,[21] they concede that for the last five plagues God does will this, at least in the sense of strengthening Pharaoh to continue in the path of rebellion. Thus there is a sense in which God does will that Pharaoh go on refusing to let the people go, and there is a sense in which he does will that Pharaoh release the people. For he commands, "Let my people go." This illustrates why theologians talk about the "will of command" ("Let my people go!") and the "will of decree" ("God hardened Pharaoh's heart").

The exodus is not a unique instance of God's acting in this way. When the people of Israel reached the land of Sihon king of Heshbon, Moses sent messengers "with words of peace saying, Let me pass through your land; I will travel only on the highway" (Deut. 2:26–27). Even though this request should have led Sihon to treat the people of God with respect, as God willed

19. This is illustrated also in the way the Lord worked so that the Egyptians hated his people, and then worked again so that the Israelites found favor with the Egyptians. Psalm 105:25, "[God] turned their hearts to hate his people, to deal craftily with his servants." Exodus 12:36, "The LORD had given the people favor in the sight of the Egyptians, so that they let them have what they asked."

20. Roger T. Forster and V. Paul Marston, *God's Strategy in Human History* (Wheaton: Tyndale, 1973), 73.

21. But they are probably wrong about this. The argument from the passive voice ("Pharaoh's heart *was hardened*") that God was not the one hardening will not work. The text implies that *God* is the one hardening even when the passive voice is used. We know this because the passive verb is followed by the phrase *as the Lord had said* which refers to Exodus 4:21 and 7:3, where God had promised beforehand that he would harden Pharaoh's heart.

for his people to be blessed rather than attacked, nevertheless "Sihon the king of Heshbon would not let us pass by him; for the LORD your God hardened his spirit and made his heart obstinate, that he might give him into your hand, as at this day" (Deut. 2:30). It was God's will (in one sense) that Sihon act in a way that was contrary to God's will (in another sense) that Israel be blessed and not cursed.

Similarly the conquest of the cities of Canaan is owing to God's willing that the kings of the land resist Joshua rather than make peace with him. "Joshua waged war a long time with all these kings. There was not a city which made peace with the sons of Israel except the Hivites living in Gibeon; they took them all in battle. For it was of the Lord to harden their hearts, to meet Israel in battle in order that he might utterly destroy them, that they might receive no mercy, but that he might destroy them, just as the Lord had commanded Moses" (Josh. 11:19–20). In view of this it is difficult to imagine what Guy means when he says that the "will of God" is always to be thought of in terms of loving desire and intention[22] rather than in terms of God's effective purpose of judgment. What seems more plain is that when the time has come for judgment God wills that the guilty do things that are against his revealed will, like cursing Israel rather than blessing her.

The hardening work of God was not limited to non-Israelites. In fact it plays a central role in the life of Israel in this period of history. In Romans 11:7–9 Paul speaks of Israel's failure to obtain the righteousness and salvation it desired: Israel failed to obtain what it sought. The elect obtained it, but the rest were hardened, as it is written, "God gave them a spirit of stupor, eyes that should not see and ears that should not hear, down to this very day." Even though it is the command of God that his people see and hear and respond in faith (Isa. 42:18), nevertheless God also has his reasons for sending a spirit of stupor at times so that some will not obey his command.

Jesus expressed this same truth when he explained that one of the purposes of speaking in parables to the Jews of his day was to bring about this judicial blinding or stupor. In Mark 4:11–12 he said to his disciples, "To you has been given the secret of the kingdom of God, but for those outside everything is in parables; so that they may indeed see but not perceive, and may indeed hear but not understand; lest they should turn again, and be forgiven." Here again God wills that a condition prevail that he regards as blameworthy. His will is that they turn and be forgiven (Mark 1:15), but he acts in a way to restrict the fulfillment of that will.

Paul pictures this divine hardening as part of an overarching plan that will involve salvation for Jew and Gentile. In Romans 11:25–26 he says to his Gentile readers, "Lest you be wise in your own conceits, I want you to understand this mystery, brethren: a hardening has come upon part of Israel, until

---

22. See note 12.

the full number of the Gentiles come in, and so all Israel will be saved." The fact that the hardening has an appointed end—"until the full number of the Gentiles comes in"—shows that it is part of God's plan rather than a merely contingent event outside God's purpose. Nevertheless Paul expresses not only his but also God's heart when he says in Romans 10:1, "My heart's desire and prayer to God for them [Israel] is their salvation." God holds out his hands to a rebellious people (Rom. 10:21), but ordains a hardening that consigns them for a time to disobedience.

This is the point of Romans 11:31–32. Paul speaks to his Gentile readers again about the disobedience of Israel in rejecting their Messiah: "So they [Israel] have now been disobedient in order that by the mercy shown to you [Gentiles] they also may receive mercy." When Paul says that Israel was disobedient "in order that" Gentiles might get the benefits of the gospel, whose purpose does he have in mind? It can only be God's. For Israel did not conceive of their own disobedience as a way of blessing the Gentiles or winning mercy for themselves in such a roundabout fashion. The point of Romans 11:31 therefore is that God's hardening of Israel is not an end in itself, but is part of a saving purpose that will embrace all the nations. But in the short run we have to say that he wills a condition (hardness of heart) that he commands people to strive against ("Do not harden your heart" [Heb. 3:8, 15; 4:7]).

God's Right to Restrain Evil and His Will Not to Restrain

Another line of biblical evidence that God sometimes wills to bring about what he disapproves is his choosing to use or not to use his right to restrain evil in the human heart.

Proverbs 21:1 says, "The king's heart is like channels of water in the hands of the Lord; he turns it wherever he wishes." An illustration of this divine right over the king's heart is given in Genesis 20. Abraham is sojourning in Gerar and says to Abimelech that Sarah is his sister. So Abimelech takes her as part of his harem. But God is displeased and warns him in a dream that she is married to Abraham. Abimelech protests to God that he had taken her in his integrity. And God says (in verse 6), "Yes, I know that in the integrity of your heart you have done this, and I also kept you from sinning against me; therefore I did not let you touch her."

What is apparent here is that God has the right and the power to restrain the sins of secular rulers. When he does, it is his will to do it. And when he does not, it is his will not to. Sometimes God wills that sins be restrained and sometimes he wills that they increase more than if he restrained them.[23]

---

23. Other examples of God stirring up the hearts of kings to do his will include 1 Chronicles 5:25–26 (= 2 Kings 15:19) and 2 Chronicles 36:22–23 (= Ezra 1:1–3).

It is not an unjust infringement on human agency that the Creator has the right and power to restrain the evil actions of his creatures. Psalm 33:10–11 says, "The LORD brings the counsel of the nations to nought; he frustrates the plans of the peoples. The counsel of the LORD stands for ever, the thoughts of his heart to all generations." Sometimes God frustrates the will of rulers by making their plans fail. Sometimes he does so by influencing their hearts the way he did Abimelech, without them even knowing it.

But there are times when God does not use this right because he intends for human evil to run its course. For example, God meant to put the sons of Eli to death. Therefore he willed that they not listen to their father's counsel: "Now Eli was very old; and he heard all that his sons were doing to all Israel, and how they lay with the women who served at the doorway of the tent of meeting. And he said to them, 'Why do you do such things, the evil things that I hear from all these people? No, my sons; for the report is not good which I hear the Lord's people circulating. If one man sins against another, God will mediate for him; but if a man sins against the Lord, who can intercede for him?' But they would not listen to the voice of their father, for the Lord desired to put them to death" (1 Sam. 2:22–25).

Why would the sons of Eli not give heed to their father's good counsel? The answer of the text is "*because* the Lord desired to put them to death." This makes sense only if the Lord had the right and the power to restrain their disobedience—a right and power that he willed not to use. Thus we must say that in one sense God willed that the sons of Eli go on doing what he commanded them not to do; dishonoring their father and committing sexual immorality.

Moreover the word for "desired" in the clause the Lord desired to put them to death, is the same Hebrew word *(haphez)* used in Ezekiel 18:23, 32 and 33:11, where God asserts that he does not desire the death of the wicked. God desired to put the sons of Eli to death, but he does not desire the death of the wicked. This is a strong warning to us not to take an assertion like Ezekiel 18:23 and assume we know the precise meaning without letting other Scripture like 1 Samuel 2:25 have a say. The upshot of putting the two together is that in one sense God may desire the death of the wicked and in another sense he may not.

Another illustration of God's choosing not to use his right to restrain evil is found in Romans 1:24–28. Three times Paul says that God hands people over *(paredōken)* to sink further into corruption:

> "God handed them over to the lusts of their hearts to impurity, to the dishonoring of their bodies among themselves" (v. 24)
> "God handed them over to dishonorable passions" (v. 26)

"And since they did not see fit to acknowledge God, God handed them over to a base mind and to improper conduct" (v. 28)

God has the right and the power to restrain this evil the way he did for Abimelech. But he did not will to do that. Rather his will in this case was to punish, and part of God's punishment on evil is sometimes willing that evil increase. But this means that God chooses for behavior to come about that he commands not to happen. The fact that God's willing is punitive does not change that. And the fact that it is justifiably punitive is one of the points of this chapter. There are other examples we could give,[24] but we pass on to a different line of evidence.

Does God Delight in the Punishment of the Wicked?

We just saw that God "desired" to put the sons of Eli to death, and that the word for desire is the same one used in Ezekiel 18:23 when God says he does not delight in the death of the wicked. Another illustration of this complex desiring is found in Deuteronomy 28:63. Moses is warning of coming judgment on unrepentant Israel. What he says is strikingly different (not contradictory, I will argue) from Ezekiel 18:23. "And as the Lord took delight in doing you good and multiplying you, so the Lord will take delight in bringing ruin upon you and destroying you."

Here an even stronger word for joy *(yasis)* is used when it says that God will "take delight over you to cause you to perish and to destroy you." We are faced with the inescapable biblical fact that in some sense God does not

---

24. Other examples of God's not restraining evil because he planned to use it could be given.

1. "The Lord had ordained to defeat the good counsel of Ahithophel so that the Lord might bring evil upon Absalom" (2 Sam. 7:14).

2. When Rehoboam, the son of Solomon, was considering how to rule the people, he took into consideration the will of the people that he lighten the yoke that Solomon had put on them (1 Kings 12:9). He also consulted with the young and with the old men. He decided to follow the counsel of the young who said to make the yoke harder. Why did this come about? First Kings 12:15 gives the answer: "So the king did not hearken to the people; for *it was a turn of affairs brought about by the* LORD *that he might fulfill his word,* which the LORD spoke by Ahijah the Shilonite to Jeroboam the son of Nebat." This is important too show again (as with Revelation 17:17) that the fulfillment of prophecy (1 Kings 11:29–39) is by a work of the Lord: "it was a turn of affairs brought about by the Lord." Prophecy is not mere foreknowledge of what will come about somehow on its own. Prophecy is an expression of what God intends to bring about in the future.

3. To his father's dismay Samson insisted that he take a wife for him from the Philistines. His father counseled against it just as Eli tried to restrain the evil of his sons. But Samson prevailed. Why? "His father and mother did not know that *it was of the Lord,* for He was seeking an occasion against the Philistines" (Judg. 14:4).

4. In Deuteronomy 29:2–4 Moses explains why the people have not been more responsive to God and why they have gone their own way so often: "You have seen all that the LORD did before your eyes in the land of Egypt . . . the signs, and those great wonders; but to this day *the* LORD *has not given you a mind to understand, or eyes to see, or ears to hear.*"

delight in the death of the wicked (Ezek. 18), and in some sense he does (Deut. 28:63; 2 Sam. 2:25).[25]

How Extensive Is the Sovereign Will of God?

Behind this complex relationship of two wills in God is the foundational biblical premise that God is indeed sovereign in a way that makes him ruler of all actions. Forster and Marston try to overcome the tension between God's will of decree and God's will of command by asserting that there is no such thing as God's sovereign will of decree: "Nothing in Scripture suggests that there is some kind of will or plan of God which is inviolable."[26] This is a remarkable claim. Without claiming to be exhaustive it will be fair to touch briefly on some Scriptures that do indeed "suggest that there is some kind of will or plan of God which is inviolable."

There are passages that ascribe to God the final control over all calamities and disasters wrought by nature or by man:

> "Does evil befall a city, unless the LORD has done it?" (Amos 3:6)

> "I am the LORD, and there is no other. I form light and create darkness, I make weal and create woe, I am the LORD, who do all these things." (Isa. 45:7)

> "Who has commanded and it came to pass, unless the Lord has ordained it? Is it not from the mouth of the Most High that good and evil come?" (Lam. 3:37–38)

Noteworthy in these texts is that the calamities in view involve human hostilities and cruelties that God would disapprove of even as he wills that they be.

The apostle Peter wrote concerning God's involvement in the sufferings of his people at the hands of their antagonists. In his first letter he spoke of the "will of God" in two senses. It was something to be pursued and lived up to on the one hand. "Such is the will of God, that by doing right you may silence

---

25. One should also take heed to the texts that portray God laughing over the ruin of the defiant (Prov. 1:24–26; Isa. 30:31; Rev. 18:20).

26. Forster and Marston, *God's Strategy in Human History*, 32. Their favorite text to demonstrate that God's will for people is contingent and not effectual is Luke 7:30, "The Pharisees and the lawyers rejected the purpose of God for themselves, not having been baptized by [John]" (RSV). However the phrase *for themselves*, because of its location in the word order, very likely does not modify "the purpose of God" (as the Revised Standard Version might suggest). Rather it probably modifies "rejected." Thus Luke would be saying that the plan of salvation preached by John the Baptist was accepted by some and rejected by others "for themselves." The text cannot prove one way or the other whether God has a specific plan for each life that can be successfully frustrated.

the ignorance of foolish men" (1 Pet. 2:15). "Live the rest of the time in the flesh no longer for the lusts of men but for the will of God" (4:2). On the other hand the will of God was not his moral instruction, but the state of affairs that he sovereignly brought about. "For it is better to suffer for doing right, if that should be God's will, than for doing wrong" (3:17). "Let those who suffer according to God's will do right and entrust their souls to a faithful Creator" (4:19). And in this context, the suffering that Peter has in mind is the suffering that comes from hostile people and therefore cannot come without sin.

In fact the New Testament saints seemed to live in the calm light of an overarching sovereignty of God concerning all the details of their lives and ministry. Paul expressed himself like this with regard to his travel plans. On taking leave of the saints in Ephesus he said, "I will return to you if God wills" (Acts 18:21). To the Corinthians he wrote, "I will come to you soon, if the Lord wills" (1 Cor. 4:19). And again, "I do not want to see you now just in passing; I hope to spend some time with you, if the Lord permits" (1 Cor. 16:7).

The writer to the Hebrews says that his intention is to leave the elementary things behind and press on to maturity. But then he pauses and adds, "And this we will do if God permits" (6:3). This is remarkable since it is hard to imagine one even thinking that God might not permit such a thing unless one had a remarkably high view of the sovereign prerogatives of God.

James warns against the pride of presumption in speaking of the simplest plans in life without a due submission to the overarching sovereignty of God. Instead of saying, "Tomorrow we will do such and such . . . you ought to say, 'If the Lord wills, we shall live and we shall do this or that'"[27] (4:15). Thus the saints in Caesarea, when they could not dissuade Paul from taking the risk to go to Jerusalem "ceased and said, 'The will of the Lord be done'" (Acts 21:14). God would decide whether Paul would be killed or not, just as James said.

This sense of living in the hands of God, right down to the details of life, was not new for the early Christians. They knew it already from the whole history of Israel, but especially from their wisdom literature. "The plans of the mind belong to man, but the answer of the tongue is from the Lord" (Prov. 16:1). "A man's mind plans his way, but the Lord directs his steps" (Prov. 16:9). "Many are the plans in the mind of a man, but it is the purpose of the Lord that will be established" (Prov. 19:21). "The lot is cast into the

---

27. In *The Grace of God, the Will of Man*, Basinger argues that belief in the absolute sovereignty of God is practically irrelevant in daily life. Of all the things that could be said against this view the most important one seems to be that James, writing under the inspiration of God, does not share it, but teaches that a life lived without a conscious submission to the sovereignty of God in everyday affairs is tantamount to "boasting in arrogance" (4:16). See also in this work, chapter 12 by Jerry Bridges.

lap, but the decision is wholly from the LORD" (Prov. 16:33). "I know, O LORD, that the way of man is not in himself, that it is not in man who walks to direct his steps" (Jer. 10:23). Jesus had no quarrel with this sense of living in the hand of God. If anything, he intensified the idea with words like those in Matthew 10:29, "Are not two sparrows sold for a penny? And not one of them will fall to the ground apart from your Father."

This confidence that the details of life were in the control of God every day was rooted in numerous prophetic expressions of God's unstoppable, unthwartable sovereign purpose. "Remember the former things of old; for I am God, and there is no other; I am God, and there is none like me, declaring the end from the beginning and from ancient times things not yet done, saying, 'My counsel shall stand, and I will accomplish all my purpose'" (Isa. 46:9–10; cf. 43:13). "All the inhabitants of the earth are accounted as nothing; and he does according to his will in the host of heaven and among the inhabitants of the earth; and none can stay his hand or say to him, 'What doest thou?'" (Dan. 4:35). "I know that thou canst do all things, and that no purpose of yours can be thwarted" (Job 42:2). "Our God is in the heavens; he does whatever he pleases" (Ps. 115:3).

One of the most precious implications of this confidence in God's inviolable sovereign will is that it provides the foundation of the "new covenant" hope for the holiness without which we will not see the Lord (Heb. 12:14). In the old covenant the law was written on stone and brought death when it met with the resistance of unrenewed hearts. But the new covenant promise is that God will not let his purposes for a holy people shipwreck on the weakness of human will. Instead he promises to do what needs to be done to make us what we ought to be. "And the LORD your God will circumcise your heart and the heart of your offspring, so that you will love the LORD your God with all your heart and with all your soul, that you may live" (Deut. 30:6). "I will put my spirit within you, and cause you to walk in my statutes and be careful to observe my ordinances" (Ezek. 36:27). "I will make with them an everlasting covenant, that I will not turn away from doing good to them; and I will put the fear of me in their hearts, that they may not turn from me" (Jer. 32:40). "Work out your salvation with fear and trembling, for it is God who is at work in you to will and to work for his good pleasure" (Phil. 2:12–13).

In view of all these texts I am unable to grasp what Forster and Marston might mean by saying, "Nothing in Scripture suggests that there is some kind of will or plan of God which is inviolable" (see n. 26). Nor can I understand how Guy can say that the "will of God" is always a desiring and intending but not a sovereign, effective willing (see n. 12). Rather the Scriptures lead us again and again to affirm that God's will is sometimes spoken of as an expression of his moral standards for human behavior and sometimes as an expression of his sovereign control even over acts that are contrary to that standard.

This means that the distinction between terms like "will of decree" and "will of command" or "sovereign will" and "moral will" is not an artificial distinction demanded by Calvinistic theology. The terms are an effort to describe the whole of biblical revelation. They are an effort to say yes to all of the Bible and not silence any of it. They are a way to say yes to the universal, saving will of 1 Timothy 2:4 and yes to the individual unconditional election of Romans 9:6–23.[28]

Does It Make Sense?

I turn now to the task of reflecting on how these two wills of God fit together and make sense—as far as this finite and fallible creature can rise to that challenge.

The first thing to affirm in view of all these texts is that God does not sin. "Holy, holy, holy is the LORD of hosts, the whole earth is full of his glory" (Isa. 6:3). "God cannot be tempted by evil and he himself does not tempt anyone" (James 1:13).[29] In ordering all things, including sinful acts, God is not

---

28. That Romans 9:23 does in fact deal with individuals and eternal destinies and not just with groups and historical roles is the thesis of Piper, *The Justification of God;* and to my knowledge the arguments presented there have not been gainsaid. From the one passing reference to this study by Pinnock in *The Grace of God, the Will of Man,* it seems that serious attention has not been paid to the arguments I gave there. Pinnock has a legitimate concern that Romans 9 be interpreted with an awareness of Romans 10 and 11 in view. He says, "I believe that if Piper had moved forward in Romans beyond Romans 9, he would have encountered Paul's earnest prayer to God that the lost be saved (10:1) and his explanation of how it happens that any are actually included or excluded—through faith or the lack of it (11:20). Romans 9 must be read in the context of the larger context of Romans 9–11" (29 n. 10). I certainly don't want to disagree that Romans 9 must be read in its context. That is why, for example on pages 9–15 and 163–65, I discussed the limits of my focus on Romans 9:1–23 within the structure of Romans 9–11. With regard to Pinnock's two specific points: it is true that we are included or excluded in salvation on the condition of faith. But that does not account for how one person comes to faith and not another. Nor does Paul's "heart's desire and prayer to God" for the salvation of the Jews in Romans 10:1 contradict the explicit statement that "a hardening has come [from God] upon part of Israel until [God lifts it after] the full number of the gentiles [appointed by God for salvation] come in" (Rom. 11:25). See also Thomas R. Schreiner, chapter 4 in this work.

29. I am aware that James 1:13–14 is a text Arminians would use against my position. There is no point in hiding each other's problem texts. I am not allowed to pick and choose any more than Arminians may not neglect all the texts I have cited. If I cannot make texts harmonize I try to let them both stand until someone wiser than I can (even if I must wait for God's final enlightenment in heaven). My effort at understanding James 1:13, in view of all the examples of God's willing that sinful actions come about, is to say that "tempt" is defined in verse 14 as being "dragged away" *(exelkomenos)* and "lured" *(deleazomenos)*. James is not thinking of temptation in terms of an object of desire being put in front of someone (e.g., he does not attribute "temptation" to Satan, the arch "tempter," but to our "desire"). For example, temptation is not the pornography on display, in James's way of thinking here; rather it is the

sinning. For as Edwards says, "It implies no contradiction to suppose that an act may be an evil act, and yet that it is a good thing that such an act should come to pass . . . As for instance, it might be an evil thing to crucify Christ, but yet it was a good thing that the crucifying of Christ came to pass."[30] The Scriptures lead us to the insight that God can will that a sinful act come to pass without willing it as an act of sin in himself.

Edwards points out that Arminians, it seems, must come to a similar conclusion.

> All must own that God sometimes wills not to hinder the breach of his own commands, because he does not in fact hinder it . . . But you will say, God wills to permit sin, as he wills the creature should be left to his freedom; and if he should hinder it, he would offer violence to the nature of his own creature. I answer, this comes nevertheless to the very same thing that I say. You say, God does not will sin absolutely; but rather than alter the law of nature and the nature of free agents, he wills it. He wills what is contrary to excellency in some particulars, for the sake of a more general excellency and order. So that the scheme of the Arminians does not help the matter.[31]

This seems right to me, and it can be illustrated again by reflecting directly on 1 Timothy 2:4, where Paul says that God wills all persons to be saved. What are we to say of the fact that God wills something that in fact does not happen? These are two possibilities. One is that there is a power in the universe greater than God's that is frustrating him by overruling what he wills. Neither Calvinist nor Arminian affirms this.

The other possibility is that God wills not to save all, even though he is willing to save all, because there is something else that he wills more, which would be lost if he exerted his sovereign power to save all. This is the solution

---

"dragging" "luring" feeling that makes a person look. He is thinking of temptation as the engagement of the emotions in strong desires for evil. This he calls the "conceiving" *(syllabousa)* stage of temptation before the actual "birth" *(tiktei)* of the act of sin (v. 15). Thus it seems to me that James is saying that God does not ever experience this kind of "being dragged away" or "being lured." And he does not directly (see n. 34) produce that "dragging" and "luring" toward evil in humans. In some way (that we may not be able to fully comprehend) God is able without blameworthy "tempting" to see to it that a person does what God ordains for him to do even if it involves evil.

But James is not saying that God cannot have objective enticements to evil put in front of him, nor that he himself does not arrange events at times so that such enticements come before us, which may lead us, through the "dragging" of our desires, to sin (which God knew and, in one sense, willed). In fact, the Bible reveals that God tests (same word as "tempt" in Greek) his people often (cf. Heb. 11:17) by arranging their circumstances so that they are presented with dangerous acts of obedience that they might sinfully fear, or sinful pleasures that they might covet. In the end what I say is that God is able to order events, if it seems wise and good to do so, such that sin comes about; yet he does so without "tempting" those who sin, as James says.

30. Edwards, "Concerning the Decrees in General, and Election in Particular," 529.
31. Ibid., 528.

that I as a Calvinist affirm along with Arminians. Both Calvinists and Arminians affirm two wills in God when they ponder deeply over 1 Timothy 2:4. Both can say that God wills for all to be saved. But then when queried why all are not saved both Calvinist and Arminian answer that God is committed to something even more valuable than saving all.

The difference between Calvinists and Arminians lies not in whether there are two wills in God, but in what they say this higher commitment is. What does God will more than saving all? The answer given by Arminians is that human self-determination and the possible resulting love relationship with God are more valuable than saving all people by sovereign, efficacious grace. The answer given by Calvinists is that the greater value is the manifestation of the full range of God's glory in wrath and mercy (Rom. 9:22–23) and the humbling of man so that he enjoys giving all credit to God for his salvation (1 Cor. 1:29).

This is crucial to see, for what it implies is that 1 Timothy 2:4 does not settle the momentous issue of God's higher commitment that restrains him from saving all. There is no mention here of free will.[32] Nor is there mention of sovereign, prevenient, efficacious grace. If all we had were this text, we could only guess what restrains God from saving all. When free will is found in this verse, it is a philosophical, metaphysical assumption, not an exegetical conclusion.[33] The assumption is that if God wills in one sense for all to be

32. In fact 2 Timothy 2:24–26 teaches that self-determination is not the decisive factor in repenting and coming to a knowledge of the truth. See note 14.

33. Clark Pinnock, it seems to me, falls victim to his own accusations in this matter of letting philosophical considerations override biblical ones. For example, he is one of a number today who are trying to refute the truth of God's knowledge of all future events as a way of preserving man's freedom from divine necessity. Pinnock, after a pilgrimage from Calvinism to Arminianism (and beyond, since classical Arminianism still affirmed that God knows all future actions), now declares, "Decisions not yet made do not exist anywhere to be known even by God. They are potential—yet to be realized but not yet actual. God can predict a great deal of what we will choose to do, but not all of it, because some of it remains hidden in the mystery of human freedom . . . God too faces possibilities in the future, and not only certainties. God too moves into a future not wholly known because not yet fixed." (*The Grace of God, the Will of Man*, 25–26).

Pinnock was pressed to this position first by neo-Arminian "logic," not Scripture. This is ironic because of how he persistently accuses others of silencing Scripture with "Calvinian logic" (19, 21, 22, 25, 26, 28). The neo-Arminian logic goes like this: "A total omniscience would necessarily mean that everything we will ever choose in the future will have been already spelled out in the divine knowledge register, and consequently the belief that we have truly significant choices to make would seem to be mistaken" (25). Thus the philosophical presuppositions that foreknowledge is incompatible with "significant choices" and that the reality of what he calls "significant choices" is more sure than the total foreknowledge of God—these two neo-Arminian (not classical Arminian) presuppositions lead him logically to reject the total foreknowledge of God. Only then does he say, "Therefore, I had to ask myself if it was biblically possible to hold that . . . free choices would not be something that can be known even by God because they are not yet settled in reality" (25). In another place he says, "Let me explain five of the doctrinal moves that *logic required* and I believed *Scripture permitted* me to make . . ." (18–19, italics added). Scripture was searched as a confirmation of what neo-Arminian logic demanded.

saved, then he cannot in another sense will that only some be saved. That assumption is not in the text, nor is it demanded by logic, nor is it taught in the rest of Scripture. Therefore 1 Timothy 2:4 does not settle the issue; it creates it. Both Arminians and Calvinists must look elsewhere to answer whether the gift of human self-determination or the glory of divine sovereignty is the reality that restrains God's will to save all people.

The Calvinists whom I admire do not claim to have simple, easy solutions to complex biblical tensions. When their writing is difficult this is because the Scriptures are difficult (as the apostle Peter admitted that, in part, they are [2 Pet. 3:16]). These Calvinists are struggling to be faithful to diverse (but not contradictory) Scriptures. Both Calvinists and Arminians feel at times that the ridicule directed against their complex expositions are in fact a ridicule against the complexity of the Scriptures.

I find the effort of Stephen Charnock (1628–1680), a chaplain to Henry Cromwell and nonconformist pastor in London, to be balanced and helpful in holding the diverse Scriptures on God's will together.

> God doth not will [sin] directly,[34] and by an efficacious will. He doth not directly will it, because he hath prohibited it by his law, which is a discovery of his will; so that if he should directly will sin, and directly prohibit it, he would will good and evil in the same manner, and there would be contradictions in God's will: to will sin absolutely, is to work it (Ps. 115:3): "God hath done whatsoever he pleased." God cannot absolutely will it, because he cannot work it. God wills good by a positive decree, be-

---

34. Arminians sometimes disparage Calvinist appeals to "secondary causes" between God's sovereign will and the immediate effecting of a sinful act (Jack Cottrell, "The Nature of Divine Sovereignty," in *The Grace of God, the Will of Man,* 100–102). But this idea of intermediate causes, different from God's ultimate causing, is not introduced because of a theological necessity but because so many Scriptures demand it. For example, God commissions an "evil spirit" between Abimelech and the men of Shechem to bring about his will (Judg. 9:22–24; Satan leads Judas to do (Luke 22:3) what Acts 2:23 says God brought about; Paul says that Satan blinds the minds of unbelievers (2 Cor. 4:4) but also says that God sends a blinding spirit of stupor (Rom. 11:8–10); Satan stirs up David to take a census (1 Chron. 21:1) which proved to be sin (2 Sam. 24:10), and yet it is written that God was in some sense the cause behind Satan (2 Sam. 24:1); Satan gets permission from God to torment Job (Job 1:12; 2:6), but when Satan had taken Job's family and made him sick Job said, "The LORD has taken" (Job 1:21), and, "Shall we receive good at the hand of the LORD and shall we not receive evil" (2:10)—to which the writer responds: "In all this Job did not sin with his lips" (1:22; 2:10). Texts like this make the theological reflections of Theodore Beza (in 1582) biblically sound: "Nothing happens anyhow or without God's most righteous decree, although God is not the author of or sharer in any sin at all. Both His power and His goodness are so great and so incomprehensible, that at a time when He applies the devil or wicked men in achieving some work, whom He afterwards justly punishes, He Himself none the less effects His holy work well and justly.—These things do not hinder but rather establish second and intermediate causes, by which all things happen. When from eternity God decreed whatever was to happen at definite moments, He at the same time also decreed the manner and way which He wished it thus to take place; to such extent, that even if some flaw is discovered in a second cause, it yet implies no flaw or fault in God's eternal counsel." Heppe, *Reformed Dogmatics,* 144–45.

cause he hath decreed to effect it. He wills evil by a private decree, because he hath decreed not to give that grace which would certainly prevent it. God doth not will sin simply, for that were to approve it, but he wills it, in order to that good his wisdom will bring forth from it. He wills not sin for itself, but for the event.[35]

Edwards, writing about eighty years later, comes to similar conclusions with somewhat different terminology.

> When a distinction is made between God's revealed will and his secret will, or his will of command and decree, "will" is certainly in that distinction taken in two senses. His will of decree, is not his will in the same sense as his will of command is. Therefore, it is no difficulty at all to suppose, that the one may be otherwise than the other: his will in both senses is his inclination. But when we say he wills virtue, or loves virtue, or the happiness of his creature; thereby is intended, that virtue, or the creature's happiness, absolutely and simply considered, is agreeable to the inclination of his nature.

> His will of decree is, his inclination to a thing, not as to that thing absolutely and simply, but with respect to the universality of things, that have been, are or shall be. So God, though he hates a thing as it is simply, may incline to it with reference to the universality of things. Though he hates sin in itself, yet he may will to permit it, for the greater promotion of holiness in this universality, including all things, and at all times. So, though he has no inclination to a creature's misery, considered absolutely, yet he may will it, for the greater promotion of happiness in this universality.[36]

Putting it in my own words, Edwards said that the infinite complexity of the divine mind is such that God has the capacity to look at the world through two lenses. He can look through a narrow lens or through a wide-angle lens. When God looks at a painful or wicked event through his narrow lens, he sees the tragedy or the sin for what it is in itself and he is angered and grieved. "I do not delight in the death of anyone, says the Lord God" (Ezek. 18:32). But when God looks at a painful or wicked event through his wide-angle lens, he sees the tragedy or the sin in relation to everything leading up to it and everything flowing out from it. He sees it in all the connections and effects that form a pattern or mosaic stretching into eternity. This mosaic, with all its (good and evil) parts he does delight in (Ps. 115:3).

God's emotional life is infinitely complex beyond our ability to fully comprehend. For example, who can comprehend that the Lord hears in one moment of time the prayers of ten million Christians around the world, and sympathizes with each one personally and individually like a caring Father (as Hebrews 4:15 says he will), even though among those ten million prayers some

35. Stephen Charnock, *Discourses upon the Existence and Attributes of God* (Grand Rapids: Baker, 1979), 148.
36. Edwards, "Concerning the Divine Decrees," 527–28.

are brokenhearted and some are bursting with joy? How can God weep with those who weep and rejoice with those who rejoice when they are both coming to him at the same time—in fact are always coming to him with no break at all? Or who can comprehend that God is angry at the sin of the world every day (Ps. 7:11), and yet every day, every moment, he is rejoicing with tremendous joy because somewhere in the world a sinner is repenting (Luke 15:7, 10, 23)? Who can comprehend that God continually burns with hot anger at the rebellion of the wicked, grieves over the unholy speech of his people (Eph. 4:29–30), yet takes pleasure in them daily (Ps. 149:4), and ceaselessly makes merry over penitent prodigals who come home?

Who of us could say what complex of emotions is not possible for God? All we have to go on here is what he has chosen to tell us in the Bible. And what he has told us is that there is a sense in which he does not experience pleasure in the judgment of the wicked, and there is a sense in which he does.

Therefore we should not stumble over the fact that God does and does not take pleasure in the death of the wicked. When Moses warns Israel that the Lord will take delight in bringing ruin upon them and destroying them if they do not repent (Deut. 28:63), he means that those who have rebelled against the Lord and moved beyond repentance will not be able to gloat that they have made the Almighty miserable. God is not defeated in the triumphs of his righteous judgment. Quite the contrary. Moses says that when they are judged they will unwittingly provide an occasion for God to rejoice in the demonstration of his justice and his power and the infinite worth of his glory (Rom. 9:22–23).[37]

When God took counsel with himself as to whether he should save all people, he consulted not only the truth of what he sees when looking through the narrow lens but also the larger truth of what he sees when all things are viewed through the wide-angle lens of his all-knowing wisdom. If, as Calvinists say, God deems it wise and good to elect unconditionally some to salvation and not others, one may legitimately ask whether the offer of salvation to all is genuine. Is it made with heart? Does it come from real compassion? Is the willing that none perish a bona fide willing of love?

The way I would give an account of this is explained by Robert L. Dabney in an essay written over a hundred years ago.[38] His treatment is very detailed

---

37. This is the way Edwards tackled the problem of how God and the saints in heaven will be happy in heaven for all eternity knowing that many millions of people are suffering in hell forever. It is not that suffering or misery in itself is pleasant to God and the saints, but that the vindication of God's infinite holiness is cherished so deeply. See John Gerstner, *Jonathan Edwards on Heaven and Hell* (Grand Rapids: Baker, 1980), 33–38.

38. Robert L. Dabney, "God's Indiscriminate Proposals of Mercy, as Related to his Power, Wisdom, and Sincerity," in *Discussions: Evangelical and Theological,* vol. 1 (1890; Edinburgh: Banner of Truth Trust, 1967), 282–313. This treatment of Dabney has been published previously in Piper, *Pleasures of God,* 145–46.

and answers many objections that go beyond the limits of this chapter. I will simply give the essence of his solution, which seems to me to be on the right track, though he, as well as I, would admit we do not "furnish an exhaustive explanation of this mystery of the divine will."[39]

Dabney uses an analogy from the life of George Washington taken from Chief Justice Marshall's *Life of Washington*. A certain Major André had jeopardized the safety of the young nation through "rash and unfortunate" treasonous acts. Marshall says of the death warrant, signed by Washington, "Perhaps on no occasion of his life did the commander-in-chief obey with more reluctance the stern mandates of duty and policy." Dabney observes that Washington's compassion for André was "real and profound." He also had "plenary power to kill or to save alive." Why then did he sign the death warrant? Dabney explains, "Washington's volition to sign the death-warrant of André did not arise from the fact that his compassion was slight or feigned, but from the fact that it was rationally counterpoised by a complex of superior judgments . . . of wisdom, duty, patriotism, and moral indignation [the wide-angle lens]."

Dabney imagines a defender of André, hearing Washington say, "I do this with the deepest reluctance and pity." Then the defender says, "Since you are supreme in this matter, and have full bodily ability to throw down that pen, we shall know by your signing this warrant that your pity is hypocritical." Dabney responds to this by saying, "The petulance of this charge would have been equal to its folly. The pity was real, but was restrained by superior elements of motive. Washington had official and bodily power to discharge the criminal, but he had not the sanctions of his own wisdom and justice."[40] The corresponding point in the case of divine election is that "the absence of volition[41] in God to save does not necessarily imply the absence of compassion."[42] God has "a true compassion, which is yet restrained, in the case of the . . . non-elect, by consistent and holy reasons, from taking the form of a volition to regenerate."[43] God's infinite wisdom regulates his whole will and guides and harmonizes (not suppresses) all its active principles."[44]

In other words, God has a real and deep compassion for perishing sinners. Jeremiah points to this reality in God's heart. In Lamentations 3:32–33 he speaks of the judgment that God has brought upon Jerusalem: "Though he causes grief, he will have compassion according to the abundance of his steadfast

39. Dabney, "God's Indiscriminate Proposals of Mercy," 309.
40. Ibid., 285.
41. Dabney is using the word *volition* as "effective volition" and as distinct from willings and wishings and desirings and yearnings that one can have short of an effective volition that carries into action.
42. Dabney, "God's Indiscriminate Proposals of Mercy," 299.
43. Ibid., 307.
44. Ibid., 309.

love; for he does not willingly afflict or grieve the sons of men." The word willingly translates a composite Hebrew word *(milibo)* which means literally "from his heart" (cf. 1 Kings 12:33). It appears that this is Jeremiah's way of saying that God does will the affliction that he caused, but he does not will it in the same way he wills compassion. The affliction did not come "from his heart." Jeremiah was trying, as we are, to come to terms with the way a sovereign God wills two different things, affliction and compassion.

God's expression of pity and his entreaties have heart in them. There is a genuine inclination in God's heart to spare those who have committed treason against his kingdom. But his motivation is complex, and not every true element in it rises to the level of effective choice. In his great and mysterious heart there are kinds of longings and desires that are real—they tell us something true about his character. Yet not all of these longings govern God's actions. He is governed by the depth of his wisdom expressed through a plan that no ordinary human deliberation would ever conceive (Rom. 11:33–36; 1 Cor. 2:9). There are holy and just reasons for why the affections of God's heart have the nature and intensity and proportion that they do.

Dabney is aware that several kinds of objections can be raised against the analogy of George Washington as it is applied to God.[45] He admits that "no

45. Ibid., 287–99. He cites three kinds of objections to the analogy.

1) "While it applies to a human ruler, who is not omnipotent, it does not apply to God, who is almighty." A human ruler foresees negative effects of his pardoning and cannot overcome them and therefore is constrained to condemn. God is omnipotent and therefore is not constrained by such inability. Dabney answers, "We know that [God's] ultimate end is his own glory. But we do not know all the ways in which God may deem his glory is promoted . . . God may see in his own omniscience, a rational ground other than inability for restraining his actual [inclination] of pity towards a given sinner" (288–89). Notice how Dabney is not driven by human logic here. He is simply coming to terms with Scripture and saying in effect: the Scripture says it is this way; therefore God must have his reasons.

2) The second objection comes from advanced theological speculation: "Such a theory of motive and free agency may not be applied to the divine will, because of God's absolute simplicity of being, and the unity of his attributes with his essence, the unity and eternity of his whole will as to all events. It is feared that the parallel would misrepresent God's activities of will by a vicious anthropomorphism" (287).

The real issue here is whether God's unchangeableness is jeopardized and whether he is put at the mercy of creatures who bring about fluctuations in his heart that make him dependent on them and divided in his will. This is the concern when the historic confessions say that God is "without passions." Dabney responds by saying, "While God has no . . . mere susceptibility such that his creature can cause an effect upon it irrespective to God's own will and freedom, yet he has active principles. These are not passions, in the sense of fluctuations or agitations, but none the less are they affections of his will, actively distinguished from the cognitions in his intelligence" (291). Moreover the actions of his creatures "are real occasions, though not efficient causes, of the action both of the divine affections and will" (291). In other words, God is not at the mercy of his creatures, because, even though he genuinely responds to their actions with affections and choices, this response is always according to God's prior willing in complete freedom. Thus he is not forced to respond by others, nor is he, as it were, cornered into a frustrated compassion that he did not anticipate.

analogy can be perfect between the actions of a finite and the infinite intelligence and will."[46] Yet I think he is right to say that the objections do not overthrow the essential truth that there can be, in a noble and great heart (even a divine heart), sincere compassion for a criminal that is nevertheless not set free.

Therefore I affirm with John 3:16 and 1 Timothy 2:4 that God loves the world with a deep compassion that desires the salvation of all men. Yet I also affirm that God has chosen from before the foundation of the world whom he will save from sin. Since not all people are saved we must choose whether we believe (with the Arminians) that God's will to save all people is restrained by his commitment to human self-determination or whether we believe (with the Calvinists) that God's will to save all people is restrained by his commitment to the glorification of his sovereign grace (Eph. 1:6, 12, 14; Rom. 9:22–23).

This decision should not be made on the basis of metaphysical assumptions about what we think human accountability requires.[47] It should be made on the basis of what the Scriptures teach. I do not find in the Bible that human beings have the ultimate power of self-determination. As far as I can tell it is a philosophical inference based on metaphysical presuppositions. This book aims to show that the sovereignty of God's grace in salvation is taught in Scripture.

God's simplicity and unity should not be taken to mean what the Bible forbids that it mean: "The Bible always speaks of God's attributes as distinct, and yet not dividing his unity; of his intelligence and will as different; of his wrath, love, pity, wisdom, as not the same activities of the Infinite Spirit" (290). The unity of God's Spirit lies not in his having no affections, nor in all his affections being one simple act; rather his unity lies in the glorious harmony and proportion of all that he is—each affection and propensity revealing something of the unified, harmonious complexity of the infinite Mind.

3) The third kind of objection to applying the analogy of George Washington to God is that "no such balancing of subjective motives takes place without inward strivings, which would be inconsistent with God's immutability and blessedness" (287). Dabney agrees that this is difficult to imagine—that God is moved by all the energy of affections and yet shows all the equanimity of deity. But it is not impossible. He observes wisely that the more pure and steady a person's affections and thoughts are, the less struggle is involved in adjusting them into a rational and righteous decision.

He imagines a man of more unstable condition than the "majestic calmness" of Washington facing the same choice: "He would have shown far more agitation; he would perhaps have thrown down the pen and snatched it again, and trembled and wept. But this would not have proved a deeper compassion than Washington's. His shallow nature was not capable of such depths of sentiment in any virtuous direction as filled the profounder soul. The cause of the difference would have been in this, that Washington's was a grander and wiser as well as a more feeling soul" (298).

Dabney cites an analogy of how deepening mixed affections does not have to result in internal strife and agitation: "Dying saints have sometimes declared that their love for their families was never before so profound and tender; and yet were enabled by dying grace to bid them a final farewell with joyful calmness. If, then, the ennobling of the affections enables the will to adjust the balance between them with less agitation, what will the result be when the wisdom is that of omniscience, the virtue is that of infinite holiness, and the self-command that of omnipotence?" (299).

46. Ibid., 287.

47. For an example of the way philosophical assumptions seem to exert undue limits on what the Scriptures can teach, see note 33.

My contribution has simply been to show that God's will for all people to be saved is not at odds with the sovereignty of God's grace in election. That is, my answer to the question about what restrains God's will to save all people is his supreme commitment to uphold and display the full range of his glory through the sovereign demonstration of his wrath and mercy for the enjoyment of his elect and believing people from every tribe and tongue and nation.

6

Perseverance of the Saints: A Case Study from the Warning Passages in Hebrews

WAYNE GRUDEM

For centuries Christians have been puzzled by Hebrews 6:4–6:

> For it is impossible to restore again to repentance those who have once been enlightened, who have tasted the heavenly gift, and have become partakers of the Holy Spirit, and have tasted the goodness of the word of God and the powers of the age to come, if they then commit apostasy, since they crucify the Son of God on their own account and hold him up to contempt.[1]

Were these people really saved in the first place? And if they were, does this passage prove that true Christians can lose their salvation? That is the conclusion many Christians have reached while pondering this passage. Others have continued to believe that genuine Christians cannot lose their salvation,[2] but they have done so only by saying that the cumulative force of passages outside the Book of Hebrews is so strong that this difficult passage is not enough to overturn their belief.

In this chapter, I hope to demonstrate that people who hold that true Christians can never lose their salvation do not have to look outside of Hebrews in

---

1. All Scripture quotations in this chapter are taken from the Revised Standard Version unless otherwise specified. I have adopted the commonly accepted sense of the complex syntax of this passage (as reflected, for example in the Revised Standard Version, New International Version, and New American Standard Bible), although some other formulations have been suggested. See the discussion in William L. Lane, *Hebrews 1–8*, Word Biblical Commentary (Dallas: Word, 1991), 132.

2. Some people object to using the phrase *lose their salvation* in discussing Hebrews; I discuss this phrase in the section "Definition of the Question," 134–37.

133

order to find doctrinal ammunition to hold these verses at bay. Rather, by focusing our attention within the Book of Hebrews itself we can see that this passage in its immediate context, and within the larger context of the book, is consistent with the Reformed doctrine of the perseverance of the saints.

At the end of the chapter, I will also examine some other warning passages in Hebrews (2:1–4; 3:6–4:13; 10:26–31; 12:25) to compare their teachings with that of 6:4–6.

The plan of this chapter is as follows:

I. Analysis of Hebrews 6:4–6 in its immediate context
   A. Definition of the question
   B. The meanings of the descriptive terms (vv. 4–6)
      1. The argument that these people were once saved
      2. The argument that the terms alone are inconclusive
      3. Other views of 6:4–6
      4. Conclusion regarding the positive terms in 6:4–6
      5. Why it is impossible to restore such people to repentance
   C. The metaphor of the field (vv. 7–8)
   D. Better things, that is, things that belong to salvation (vv. 9–12)
   E. Comparison with the earlier state of those who fell away elsewhere in Hebrews (chaps. 3–4)
   F. Comparison with language describing the saved elsewhere in Hebrews
   G. Conclusions regarding Hebrews 6:4–6
II. Analysis of other warning passages in Hebrews
   A. Hebrews 2:1–4
   B. Hebrews 3:6–4:13
   C. Hebrews 10:26–31
   D. Hebrews 12:25
III. Comparison with related passages in the rest of the New Testament
IV. Conclusions for the doctrine of perseverance of the saints

Analysis of Hebrews 6:4–6 in Its Immediate Context

Definition of the Question

It is important that we define clearly the question that has made this such a disputed passage. The question is a theological one, and for purposes of clarity in discussion I will introduce here some theological concepts on which I think there is broad agreement, even among people who take widely differing positions on the meaning of Hebrews 6:4–6. The precise question under consideration is *whether these verses describe people who had experienced the decisive beginning stages of a genuine Christian life, and who then had fallen away and lost their salvation.*[3]

But what do we mean by "the decisive beginning stages of a genuine Christian life"? And what do we mean by "lost their salvation"? No matter what position people take on Hebrews 6:4–6, or on the question of the perseverance of the saints, it should not affect their definition of the beginning of the Christian life, for all theological traditions within evangelical Protestantism (and many others) have agreed that the beginning of the Christian life includes at least the following elements:

1. Regeneration (being "born again")[4]
2. Conversion (which includes repentance from sins and faith in Christ)[5]
3. Justification (God declares us righteous in his sight)
4. Adoption (God makes us members of his family)
5. The beginning of sanctification (some initial break with actual sin, so that a new pattern of life is begun)

In this list, items 1, 3, and 4 (regeneration, justification, and adoption) are entirely works of God. Item 2 (repentance and faith) is entirely a work of

3. I think that lack of clarity in definition of terms has been a major source of controversy regarding this passage: it does little good for interpreters to argue about whether these people were "saved" if they assume different definitions of the word *saved* but never make their definitions explicit. My procedure in this first section is not a matter of putting theology before exegesis; it is matter of putting definition before discussion, for the sake of clarity.

4. Some would place regeneration before conversion and some after. The order is not important for our argument, since all would agree that regeneration is an essential element of a genuine beginning to the Christian life.

5. Some evangelicals deny that repentance is necessary for experiencing justification and the other initial elements of the Christian life mentioned in this list (for example, Lewis Sperry Chafer says, "The New Testament does not impose repentance upon the unsaved as a condition of salvation" [*Systematic Theology*, 7 vols. (Dallas: Dallas Seminary Press, 1947–1948), 3:376]). But that difference need not concern us here, since they would agree on the other elements listed, and my general argument will work on the basis of these other elements even if the element of repentance is not included.

However, most evangelicals, including this author, understand repentance from sins to be an essential part of true conversion and argue that no one can genuinely trust in Christ as a Savior *from his or her sins* unless the person has repented of those sins. Therefore, although justification is by faith alone, it is not by faith that is alone—faith is always accompanied by repentance, and always results in a changed pattern of life. The Westminster Confession of Faith aptly says:

Faith, thus receiving and resting on Christ and his righteousness, is alone the instrument of justification: yet is it not alone in the person justified, but is ever accompanied with all other saving graces, and is no dead faith, but worketh by love (11.2).

Although repentance be not to be rested in, as any satisfaction for sin, or any cause of the pardon thereof, which is the act of God's free grace in Christ; yet it is of such necessity to all sinners, that none may expect pardon without it (15.3).

man.[6] Item 5 (sanctification) is a work in which God and man cooperate (God empowers us to obey, and we obey).[7] No matter what view people take of Hebrews 6, they will also agree that these five elements come together as a package—that any person who experiences one of these elements will experience all five of them. Therefore it follows that if the people described in Hebrews 6:4–6 have genuinely experienced any one of these elements, we may conclude that they have experienced all of them, and therefore they have experienced the decisive beginning stages of a genuine Christian life.

It will be cumbersome to reproduce this list again and again in subsequent discussion, so, for the purpose of this chapter, I will use the summary phrase *once saved* (or simply *saved*) to refer to people who have experienced these things. I realize that salvation has a past, a present, and a future aspect in New Testament thought: We have been saved (at the time of conversion), we are being saved (sanctification continues as a process throughout our earthly lives, as does God's protection), and we will be saved (we will in the future experience death, bodily resurrection, final rewards, and eternal life with God). However, when I speak of people who were "saved" (in the past), I am referring only to those decisive beginning stages of the Christian life, as already defined.[8] I will also use the expression *to become a Christian* to refer to the experience of these five initial elements.

6. Although many would argue that God enables us to repent and believe, all would agree that we repent and we believe; God does not repent and believe for us.

7. Some theologians say that sanctification is entirely a work of God, but this difference is only a matter of definition, since they would define sanctification more narrowly, to include only the internal change of heart that God alone can bring about. This difference in definition will not affect my argument.

8. Scot McKnight, "The Warning Passages in Hebrews: A Formal Analysis and Theological Conclusions," *Trinity J* 13 n.s. (1992): 21–59, argues (55–58) that "salvation" *(sōtēria)* in Hebrews is primarily a future concept: for example, Christ "will appear a second time . . . to save those who are eagerly waiting for him" (9:28; cf. 1:14). I agree that there is a strong future-oriented aspect to salvation in Hebrews (as in the New Testament generally), but we must not forget that the author also sees past and present Christian experiences as part of the overall process of salvation. In 2:3, "salvation" is something that is primarily present, since it was proclaimed by the Lord, was manifested in miracles, and is not now to be neglected: "How shall we escape if we neglect such a great salvation?" In other verses, *sōtēria* is used to refer to the whole of the Christian experience (past, present, future): Christ is "the pioneer of their salvation" (2:10); he became "the source of eternal salvation" (5:9); the readers at the present time possess "better things . . . things that accompany salvation" (6:9); "he is able for all time [or: completely] to save *(sōzō)* those who draw near to God through him" (7:25). If we add verses that use other terms than *sōtēria* and *sōzō*, there are dozens of descriptions of past or present aspects of the Christian life in Hebrews (see 141–52). McKnight agrees that it is appropriate to speak of "the present dimensions of salvation that have already been inaugurated and experienced" (58).

My only concern at this point is to find a brief word or phrase that will summarize the Christian's experience of these decisive beginning stages of a genuine Christian life. The word *salvation* is a broad term that can refer to past, present, or future experiences, or to the whole of the Christian experience (from the point of conversion to enjoyment of the future eternal state), both in

In a corresponding way, the phrase *lost their salvation* would mean that all of these past and present elements of salvation have been removed from people's lives: If people have in fact lost their salvation, it would mean that in their own experience they no longer have (2) repentance from sins or faith in Christ, and they no longer have (5) a pattern of increasing sanctification in conduct of life. With respect to divine activity, it would mean that God had withdrawn (1) their regeneration (they are no longer born again, but are once again dead in trespasses and sins), (3) their justification (they no longer have forgiveness of sins), (4) their adoption (they are no longer members of God's family), and (5) his internal work of sanctification.

With these definitions in mind, the precise question may now be stated in very brief form: *Does Hebrews 6:4–6 describe people who were once saved but have lost their salvation?*

The Meanings of the Descriptive Terms (vv. 4–6)

The Argument That These People Were Once Saved

If we confine our attention to verses 4–6, a good case can be made for viewing these people as those who were once truly saved.[9]

First, the author says they have "once been enlightened" (Heb. 6:4). One could argue that the word *enlightened (phōtizō)* means "heard and believed the gospel," because in Hebrews 10:32 the author uses the same word to refer to the time when the readers became Christians:

> But recall the former days when, after you were *enlightened*, you endured a hard struggle with sufferings, sometimes being publicly exposed to abuse and affliction, and sometimes being partners with those so treated. (10:32–33)

Even if *phōtizō* does not always mean "heard and believed the gospel" for other New Testament writers, one could argue that it means that for the

---

contemporary English and in theological studies generally. The Greek term *sōtēria* in the New Testament can similarly summarize the whole of the Christian life (John 4:22; Acts 4:12; 13:26, 47; 28:28; Rom. 1:16; Eph. 1:13; 2 Tim. 2:10; Jude 3; also the verses from Hebrews in the previous paragraph). Therefore, when used with reference to past Christian experience, the terms *saved* and *once saved* seem appropriate as summary terms for these decisive beginning stages of the Christian life, especially when they have been defined clearly at the outset of the discussion.

9. This is the view of several interpreters, including Grant R. Osborne, "Soteriology in the Epistle to the Hebrews," in *Grace Unlimited*, ed. Clark H. Pinnock (Minneapolis: Bethany House, 1975), 148–53; I. Howard Marshall, *Kept by the Power of God* (London: Epworth, 1969), 136–41; Lane, *Hebrews 1–8*, 132–33, 141–42; McKnight, "Warning Passages," 24, 43–48; and Harold W. Attridge, *The Epistle to the Hebrews*, Hermeneia (Philadelphia: Fortress, 1989), 169–70.

author of Hebrews, as this other passage shows. In addition, 2 Corinthians 4 provides a close conceptual parallel: although the verb *phōtizō* is not used, the cognate noun *phōtismos* (illumination, enlightenment) is used twice with reference to conversion:

> In their case the god of this world has blinded the minds of the unbelievers, to keep them from seeing the *light* of the gospel of the glory of Christ. . . . For it is the God who said, "Let light shine out of darkness," who has shone in our hearts to give the *light* of the knowledge of the glory of God in the face of Christ. (2 Cor. 4:4, 6)

Moreover, one could argue that in the phrase *have once been enlightened* the word *once (hapax)* indicates a decisive, once-for-all enlightenment that occurs at the beginning of the Christian life. That the word *hapax* can be used to describe a one-time, never-to-be-repeated event is clear, for example, from its use in Hebrews 9:26–28:

> But as it is, he has appeared *once for all* at the end of the age to put away sin by the sacrifice of himself. And just as it is appointed for men to die *once*, and after that comes judgment, so Christ, having been offered *once* to bear the sins of many, will appear a second time, not to deal with sin but to save those who are eagerly waiting for him.[10]

The text (6:4–5) further says that these people "have tasted the heavenly gift" and that they "have tasted the goodness of the word of God and the powers of the age to come." One can argue that the term *taste (geuomai)* implies a full and complete experiencing of something, since the author uses the same term when he[11] speaks of Christ's experience of death: "so that by the grace of God he might *taste* death for every one" (Heb. 2:9). Whether "the heavenly gift" means the Holy Spirit (as in Acts 2:38; 8:20; 10:45; 11:17) or justification (as in Rom. 5:15, 17), the fact that these people have tasted this gift means that they have truly experienced the indwelling of the Holy Spirit that accompanies salvation (see Rom. 8:9, 11), or that they have truly experienced justification.[12]

---

10. Compare also Hebrews 10:2: "If the worshipers had *once* been cleansed, they would no longer have any consciousness of sin."

11. Although the author of Hebrews is anonymous, I have referred to him as "he," since he identifies himself as a man by use of a masculine participle to refer to himself in the Greek text of 11:32, "time would fail me *telling (diēgoumenon)* . . ." A woman would have used the feminine participle *diēgoumenēn*. Someone might object that this masculine participle is just part of the female author's "camouflage," but this objection is not persuasive, for such deliberate deception would be morally objectionable for any Christian, not least an author of Scripture.

12. The actual phrase used in Hebrews 6:4, "the heavenly gift" *(tēs dōreas tēs epouraniou)*, does not occur elsewhere in the New Testament. However, the verses just mentioned do use the same word *dōrea* (gift) to refer to the Holy Spirit or to justification.

The statement that these people "have tasted the goodness of the Word of God and the powers of the age to come" may also be taken to indicate that they had truly experienced and taken into themselves the Word of God and the power of God, and therefore that they had experienced salvation.

The text also says that these people "have become *partakers* of the Holy Spirit" (Heb. 6:4). One could readily argue that the term *partaker (metochos)* indicates a saving participation in the Holy Spirit, just as the same term indicates a saving participation in Christ in Hebrews 3:14: "For we have become partakers *(metochos)* of Christ, if we hold fast the beginning of our assurance firm until the end" (NASB).

Finally, the text says "it is impossible to restore again to repentance" people who have experienced these things and then have committed apostasy. One could argue that if this is a repentance to which people need to be restored again, then it must be genuine repentance, what the New Testament elsewhere calls "*repentance* unto life" (Acts 11:18), and what the author of Hebrews calls "a foundation of *repentance* from dead works and of faith toward God" (6:1).

The cumulative force of these terms can also be used as an argument to show that these people were genuine Christians before falling away. Even if someone is not persuaded by any single phrase, the phrases taken together, one could argue, must indicate genuine salvation: the people were enlightened, they repented, they tasted salvation (or the Holy Spirit), they tasted the Word of God and the powers of the age to come, and they became partakers of the Holy Spirit. What more could the author say to indicate a genuine experience of salvation?

The Argument That the Terms Alone Are Inconclusive

A different interpretation of the phrases in Hebrews 6:4–6 is possible, however. Such an interpretation would not argue that the terms show the people described to be unbelievers, for (until the mention of apostasy) there is nothing negative in the description: the terms all indicate positive events that are generally experienced by people who become Christians. But this alternative view would argue that the terms in verses 4–6 by themselves are inconclusive, for they speak of events that are experienced both by genuine Christians and by some people who participate in the fellowship of a church but are never really saved.[13] Therefore (according to this interpretation), when we read about people who

13. Several elements of this second interpretation, if not its exact formulation, are found in many interpreters who conclude (as I do) that the people in 6:4–6 were never really saved. In order to do this, they reason not from the terms in 6:4–6 (which by themselves are inconclusive), but from other evidence in the larger context (whether from verses 7–12, where I find the most persuasive exegetical evidence, or elsewhere). See especially the excellent discussion in John

have once been enlightened,
have tasted the heavenly gift,
have become partakers of the Holy Spirit,
have tasted the goodness of the Word of God and the powers of the age
to come, and
have repented,

we still cannot know, on the basis of that information alone, if they really have experienced the decisive beginning stages of the Christian life. Whether they truly have become Christians can be known only if we learn other factors—whether they have trusted in Christ for salvation, for example, and whether God has given them regeneration and forgiven their sins and adopted them into his family, and whether their lives show fruit that gives evidence of true salvation.[14]

This second interpretation (which is the interpretation supported in this chapter) would argue that the first view has been premature in reaching the conclusion that the terms must describe genuine saving faith and true regeneration. It would argue, instead, that a closer examination of the terms used will show them to be *inconclusive* regarding the question of whether they indicate genuine salvation. The positive experiences in 6:4–6, therefore, simply put people in a category well described by D. A. Carson: "Is there N[ew] T[estament] warrant for thinking that, *as far as Christian observers are con-*

Owen, *An Exposition of Hebrews*, 7 vols. in 4 (1855; Marshallton, Del.: National Foundation for Christian Education, 1969), 3:68–91. See also Roger Nicole, "Some Comments on Hebrews 6:4–6 and the Doctrine of the Perseverance of God with the Saints," in *Current Issues in Biblical and Patristic Interpretation*, Festschrift for Merrill Tenney, ed. Gerald F. Hawthorne (Grand Rapids: Eerdmans, 1975), 355–64; Philip Edgcumbe Hughes, *A Commentary on the Epistle to the Hebrews* (Grand Rapids: Eerdmans, 1977), 206–22; F. F. Bruce, *The Epistle to the Hebrews*, rev. ed., NICNT (Grand Rapids: Eerdmans, 1990), 144–50; Robert A. Peterson, "Apostasy," *Presbyterion* 19,1 (1993): 17–31; Leon Morris, "Hebrews," in *The Expositor's Bible Commentary*, vol. 12, ed. Frank E. Gaebelein (Grand Rapids: Zondervan, 1981), 54–56; John Calvin, *The Epistle of Paul the Apostle to the Hebrews and the First and Second Epistles of St. Peter*, trans. William B. Johnson, ed. D. W. Torrance and T. F. Torrance (Grand Rapids: Eerdmans, 1963), 74–77.

14. It is important to distinguish this second position from the view McKnight calls the "phenomenological-false believer view" ("Warning Passages," 23–24), a position I do not hold or argue for. According to McKnight, the "phenomenological-false believer view" argues that the people in 6:4–6 had given outward indications (phenomena) of saving faith but were not really saved: they were "persons who had the signs of faith but did not in fact have genuine faith" (23). This is certainly not my position, for one of the fundamental claims of this chapter is that the people in 6:4–6 *did not have any of the signs of true saving faith* (see the following discussion), and the author of Hebrews makes that clear in several ways. (I will argue from 6:7–12 that the people in 6:4–6 were unbelievers, but I do not think there is evidence to say that they were "false believers," that is, people who gave indications of faith but did not have it. Rather, their affiliation with the church and apparent agreement with its teachings meant that one could not tell, until they fell away, whether they were believers or not.)

cerned, some people are not clearly either 'in' or 'out,' that the step of conversion is not always luminously clear?"[15]

We now turn to such a reexamination of these terms to see if such a position is justified.

(1) *Enlightened.* It is true that the word *phōtizō* is used in Hebrews 10:32 to speak of an event that happened near the beginning of the Christian lives of the hearers, but that does not prove that it means "heard and believed the gospel," for "learned about the gospel" would fit just as well: "after you were *enlightened,* you endured a hard struggle with sufferings."[16] In fact, the term *phōtizō* does not carry a sense of "believed the gospel" or "came to faith" in any of its other New Testament uses.[17] It occurs eleven times in the New Testament, sometimes just referring to a literal giving of light by a lamp (Luke 11:36), and other times referring to learning in general, not specifically a learning that results in salvation. For example, *phōtizō* is used in John 1:9 of "enlightening" every man that comes into the world, in 1 Corinthians 4:5 of the enlightening that comes at the final judgment (God will "bring to light the things now hidden in darkness"), and in Ephesians 1:18 of the enlightening that accompanies growth in the Christian life ("having the eyes of your hearts enlightened"). With respect to the noun *phōtismos* in 2 Corinthians 4:4–6, it is true that Paul here gives an extended metaphor that pictures conversion in terms of seeing the "light" of the gospel. This is, I think, the best argument that *phōtizō* in Hebrews 6:4 could mean "converted." Yet even in 2 Corinthians 4, it is not the term *phōtismos* itself that gives the meaning *converted,* but the entire metaphor of giving light that Paul has constructed using several different terms (*phōs* [light], *lampō,* [shine], *phōtismos* [illumination, light]), none of which elsewhere is a technical term meaning conversion.

Therefore, contrary to the assertion of several interpreters, in the New Testament world, *phōtizō* is not a technical term that means "hear and believe the gospel" or "come to saving faith."[18] It refers to learning and understanding, and therefore the most that can confidently be claimed for it in

15. D. A. Carson, "Reflections on Christian Assurance," *WTJ* 54 (1992): 18 (also chap. 10 in this work).

16. Here the parallel with "receiving the knowledge of the truth" in verse 26 would indicate that receiving knowledge of the gospel is all that the author means (see the fuller discussion of Heb. 10:32, 144–52).

17. BAGD, 872–73, define *phōtizō* as "enlighten, give light to, shed light upon," but give no sense such as "bring to faith" or (in the passive voice) "come to faith, believe" or "be converted."

18. McKnight, "Warning Passages," 46, says that *phōtizō* "regularly signifies conversion in early Christian literature," and for support he cites "the full listing of evidence" in Attridge, *Hebrews,* 169–70, especially note 43. Attridge lists twenty-three references on 169 n. 23 (without citing them). Attridge's own claim is not exactly that they speak of conversion, but of "the reception of a salvific message" (169), a sense not really incompatible with my own position. However, when I looked up Attridge's references, I discovered that it is difficult to find any of them that clearly show *phōtizō* even to mean "the reception of a salvific message" (but

Hebrews 6:4 is that it speaks of "those who have heard and understood the gospel."[19] Certainly such intellectal understanding of the facts of the gospel

---

probably the last one does). None of them use *phōtizō* to mean "come to saving faith," and in eight of the twenty-three *phōtizō* does not even occur:

Judg. 13:8 (A): Manoah asks God to let the angel come once more "and *instruct* us what we shall do about the child to be born"

2 Kings (LXX 4 Kings) 12:2: "Joash did what was right in the sight of the Lord all the days that Jehoiada the priest *instructed* him"

Ps. 34:5 (LXX 33:5): "Draw near to him, and be enlightened, and your faces will not be ashamed"

Ps. 119:130 (LXX 118:130): "The manifestation of your words will *enlighten*, and will instruct the simple"

Isa. 60:1: "Be *enlightened*, be *enlightened*, O Jerusalem, for your light has come"

Isa. 60:19: "No more shall the rising of the moon *give light to* your night"

Mic. 7:8: "Do not rejoice against me, my enemy . . . for though I sit in darkness, the Lord shall *give light to* me."

1 En. 5:8: "Then there will be given to the chosen *light* and grace"

Dead Sea Scrolls, 1 QS 4:2 (written in Hebrew; *phōtizō* does not occur)

Dead Sea Scrolls, 1 QS 11:2 (written in Hebrew; *phōtizō* does not occur)

Philo, *Fug.* 139: the ordinance of Scripture "*enlighten*s and sweetens the soul"

1 Cor. 4:5: when the Lord comes he "will *bring to light* the things now hidden in darkness and will disclose the purposes of the heart"

2 Cor. 4:4–6: (*phōtizo* does not occur)

Eph. 1:18: Paul prays that Christians may have "the eyes of your hearts *enlightened*"

Eph. 3:9: Paul was given grace "*to make men see* what is the plan of the mystery" [of theGentile inclusion in the church]

2 Tim. 1:10: Christ "abolished death and *brought* life and immortality *to light*"

John 1:9: the Word "*enlightens* every man who comes into the world"

1 Peter 2:9: (*phōtizō* does not occur)

2 Peter 1:10: (*phōtizō* does not occur)

James 1:17: (*phōtizō* does not occur)

1 Clement 36:2: (*phōtizō* does not occur)

1 Clement 59:2: (*phōtizō* does not occur)

Ignatius *To the Romans* (Attridge cites no reference but *passim* [throughout]).

In fact, *phōtizō* occurs only in the inscription of this epistle: "to the Church beloved and *enlightened* by the will of him who has willed all things which are."

Attridge (169) may have been talking not about *phōtizō* but about the metaphor of "enlightening," but that is inconclusive regarding the meaning of *phōtizō* in Hebrews 6:4.

In later Christian literature *phōtizō* was sometimes used as a synonym for baptism (see G. W. H. Lampe, *A Patristic Greek Lexicon* [Oxford: Clarendon, 1961], 1508–9 (12.B.4.c.8), but these occurrences are all after the time of the New Testament, and much less relevant in assessing New Testament meanings.

Therefore I must agree with the entry on *phōtizō* in BAGD (872–73; see previous footnote): there are no examples from the New Testament period where *phōtizō* signifies conversion.

19. McKnight criticizes Nicole for "moving from what is a possible meaning of an expression ('to be enlightened' can perhaps mean simply 'being exposed to something') to a conclusion that such is the meaning here without offering any evidence" ("Warning Passages," 49). However, the same can be said of McKnight: he asserts that "enlightened" means "converted," but does not show why *in the context of Hebrews 6:4* it cannot mean simply "heard and understood the gospel." A better approach is to say that the term by itself is inconclusive, and more information from the context is needed to decide the spiritual state of the people.

is an important step toward saving faith, but it does not itself constitute the element of personal trust in Christ that is essential to faith.

Objection regarding examples of words used outside of Hebrews. At this point someone may object that, in seeking to understand the meaning of *phōtizō* in Hebrews 6:4 (or any other word in Hebrews 6, for that matter), we should confine ourselves to looking at examples of the same word *as used in Hebrews only.*[20] In this case, then, we should look only at *phōtizō* in Hebrews 10:32 (its only other occurence in Hebrews) to find evidence for what it means in 6:4. But such an objection is invalid for several reasons:

(1) Greek-speaking people in the first-century world shared a common stock of words that were understandable by everyone who spoke Greek. This is why, for example, Paul could write an epistle to people he had never visited (the Christians in Rome) and expect that they would understand him. They did not have to acquire some kind of special "Pauline vocabulary" before they could read Romans; they simply had to read the words he wrote, words they already knew. This is also why people who could read Hebrews could also read and understand James or Matthew or Philippians (or the Septuagint, or secular writers such as Diodorus Siculus or Strabo or Polybius)—the linguistic stock available to be used by these writers was largely the same. Therefore any examples of Greek terms used in any first-century literature are useful for gaining a sense of the range of meanings that might attach to a word (though those authors closest in time and who share the most social and cultural background are most useful).

(2) When a word can take several senses (as most words can), it is incorrect to assume that the use of a word in one sense by an author precludes him from using that word in other senses elsewhere. For example, Paul uses the word *nomos,* "law," in several senses.[21]

(3) Of course, every writer can develop a preference for certain words and certain senses of words, and some words are naturally used more often when writers specialize in a certain subject matter (as with the religious terms and Old Testament terms used by New Testament writers). For this reason, when we have several examples (not just one or two) of one word used in one way by a particular author (for example, *dikaioō,* "justify" in Paul), we may conclude that this is a common sense of the word in that author (but even then

20. This objection has been raised frequently by seminary students when I have taught on this section of Hebrews, so I include a discussion of it at this point.

21. I used the word *saved* in three senses earlier in this chapter (136-39), and I am using it in a fourth sense when say that I *saved* [stored in long-term memory] this file on my computer, and in a fifth sense when I say that I *saved* [did not spend] money by deciding not to buy coffee this morning. Someone could read this chapter and compile over thirty examples of my use of "saved" to refer to Christian salvation, but that still would not prove that I had to use "saved" to refer to Christian salvation in this footnote, when talking about computer files or money.

we should not claim a sense that is unprecedented, but one that is among the possible senses attested elsewhere). In this way, the meaning attaching to other uses of a word by the same author should be given somewhat greater weight.[22] But we cannot establish a specialized sense for *phōtizō* in Hebrews in this way, for it is used only one other time in Hebrews, while it occurs nine other times in the rest of the New Testament.

(4) Greek lexicons do not generally define words with reference to unique meanings in each New Testament author. They do not have special sections, for example, for "the meaning of *phōtizō* in Luke," and "the meaning of *phōtizō* in John" and "the meaning of *phōtizō* in Hebrews," but rather list the various meanings *phōtizō* could take in all of first-century Christian literature, and also in Jewish and pagan literature at the time of the New Testament.

(5) Looking only, or even primarily, at the uses of terms by the same author would make it impossible to do exegesis even in this passage, which has many terms that occur only once in Hebrews (for example, the terms for "gift," "commit apostasy," "renew," "crucify again," and "hold up to contempt"). Sound exegesis will examine these same Greek terms as they are used in the rest of the New Testament, and in the first century generally, to gain information on the possible meanings attaching to them.[23]

(6) Looking only at *phōtizō* in Hebrews 10:32 would not change our argument here in any significant way, for the sense "heard and understood the gospel" fits just as well there.[24]

(2) *Once.* It is incorrect to claim that the term *hapax* (once) must indicate an event that happens once for all time and can never be repeated.[25] *Hapax* is used, for example, in Hebrews 9:7 to speak of the fact that the high priest enters into the Holy of Holies "*once* a year," an event that was repeated year after year. In Philippians 4:16 Paul uses *hapax* to say that the Philippians had sent him a gift "*once* and again"—the event was repeated when they sent the

22. For example, I give somewhat greater weight to the use of *kreisson*, "better," by the author of Hebrews (157–60) below, because thirteen of the nineteen New Testament occurrences are in Hebrews.

23. The examination of occurrences of words outside of Hebrews should be recognized as valid by every interpreter, no matter what his or her position is on Hebrews 6 or on the question of whether Christians can lose their salvation. The question of using *meanings of words* outside Hebrews is different from the question of using *doctrinal conclusions* from other New Testament books to influence our decision on 6:4–6. As I mentioned at the beginning of the chapter, my goal in this chapter is first to construct an exegetical argument from the teaching material within Hebrews alone, before comparing it with other New Testament material. My purpose in this is to enable the arguments here to be considered fairly by people who approach the text with widely differing theological convictions on whether Christians can lose their salvation.

24. See further discussion of Hebrews 10:32, 163–64, 179.

25. Lane is representative of many commentators when he says that *hapax* "conveys the notion of definitive occurrence" (*Hebrews*, 141), but this is not borne out by an examination of the actual use of the word.

second gift. In places where *hapax* does refer to something that can never be repeated (for example, Heb. 9:26-28), that idea is derived from other indications in the context, not from any sense inherent in this word itself. Therefore, this word does not in itself mean that something happened "once for all time" and can never be repeated, but simply that it happened "once," without specifying whether it will be repeated.[26]

(3) *Tasted.* Inherent in the idea of *geuomai* when it means "taste" are two factors: (1) the tasting is temporary, and (2) a more permanent experience of the thing might or might not follow.[27] With regard to literal tasting of food or drink, for example, *geuomai* is used in Matthew 27:34 to say that those crucifying Jesus "offered him wine to drink, mingled with gall; but when he *tasted* it, he would not drink it" (cf. John 2:9).

This is also true when *geuomai* is used in the figurative sense of "come to know something" (BAGD, 157, 2). For example, a very good parallel to Hebrews 6:4–6 is found in Josephus (*The Jewish War* 2.158), who speaks about the theological views of the Essenes "whereby they irresistibly attract all who have *once tasted* (*tois hapax geusamenois*) their philosophy."[28] Here Josephus makes it clear that those who have "once tasted" have not yet made the Essene philosophy their own, but are strongly attracted to it. By analogy, in Hebrews 6 those who have "tasted" the heavenly gift and the goodness of the word of God and the powers of the age to come may be strongly attracted to these things, or they may not be, but *mere tasting does not mean that they have made these things their own possession.*

Those who hold the first interpretation may object that *geuomai* has a stronger sense than this: the example of Jesus tasting death in Hebrews 2:9 shows that tasting is "genuinely experiencing" the thing tasted, for Jesus really died. In response, I can agree that a "real experience" of the thing tasted is in view not only in Hebrews 2:9 but also in every example of *geuomai* mentioned (a real experience of wine, of Essene philosophy, of freedom,

26. This is not the same word as *ephapax*, which is more regularly used in the New Testament of nonrepeatable events (Rom. 6:10; Heb. 7:27; 9:12; 10:10; cf. BAGD, 330, 2).

27. The discussions in the commentaries about whether tasting involves a partial or full experience of the thing tasted do not focus the issue well: Of course there is some kind of experience in all tasting of things (or ideas). The fact more important for our discussion is that the common factor in all instances of tasting is that the tasting is a temporary experience, not a continuing one, and it sometimes (or often) results in no permanent experience or permanent change in the person doing the tasting. The author of Hebrews clearly does not say the people were *transformed* by the heavenly gift or *made alive* by the word of God, or use some similar expression. They *tasted* these things.

28. BAGD, 157, 2, give other examples of *geuomai* in this sense, such as Herodotus 6.5, where the people of Miletus had "tasted of freedom," but they certainly did not possess freedom as their own. They also cite Dio Chrysostom 32.72, where he speaks of the people of Alexandria in a time when they "had a taste of warfare" in an encounter with Roman troops who were harassing them and not actually engaging in genuine war. These examples indicate only a temporary sampling.

or of military conflict). Similarily, in Hebrews 6:4–6 the people had a genuine experience of the heavenly gift and the word of God and the powers of the age to come. But that is not the point. The question is whether they had a *saving* experience of these things, whether the experience was one that brought regeneration, saving faith, justification, etc.

Of course, if it could be shown that "the heavenly gift" was salvation, then a "real experience" of salvation would have to be understood as the beginning of the Christian life. But the exact phrase *hē dōrea tēs epouraniou* (the heavenly gift) occurs nowhere else in the New Testament, so it would be impossible to prove from other examples of the phrase that "the heavenly gift" means salvation. In fact, the word *dōrea* by itself does refer to the Holy Spirit elsewhere (Acts 2:38; 8:20; 10:45; 11:17), and the Holy Spirit has been sent from heaven (Acts 2:33; 1 Pet. 1:12), so it is likely that Hebrews 6:4 means that those who "tasted the heavenly gift" had some experience of the power of the Holy Spirit—perhaps in convicting them of sin (cf. John 16:8), perhaps in casting a demon out of them (cf. Matt. 12:28), or perhaps in receiving some kind of healing (cf. Luke 4:14, 40; 1 Cor. 12:9).[29] But such experiences of the Holy Spirit do not themselves indicate salvation, for it is possible to "resist the Holy Spirit" (Acts 7:51), and even, for those who are under conviction from the Holy Spirit, to resist so strongly that one commits "blasphemy against the Spirit" (Matt. 12:31).

The other things tasted can be understood similarly. To taste "the goodness of the word of God" is to come to know and even feel something of its truthfulness and power. But this is not the same as believing it for eternal life. To taste "the powers of the age to come" probably means to feel something of the new covenant power of the Holy Spirit in conviction of sin, having demons cast out, experiencing healing (see the verses previously listed). Such tasting of "the powers of the age to come" may even include preaching the gospel so that people are saved (cf. Phil. 1:15–18: some preach from wrong motives), or prophesying and working miracles and casting out demons in Christ's name (Matt. 7:22–23). But these experiences do not necessarily indicate that the person is saved (Jesus says, "I never knew you; depart from me, you evildoers" [Matt. 7:23]).[30]

29. The fact that the Holy Spirit is mentioned directly in the following phrase does not prevent "the heavenly gift" from meaning the Holy Spirit, or the working of the Holy Spirit, for the author could be varying his method of expression while repeating similar ideas for emphasis.

30. One more consideration may be mentioned here, even though it applies to each of the positive terms in 6:4–6. If the author had wanted to emphasize the continuing results of the tasting (or enlightening, or partaking), he could easily have done so with the use of perfect participles, but he used aorist participles instead for all of these experiences, thereby indicating only that the enlightening, tasting, and partaking *happened*, without signifying anything about continuing results from any of these events. This does not, of course, prove that the effects lasted only a short time, but only that the author did not specify continuing results when he could easily have done so.

Here also the nature of "tasting" is relevant. As we have noted, the New Testament examples of tasting show that the tasting is temporary, and a more permanent experience of the thing tasted might or might not follow. In these verses, this means that the tasting of the heavenly gift, and the word of God, and the coming powers, was temporary, and we cannot tell from the mere fact of such tasting if a more permanent experience of these things followed or not.

(4) *Partakers of the Holy Spirit.* In the phrase "have become *partakers of the Holy Spirit*," the first question is the exact meaning of the word *metochos*, "partaker." It is not always clear to English-speaking readers that this term has a range of meaning and may imply very close participation and attachment, or may imply only a loose association with the other person or persons named.

For example, to become "partakers (*metochoi*) of Christ" (literal translation of Heb. 3:14) is to have a saving participation in the salvation he brings. On the other hand, *metochos* can also be used in a looser sense, to refer to associates or companions. We read that when the disciples took in a great catch of fish so that their nets were breaking, "they beckoned to their *partners* (*metochoi*) in the other boat to come and help them" (Luke 5:7). Here it refers to those who were companions or partners with Peter and the other disciples in their fishing work. Hebrews 1:9 (quoting Ps. 45:7) also uses *metochos* to speak of "comrades" (RSV) or "companions" (NIV, NASB): "God, your God, has set you above your *companions*" (NIV). Ephesians 5:7 uses a closely related word (*summetochos*, a compound of *metochos*) when Paul warns Christians about the sinful acts of unbelievers and says, "do not *associate* [literally, do not be partners] with them" (Eph. 5:7). So the term *metochos* commonly means someone who shares or participates in something with someone else.[31]

What does it mean to become a "partaker" (or sharer) in the Holy Spirit? It cannot mean that people are given a share of the very being of the Holy Spirit, because, as God, the Holy Spirit cannot be divided into parts and cannot give away any share of his being, and because the term *metochos* never means "to have a share of the being of another person." Therefore *to become a "partaker" of the Holy Spirit means to be associated in some way with the*

---

31. Some instances of *metochos* from the Septuagint also provide examples where it refers only to companionship, not to any kind of regenerating or life-changing experience with God or with the Holy Spirit. For instance, in 1 Kings 20:30, Saul accuses Jonathan of being a "partner" with David. In Psalm 119:63, the psalmist says he is a "companion" of all those who fear God. Ecclesiastes 4:10 says that two are better than one, for if they fall, the one will lift up his "partner." Proverbs 28:24, in the translations of Aquila, Symmachus, and Theodotian, uses this word to say that a man who rejects his father or mother is a "companion" of ungodly men.

BAGD define *metochos* as (1) (as adjective) "sharing or participating in," or (2) (as substantive) "partner, companion" (514).

147

work of the Holy Spirit and to share in some of the benefits the Holy Spirit gives. Sometimes interpreters assume that the phrase means "to receive the regenerating work of the Holy Spirit," and certainly that is one way of being a "partaker" of the Holy Spirit. But regeneration is not the only way people partake in the Holy Spirit or receive some of his benefits, and therefore we cannot assume that regeneration is the sense intended here. The phrase could instead refer to receiving some of the other benefits or influences of the Holy Spirit. For example, the phrase may mean simply that these people had come into the church and there had experienced some of the benefits of the Holy Spirit in answers to prayer or even in using some spiritual gifts. All that we can say with confidence is that *they were partakers of some of the benefits that the Holy Spirit gives.*[32]

The example of the fishing companions in Luke 5:7 provides a good analogy: Peter and the disciples could be associated with those companions and to some degree be influenced by them and even gain some benefits from them without having a thoroughgoing change of life caused by that association. Another close analogy is found in Ignatius, *To the Ephesians* (ca. A.D. 110) 11:2, in which he writes from prison and expresses thanks for the prayers of the Ephesians, "in which may I always be a sharer *(metochos)*"—he wanted always to benefit from their prayers. So the word *metochos* allows for a range of influence from fairly weak to fairly strong, for it only means "one who participates with or shares with or accompanies in some activity." Therefore all we can say is that the people spoken of in Hebrews 6 had been associated with the church and as such had been associated with the work of the Holy Spirit, and no doubt influenced by him in some ways (whether weak or strong) in their lives. We cannot with confidence say more than that.

(5) *Repentance.* Since the author implies that it would be desirable to "restore again to repentance" these people once they fall away, the repentance that they once had must be some kind of sorrow for sins committed. This is an important step in coming to Christ, for until people see their own sinfulness, they will see no need to have faith that Jesus will forgive their own personal sins. Therefore repentance from sins must precede or accompany all

---

32. Someone may object that it seems strange to say that becoming a partaker of Christ (3:14) means to become a Christian but becoming a "partaker of the Holy Spirit" (6:4) does not. But I think the question is resolved when we realize that *metochos* does not in itself mean anything so specific as "partook of saving benefits from (someone)," but only "partook of some influence or benefit from (someone)." The exact kind of benefit or influence is determined by each circumstance and association. With respect to Christ, his primary role with respect to the world today is to bring salvation to people, and becoming a "partaker of Christ" would naturally be understood to mean becoming a Christian. But with respect to the Holy Spirit, he has several roles in the world today, among them distributing of spiritual gifts, convicting of sin, and empowering for ministry, as well as causing regeneration. Therefore to become a "partaker of the Holy Spirit" would naturally be understood by the readers to mean partaking in *some* of the benefits that he gives, not all of which include salvation.

genuine saving faith.[33] But repentance itself is not saving faith. In this very paragraph, the author distinguishes "repentance from dead works" from "faith toward God" (v. 1), showing that there is a distinction between them.[34]

Moreover, it is possible to have a kind of repentance that falls short of saving repentance, a repentance that is not accompanied by saving faith. For example, Hebrews 12:17 uses *metanoia* to speak of the change of mind that Esau sought concerning the sale of his birthright. This would not have been a repentance that brought him to salvation, but simply an undoing of the transaction regarding his birthright.[35] Another example of repentance that is not saving repentance is found in the conduct of Judas: "When Judas, his betrayer, saw that he was condemned, he *repented*[36] and brought back the thirty pieces of silver to the chief priests and the elders" (Matt. 27:3). Judas "repented," but he did not have saving faith (see John 6:70–71; 13:27; Acts 1:16–20; Matt. 27:5). When Paul says that "godly grief produces a repentance that leads to salvation" (2 Cor. 7:10), this suggests at least that there can be a repentance that does not lead to salvation. We conclude that "repentance" means a sorrow for actions that have been done or for sins that have been committed, and a resolve to forsake those sins. But not all repentance includes an inward, heartfelt *repentance toward God* that accompanies saving faith.

Whether or not repentance is a genuine saving repentance, a "repentance unto life" (Acts 11:18) may not always be evident right away. Another good parallel is seen in the false teachers described in 2 Peter 2:20–22: They had "escaped the defilements of the world through the knowledge of our Lord and Savior Jesus Christ" (v. 20), which indicates that there had been both knowledge of the gospel and repentance (they had escaped the defilements of the world). But then they had turned back to their previous ways. Moreover, they had never really been saved, for Peter says, "It has happened to them according to the true proverb, The dog turns back to his own vomit, and the sow is washed only to wallow in the mire" (v. 22)—in other words, the repentance was only an outward cleansing, and did not change their true nature.

33. See note 5.
34. Repentance and faith are also connected but distinguished in Mark 1:15 ("repent, and believe in the gospel"); Acts 19:4; 20:21; compare also Acts 26:20 ("repent and turn to God").
35. The verb *to repent* (Greek *metanoeō*, cognate to *metanoia*) is sometimes used to refer not to saving repentance but to sorrow for individual offenses, as in Luke 17:3–4: "if your brother sins, rebuke him, and if he *repents* forgive him; and if he sins against you seven times in the day, and turns to you seven times, and says, 'I *repent*,' you must forgive him." This is not repentance unto salvation but simply regret for wrongs done.
36. The verb here is not the noun *metanoia* or the cognate verb *metanoeō* but *metamelomai*, another term for repentance used in the New Testament. The ideas of changing one's mind and feeling regret for past actions are present in both words.

In fact, the idea that there can be a nonsaving kind of repentance is parallel to the idea that there can be a nonsaving kind of faith. There is a kind of intellectual belief that involves knowledge and approval, but not personal trust (see, for example, the "belief" of Nicodemus, Agrippa, and demons in John 3:2; Acts 26:27–28; James 2:19; compare also 1 Cor. 15:2; 1 Tim. 1:19).

But someone may object, if the repentance mentioned in Hebrews 6:4 is not genuine saving repentance, why would the author think it desirable to "restore" people to such repentance? The answer is that the author is not concerned—or able—to specify whether the "repentance" he describes in verses 4–6 had led to salvation or not. That is because the real nature of repentance is not always evident from outward observation. The author is simply saying that if someone has a sorrow for sin and a decision to forsake that sin, and then comes to understand the gospel and experience various blessings of the Holy Spirit's work (no doubt in fellowship with the church), and then turns away, it will not be possible to restore such a person again to a place of sorrow for sin—there will be a hardness of heart incompatible with repentance.[37] But none of this implies that the original repentance had necessarily led to saving faith and a forgiveness of sins. That is not specified, and we cannot therefore draw a conclusion on the basis of the term *repentance* itself.

Other Views of 6:4–6

Three other less common views can be mentioned here. (1) *The community view.* Verlyn D. Verbrugge proposes that 6:4–6 speaks not of individuals at all, but of a Christian community that is in danger of falling away.[38] Most interpreters mention this proposal as interesting, but few have been persuaded by it. McKnight rightly objects that both the warnings (3:12; 4:1; 10:28–29) and the exhortations to persevere (Heb.11 gives many positive models) assume that the author is concerned with individual apostasy, and also that Verbrugge's argument for Isaiah 5:1–7 as the background to 6:7–8 is not convincing.[39] Furthermore, verses 7–8 picture land that is completely blessed or completely cursed, an idea suitable to a picture of individual believers, but incompatible with either possibility that Verbrugge foresees (communal faithfulness with some apostates present, or communal apostasy with some faithful believers present). Finally, the enlightening, tasting, partaking, and repenting are best understood as individual experiences that precede saving faith, and there is nothing in the context that

---

37. Morris understands a reference to a specific kind of repentance, "a repentance that means leaving the backsliding into which the person has fallen" ("Hebrews," 55).

38. Verlyn D. Verbrugge, "Towards a New Interpretation of Hebrews 6:4–6," *CTJ* 15 (1980): 61–73.

39. McKnight, "Warning Passages," 54.

would let the readers know that the author intends to be speaking of a community here.

(2) *The Christian maturity view.* Thomas K. Oberholtzer argues that the warning is addressed to true Christians, but says the warning is not against apostasy but against failing to press on to maturity in the Christian life. Therefore the judgments that would follow are only loss of reward, not loss of salvation.[40] However, Oberholtzer's argument fails to be persuasive for the following reasons: (a) He says the metaphor of fiery judgment in verse 8 refers only to loss of reward, not eternal condemnation, because the thorns are burned, not the ground (326). But this overlooks the feminine singular relative pronoun *hēs* (v. 8), which must refer to the ground *(gē),* not the plural "thorns and thistles." The final end of the ground is "to be burned," which surely signifies not loss of reward but eternal condemnation. (b) His translation of verse 9, "better things that accompany salvation" (327; he follows the RSV), fails to account for the epexegetical *kai* in that phrase, and therefore fails to take account of the fact that the "better things" are better precisely because they accompany salvation. This means that the people in 6:4–6 do not have salvation, contrary to Oberholtzer's contention.[41] (c) He incorrectly minimizes the sense of *adynatos,* "impossible," in verse 4, saying that it means that those who fail to press on to maturity also fall away from "worship participation in God's house" and thereby put themselves "beyond encouragement by others in the community" (323). But *adynatos* has a much stronger sense than this: Oberholtzer's view essentially makes it mean "difficult" or "unlikely."[42] In addition, it is simply not true that it is *impossible* to restore to repentance Christians who at one point in their lives fail to press on to maturity—this would be a new doctrine of "grow now or remain immature forever," which the Bible nowhere teaches. (d) Oberholtzer incorrectly minimizes the seriousness of the sin in verse 6: "they crucify the Son of God on their own account and hold him up to contempt." This is a public repudiation and mockery of Christ[43] characteristic only of hardhearted unbelievers; it is not simply a failure to press on to Christian maturity. (e) His argument that the context is one of encouraging the readers to press on to maturity (5:11–

---

40. Thomas K. Oberholtzer, "The Thorn-Infested Ground in Hebrews 6:4–12," *BibSac* 145 (July-September 1988): 319–28. At several crucial points in his argument Oberholtzer cites Zane C. Hodges, "Hebrews," in *The Bible Knowledge Commentary,* ed. John F. Walvoord and Roy B. Zuck (Wheaton, Ill.: Victor, 1983), 794–96, whose position Oberholtzer follows quite closely. (The entire position is compatible with Hodges's view that saving faith need not be the kind of faith that results in a changed life; therefore, the people in 6:4–6 were truly saved [though they were immature]: even though they do not now press on to maturity, and even though they bear no good fruit [v. 8], they will still be saved eternally and only experience a loss of reward.)

41. See the full discussion of this verse (157–60).

42. See pages 153–54 for a discussion of *adynatos.*

43. See the extensive discussion of this sin in McKnight, "Warning Passages," 36–43.

6:3) is correct, but that fact (recognized by all interpreters) does not require his understanding of 6:4–6. Several solutions have been proposed, and one definite possibility is to see this progression of thought: Let us go on to maturity (5:11–6:3), *for* those who do not go on may fall away (6:4–8), *and* even you who are clearly saved need to persevere earnestly (6:9–12).

Therfore, because he overlooks or misunderstands several key terms, Oberholtzer's view is not convincing.

(3) *The hypothetical view.* Thomas Hewitt adopts a "hypothetical" view of these verses, that is, that the writer is telling what would happen if a true Christian could ever fall away, even though in fact that could never happen: "the writer is dealing with supposition and not with fact, so that he may correct wrong ideas."[44] But surely it would be useless to warn the readers against something that could never happen, and that without telling them that it could never happen. Nicole says, "When there is an insuperable barrier there is no need to give warning concerning dangers on the other side!"[45]

Each of these three alternative views, then, deserves mention, but none of them has enough evidence to be persuasive.

Conclusion Regarding the Positive Terms in Hebrews 6:4–6

At this point we may ask what kind of person is described by all of these terms. On the basis of the terms alone, a reasonable argument can be made that these were genuine Christians before they fell away (137–39). On the other hand, the foregoing discussion has shown that all of the terms can be used to describe either Christians or non-Christians who have heard the gospel and been attracted to it, and who have affiliated closely with the activities of a church. Therefore, on the question of whether these people were really saved before they fell away, our decision must be that *the terms by themselves are inconclusive.* If any other decision is to be reached, it will have to be on the basis of other factors found in the context of the passage.[46]

---

44. Thomas Hewitt, *The Epistle to the Hebrews*, TNTC (Grand Rapids: Eerdmans, 1960), 110–11.

45. Nicole, "Some Comments," 356.

46. Someone may object that, though the terms in 6:4–6 *sometimes* have nonsalvific meanings, these meanings are less common and therefore less likely, and at this point we should simply ask what meaning for the terms is *most likely* and use that understanding in our exegesis. (McKnight, for example, says, "If one used these descriptions neutrally most Christian congregations would unanimously think that regenerate Christians were in view" [48 n. 104].)

But this objection misunderstands the nature of exegesis. When dealing with terms that have a range of meanings, no responsible exegete will say that one meaning is "more likely" until he or she has examined the context in which a term occurs. Words derive their specific sense (within a possible range) from the context, and, among the possible meanings (those that have been attested elsewhere), there is no such thing as a "more likely" meaning for a term apart from its context. In this case, the most relevant context includes the author's continuation of this discussion in verses 7–12.

What then has happened to these people? They are at least people who have been affiliated closely with the fellowship of the church. They have had some sorrow for sin and a decision to forsake their sin (*repentance*). They have clearly understood the gospel and given some assent to it (they have been *enlightened*). They have come to appreciate the attractiveness of the Christian life and the change that comes about in people's lives because of becoming a Christian, and they have probably had answers to prayer in their own lives and felt the power of the Holy Spirit at work, perhaps even using some spiritual gifts (they have become "associated with" the work of the Holy Spirit or have become "*partakers*" of the Holy Spirit and have tasted the heavenly gift and the powers of the age to come). They have been exposed to the true preaching of the Word and have appreciated much of its teachings (they have *tasted* the goodness of the Word of God).

These factors are all positive, and people who have experienced these things may be genuine Christians. But these factors alone are not enough to give conclusive evidence of any of the decisive beginning stages of the Christian life (regeneration, saving faith and repentance unto life, justification, adoption, initial sanctification). In fact, *these experiences are all preliminary to those decisive beginning stages of the Christian life.* The actual spiritual status of those who have experienced these things is still unclear.

Why It Is Impossible to Restore Such People to Repentance

In spite of all these positive experiences, "if [47] they then commit apostasy"[48] and "crucify the Son of God on their own account and hold him up to contempt" (6:6), they are willfully rejecting these blessings and turning decidedly against them. The sin in view involves determined rejection of Christ and probably public ridicule of him: they "crucify the Son of God" and "hold him up to contempt" (v. 6).[49]

47. Grammatically it is possible to translate the participle *parapesontas* in verse 6 temporally rather than causally: "It is impossible to restore" them "*while* they are crucifying the Son of God on their own account . . ." But the sense *because* is much better: "To say that they cannot be brought to repentance so long as they persist in their renunciation of Christ would be a truism hardly worth putting into words" (Bruce, *Hebrews,* 149).

48. The Revised Standard Version translation "commit apostasy" is a bit too specific for the word *parapiptō*, which simply means "to fall beside, go astray, miss," or "to become lost" (BAGD, 621); compare the New American Standard Bible ("have fallen away") and New International Version ("fall away"). However, the context does indicate that the falling away is so serious it could be rightly called "apostasy" (see next footnote).

49. McKnight says the sin is apostasy in the specific sense of "a willful rejection of God and his Son, Jesus the Messiah, and open denunciation of God and his ethical standards" ("Warning Passages," 39). McKnight's "synthetic perspective" is helpful in that it gives more insight into the nature of the falling away that the author warns against in several places (36–43), and he rightly points out several textual indicators that support the idea that the same or a similar sin of apostasy is in view in the passages he examines (though I do not think that is the only sin the author warns against, either in these passages or in the rest of the epistle).

If this happens, the author says it will be impossible[50] to restore them again to any kind of repentance or sorrow for sin. This is probably because their hearts will be hardened and their consciences calloused. What more could be done to bring them to salvation? If someone tells them Scripture is true they will say that they know it but they have decided to reject it. If someone tells them God answers prayer and changes lives they will respond that they have experienced that as well, but they want nothing of it. If someone tells them that the Holy Spirit is powerful to work in people's lives and the gift of eternal life is good beyond description, they will say that they understand that, but they want nothing of it. If someone tells them repentance from sins will lead to a better life, they will say that they know that but they do not want that kind of better life. Their repeated familiarity with the things of God and their experience of many influences of the Holy Spirit has simply served to harden them against conversion.

F. F. Bruce reaches a similar conclusion:

> In these verses he is not questioning the perseverance of the saints; we might say that rather he is insisting that those who persevere are the true saints. But in fact he is stating a practical truth that has verified itself repeatedly in the experience of the church. Those who have shared the covenant privileges of the people of God, and then deliberately renounce them, are the most difficult persons of all to reclaim for the faith.[51]

The author knows that there are some in the community to which he writes who are in danger of falling away in just this way (see 2:3; 3:8, 12, 14–15; 4:1, 7, 11; 10:26, 29, 35–36, 38–39; 12:3, 15–17). He wants to warn them that, although they have participated in the fellowship of the church and experienced a number of God's blessings in their lives, yet if they fall away after all that, they will not be saved. This does not necessarily imply that he thinks that true Christians could fall away, for he is especially writing to warn those whose spiritual status is not yet clear.

The Metaphor of the Field (vv. 7–8)

Verses 7–8 are connected to verses 4–6 with *gar* (for, because), indicating

---

50. The author does not say whether he means it is impossible for God (*adynatos* has this sense in Heb. 6:18 and 10:4) or simply impossible for men but possible for God (*adynatos* has this sense in Matt. 19:26; Mark 10:27; Luke 18:27). It does not matter which is intended, for the author's point is that the readers should not expect such renewal to repentance to happen: it is not within the range of God's ordinary ways of working with man. McKnight understands "impossible" to mean, "God will not work in them any longer so it is impossible for them to be restored" (33 n. 39).

51. Bruce, *Hebrews*, 144.

that the author is providing a reason or an explanation to support what he has said in verses 4–6:

> *For* land which has drunk the rain that often falls upon it, and brings forth vegetation useful to those for whose sake it is cultivated, receives a blessing from God. But if it bears thorns and thistles, it is worthless and near to being cursed; its end is to be burned.

Since the author intends this metaphor as an explanation of verses 4–6, the frequent rain best corresponds to the blessings that came from God into the lives of these people: the enlightening, the tasting of the heavenly gift and the word of God and the powers of the age to come, and the partaking in the work of the Holy Spirit. But the parallel with rain is revealing, for rain falls on all kinds of ground, and when the ground is still bare, one cannot tell what kind of vegetation will appear as a result of the rain. If the rain falls on ground that responds positively ("brings forth vegetation useful to those for whose sake it is cultivated"), then it "receives a blessing from God" (v. 7). But the same rain (in terms of the metaphor, the same events of being enlightened, tasting, and partaking) can fall on unresponsive ground, ground that only brings forth thorns and thistles. The difference was not in the kinds of events experienced but in the kinds of ground the rain fell on. The way the ground responds to the rain reveals the kind of ground it was in the first place.[52]

Therefore this metaphor provides significant help in solving the puzzle of verses 4–6. The phrase "if it bears thorns and thistles" in verse 8 corresponds directly to "if they then commit apostasy" in verse 6. When the land bears thorns and thistles, "it is worthless and near to being cursed; its end is to be burned" (v. 8). In sharp contrast to the "blessing from God" on the fruitful land in verse 7, these consequences (being cursed and burned) are a picture of final judgment from God. Moreover, it is not just the thorns and thistles that are burned up (which might fit a picture of loss of reward for a Christian who is finally saved), but the land itself.[53] In this sense, *these people who fall away are like land that bears thorns and thistles*—the final state (the *telos* [end]) of both is cursing and fiery judgment.

Was the land that received much rain good land or bad when it began to receive the rain? Before it bore a crop its status was uncertain, because no

---

52. Though grammatically the same word, "ground" *(gē)*, is referred to in verses 7 and 8, the "but" *(de)* and the conditional sense of the participle in verse 8 ("but if it bears thorns and thistles . . .") show that the author is not thinking of the same piece of land at all, for he clearly thinks of two distinct possibilities for two very different kinds of ground.

53. In verse 8, the singular adjective *adokimos* (worthless) and the singular relative pronoun *hēs* (of which) cannot refer to the plural nouns *akanthas* and *tribolous* (thorns and thistles), but must both refer to the singular noun *gē* (land), which is understood but not repeated in verse 8 as the noun modified by the participle *ekpherousa* (bearing).

vegetation had appeared. But once the thorns appeared, they revealed the true nature of the land—it had been bad land all along. In exactly the same way, were the people in verses 4–6 truly saved when they were enlightened, and tasted, and partook of the Holy Spirit? At that point their status was uncertain because these experiences were all things they had received, but these experiences did not yet give any indication of their response, of the kind of fruit they would bear, whether good or bad.[54] But once they fell away and held Christ up to contempt, this bad fruit in a similar way revealed what their true status was all along: they had never truly been saved in the first place.[55]

Now someone may object that another understanding of the metaphor is possible: perhaps those who fell away only became like land that bore thorns after they fell away; perhaps they were like good land (they were "saved") before they fell away. But the author's language is not consistent with this interpretation: (1) There is no indication of good fruit-bearing before falling away, so this view is simply speculation with no data to support it. (2) The author uses present participles to indicate a continuous process of bearing that we could paraphrase as follows:

"having drunk and continuing to bear" (piousa . . . kai tiktousa) useful vegetation (v. 7),

or

"having drunk and continuing to bear" (ekpherousa) thorns and thistles (v. 8).[56]

The idea of land that once bore good fruit and now bears thorns is not compatible with this picture.

The implication is this: While the positive experiences listed in verses 4–6 do not provide us enough information to know whether the people were truly saved or not, the committing of apostasy and holding Christ up to contempt do reveal the true nature of those who fall away: all along they have been like bad ground that can only bear bad fruit. If the metaphor of the

54. It is true that repentance was a kind of response, but an individual experience of repentance may or may not be the life-changing kind of repentance that accompanies saving faith. It is also significant that the author's syntax treats "repentance" differently from the other five elements, all of which are expressed by a series of aorist participles, and all of which are the blessings that the author is emphasizing and basing his argument on (they are the things that have been received as the ground receives rain).

55. The author's metaphor here is consistent with other metaphors in Scripture where good fruit is a sign of true spiritual life and fruitlessness or bad fruit is a sign given by unbelievers (for example, Matt. 3:8–10; 7:15–20; 12:33–35).

56. The resumption of piousa . . . kai is assumed in verse 8, to enable the contrast with ekpherousa.

thorn-bearing land explains verses 4–6 (as it surely does), then their falling away shows that they were never saved in the first place.

Better Things, Things That Belong to Salvation (vv. 9–12)

Though the author has been speaking harshly about the possibility of falling away, in verse 9 he returns to speak of the most common situation among his readers, most of whom he thinks to be genuine Christians (he now speaks of them as "you").[57] He says, "Even though we speak like this, dear friends, we are confident of *better things* in your case—*things that accompany salvation*" (NIV). We may also translate the last phrase, "things that *belong to* salvation."[58]

What exactly does the author refer to when he speaks of these "better things"? Verses 10–12 explain verse 9 (note the *gar*, "for," connecting verse 10 to verse 9), and these verses mention several "better things." In verse 10 he mentions work and love and service in their lives: "Your *work* and the *love* which you showed for his sake in *serving the saints,* as you still do." In verse 11 he mentions full assurance of hope, which some have and which he wants all to have: "And we desire each one of you to show the same earnestness in realizing the full assurance of *hope* until the end." In verse 12 he says that those who realize this "full assurance of hope" will have faith and pa-

---

57. The author's shift in perspective is abrupt and is emphasized repeatedly. He had been speaking in the third person:
"those who have once been enlightened" (v. 4)
"if they then commit apostasy" (v. 6)
"they crucify" (v. 6)
But now in verse 9 he switches to the second person:
"in your case . . ." (v. 9)
"your work" (v. 10)
"the love which you showed" (v. 10)
"as you still do" (v. 10)
"each one of you" (v. 11)
"so that you may not be sluggish" (v. 12)
Therefore no analysis of the "audience" for the warning passages should assume that the *audience* for the epistle (which is of course a single group in a single location) is the same as the *subjects* who commit apostasy in 6:4–6, for 6:9 clearly distinguishes them (see 10:39, similarly). The author warns the readers in general because he thinks there are a few among them who may fall away, but this does not mean that he thinks they all fall in the category of people described in 6:4–6; to the contrary, he says that, for the most part, they do not.

58. Regarding the translation of *echomena*, BAGD, 334, 3, translate the middle voice of *echō* as "hold oneself fast, cling to," and list Hebrews 6:9 as the only New Testament example of this form used "of inner belonging and close association." They translate Hebrews 6:9 as "things that belong to salvation" (cf. LSJ, 750, C: "hold oneself fast, cling closely"). Following BAGD, I have adopted the sense *belonging to* in my discussion, but I have also at times followed the New International Version, "accompany," which gives a somewhat similar sense and does not affect the argument.

tience: "so that you may not be sluggish, but imitators of those who through *faith* and *patience* inherit the promises." In this way he reassures those who are genuine believers—those who show fruit in their lives and show love for other Christians, who show hope and genuine faith.

But the question is "better things" than what? What contrast is in the author's mind? There are two possible interpretations: (1) better things than being burned in judgment (v. 8),[59] or (2) better things than the good experiences of being enlightened, tasting, and partaking (vv. 4–5).

The first interpretation seems unlikely, because (a) the adjective *kreisson,* "better," in Hebrews[60] is regularly used to contrast something better with something good (better covenant, better promises, better sacrifices, better possession, better country), not something better with something bad. Therefore it is unlikely that he would say, "In your case we feel sure of something better than final judgment." (b) If the author had wanted to say, "I am convinced of something better than judgment for you, because you will be saved, not burned in judgment," he probably would not have used the plural *ta kreissona* (better things), but would have rather used a singular expression like "something better" (compare the singular *kreitton ti* in Heb. 11:40), in order to say "something better for you, that is, salvation."[61] (c) The better things he mentions are best understood not as future better things (future salvation rather than future judgment), but as present better things, because the present participle *echomena* in the phrase *kai echomena sōtērias* is most naturally understood as giving a sense of present duration over time, "things *now presently* belonging to salvation, and continuing to belong to salvation." (d) He had no need to assure them that they had not yet fallen away (both author and readers knew that, for the readers were still listening to him). Therefore his concern is not to tell them, "I am convinced of something better than that you have fallen away," and his contrast is not with falling away, but with the positive experiences in verses 4–5.

But the second interpretation fits quite well: (a) On this interpretation these things are better than the good things mentioned in verses 4–6: enlight-

59. Another interpretation would be, better things than receiving blessings and then falling away (v. 6), but this would essentially be the same as the first interpretation, since those who fall away in verse 6 are explained by the metaphor in verses 7–8.

60. The author uses both spellings *kreisson* and *kreitton.* Thirteen of the nineteen occurrences in the New Testament are found in Hebrews, providing us with enough examples to see a pattern of emphasis or meaning.

61. Lane, *Hebrews 1–8,* 144, says that the definite article in the phrase *ta kreissona* (the better things) "is significant and looks back on the better of the two options contemplated in vv. 7–8." However, the definite article does not require this sense here (it is not translated in this way by the Revised Standard Version, New International Version, or New American Standard Bible), and is better understood as making the adjective substantial and giving the sense, "better (things)" (see BDF, §263 (3); A. T. Robertson, *A Grammar of the Greek New Testament in the Light of Historical Research* (Nashville: Broadman, [4]1934), 762–63; cf. 1 Cor. 1:27; 12:1).

ening, tasting, and partaking, so the author's usual sense of "better" in contrast to what is "good" is found here as well. (b) The author does not say that these "better things" are salvation (which would be a contrast to judgment), but that they are things that "accompany salvation" or "belong to salvation." This is consistent with understanding the "better things" to be the virtues such as love, service, faith, and hope that he mentions in verses 10–12, all of which do belong to the Christian's experience of salvation, and all of which provide an appropriate comparison to the positive experiences in verses 4–6. (c) Since things like love and service and faith in verses 10–12 are the kinds of good fruit that do give evidence of salvation, it is reasonable to think that the author would say that these are "better" than the enlightening, tasting, and partaking in verses 4–6, which in themselves do not give evidence of salvation.

We may conclude that in verse 9 the author says he is confident that most of his readers have better things than the people he described in verses 4–6, and *these things are better in that his readers also have things that belong to salvation.*[62] This implies that the blessings in verses 4–6 were not things that belong to salvation. This point is valid whether we translate the phrase *kai echomena sōtērias* as "*that is,* things that belong to salvation" or "*and* things that belong to salvation."[63]

In this way verse 9 provides a crucial key for understanding this whole passage. If the author had meant to say that the people mentioned in verses 4–6 were truly saved, then it is very difficult to understand why he would say in verse 9 that he is convinced of better things for his readers, that is, things that belong to salvation. *In writing this he shows that the people that he speaks of in verses 4–6, while they had many blessings, did not have salvation.*

One more point must be noted. This whole section in 6:9–12 makes it evident that "the author was making a distinction, and that he postulated a group of believers who would not be subject to a fall such as he described in

---

62. "Salvation" in this verse is not restricted to past, present, or future aspects of the Christian's experience, so it is best to understand it here in a broad sense, to refer to the whole of the Christian life (as in 2:10 and 5:9); see discussion of the term *salvation,* 134–37.

63. I have translated the *kai* as epexegetical (that is). As such it indicates that "belonging to salvation" explains further what the author means by "better things." The New International Version treats the *kai* as epexegetical: "better things in your case—things that accompany salvation." However, the Revised Standard Version translation, "better things that belong to salvation," ignores the *kai* altogether and thereby obscures the fact that these better things stand in clear contrast to the good things mentioned in the previous verses.

It is also possible to translate *kai* here as "and," in which case the sense would be, "better things, *and* things belonging to salvation." (The New American Standard Bible treats the *kai* this way: "better things concerning you, and things that accompany [mg: or, belong to] salvation.")

The difference in translation makes no difference in my argument, because in the first case, the things are better precisely in the fact that they belong to salvation, and this implies that the other things did not belong to salvation. In the second case the things still form a contrast to those things mentioned in verses 4–6, and this implies that the things in verses 4–6 did not belong to salvation.

verses 4–6."[64] This means that we cannot conclude that he thinks the falling away in verses 4–6 is a possibility for all Christians (a doctrinal conclusion different from the position of those who use this passage to argue that any Christian could lose salvation). Here the author thinks that most of his readers are in a different category—they have fruit in their lives that gives them grounds for assurance of their salvation.[65]

At this point it is appropriate to draw the following conclusions from verses 7–12: Verses 7–8 describe the people in verses 4–6 as unfruitful land that repeatedly bears thorns and thistles, and thus indicate that they were never saved. Verses 9–12 say that the readers, in general, have better things than the temporary experiences of verses 4–6, and that those better things include salvation. Therefore both verses 7–8 and verse 9 indicate that the people in verses 4–6 who fell away never had salvation.

Comparison with the Earlier State of Those Who Fell Away Elsewhere in Hebrews (chaps. 3–4)

In Hebrews 3–4, the author frequently compares his readers to the people of Israel wandering in the wilderness. As he does in chapter 6, he warns his readers in chapters 3–4 not to fall away. But in chapters 3–4 he gives more explicit statements about the initial spiritual state of those who eventually fell away. The parallels are instructive, for they show that the author believed that the people who fell away in the wilderness had several blessings similar to the enlightening, tasting, and partaking in 6:4–6, but never were saved.

For example, the fact that the people in 6:4–6 had been "enlightened" (6:4) means at least that they had heard and understood the gospel. Similarly, the author has already noted that many Israelites with Moses had heard the gospel (in old covenant form) but had never come to saving faith: "For good news came to us just as to them; but the message which they heard did not benefit them, because it did not meet with faith in the hearers" (4:2). Moreover, the fact that the people in 6:4–6 had "tasted the goodness of the word of God and the powers of the age to come" (6:5) means at least that they had come to know by personal experience something of the excellent qualities of God's Word, and something of God's great power breaking into their lives. But the author has also noted similar experiences in the lives of unbelieving Israelites who were with Moses: They had experienced remarkable miracles (what could even be called "the powers of the age to come") in the plagues on Egypt, the parting of the Red Sea, the manna from heaven, the water from the rock, and even the very presence of the glory of God among them in the

64. Nicole, "Some Comments," 362.
65. This conclusion should follow even for those who think 6:4–6 describes true Christians who lost their salvation: verses 9–12 describe the majority of Christians, who are in a different category than that.

pillar of cloud by day and fire by night. Yet they had never been truly saved: "your fathers put me to the test and saw my works for forty years. Therefore I was provoked with that generation, and said, *'They always go astray in their hearts; they have not known my ways'*" (3:9–10). He does not say that they once had believing hearts and then went astray, but rather, "They *always* go astray in their hearts." He does not say that they had previously known God's ways and then had turned astray, but rather, "they *have not known* my ways." They had heard the good news, heard the voice of God, tasted the powers of the age to come, but they had never believed.

In a similar way, the author says, "Who were they that heard and yet were rebellious? Was it not all those who left Egypt under the leadership of Moses? And with whom was he provoked forty years? Was it not with those who sinned, whose bodies fell in the wilderness? And to whom did he swear that they should never enter his rest, but to those who were disobedient? So we see that they were unable to enter because of unbelief" (3:16–19). Here they had left Egypt—they had been "redeemed" in the great exodus from Egypt. But they were rebellious and continued in unbelief.

The point of this is simply to say that the people of 6:4–6 have some experiences that are compatible not only with the situation of those who are saved, but also with the situation of some who notoriously fell away, and the author tells us in explicit language that the Israelites who fell away were never saved in the first place. This conclusion is consistent with our earlier evidence that the people who fell away in 6:4–6 were never saved in the first place either. Furthermore, this passage resembles what we found in 6:4–6 regarding the kinds of people the author discusses, for in chapters 3–4 only two kinds of people are in his mind: those who do not believe and fall away, and those who believe and persevere. He contemplates no third category (people who first believe and later fall away), either here or in 6:4–6.

Comparison with Language Describing the Saved Elsewhere in Hebrews

At this point we can broaden our investigation to examine language the author uses to describe those who are clearly saved elsewhere in the entire Book of Hebrews.[66] This may help us to see whether or not the descriptions in 6:4–6 match the descriptions he elsewhere gives to those who are saved.

66. I am grateful to my colleague Scot McKnight ("Warning Passages") for his work in viewing Hebrews 6:4–6 and 10:26–29 not in isolation, but in the light of all the passages in Hebrews that warn against falling away. His article gave me the idea to look in a similarly synthetic way at all of the descriptions of the saved in Hebrews. Though my doctrinal conclusion in this chapter is different from his, and though I differ with him at a number of points in this chapter, I found that his analysis provided me with helpful insight at many other points (several of which I have already cited).

What verses in Hebrews shall we count as descriptions of those who are saved? It would not be legitimate to count passages where the author warns against certain kinds of conduct (unbelief, falling away, disobedience), because he sees these as uncharacteristic of the Christian life. It would, however, be legitimate to count passages where he encourages certain kinds of conduct (faith, persevering, obedience), because he counts these as characteristic of the Christian life. In addition, it would certainly be legitimate to count verses that speak of things that God has done in the lives of those who are saved (forgiven their sins, cleansed their consciences). Finally, except for passages that warn against certain kinds of conduct, it would be legitimate to count passages that speak in the first or second person of the author and the readers ("we, us," and "you"), since the author's overall approach is to consider himself and his readers generally to be believers.[67] But it would not be legitimate to count passages in which the spiritual state of the people mentioned is in doubt or uncertain.[68] With these criteria in mind, we can compile the following list of descriptions of the saved in Hebrews.

We begin with several descriptions of what God has done in the lives of those who are saved.

1. God has forgiven their sins. The author applies to Christians the Lord's new covenant promise in Jeremiah, "I will remember their sins and their misdeeds no more" (Heb. 10:17; also 8:12).

2. God has cleansed their consciences. In contrast to the ineffectual sacrifices of the old covenant, the author says, "how much more shall the blood of Christ, who through the eternal Spirit offered himself without blemish to God, purify your conscience from dead works to serve the living God" (9:14). He encourages believers to "draw near" to God "with a true heart in full assurance of faith, with our hearts sprinkled clean from an evil conscience" (10:22). This cleansed conscience results from sins forgiven and it allows the saved to come into God's presence without fear of condemnation.

3. God has written his laws on their hearts. God had promised to do this for members of the new covenant, for he had said, "I will put my laws into their minds, and write them on their hearts" (8:10). The author says this is true of the saved, for he applies this statement to them in 10:16: "I will put my laws on their hearts, and write them on their minds."

67. I realize that he frequently warns them not to fall away, but this is simply because he knows there are some in the congregation whose spiritual status is unclear. He approaches them generally as believers with the possibility that there may be some unbelievers among them. His general approach is not, "You are all unbelievers" or "You have all fallen away," but, "Take care, brethren, lest there be in any of you an evil, unbelieving heart, leading you to fall away from the living God. But exhort one another every day, as long as it is called 'today,' that none of you may be hardened by the deceitfulness of sin" (Heb. 3:12–13).

68. I have not included material from the disputed passages 6:4–6 or 10:26–31, since I am here trying to gain a broader perspective from the rest of Hebrews that may help in understanding these passages.

162

4. God is producing holiness of life in them. The author uses a present participle to speak of the saved as those who "are being sanctified" (2:11 and 10:14; NASB mg). Part of this sanctifying process is God's fatherly discipline, for "he disciplines us for our good, that we may share his holiness" (12:10). The author also tells Christians that he hopes that God will "equip you with everything good that you may do his will, working in you that which is pleasing in his sight, through Jesus Christ; to whom be glory for ever and ever" (13:21).[69]

5. God has given them an unshakable kingdom. The author exhorts his readers, "let us be grateful for receiving a kingdom that cannot be shaken" (12:28). He reminds them, "you joyfully accepted the plundering of your property, since you knew that you yourselves had a better possession and an abiding one" (10:34; cf. 11:16).

6. God is pleased with them. This is the dominant theme of Hebrews 11: those who have faith are pleasing to God. "By faith Enoch was taken up so that he should not see death; and he was not found, because God had taken him. Now before he was taken *he was attested as having pleased God*" (11:5). The general truth is then summarized in 11:6: "And without faith it is impossible *to please him.*" The implication is that with faith, which the author encourages the readers to have, it is possible to please God. Similarly, the author quotes the Lord's statement, "but my righteous one shall live by faith, and if he shrinks back, my soul has no pleasure in him" (10:38)—implying that God does have pleasure in those who live by faith and do not shrink back. Moreover, believers are able to "offer to God *acceptable (euarestōs,* pleasing) worship, with reverence and awe" (12:28), and when they "do good" and share their goods with others, "such sacrifices are *pleasing* to God" (13:16). The author hopes that God will continue to work in the readers "that which is *pleasing* in his sight" (13:21).

We now turn from these six descriptions of what God has done in the lives of the saved to descriptions of actions or qualities that characterize their lives.

7. The saved have been enlightened. Speaking to his readers, the majority of whom he considers to be saved, the writer says, "But recall the former days when, *after you were enlightened,* you endured a hard struggle with sufferings, sometimes being publicly exposed to abuse and affliction, and some-

---

69. The author also sees a completed past aspect of sanctification: He says, "we *have been sanctified (hēgiasmenoi esmen)* through the offering of the body of Jesus Christ once for all" (10:10). This perfect tense speaks of a completed past activity with continuing present results: the saved have been made holy (in some sense, perhaps in a moral sense of initial sanctification, or perhaps in an Old Testament ceremonial sense of being made fit to come before God in worship) and they still bear the results of that initial sanctifying work. (In a similar way, the apostle Paul can also call believers "those who have been sanctified *[tois hēgisamenois]*"; see Acts 20:32).

times being partners with those so treated" (10:32–33). This shows that true Christians have been "enlightened." But we must realize that in this context the phrase almost certainly means "heard the gospel." This is because the two paragraphs (10:26–31 and 10:32–39) form a clear contrast with each other, and they show two different responses to the gospel.

> Response A: For if we sin deliberately after receiving the knowledge of the truth, there no longer remains a sacrifice for sins, but a fearful prospect of judgment. (10:26–27)

Here, "receiving the knowledge of the truth" simply means hearing and understanding the gospel, and probably also giving mental agreement or approval to it.[70] Therefore this response is (1) hear the gospel, and after hearing it (2) sin deliberately. This leads to (3) judgment. The author places this response in clear contrast to

> Response B: But recall the former days when, *after you were enlightened,* you endured a hard struggle with sufferings. . . . Therefore do not throw away your confidence, which has a great reward. . . . We are not of those who shrink back and are destroyed, but of those who *have faith* and keep their souls. (10:32, 35, 39)

This response is (1) hear the gospel, and after hearing it (2) endure with confidence and faith. This leads to (3) great reward and final salvation of their souls.

In this way, the author says that true Christians have been enlightened, but we must realize that the contrast with 10:26 shows that the enlightening means only hearing and understanding the gospel, and does not necessarily imply that they actually believed it. In this way, we can conclude that in Hebrews all true Christians have been enlightened, but not all who have been enlightened are true Christians.

8. *The saved have faith.* This is probably the dominant description of the saved in Hebrews. The saved are not merely those who have heard the gospel, but those who have responded to it with faith. With respect to a past experience of coming to faith, the author can say, "We who *have believed (hoi pisteusantes)* enter that rest" (4:3).

---

70. A good parallel is found in Mark 4:16–17, which speaks of people who, "when they hear the word, immediately receive it with joy." This certainly includes as much as "receiving the knowledge of the truth" in Hebrews 10:26, and probably more: in both passages the people "receive" what they have heard (the verb *lambanō* is used in both verses), and in Mark 4, they even receive it "with joy." But in Mark 4 these people had no genuine spiritual life, because Jesus says in the next verse, "they have no root in themselves" (v. 17, indicating no source of spiritual life or nourishment in themselves). Therefore they "endure for a while; then, when tribulation or persecution arises on account of the word, immediately they fall away" (v. 17).

There are many exhortations to continue in faith, showing that the author considers faith an essential element of the ongoing Christian life. The author encourages the readers to be "imitators of those who through *faith* and patience inherit the promises" (6:12), and to consider the lives of their leaders and "imitate their *faith*" (13:7)—both verses show that faith is a characteristic of those who are truly saved. The readers are encouraged to draw near to God "in full assurance of *faith*" (10:22), and to realize that the Lord says, "my righteous one shall *live by faith*" (10:38)—in other words, faith is the essential element in the Christian life. The author tells the readers, "we are not of those who shrink back and are destroyed, but of those who have faith and keep their souls" (10:39).[71] Then Hebrews 11 mentions

71. Several of these preceding verses contain *assurance of present genuine faith* and thereby stand in contrast to the view of "phenomenological faith" advocated by McKnight ("Warning Passages," 23–24). He speaks of "phenomenological believers" as people who give signs or evidence (phenomena) of faith: they are "believers in every observable sense" ("Warning Passages," 24). He says, moreover, that "phenomenological believers" think they have saving faith: "The 'phenomenological' believer experiences faith so far as he or she is capable" (24 n. 12). In addition, he thinks that no Christian in this life experiences anything other than this phenomenological faith, which may or may not be genuine saving faith: ". . . this 'phenomenological' faith is all that humans can experience in this present order of things; some of these believers persevere unto eternal life and others will not and so will be condemned. These former believers had a phenomenological faith but did not persevere; these latter believers had a phenomenological faith but did persevere and so had 'genuine' or 'true' or 'real' or 'saving' faith" (ibid.). He supports this idea by saying in Hebrews, "'believers' is used for some who may be finally damned" (ibid.).

I differ with this position at several points: (1) The word *believer* is never used in Hebrews of anyone who is finally condemned (McKnight gives no references, and the *pistis/pisteuō* word group is never used this way in Hebrews). (2) This position (as he has expressed it) says nothing about the significant differences in outward evidence and in inward perception between those who merely give intellectual agreement or superficial consent to the gospel and those who have a genuine faith that includes heartfelt personal trust in Christ. But Hebrews speaks quite differently about the *present assurance* that comes with genuine faith: "Faith is the assurance of things hoped for, the conviction of things not seen" (11:1); the author is confident that "we are of those who *have faith* and keep their souls" (10:39); we can have "*full assurance of faith*" (10:22); Noah became (long before he died) "an heir of the righteousness *which comes by faith*" (11:7). Moreover, the Old Testament heroes of the faith by their obedience gave abundant compelling evidence that they had true faith (chap. 11). By contrast, the author does not say that those who fell away had faith but did not persevere in it (as McKnight's position would say); rather, he says they never had faith: the message they heard "did not meet with faith in the hearers" (4:2; cf. 3:10, 12, 19).

(3) This position would mean that no Christian could ever have *present* assurance of salvation, but would simply have to wait and persevere until the end of life in order to have confidence that he or she would be saved. But surely the New Testament generally, and Hebrews specifically, give many grounds for assurance in addition to perseverance (see 1:14; 4:3; 6:7, 9–10, 19–20; 7:19, 25; 8:10–12; 9:24; 10:10, 14, 16–18, 19–22, 39; also the chapter on assurance by D. A. Carson elsewhere in this work, as well as Wayne Grudem, *Systematic Theology* [Grand Rapids: Zondervan, 1994], "Perseverance," chap. 40). Paul's declaration likewise gives assurance of salvation based on *present* faith: "if you confess with your lips that Jesus is Lord and *believe in your heart* that God raised him from the dead, *you will be saved*" (Rom. 10:9).

faith twenty-four times in the course of exhorting the readers to imitate the faith of Old Testament believers, for by faith "the men of old received divine approval" (11:2).[72] Therefore New Testament Christians are to run the race set before them, "looking to Jesus the pioneer and perfecter of our *faith*" (12:2).

Finally, it is important that faith continue to the end of one's life. The verse just quoted pictures a race yet to be run, a race that will continue, following in Jesus' steps, to the end of life. The author exhorts the readers to "hold fast our confidence" (3:6), to "hold our first confidence firm to the end" (3:14), and to "hold fast our confession" (4:14). (The idea of continuing in faith until the end of life is also indicated in 6:12; 11:13; and 13:7.)

9. *The saved have hope.* Closely related to faith is hope. Hope may be understood as faith directed toward the future, especially future fulfillment of God's promises. Thus, hope includes a confident expectation of future good based on trust in God's character and the truthfulness of his words.

The readers have hope, for they are encouraged to hold on to it, to "hold fast the confession of our *hope* without wavering, for he who promised is faithful" (10:23). Through a "better hope" than under the old covenant, they "draw near to God" (7:19). Their hope was also evident in their expectation of heaven: "You joyfully accepted the plundering of your property, since you knew that you yourselves had a better possession and an abiding one" (10:34), and, "we seek the city which is to come" (13:14). He encourages them to "show the same earnestness in realizing the full assurance of *hope* until the end" (6:11), and to "seize the *hope* set before us" (6:18). Christ will return "to save those who are *eagerly waiting* for him" (9:28). Such hope was also strong in the expectations of previous heroes of the faith, who "looked forward to the city which has foundations" (11:10), and who "looked to the reward" (11:26).

10. *The saved have love.* The author is sure that "God is not so unjust as to overlook your work and the *love* which you showed for his sake in serving the saints, as you still do" (6:10), and gives specific evidence of this in the fact that they were "partners" with those who were persecuted, and they "had compassion on the prisoners" (10:33–34). He tells them to "consider how to stir up one another to *love* and good works" (10:24), and says, "Let brotherly *love* continue" (13:1).

11. *The saved worship and pray.* The author encourages them, "let us offer to God acceptable *worship,* with reverence and awe" (12:28), and says, "let us continually offer up a sacrifice of *praise* to God, that is, the fruit of

---

72. McKnight helpfully observes that "of all the discontinuities of Hebrews (e.g., priesthood, covenant, sacrifice, etc.) the one dominating continuity is that the faith under the former covenant is the same kind of faith that is required of believers under the new covenant" ("Warning Passages," 32–33 n. 36).

lips that acknowledge his name" (13:15). Such worship is made possible by the amazing fact that new covenant believers have come not into the earthly temple, but "to the city of the living God, the heavenly Jerusalem" (12:22). In fact, they have come not only into the heavenly city, but into the very Holy of Holies in the temple of God in heaven: "We have confidence *to enter the sanctuary (eis tēn eisodon tōn hagiōn,* literally, "into the holy places")[73] by the blood of Jesus" (10:19).

The author says Christians have a high priest "who in every respect has been tempted as we are, yet without sin" (4:15). Therefore the saved are able to pray and be heard by God, and they are told, "Let us then with confidence *draw near to the throne of grace,* that we may receive mercy and find grace to help in time of need" (4:16; cf. 7:19, 25), and, "let us draw near with a true heart in full assurance of faith" (10:22).

12. The saved obey God. Just as the faith of Old Testament believers led to bold obedience, as when Noah built an ark (11:7), or when "Abraham *obeyed* when he was called to go out to a place which he was to receive as an inheritance" (11:8), or when he offered up Isaac (11:17), or when Moses chose to avoid "the fleeting pleasures of sin" (11:25), so new covenant believers are to "do the will of God" (10:36), and to "*strive . . . for* the *holiness* without which no one will see the Lord" (12:14). Their discipline by God will lead to "holiness" and "the peaceful fruit of righteousness" (12:10–11). So strong is the expectation of obedience that the author can say that those who are saved are those who obey: Jesus is "the source of eternal salvation to *all who obey him*" (5:9).

13. The saved persevere. As McKnight so clearly demonstrated,[74] again and again the author of Hebrews emphasizes that those who are saved are those who continue in faith to the end of their lives, those who persevere in their allegiance to Christ. "We are his house *if* we hold fast our confidence and pride in our hope" (3:6). Moreover, "we share in Christ, if only we hold our first confidence *firm to the end*" (3:14). The author exhorts his readers to "show the same earnestness in realizing the full assurance of hope *until the end*" (6:11), and says, "Let us hold fast the confession of our hope *without wavering*" (10:23). They "have need of endurance" (10:36); they are not to "shrink back" (10:39); they are to "run *with perseverance*" (12:1); they should not "grow weary or fainthearted" (12:3); they are not to "lose courage" (12:5); they "have to *endure*" (12:7), just as many of them had previously "endured a hard struggle with sufferings" (10:32), and had not abandoned their faith.

---

73. In Hebrews, "the holy places" *(ta hagia)* refers to the Holy of Holies, using the imagery of the Old Testament temple to speak of the greater heavenly reality in the very presence of God: see *ta hagia* in 8:2; 9:8, 25; 10:19; 13:11.
74. See note 72.

14. The saved enter God's rest. The author says that "we who have believed enter that rest" (4:3), and also, "Let us therefore strive to enter that rest" (4:11). He is concerned "lest any of you be judged to have failed to reach it" (4:1).

15. The saved know God. In the new covenant age, "they shall not teach every one his fellow or every one his brother, saying, 'Know the Lord,' for all shall know me, from the least of them to the greatest" (8:11).

16. The saved are God's house, his children, and his people. The author uses various Old Testament metaphors and themes to characterize the saved. They are God's house, for he says, "And we are his house if we hold fast our confidence and pride in our hope" (3:6). They are God's children, for they are the "many sons" who are brought to glory (2:10), and Christ can call them "my brothers" (2:12 NIV) and "the children God has given me" (2:13). And they are God's own people, for he says, "I will be their God, and they shall be my people" (8:10).

17. The saved share in Christ. In exhorting the readers to persevere in their faith, the author tells them, "For we share in Christ, if only we hold our first confidence firm to the end" (3:14).

18. The saved will receive future salvation. The author refers to Christians as "those who are to obtain salvation" (1:14), and says that Christ is "able for all time to save those who draw near to God through him" (7:25). Christ is "the source of eternal salvation to all who obey him" (5:9), and he will return "to save those who are eagerly waiting for him" (9:28).

We can summarize these descriptions of the saved in the following list:

1. God has forgiven their sins
2. God has cleansed their consciences
3. God has written his laws on their hearts
4. God is producing holiness of life in them
5. God has given them an unshakable kingdom
6. God is pleased with them
7. They have been enlightened
8. They have faith
9. They have hope
10. They have love
11. They worship and pray
12. They obey God
13. They persevere
14. They enter God's rest
15. They know God
16. They are God's house, his children, and his people
17. They share in Christ
18. They will receive future salvation

Before we compare this list to 6:4–6, one conclusion we may draw is that, while perseverance in the faith is certainly one characteristic of the saved, it is not the only distinguishing characteristic. And falling away is only one of many characteristics of the lost.[75] This is because the actions of persevering and falling away do not occur in a vacuum—they occur in the context of a life that has qualities which lead one to persevere or to fall away. For example, the author warns, "do not harden your hearts" (3:8) because he knows that hard hearts are involved when people fall away: "Take care, brethren, lest there be in any of you an evil, unbelieving heart, leading you to fall away from the living God" (3:12).[76] He knows that those who failed to enter God's rest did not just arbitrarily and unpredictably turn away from God's invitation, but they did so because there was no faith in their hearts: "they were unable to enter because of unbelief" (3:19), and "the message which they heard did not benefit them, because it did not meet with faith in the hearers" (4:2). Therefore we must realize that the characteristics of the saved and the lost cannot be mixed and matched; they hold together in an integral relationship in each of two radically different kinds of life.

It is interesting that only one item on this list (they have been enlightened) is found in 6:4–6. And that item is seen, from the context of 10:32 and from the sense of the word *phōtizō*, to be true not only of Christians but also of others who hear the gospel but then reject it.[77] Not one of the other characteristics by which the author describes genuine Christians is found in 6:4–6:

> For it is impossible to restore again to repentance those who have once been enlightened, who have tasted the heavenly gift, and have become partakers of the Holy Spirit, and have tasted the goodness of the word of God and the powers of the age to come, if they then commit apostasy, since they crucify the Son of God on their own account and hold him up to contempt.

This fact makes us realize that some of the statements that interpreters have made about Hebrews 6:4–6 in the past have been quite unguarded, and in fact have not been accurate. For example, a statement such as, "There is no more powerful description of a true Christian in the New Testament" is certainly an overstatement. The Book of Hebrews itself gives many more

---

75. I have not listed the descriptions that the author gives for the lost in Hebrews, but they parallel the descriptions of the saved in many cases. For example: God has not forgiven their sins; God takes no pleasure in them; they have no faith and no hope; they are disobedient, do not worship or pray, do not enter God's rest, fall away, and will receive future judgment.

76. The connection between an unbelieving heart and falling away is clear whether we translate *en* plus the dative articular infinitive *tō apostēnai* to denote cause (as RSV), manner or attendant circumstance (NASB, "in falling away from the living God") or some kind of adjectival relationship (NIV, "that turns away from the living God").

77. See discussion, 141–44.

powerful and detailed descriptions, one of which occurs immediately in 6:9–12. In several other places, when the author wants to, he can give much more clear descriptions of genuine Christians.

Nor is it true that 6:4–6 provides the most detailed description of a Christian that the author could give. For example, if the author had wanted to say that it is impossible to restore again to salvation those who have become genuine Christians and have then fallen away, his descriptions of true Christians elsewhere show that he could have said something like this:

> For it is impossible to restore again to faith those who have believed the message they heard, and have entered God's rest, and whose sins have been forgiven and whose consciences have been cleansed by the blood of Jesus, and who have had God's laws written on their hearts, and who have shown love in serving the saints, and who have persevered in hardship, and who have come into the Holy of Holies and drawn near to God and come boldly before the throne of grace, and who have offered to God acceptable worship with reverence and awe, and have become God's children and his house and his people, if they then commit apostasy. . . .

If that description or anything like it had been written, then we could rightly say, "No more clear description of genuine Christians could be given." But the fact remains that the actual phrases of Hebrews 6:4–6 are far different from this. And this gives one more indication that persons other than genuine Christians are being described here.[78]

At this point someone may object that we must also compare Hebrews 6:4–6 with the descriptions of the lost that are found elsewhere in Hebrews. Is it not true that no decisive description of the lost is given in the following phrases?

"who have once been enlightened"

"who have tasted the heavenly gift"

"and have become partakers of the Holy Spirit"

"and have tasted the goodness of the word of God and the powers of the age to come"

and the implication that they had previously repented

78. At this point someone may object that these descriptions in 6:4–6, while not used to refer to Christians elsewhere in Hebrews, are nevertheless valid descriptions of genuine Christians. Yet it must be remembered that this suggestion remains only a suggestion until it can be proven by a careful investigation of the specific words and phrases found in verses 4–6. Moreover, it must be recognized that, except for the individual words *enlightened (phōtizō)* and *repentance (metanoia)*, none of the phrases that describe people in verses 4–6 occurs anywhere else in the New Testament.

In response, I agree that the phrases alone do not match the author's descriptions of the lost, and they do not indicate that these people are lost (before they commit apostasy). But that is just the point: *Before they commit apostasy their spiritual status is uncertain.* It remains to be seen whether they are among the saved or the lost. They have not yet given decisive indications either way. That is the reason the author warns them not to turn away—they are still at a point where a decision to be among the saved or the lost must be made.

Now some might argue that a few of the pre-apostasy conditions of these people were similar to one or another of these characteristics of the saved. For example, one could argue that "repentance" is similar to (12) obedience, or that it is connected to (8) faith. One could argue that being "enlightened" is similar to (8) faith. And one could argue that becoming a partaker of the Holy Spirit is similar to (17) sharing in Christ or (2) having a cleansed conscience or (3) having God's laws on one's heart. Moreover, one could argue that tasting the heavenly gift is similar to (5) receiving a heavenly kingdom, and that tasting "the goodness of the word of God and the powers of the age to come" is similar to (11) genuine worship and prayer, or (8) faith, or (15) knowing God.

But wherever there are similarities it is certain that there are also differences. We cannot just assume that being "enlightened" is the same as having genuine saving faith, or that "repentance" is the same as true obedience, unless this can be proven from a careful analysis of the meanings and contexts of the precise words the author used. And our analysis of these phrases (148–50) has shown that none of these phrases is a clear indication of any elements in the distinctive beginning stages of the Christian life: "Repentance" does not necessarily imply obedience or saving faith; being "enlightened" is not the same as saving faith; being a "partaker" in the Holy Spirit is not the same as sharing in Christ or having a cleansed conscience; and "tasting" the heavenly gift is not the same as receiving a heavenly kingdom. To assume that these things are the same is to fail to give adequate attention to the actual words that the author used.

Conclusions Regarding Hebrews 6:4–6

We began with the question: Does Hebrews 6:4–6 describe people who had experienced the decisive beginning stages of a genuine Christian life, and who then had fallen away and lost their salvation? Careful analysis of the terms used to describe these people before they fell away showed that, while the terms could be used to apply to genuine Christians, they could also be used to apply to people who were not yet Christians but who had simply heard the gospel and had experienced several of the blessings of the Holy

Spirit's work in the Christian community. In other words, these terms tell us that the people had experienced many of the preliminary stages that often precede the beginning of the Christian life, but they do not tell us that the people had experienced any of the decisive beginning stages of the Christian life. Therefore, the spiritual status of these people before they fell away could not be determined on the basis of the terms in 6:4–6 alone.

However, an examination of the metaphor of the field in verses 7–8, which the author uses to explain verses 4–6, showed that the people in 4–6 were like a field that received frequent rain but only bore thorns and thistles. This indicated that, in the author's mind, the people in 4–6 had received many blessings but had never borne good fruit because they had been like bad ground the entire time: There had never been true spiritual life in them.

An examination of verses 9–12 led us to a similar conclusion. Though the author had been speaking of the possibility of some of his readers falling away, his view of most of them was much different: He felt sure that, in general, his readers were in possession of "better things" than the preliminary experiences in 4–6, and that the better things were in fact "things belonging to salvation." This implied that the blessings of 4–6, while positive, nevertheless did not belong to salvation. Then in verses 10–12 the author names those "better things" as the good fruits of work, love, service for others, hope, faith, and patience.

A comparison with chapters 3 and 4 showed that the author thought of the rebellious people of Israel in the wilderness as people who had experiences similar to being enlightened, tasting the blessings of redemption, tasting the goodness of the word of God, and associating with, seeing, and benefiting from some of the works of the Holy Spirit—yet they never had faith (4:2), they always went astray in their hearts (3:10), and they had never known God's ways (3:10). This example provided a parallel case of another group of people who had many remarkable experiences of blessing from God, but were never really saved.

Then an examination of descriptive terms used by the author to describe Christians elsewhere in Hebrews revealed that only one term in 6:4–6 ("enlightened") was used elsewhere to describe believers, and that term referred only to hearing and understanding the gospel, not to any of the decisive beginning stages of the Christian life. The most significant finding was that none of the other seventeen descriptions of true Christians in Hebrews was used in 6:4–6. This indicated that if the author had wanted to say that it is impossible for true Christians who fall away to come back to salvation, he certainly could have done so clearly, but he did not. In 6:4–6 he chose to use language that does not describe those who are truly saved.

Therefore, confining our attention to the Book of Hebrews itself, and examining 6:4–6 in its immediate and broader context within the book, leads us to the conclusion that the people in this passage who experienced many blessings and then fell away had never truly been saved in the first place.

Analysis of Other Warning Passages in Hebrews

Hebrews 2:1–4

We can now turn our attention to the remaining warning passages in Hebrews, comparing their teaching to that of 6:4–6.

In Hebrews 2:1–4, the author warns against drifting away after hearing the gospel:

> Therefore we must pay the closer attention to what we have heard, *lest we drift away from it.* For if the message declared by angels was valid and every transgression or disobedience received a just retribution, how shall we escape *if we neglect such a great salvation?* It was declared at first by the Lord, and it was attested to us by those who heard him, while God also bore witness by signs and wonders and various miracles and by gifts of the Holy Spirit distributed according to his own will.

This text has not created controversy regarding the doctrine of the perseverance of the saints, for it contains no phrases that might indicate the decisive beginning stages of the Christian life. The only possible exception to this is the first person plural, "we." Someone could argue that the author in this use of "we" implies that any Christian might "drift away" from the gospel and "neglect" this great salvation.

But this is not a necessary inference from the expression. The author needs some way of speaking about himself and his readers as an entire group, and the use of the first person plural is an ordinary conversational convention for doing that. It does not imply that everyone in the group is subject to everything discussed using this convention, but only that some (at least) are included. In this case, the author knows that some among his readers are in danger of falling away, but he does not know specifically who they are, so he includes this general kind of warning at several places in the epistle.[79] The passage is similar to 6:4–6 in that the people warned are those who have *heard* the gospel message and *experienced miracles* (this is similar to tasting the

---

79. Similar "we" statements are found in other warnings in Hebrews:
"And we are his house if we hold fast our confidence and pride in our hope" (3:6).
"For we share in Christ, if only we hold our first confidence firm to the end" (3:14).
"For if we sin deliberately after receiving the knowledge of the truth, there no longer remains a sacrifice for sins, but a fearful prospect of judgment" (10:26–27).
"For if they did not escape when they refused him who warned them on earth, much less shall we escape if we reject him who warns from heaven" (12:25).

goodness of the word of God and the powers of the age to come). As in 6:4–6, we cannot tell whether people who have had such experiences are believers or not. They are simply warned against drifting away after these experiences.

Hebrews 3:6–4:13

This passage is an extended comparison between the readers and the people of Israel in the wilderness. Only a brief analysis is necessary, since we discussed earlier the fact that the people heard the word of God, experienced miracles, saw the works of God for forty years, and yet never believed.[80]

When the author speaks directly about the present situation of his readers, however, some strong warnings are included.

> . . . Christ was faithful over God's house as a son. And *we are his house if we hold fast our confidence and pride in our hope.* Therefore, as the Holy Spirit says, "Today, when you hear his voice, *do not harden your hearts* as in the rebellion, on the day of testing in the wilderness, where your fathers put me to the test and saw my works for forty years. Therefore I was provoked with that generation, and said, 'They always go astray in their hearts; they have not known my ways.' As I swore in my wrath, 'They shall never enter my rest.'" *Take care, brethren, lest there be in any of you an evil, unbelieving heart, leading you to fall away from the living God.* But exhort one another every day, as long as it is called "today," that none of you may be hardened by the deceitfulness of sin. *For we share in Christ, if only we hold our first confidence firm to the end,* while it is said, "Today, when you hear his voice, *do not harden your hearts* as in the rebellion." Who were they that heard and yet were rebellious? Was it not all those who left Egypt under the leadership of Moses? And with whom was he provoked forty years? Was it not with those who sinned, whose bodies fell in the wilderness? And to whom did he swear that they should never enter his rest, but to those who were disobedient? So we see that they were unable to enter because of unbelief. (Heb. 3:6–19)

The warnings are continued in chapter 4:

> Therefore, while the promise of entering his rest remains, let us fear *lest any of you be judged to have failed to reach it.* For good news came to us just as to them; but the message which they heard did not benefit them, because it *did not meet with faith in the hearers.* . . . *Let us therefore strive to enter that rest, that no one fall by the same sort of disobedience.* (4:1–2, 11)

In these sections the repeated warning is against hardening their hearts against the message that they have heard (3:8, 12, 15; 4:7). The hardness of

---

80. See 160–61.

heart accompanies unbelief and falling away from the living God (3:12, 19; 4:2), and also is evident in disobedience (4:6, 11).

For our purposes 3:14 is especially relevant: For *we have become partakers of Christ, if* we hold fast the beginning of our assurance firm to the end" (NASB). This verse provides an excellent perspective on the doctrine of perseverance. How do we know if "we *have become* partakers[81] of Christ"? How do we know if this being joined to Christ *has happened to us at some time in the past?*[82] One way in which we know that we have come to genuine faith in Christ is if we continue in faith until the end of our lives. D. A. Carson writes,

> . . . close attention to the tenses in Hebrews 3:14 reveals an extra ingredient in this verse. We have become *(gegonamen)*—in the past!—partakers of Christ if we now, in the present, hold firmly to the confidence we had at first. It follows from this verse that although perseverance is mandated, it is also the evidence of what has taken place in the past. . . . If persevering shows we have (already) come to share in Christ, it can only be because sharing in Christ has perseverance for its inevitable fruit.[83]

Therefore, far from saying that those who have been saved can lose their salvation, this verse says that only those who persevere in the Christian life were ever truly saved (savingly participated in Christ) in the first place. And the implication is that those who fall away never did become partakers in Christ—those who fall away show that they never were saved.

However, attention to the context of Hebrews 3:14 will keep us from using this and similar passages in a pastorally inappropriate way. We must remember that there are other evidences elsewhere in the Scripture that give Christians assurance of salvation,[84] so we should not think or teach that assurance that we belong to Christ is impossible until we die. Nevertheless, continuing in faith is the one means of assurance that is named here by the author of Hebrews. He mentions this to warn his readers that they should not fall away from Christ, because he is writing to a situation where such a warning is needed (see 3:12). In fact, in all of the passages in which continuing to believe in Christ to the end of our lives is mentioned as one indication of genuine faith, *the purpose is never to make those who are presently trusting in Christ worry that sometime in the future they might fall away* (and we

81. Here the context indicates that *metochos*, "partaker," is used in the sense of having a saving interest in Christ, because it is parallel to entering God's eschatological rest, and accompanies holding one's confidence firm to the end.

82. The author uses the perfect tense verb *gegonamen*, "we have become" (at some time in the past, with results that continue into the present).

83. D. A. Carson, *Exegetical Fallacies* (Grand Rapids: Baker, 1984), 88.

84. See the discussion of assurance and of evidences of salvation in chapter 10 by D. A. Carson in this work.

should never use these passages that way either). Rather, the purpose is always to warn those who are thinking of falling away or have fallen away that if they do this it is a strong indication that they were never saved in the first place.

Hebrews 10:26–31

Our analysis of this passage can be much more brief, since it has several similarities to 6:4–6:

For if we sin deliberately[85] after *receiving the knowledge of the truth*, there no longer remains a sacrifice for sins, but a fearful prospect of judgment, and a fury of fire which will consume the adversaries. A man who has violated the law of Moses dies without mercy at the testimony of two or three witnesses. How much worse punishment do you think will be deserved by the man who has spurned the Son of God, and profaned the blood of the covenant by which *he was sanctified,* and outraged the Spirit of grace? For we know him who said, "Vengeance is mine, I will repay." And again, "The Lord will judge his people." It is a fearful thing to fall into the hands of the living God.

As with 6:4–6, a reasonable argument can be made that these people were genuine Christians before they rejected Christ and fell away. On the view that these people were once saved, "if we sin deliberately" implies that the author thinks that he himself or anyone among his readers might actually fall into such sin. Also according to this view, "receiving the knowledge of the truth" is equivalent to coming to saving faith, and "sanctified" refers to the initial break with actual sin that occurs at the beginning of the Christian life.

But once again it must be said that none of these phrases gives a decisive indication of the spiritual state of a person. As was true with 2:1–4, the use of "we" is a verbal convention that enables the author to speak of his readers in general, without implying that every one of them is in the situation described in the "we" clauses.[86]

To "receive the knowledge of the truth" simply means to hear and understand the gospel, and probably also to give mental agreement or approval to it.[87] In this way, the phrase is similar in meaning to "enlightened" in 6:4. But

85. The present participle indicates an ongoing pattern of sin; the New International Version translates, "If we deliberately *keep on sinning* after we have received the knowledge of the truth, no sacrifice for sins is left" (Heb. 10:26). Willful and persistent rejection of the truth and living in rebellion against it are in view in this verse.
86. See 173–74.
87. See the discussion of Hebrews 10:32, 163–64.

this is not the same as saving faith, which must include the hearer's individual trust in Christ as a person.

When the author talks about the blood of the covenant "that sanctified him," the word *sanctified* need not refer to the internal moral purification that comes with salvation, for the term *hagiazō* has a broader range than that, both in Hebrews and in the New Testament generally. For example, Hebrews 9:13 says, "The blood of goats and bulls and the ashes of a heifer sprinkled on those who are ceremonially unclean *sanctify (hagiazō)* them so that they are outwardly clean" (NIV). The author of Hebrews says that an Old Testament ceremony of sacrificial sprinkling *sanctified* people[88]—that is, it made them ceremonially clean, so that they could once again worship with God's people. But it was only outward sanctification, not the internal sanctification that accompanies true salvation.

Another nonsaving sense of *hagiazō*, "sanctify," is found in 1 Corinthians 7:14: "For the unbelieving husband has been *sanctified* through his wife, and the unbelieving wife has been *sanctified* through her believing husband. Otherwise your children would be unclean, but as it is, they are holy" (NIV). Here the sense is not that the unbeliever has been saved, but that some positive moral influence has been brought to bear on him or her.

Jesus also uses *hagiazō* to refer to ceremonial purification: "You blind fools! For which is greater, the gold or the temple that has *made* the gold sacred? . . . Which is greater, the gift or the altar that *makes* the gift sacred?" (Matt. 23:17, 19). In both cases, *hagiazō* is used in the sense "make sacred" or "make ceremonially pure." In 1 Timothy 4:5, Paul uses *hagiazō* to say that food can be "*consecrated* by the word of God and prayer." And Peter says Christians are to "*reverence (hagiazō)* Christ as Lord" (1 Pet. 3:15) in their hearts—the sense is "to think of as holy."

These other examples do not of course prove that *hagiazō* in Hebrews 10:29 must refer to something other than the internal sanctification that accompanies salvation, but they mean that we should not assume that *hagiazō* means saving sanctification either. Moreover, the entire context in which 10:29 occurs, from 9:1 to 10:39, is concerned with parallels between the Old Testament Levitical sacrifices and the better new covenant sacrifice of Christ. Because a ceremonial focus pervades this context, a ceremonial sense of "sanctify" would be appropriate in 10:29. This is especially true in the immediate context of 10:19–31, for the author is speaking of the fact that the congregation in general has a "new and living way" (10:20) available by the

---

88. The most fitting Old Testament background is Numbers 19:9–19, where the ashes of a heifer that had been sacrificed are mixed with water and sprinkled on persons who have come into contact with a dead body. After this has been done, the cleansed persons are once again permitted to enter the assembly of the Lord's people. But the general point the author is making is that ceremonial sprinkling in the Old Testament made people able once again to worship with God's people.

blood of Jesus, and therefore can "enter the sanctuary" (10:19) and "draw near" (10:22) into God's presence.[89]

But the author of Hebrews knows that some may fall away, even though *they assemble with the congregation of believers* and so share in this great privilege of coming before God. So he says, "not neglecting to meet together, as is the habit of some, but encouraging one another" (10:25). The reason to encourage one another is the warning in 10:26, "For if we sin deliberately after receiving the knowledge of the truth." In such a context, it is appropriate to understand "profaned the blood of the covenant by which he was *sanctified*" to mean "*by which he was given the privilege of coming before God with the congregation of God's people.*" In this sense, the blood of Christ opened up a new way of access to God for the congregation—it "sanctified" them in a parallel to the Old Testament ceremonial sense—and this person, by associating with the congregation, was also "sanctified" in that sense: He or she had the privilege of coming before God in worship.[90] But then deliberate, continual sin, by which the person has "spurned the Son of God" and "outraged the Spirit of grace" (10:29), in spite of this great privilege, will certainly result in "a fearful prospect of judgment" (10:27).[91]

As he did in 6:4–12, the author follows his severe warning with a contrasting passage in which he comforts the readers with a reassurance that he does not think they are among those who will fall away. He reminds them that

89. In this context of congregational worship, there is a parallel to the action of Moses in throwing "the blood of the covenant" (Exod. 24:8) on the whole congregation to seal the covenant to them, even though certainly there were unbelievers in the congregation: all could stand in the congregation assembled before the Lord.

90. Regarding *hagiazō* in Hebrews 10:29, A. H. Strong, *Systematic Theology* (Valley Forge, Penn.: Judson, 1907), 884, says it refers to "external sanctification, like that of the ancient Israelites, by outward connection with God's people." Peterson says, "In view of the contrast here between Old and New Covenants, I take 'sanctified' here to mean set apart covenantally as belonging to God" ("Apostasy," 25).

91. There is an entirely different understanding of the phrase *by which he was sanctified* in 10:29 that should be mentioned at this point. Against the Old Testament background in which *hagiazō* meant "to make fit to come before God," the phrase may refer not to the deliberate sinner but to Christ: "How much worse punishment do you think will be deserved by the man who has spurned the Son of God, and profaned the blood of the covenant by which he [Christ] was sanctified, and outraged the Spirit of grace?" Grammatically, *en hō hēgiasthē* could just as easily refer to "the Son of God" in the previous phrase. Though Hebrews does not elsewhere say that Christ was "sanctified," Jesus does say this about himself in John 17:19 ("for their sake I consecrate [*hagiazō*] myself"). Conceptually, the author does speak of Christ elsewhere as being "made perfect" (2:10; 5:9), and speaks of his blood as the means through which he entered the Holy Place in heaven (9:12). This interpretation is favored by Nicole, "Some Comments," 356 n. 1, following Owen. Although I have not adopted this interpretation, it is certainly possible, and deserves further consideration. Another possibility is to understand "profaned the blood of the covenant" to mean that this person falsely took the blood of the communion cup, thus profaning it (so Hughes, *Hebrews*, 423). Yet another possibility is to translate *en hō hēgiasthē* impersonally, "by which *one* is sanctified" (mentioned but not adopted by McKnight, "Warning Passages," 43 n. 80).

they have endured in the face of persecution (10:32–34), encourages them to persevere (10:35–38), and then concludes, "But we are not of those who shrink back and are destroyed, but of those who have faith and keep their souls." He follows a consistent pattern in the epistle, indicating that he knows of only two categories of people: (1) those who do not have faith and fall away ("shrink back") and (2) those who believe ("have faith") and persevere. He knows of no third category (those who have faith and then fall away). Once again, then, this concluding passage (10:32–39) supports the idea that those who fell away in the preceding warning passage (10:26–31) were never part of those who "have faith" in the first place. We conclude that there is no decisive consideration in Hebrews 10:26–31 to make us think that it refers to someone who was genuinely saved. It refers rather to someone who heard and understood the gospel, and joined in worship before God with the assembly of Christians, but who rejected this great privilege and therefore became liable to "a fearful prospect of judgment" (10:27).

Hebrews 12:25

Here the author gives a final warning:

> See that you do not refuse him who is speaking. For if they did not escape when they refused him who warned them on earth, much less shall we escape *if we reject him who warns from heaven.*

No new issues arise in this warning text, but once again we should notice that the warning is against *rejecting the message that has been heard.* This is the same warning that he has issued throughout the epistle (2:1; 3:7–8, 15; 4:1–2; 6:4–5; 10:26). Those who are in danger of falling away are those who have heard and understood the message, and have associated with the congregation of believers, but have given no clear indication of their response or their internal spiritual state. But neither in this nor in any of the other warning passages do we find indications that true Christians can lose their salvation.

Comparison with Related Passages in the Rest of the New Testament

To this point I have not brought into the discussion any considerations from the doctrinal teachings in the rest of Scripture on the perseverance of the saints. But the question we are investigating is ultimately a theological one, and therefore, for Christians who think that the whole Bible is our absolute authority in doctrine, it is necessary at some point to compare the exegetical conclusions on 6:4–6 and the other warning passages with the teachings of the rest of Scripture (which really forms the larger "context" in which any passage appears). Far from being inappropriate, I think this procedure is necessary for right exegesis in general, and especially for exegesis that attempts to contribute to understanding doctrinal questions. John Owen observed this long ago: "And so usually doth it fall out, very unhappily, with men who think they see some peculiar opinion or persuasion in some *singular text* of Scripture, and will not bring their interpretations of it unto the analogy of faith, whereby they might see how contrary it is to the whole design and current of the word in other places."[92]

In fact, the idea that we should not attempt to find exegetical conclusions that are consistent with the teachings of other passages is an artificial restriction that none of the original readers faced, for they all had knowledge of the Old Testament and of the apostolic teaching that they had received (which was consistent with the content of our New Testament), and that knowledge influenced their understanding of each epistle they read.

I will not discuss the substantial weight of biblical evidence that teaches that genuine Christians cannot lose their salvation. I have argued this at length elsewhere,[93] as have many others. But it must be said that those who take the view that 6:4–6 describes genuine Christians who lost their salvation have an obligation not only to give a reasonable explanation of 6:4–6, but also of those other passages which repeatedly teach that true Christians will certainly persevere (for example, John 6:38–40; 10:27–29; Rom. 8:1, 30; Eph. 1:13–14; 4:30; Phil. 1:6; 1 Pet. 1:5; and passages on eternal life: John 3:36; 5:24; 6:4–7; 10:28; 1 John 5:13).[94]

92. Owen, *Hebrews*, 3:69. For Owen, the "analogy of faith" meant a comparison of one's conclusions on one passage with the teaching of other related passages in Scripture.

93. See Grudem, *Systematic Theology*, chap. 40; also *The First Epistle of Peter*, TNTC (Grand Rapids: Eerdmans, 1988), 58–59.

94. McKnight criticizes Nicole because, regarding the meaning of "repentance" in Hebrews 6:6, he says Nicole "prefers an explanation that is extremely difficult (and I would say 'impossible') over giving up his theological position! This is a confession of eisegesis, not responsible exegesis" (52).

The problem is not as simple as McKnight claims: Nicole has given thirteen other verses from the New Testament that provide strong support for the idea that Christians cannot lose their salvation, and he says that these verses "constitute only a fraction of the scriptural support for perseverance" (358). McKnight, however, gives no alternative explanation for these verses. From Nicole's perspective (and mine), the exegetical difficulties involved in denying that these other verses teach perseverance would be far greater than the exegetical difficulties of saying that *metanoia* in Hebrews 6:6 need not mean saving repentance. McKnight presents Nicole's method as a question of theology versus exegesis, but it is really a question of exegesis against exegesis. In order to solve a theological problem (which is part of Nicole's purpose, and McKnight's), at some point every Christian must attempt to formulate a synthesis in which all relevant biblical passages are understood in a way that yields a consistent formulation. With respect to this difficult doctrine of perseverance, Nicole has made a significant attempt at such synthesis, while McKnight has not made such an attempt; therefore it seems to me that his criticism of Nicole in this regard is unduly severe.

But is our basic claim that 6:4–6 describes unsaved people consistent with other passages in the New Testament? Does the New Testament speak elsewhere of people who had heard and agreed with the gospel, and had associated with the church, but never had been truly converted? It does in a number of places. For example, Jesus speaks of people who give an initial impression of faith but then fall away:

> And these in like manner are the ones sown upon rocky ground, who, when they *hear the word,* immediately *receive it with joy;* and they have no root in themselves, but *endure for a while;* then, when tribulation or persecution arises on account of the word, immediately they fall away. (Mark 4:16–17)

They "hear the word" (they are enlightened) and they respond with joy (this is at least tasting the heavenly gift and the goodness of the word of God). But they were never truly saved, for Jesus says, "they have no root in themselves." They fall away and are lost.

As for becoming "partakers of the Holy Spirit," Jesus also speaks of those who so strongly resist the conviction of the Holy Spirit that they commit blasphemy against him: "And whoever says a word against the Son of man will be forgiven; but whoever speaks against the Holy Spirit will not be forgiven, either in this age or in the age to come" (Matt. 12:32). And the people who say on the last day, "Lord, Lord, did we not prophesy in your name, and cast out demons in your name, and do many mighty works in your name?" (Matt. 7:22) were never born again, for Jesus says to them, "I never knew you; depart from me, you evildoers" (v. 23). (Note that he does not say to them, "I knew you once but now I do not know you," but rather, "I never knew you.")

Similarly, Stephen says to the unbelieving Jews, "you always resist the Holy Spirit" (Acts 7:51). There was a convicting work of the Holy Spirit that they experienced (we might say they tasted it, or became partakers in it), but they stubbornly rejected it.

John also writes of people who associated for a time with the church, but their falling away demonstrated that they never were truly part of the community of believers: "They went out from us, but they were not of us; for if they had been of us, they would have continued with us; but they went out, that it might be plain that they all are not of us" (1 John 2:19).

When we put together the testimony of these verses, we realize that there are people who have genuine spiritual experiences that are at least as strong as those mentioned in Hebrews 6:4–6, but who have never truly experienced salvation. Therefore our interpretation of 6:4–6 does not make it a unique or unusual passage in the New Testament generally, but one that fits well with other sections of the New Testament.

Conclusions for the Doctrine of Perseverance of the Saints

The Book of Hebrews contributes helpfully to the traditional Reformed doctrine of the perseverance of the saints. It certainly does not contradict it. The doctrine of the perseverance of the saints teaches that all those who are truly born again will be kept by God's power and will persevere as Christians until the end of their lives, and also that only those who persevere until the end are truly born again. The first half of the doctrine is taught frequently in Hebrews, as Nicole has so eloquently affirmed with reference to many passages on God's faithfulness, Christ's redemptive work, and the status of believers,[95] but that has not been our focus in this study. The second half of the doctrine is affirmed quite directly in 3:14, but it is also reinforced by the author's frequent exhortations to continue in faith, to press on to maturity, and not to fall away. In fact, Reformed Christians, in studying Hebrews, would do well to recognize that such strong moral exhortations to press on and not fall away are consistent with a belief in God's sovereign power to keep his own children safe for eternity, for God's sovereignty often works through human means such as warnings and exhortations: These warnings will often be the very means God uses to keep his own from turning away. This does not imply that a true believer could lose salvation, but it does imply that the impossibility of losing salvation does not rest ultimately in any inherent ability in the believer himself or herself, but in the power of God at work, usually in many different internal and external ways, in the believer's life.

---

95. See especially Nicole, "Some Comments," 359; see also note 71.

7

The Meaning of Foreknowledge

S. M. BAUGH

In the past, Calvinists and Arminians have agreed that God's knowledge is "eternal, immutable, and infinite."[1] But this tenet is an Achilles' heel for Arminianism. If God infallibly foreknows the free choices of humans, then these choices must be certain in a way that excludes the Arminian (libertarian) conception of free will. Let us say that God knows from eternity that Jones will choose soup from next Tuesday's lunch menu; how can Jones choose salad instead? If he does, God would have been mistaken. If God's knowledge is certain, Jones's choice of soup is somehow inevitable. "And if the future is inevitable, then the apparent experience of free choice is an illusion."[2]

Arminian theologians have responded in different ways to this conundrum. Arminius himself simply admitted the problem and chose to live with it.[3] Others admit that God's foreknowledge makes human decisions "in

1. Jacobus Arminius, "A Discussion on the Subject of Predestination," in *The Writings of James Arminius,* trans. James Nichols and W. R. Bagnall, 3 vols. (Grand Rapids: Baker, 1956), 3:66. On the Calvinist side: "His knowledge is infinite, infallible, and independent upon the creature, so as nothing is to Him contingent, or uncertain." Westminster Confession of Faith, 2.2.

2. Richard Rice, "Divine Foreknowledge and Free-Will Theism," in *The Grace of God, the Will of Man: A Case for Arminianism,* ed. Clark H. Pinnock (Grand Rapids: Zondervan, 1989), 127.

3. "But I do not understand the mode in which He knows future contingencies, and especially those which belong to the free-will of creatures." Arminius, "Discussion," 3:66. But see page 67, where he proposes a (temporal?) sequence in God's knowledge.

some sense certain," but fail to grapple further with the implications of this admission;[4] some settle for the notion of middle knowledge;[5] others ignore the problem.[6]

But more recent writers, wrestling specifically with this contradiction within Arminianism, have adopted a position that moves them beyond the boundaries of classic Arminianism, indeed, of Christianity. Clark H. Pinnock, for example, describes how his own thinking began to shift when he grasped divine omniscience's threat to a supposed human autonomy of will.[7] Since, for him, libertarian freedom is "one of the deepest of all human intuitions,"[8] and therefore a nonnegotiable truth more important to him than God's omniscience, he was moved to conclude:

> Decisions not yet made do not exist anywhere to be known even by God. They are potential—yet to be realized but not yet actual. God can predict a great deal of what we will choose to do, but not all of it, because some of it remains hidden in the mystery of human freedom. . . . The God of the Bible displays an openness to the future (i.e., ignorance of the future) that the traditional view of omniscience simply cannot accommodate.[9]

Pinnock, the Seventh-day Adventist theologian Richard Rice,[10] and others in evangelical circles[11] are following process theology in this outright denial

---

4. Jack W. Cottrell, *What the Bible Says about God the Ruler* (Joplin, Mo.: College Press, 1984), 225; H. Orton Wiley, *Christian Theology* (Kansas City: Beacon Hill, 1959), 1:354–57.

5. Cf. William Lane Craig, *Divine Foreknowledge and Human Freedom,* Brill's Studies in Intellectual History, 19 (Leiden: Brill, 1991).

6. "Whether God has actively foreknown each individual—both the elect and the reprobate—may remain a moot question." Robert Shank, *Elect in the Son: A Study of the Doctrine of Election* (Minneapolis: Bethany House, 1970), 155.

7. Pinnock, "From Augustine to Arminius: A Pilgrimage in Theology," in *Grace of God,* 25.

8. Clark H. Pinnock, "Responsible Freedom and the Flow of Biblical History," in *Grace Unlimited,* ed. Clark H. Pinnock (Minneapolis: Bethany Fellowship, 1975), 95.

9. Pinnock, "Augustine to Arminius," 25–26.

10. "Not even God knows the future in all its details. Some parts remain indefinite until they actually occur, and so they can't be known in advance." Richard Rice, *God's Foreknowledge and Man's Free Will* (Minneapolis: Bethany House, 1980), 10.

11. For example, Frederick Sontag: "To know all in nature and in human action that is possible is of course to know certain tendencies toward actualization, certain odds (as Las Vegas would say) for various actualizations to result. God is not startled and is never struck dumb as the future unfolds, but an element of surprise embraces the divine knowledge just as it does ours even when we think our predictive powers are at their height. Were you a god, would you not find it dull to fix the future irrevocably from eternity?" ("Does Omnipotence Necessarily Entail Omniscience?" *JETS* 34 [December 1991]: 508). Sontag has adopted other debatable positions such as an implied neutering of God in his careful avoidance of the masculine pronoun for God ("just as *deity* had to know every option open to *it* . . ."), and, elsewhere, a nonbiblical view on homosexuality ("God cannot be seen as utterly opposed to this [homosexuality] . . ." Sontag, "Barth, Romans and Feminist Theology," *EQ* 68 [October 1991]: 313–29; see 321). Has the term *evangelical* been stretched beyond all definition?

of divine foreknowledge.[12] And, although Pinnock and Rice herald their view as a new insight specially fitted for our day, they certainly must know (as does process theologian Charles Hartshorne) that this view is nothing other than the hallmark doctrine of the old Socinian heresy, the forerunner of modern Unitarianism.[13] Hence Pinnock and Rice are accurately labeled neo-Socinian in regards to foreknowledge.[14]

In this chapter, we will focus on some of the key New Testament passages that specifically bear on God's foreknowledge. But first, we will sketch the Old Testament and Greco-Roman background relating to the issue.

Old Testament Background

In the Old Testament, there was no question that God's knowledge is vast, outnumbering the sand and the stars (Ps. 139:18), for "great is our Lord, and abundant in strength; his insight cannot be measured!" (Ps. 147:5).[15] There is an intimacy about God's knowledge: it reaches even to people's thoughts (Ps. 139:2) and to the motives of the heart (Prov. 16:2; Isa. 66:18).

The most extended teaching on God's foreknowledge is in Isaiah, where God argues that knowledge of future human history marks him as the true God. To the idols, God throws down this gauntlet: "Declare future events that we may know that you are gods" (Isa. 41:23). But they cannot, for they are "nothings," mere blocks of wood (Isa. 41:20–29; 42:9; 44:7, 25; 45:21).

Included in God's prescience is Cyrus's restoration of Israel from captivity (Isa. 44:24–45:13; cf. Ezra 1:1–4). But how can this be? How can God know the future free actions of a human? Whatever answer is given must take into account God's sovereignty: "The king's heart is in the hand of Yahweh; he directs it like a canal wherever he pleases" (Prov. 21:1);[16] and, "The mind of man plans his way, but Yahweh directs his steps" (Prov. 16:9; cf. Ps. 33:10; Dan. 4:35). Yahweh is Cyrus's Maker, his Potter. And as such, he directs

---

12. Compare, for example: "In each moment of God's life there are new, unforeseen happenings in the world which only then have become knowable. Hence, God's concrete knowledge is dependent upon the decisions made by the worldly actualities." John B. Cobb Jr. and David Roy Griffin, *Process Theology: An Introductory Exposition* (Philadelphia: Westminster, 1976), 47. Cf. Charles Hartshorne, *Omnipotence and Other Theological Mistakes* (Albany: State University of New York, 1984), 26–27, 38–39.

13. See Faustus Socinus, "Praelectiones Theologicae," in *Omnia Opera*, vol. 1 (Irenopolis, 1656), chaps. 10–11; Francis Turretin, *Institutes of Elenctic Theology*, vol. 1 (Phillipsburg, N. J.: Presbyterian and Reformed, 1992), 208–12; and Hartshorne, *Omnipotence*, 27, 38–39. On the connection between Unitarianism and Socinianism see E. M. Wilbur, *A History of Unitarianism: Socinianism and Its Antecedents* (Cambridge: Harvard University Press, 1945).

14. This point was made to both Pinnock and Rice in public debate by Robert B. Strimple; see Strimple, "God's Sovereignty and Man's Free Will: How 'New' Is 'New Model' Evangelicalism?" *Modern Reformation* (January/February 1993): 8–13.

15. Unless otherwise indicated, all translations are the author's.

16. For examples, see 2 Kings 19:25–28 and Acts 4:27–28.

S. M. Baugh

Cyrus's decisions to his own good ends. This is God's right: "Will the clay say to its Potter, 'What are you doing?'" (Isa. 45:9; cf. Rom. 9:20–21).

Another remarkable example of divine foreknowledge is expressed in Jeremiah 1:5, where God says to Jeremiah:

I knew[17] you before I formed you in the womb,
I consecrated you before you emerged from the womb;
I have given you as prophet to the nations.

The first two lines are closely parallel in the number of syllables and word order, but there is a subtle development here, as is usual with Hebrew poetic parallelism.[18] The first line speaks of God's knowledge of Jeremiah before his conception in the womb, whereas the second line moves forward to a point after Jermiah's conception, but still prior to his birth. Jeremiah was "known" before conception, but "consecrated" to be a prophet as a preborn infant. Then as a young man he was "given" as a prophet to the nations.

But how can God have known Jeremiah before he was even conceived? Because he personally fashioned his prophet, just as he had fashioned Adam from the dust (Gen. 2:7), and just as he fashions all people (Ps. 139:13–16; Isa. 44:24). God foreknew not only the possibility of Jeremiah's existence—he knows all possibilities indeed—but God foreknew Jeremiah by name before he was conceived, because he knew how he would shape and mold his existence.

Given this Old Testament background, we can understand why in the New Testament we have no extended discussion on the nature of God's foreknowledge. There was no need. God's knowledge is vast and perfect; nothing is hid from his eyes, past, present, or future.

But what about the Greeks and Romans in New Testament times? Not all of them read the Old Testament, so one might expect some New Testament discussion on foreknowledge for their sake. In answer, let us digress briefly to demonstrate that God's foreknowledge is one of the unseen, divine attributes God has made clear to all (Rom. 1:19–20).

Foreknowledge in Greco-Roman Antiquity

From earliest times, Greek and Roman poets and philosophers agreed that the gods had full omniscience that included foreknowledge of human affairs. One

17. As I will mention, some authorities propose the translation *I chose* in place of "I knew" (NIVmg).
18. Cf. James L. Kugel, *The Idea of Biblical Poetry: Parallelism and Its History* (New Haven and London: Yale University Press, 1981), 50–54.

186

of the earliest witnesses is Homer—whose *Iliad* and *Odyssey* were the closest things the pagans had to a Bible—who says, "The gods know everything."[19] Except for a few extreme skeptics,[20] all were convinced that *ignoratio rerum aliena naturae deorum est* (ignorance is foreign to the nature of the gods),[21] and *obscurum deo nihil potest esse* (nothing can be hidden to god).[22]

As a result of this divine knowledge, ordinary humans could acquire foreknowledge of future events through diviners of sundry sorts,[23] astrologers,[24] or prophets connected to various shrines.[25] The innate qualities of certain holy men or philosophers could also give them prescience of future events.[26] Hence in Acts 16:16, the slave girl who had "a spirit of divination"[27] would have been viewed as part of the ordinary course of affairs at that time.[28] Divine foreknowledge was so certain in the mind of some pagan thinkers that its communication through divination and other means was itself used as a main proof for the existence of the gods.[29]

New Testament Passages

When we turn to the New Testament, we can now appreciate why no New Testament author felt compelled to expand upon God's foreknowledge or omniscience; it was already quite clear from the Old Testament and general

19. *Odyssey* 4.379 and 468.
20. E.g., Carneades in Cicero *De fato* 14.33.
21. Balbus in Cicero *De natura deorum* 2.30.
22. Cotto in Cicero *De natura deorum* 3.15; cf. Cicero's statement in *De divinitatione* (1.38) to the effect that the gods *possunt futura praenoscere* (can foreknow the future).
23. E.g., Calchas son of Thestor, "the best of diviners who knew present and future events before they happened" (*Iliad* 1.69–70). Cf. Cicero's lengthy *De divinitatione*. The Romans *haruspeces, augures,* and *auspices* foretold the future through examination of sacrificial victims or portents. Cf. Acts 13:6.
24. E.g., Nero's court astrologer, Tiberius Claudius Balbillus (Suetonius *Nero* 36).
25. The most famous was the oracle of Apollo at Delphi (see, for example, Plutarch *De Pythiae oraculis* or *De defectu oraculorum* in his *Moralia*). An inscription from Ephesus mentions its temple "of the oracular Apollo of our city," making local consultations with the god about the future possible (*IEph.* 1024; A.D. 104).
26. See the discussion on foreknowledge between Apollonius of Tyana and Indian Brahmans in Philostratus *Vita Apollonius* 3.42–44; cf. Plutarch *De defectu oracularum*, 431e, on foreknowledge by any human soul, especially as death approached.
27. Luke uses an usual word for "divination" here (*python*, snake), possibly alluding to the Delphic oracle whose priestess was known as the Pythia. Such spirit contact in fortune-telling and prescience was commonly understood in antiquity; cf. Plutarch (*De Pythiae oraculus* 417A–B) and Socrates' well known personal *daemon* (Plato *Apologia* 31c–d).
28. "The mantic arts, ranging from technical divination to inspired divination, were an integral feature of the social and religious life of the Greeks during the entire Greco-Roman period." David E. Aune, *Prophecy in Early Christianity and the Ancient Mediterranean World* (Grand Rapids: Eerdmans, 1983), 47.
29. Cicero *De natura deorum* 2.3–4.

revelation.[30] Thus Jesus saw no need to elaborate when he remarked that God's knowledge embraces each bird, even the hairs on our head (Matt. 10:29–31), or that God foreknows our needs before we ask (Matt. 6:8).

Nevertheless, there are New Testament statements that mention foreknowledge and have implications for our understanding of it. In the Greek, the verb *to foreknow* occurs five times in the New Testament, and the noun *foreknowledge* in two places. Five of these speak of God's foreknowledge (Acts 2:23; Rom. 8:29; 11:2; 1 Pet. 1:2, 20).

We should also mention places in which the words *to foresee* or similar words are used. For instance, Paul says in Galatians: "Now the Scripture, since *it saw beforehand* that God would justify the Gentiles by faith, preached the gospel ahead of time to Abraham, saying: 'All the nations will be blessed in you'" (Gal. 3:8; cf. Rom. 4:23–24). In passing, we should not overlook that for Paul the words of the Bible are the words of God and vice versa. Regarding God's prescience, Paul says that the gospel beatitude was announced beforehand to Abraham on the basis of God's foreknown plan to include the nations in his free grace. For this promise to be certain, God must have foreknown all the events used to bring salvation into effect in Christ, including the free decisions of Judas, Pilate, and others. His prescience must be all-encompassing if his promises are to be trusted—and he is truth itself (John 14:6; 1 John 5:6).

Similarly, "foreseeing" is attributed to David, "since he was a prophet," in that "he saw beforehand and spoke concerning the resurrection of Christ" (Acts 2:29–31; citing Ps. 16). It is not David's powers of prescience that are underlined, but the foreknowledge of "the Spirit of Christ" who spoke through the Old Testament prophetic "pre-witness" concerning Christ (1 Pet. 1:10–12).

These passages teach God's extensive knowledge of the future in a general way. But in other places a more specific and personal content of God's foreknowledge can be discerned.

Foreknowledge in Acts 2:23

At the beginning of Peter's Pentecost sermon he says: "You nailed up and killed this man through the agency of wicked men, who was delivered over by God's fixed purpose and foreknowledge."

We should begin by observing that the object of God's foreknowledge in Acts 2:23 is primarily his own action: his "delivering over" of Christ. God had an active role in Christ's death in that "he did not spare his own Son . . .

---

30. God's foreknowledge and sovereign control of history was also taught at Qumran: "From the God of knowledge is all the present and future, and before they came to pass he prepared all their design" ("Community Rule," 1QS 3.15; cf. 11.11, 17–20).

but delivered him over on behalf of us all" (Rom. 8:32). Peter clearly says that God knew ahead of time that he would allow Christ to be killed (cf. John 10:17–18), and Peter reinforces the point by citing David's witness to the whole affair in various psalms: "since he was a prophet . . . he foresaw . . ." (Acts 2:29–31). Christ's death did not take God by surprise.

Furthermore, God also foreknew the free decisions of Christ's murderers: "You killed this man." God had no doubt that there would be people willing to crucify Christ, evidenced, for example, in Psalm 22. Why then did they choose to kill him? The biblical witness is united in pointing to God's predestined initiative in their actions: "Herod and Pontius Pilate . . . have assembled . . . to accomplish whatsoever your hand and purpose predestined to occur" (Acts 4:27–28); "The Son of Man is about to depart in accordance with what has been determined" (Luke 22:22); "He must . . . be killed" (Matt. 16:21) in accordance with prophecy (Luke 24:46; Acts 3:18); and so on.

The way Peter expresses God's resolve in Acts 2:23 is with the word *boulē*, "purpose." This word has a range of meanings revolving around the act of deliberation over a matter.[31] When used of God, *boulē* frequently refers to his purpose foreordained to accomplish his planned redemption (Acts 4:28), which was carried forward in earlier generations by saints such as David (Acts 13:36). It is explicitly something that results from his will (Eph. 1:11), and by putting himself under oath, God has demonstrated that this purpose is unchangeable (Heb. 6:17; cf. Luke 1:72–73; Isa. 55:11).

We can take the phrase *fixed purpose* in Acts 2:23 to refer to God's determined resolve to hand his Son over that he might save his people. This is especially clear because of the modifying participle (*hōrismenē*), translated "fixed," which communicates in this form something settled or determined (cf. Luke 22:22).[32] God was determined to accomplish his purpose, and it was thereby certain to occur.

And we can conclusively infer from Peter's remark that Christ "was delivered over by God's fixed purpose and foreknowledge," that God had clear prescience of all that surrounded Christ's death, not through mere foresight of decisions beyond his control, but because he had determined to bring it about. God's foreknowledge is joined to his will. This is further confirmed as the only legitimate interpretation of Acts 2:23 when we appreciate the sensitive use of the Greek article in the phrase *God's fixed purpose and fore-*

---

31. "Deliberation" (1 Cor. 4:5); the product of deliberation, a "decision," or a "plan" developed to meet a specific problem (Acts 27:12, 42; Luke 23:51); when used of God, his standing "advice" or "counsel" that one is obliged to follow (Luke 7:30; Acts 5:38; 20:27), found also at Qumran: "united with the counsel of God" (1QS 1.8) expressing entrance into the covenant. Cf. *TDNT*, 1:633–36.

32. The same verb with the prefix (*pro-*, fore- or pre-) is the term translated "pre*destine*" or "fore*ordain*" (e.g., Acts 4:28).

knowledge. By using one article for the two nouns *purpose* and *foreknowledge*, Peter is expressing a close interconnection between the two.[33] God's foreknowledge of the events of Christ's death included his planning and willing them to occur.

Hence the certainty of God's knowledge of the event was conditioned not because he merely observed the "pure contingency" of the human decisions involved. It was certain and foreknown because God had determined to accomplish it:

> I am God, there is none like me. I declare the outcome from the beginning and from antiquity things which have not yet been done, saying, "My purpose will be established, and I will do all my good pleasure." (Isa. 46:9–10)

Only Calvinism accounts for the biblical union of God's foreknowledge and will: "But as God sees things possible in the glass of his own power, so he sees things future in the glass of his own will."[34]

Acts 2:23 also implies another truth integral to Calvinism that must not be (and is too often) overlooked: Humans possess genuine, unforced volition[35] and are thereby morally responsible. Although God accomplished his fixed purpose by handing Christ over to the cross, he himself did not crucify him: "You nailed up and killed this man through the agency of wicked men." Peter's hearers and their agents were both the culpable participants in Christ's death. God ordains all that comes to pass, but "neither is God the author of sin, nor is violence offered to the will of the creatures; nor is the liberty or contingency of second causes taken away, but rather established."[36]

Foreknowledge in Romans 8:29

When we turn to Romans, we encounter another aspect of God's foreknowledge:

> . . . God blends all things for good on behalf of those who are called according to his plan. For those whom he foreknew, he also predestined for conformity

33. Called "hendiadys." Frederic Godet failed to appreciate the Greek idiom when he said that "foreknowledge is expressly distinguished from the *fixed decree*," in Acts 2:23 (*Commentary on Romans* [reprint; Grand Rapids: Kregel, 1977], 325). In point of fact, the two nouns are expressly united.

34. Stephen Charnock, *The Existence and Attributes of God* (reprint; Ann Arbor: Puritan Book Club, 1958), 205. Cf. John Calvin, *Institutes*, 3.23.6; Louis Berkhof, *Systematic Theology* (Grand Rapids: Eerdmans, 1939), 67–68.

35. "Natural liberty" in the historic Westminster Confession of Faith, chap. 9, "Of Free-Will."

36. Westminster Confession of Faith 3.1. Cf. Charnock, *Existence and Attributes*, 219; Berkhof, *Systematic Theology*, 67–68.

to the image of his Son, so that he might be the Firstborn among many brothers. (Rom. 8:28–29)

Precognition of historical events through divine and human actions is that which was foreknown in Acts 2:23. But in Romans 8:29, the objects of God's foreknowledge are personal, so we must ask whether there is a different meaning for "foreknow" than intellectual precognition.

Put another way, we could ask, "Whom does God not foreknow cognitively?" The answer is no one, but in Romans 8:29 Paul says specifically that the objects of God's foreknowledge were predestined for salvation. For this reason, interpreters limit the verb *proginōskō* (I foreknow) to certain people in Romans 8:29, and two main lines of interpretation result.

The first interpretation is the classic Arminian (et al.) notion that God foreknows the faith of certain individuals whose decision to believe arises solely from their libertarian will, and God predestines them on the basis of this foreseen faith *(praescientia fidei)*.[37] The other interpretation takes the verb *he foreknew* to refer to some activity more personal than intellectual precognition of faith or anything else in the believer. Instead, they render *proginōskō* as "he chose," "he loved," "he predestinated," and related terms.[38]

The latter interpretation is advanced in the great majority of reference works[39] and by almost all commentators on Romans.[40] Nevertheless, some Arminians still complain that this is "an arbitrary definition" defended by those who are trying "to avoid the clear (Arminian) implications of God's foreknowledge,"[41] so we should examine the matter briefly.

One way to hone one's understanding of a word is to contrast it with its antonym. That "he foreknew" in Romans 8:29 cannot refer to mere intellectual apprehension is demonstrated by use of negation: "Those of whom God was not previously cognizant are the ones he did not predestine . . ." This is

37. E.g., Godet, *Commentary,* 325; Cottrell, "Conditional Election," 58–59. But compare Arminius himself: "Hence he is not in error who says that foreknowledge or prescience of faith in Christ is signified in Romans viii, 29, unless he adds the assertion that the faith, referred to, results from our own strength and is not produced in us by the free gift of God. . . . For He foreknew that they would believe by His own gift, which decree was prepared by Predestination." *Writings,* 3:315–16.

38. "(Whom he foreknew) expressed the loving appropriation, or adoption, of the person by God." Francis Pieper, *Christian Dogmatics* (Saint Louis: Concordia, 1953), 3:489. Pieper's discussion of the vocabulary and issues (485–90) is an especially thorough and perceptive one from a classic Lutheran perspective.

39. BAGD; *TDNT,* 1:698; *NIDNTT,* 1:693, Louw and Nida, 30.100.

40. Althaus, Barrett, Black, Bruce, Cranfield, Dunn, Käsemann, Leenhardt, Morris (almost reluctantly), Murray, and many earlier scholars.

41. Cottrell, "Conditional Election," 71 n. 21. Cf. Godet, *Commentary,* 324. Popular treatments by Roger T. Forster and V. Paul Marston (*God's Strategy in Human History* [Wheaton: Tyndale House, 1973], 178–208) and Roy Elseth (*Did God Know?* [St. Paul: Calvary United Church, 1977], 55–61) go to some lengths to oppose "foreknow" as implying God's choice.

clearly not the corollary of what Paul does say. Was it through God's ignorance of them that some people were not predestined to glory?

Nevertheless, it seems redundant to say that *proginōskō* means "chose" or "predestine" in Romans 8:29, since these ideas are already clearly stated otherwise in the passage. And if "foreknow" means "forelove," Paul could conceivably have conveyed this by saying, "Those whom he loved he also predestined."

What then does *proginōskō* mean in Romans 8:29? First, it does have a different meaning here than in other places in the New Testament (Acts 26:5; 2 Pet. 3:17), since the knower or the objects of knowledge are different. Secondly, we can legitimately understand the meaning of *proginōskō*, "I foreknow," by studying the verb without the prefix *pro-*, "fore-." This prefix merely indicates temporal priority, much like *proeuangelizomai*, "preach the gospel earlier"; *promerimnaō*, "worry beforehand" without substantially altering the meaning of *ginōskō*, "I know."

The simple verb *ginōskō* was used by the Greeks for cognition, acknowledgment, perception, or related intellectual states, and rarely with a person as the object of knowledge. Discrimination ("choose") or affection ("love") are not attested connotations for this word in nonbiblical Greek. Instead, as is frequently pointed out, we should look to the Hebrew equivalent, *yadaʿ*, for this sort of meaning for *ginōskō* in Romans 8:29.

Many Old Testament texts demonstrate how "I know" in Hebrew has a more personal connotation than mere cognition when the object of the verb is personal (e.g., Gen. 18:19; Exod. 33:17; 1 Sam. 2:12; Ps. 18:43; Prov. 9:10; Hos. 13:5). This was recognized as early as the fourth century by a Greek Father.[42]

One of the most unambiguous examples of this personal use of Hebrew "I know" is from Amos: "Only you, of all the families of the world, have I known, for this reason I will visit all your transgressions upon you" (Amos 3:2). Notice most importantly that God's knowledge of Israel is specifically given as the reason for their impending judgment. Such knowledge is not mere cognition. Even Socinians grant that God has the profoundest understanding of everyone and everything present (in their view, he is ignorant of future things). Yet here God's knowledge serves to distinguish Israel from all other equally guilty people. Hence some translate: "You only have I chosen . . ." (NIV).[43]

42. Didymus the Blind (b. A.D. 313), commenting on Psalm 18:43 (17:44 LXX), distinguishes *epistamai* (more consistently intellectual cognition) from *ginōskō* where the latter can denote "the unification and intermixing of the knower with the thing known" (*Commentary on the Psalms*, Migne 39.1264b–c). My thanks to Lee Irons for the reference and the translation.

43. "You only have Me among all the families of the earth" (NASB), seems to be altogether off-target. However, recent versions of the New American Standard Bible translate "You only have I chosen."

If we take the phrase in Amos 3:2 as "For you alone have I cared . . ." (NEB), we get closer to the concept communicated by *yāda*ᶜ, but it is not quite right. God's love and compassion lead him not to judge his people as in Amos 3:2, but to forgive them (Exod. 34:7)!

Clearly the verb in Amos 3:2 has to do with a personal relationship, illustrated in the next verse by an appointment or agreement between two travelers. I propose that we read *yāda*ᶜ here and elsewhere against the specific background of the covenantal relationship between God and people. And the covenantal notion implies, among other things, a commitment.

Israel was in covenant with God, and by breaking the Mosaic covenant they had incurred the stipulated judgments of the law (Lev. 26:14–39; Deut. 28:15–68; cf. Amos 2:4–5). God had known Israel as a people bound to him in covenant, and this special relation had made them more culpable for their iniquities. It is even possible that "to know" had a technical usage in comparable covenants (treaties) between suzerains and vassals in the ancient Near East.[44]

We can find many Old Testament examples in which covenantal commitment is expressed as "knowledge,"[45] but the clearest instance is in Daniel 11:32. In a grammatical and semantic parallel set, "covenant-breakers"[46] and "those who forsake the holy covenant" (v. 30) are contrasted with "those who know their God." "To know God" is the equivalent of "to keep, or not violate, God's covenant" here.

This is not to say that "to know" necessarily connotes or carries with it a covenantal idea everywhere it is used. Rather it would be best to say that the phrase *God knows us* expresses a relationship of commitment. And covenant is the oath-bound commitment that God has with his people: "To remember his holy *covenant*, namely, the oath he swore to Abraham" (Luke 1:72–73). This is also not to say that cognition is absent in such a personal relation, but that "to know" a person in this sense includes more than apprehension of data about a person.[47]

It only remains to demonstrate that this relational aspect of *yāda*ᶜ is carried over by New Testament writers in their use of the Greek equivalent, *gi-*

---

44. "The most obvious technical use of 'know' is that with reference to mutual recognition on the part of suzerain and vassal." H. Huffman, "The Treaty Background of Hebrew YADA'," *BASOR* 181 (February 1966): 31. Compare A. Goetze, "Hittite, "*sek-shillsak-*, '(Legally) Recognize' in the Treaties," *JCS* 22 (1968): 7–8. Goetze does not absolutely rule out the connection, though, as Botterweck implies (*TDOT*, 5:478).

45. In Proverbs 9:10, "knowledge of the Most Holy" and its parallel, "the fear of Yahweh," both express religious commitment to God (cf. Jer. 32:40). On the other hand, those who "do not know Yahweh" are covenant-breakers like the sons of Eli (1 Sam. 2:12).

46. *rasha*', "act guiltily against" (Dan. 9:5; 12:10).

47. J. A. Thompson, writing on Jeremiah 1:5, says that *yāda*ᶜ often "reached beyond mere intellectual knowledge to personal commitment." *The Book of Jeremiah*, NICOT (Grand Rapids: Eerdmans, 1980), 145.

nōskō. One clear example is when Jesus reveals his future response to false disciples at the last judgment: "I never knew you, depart from me!" (Matt. 7:23). Clearly, mere intellectual cognition is ruled out as the meaning of "know" here, since it is precisely Jesus' knowledge of their real motives and covenantal status and commitments that leads to their condemnation. Rather, he says that these people never had covenantal relations with him; the Good Shepherd did not know them as his sheep, and they did not know him (John 10:14).

Likewise the connotation of personal commitment fits Galatians 4:8–9. The Galatians were formerly "not acquainted with God"[48] and served idols instead; "but now that you have come to know God—or rather you have become known by him. . . ." The meaning *intellectual cognition* fits the verb in verse 8, but Paul is not saying that at some point God became aware of the Galatians' existence. The point is clearly that God had entered into a committed relation with them in their experience. Such knowledge of God, or rather, his knowing us, means being committed to him, which brings with it certain obligations and dangers (cf. 2 Pet. 2:20; 1 John 2:3–4; 3:1).

The classic Arminian interpretation of Romans 8:29, that God's foreknowledge of faith is in view, is clearly reading one's theology into the text. Paul does not say: "whose faith he foreknew," but "whom he foreknew." He foreknew us. This is not to say that God was ever ignorant of the fact that we would believe. But in Romans 8:29, predestination is not dependent on faith; rather, God predestines us on the basis of his gracious commitment to us before the world was.

Perhaps another rendering better expresses the concept behind Romans 8:29: "Those to whom he was previously devoted. . . ." This, again, is not to say that God's foreknowledge is devoid of intellectual cognition; to have a personal relation with someone, such as a marriage relation, includes knowledge about that person. What is more, we may wish to recall the lesson from Jeremiah 1:5; God has foreknown us because he fashioned each of us personally and intimately according to his plan. He knows far more about us than we ourselves do (Ps. 94:8–11).

That Paul refers to this concept of a committed relationship with the phrase *whom he foreknew* in Romans 8:29 is confirmed by the context. God's eternal foreknowledge, his devotion to his people before all ages, inspires the apostle to conclude with a virtual restatement of that eternal, divine commitment to us in verse 31: "If God is for us, who can be against us?" What better exhibits this divine determination to have us as his people than the fact that he delivered over his own Son on our behalf (Rom. 8:32)?

---

48. The subtle difference between *oida* in verse 8 and *ginōskō* in verse 9 should not be overlooked. *Oida* here means "be acquainted with who someone is," as found outside the New Testament (*Odyssey* 4.551; *Republic* 365e).

Paul emphasizes God's commitment to us because he is the apostle to the Gentiles, to whom was entrusted the revolutionary news that God has now extended his covenant knowledge even to the nations. And this is not some hastily devised new program, but God foreknew these very Gentiles, who are now joined with their Jewish fellow believers into a new covenant community.

Further confirmation of "foreknowledge" in Romans 8:29 as referring to a previous commitment is found in a nearby passage, Romans 11:1–2, where *proginōskō* can have only this meaning: "God has not rejected his people, has he? No way! For I also am an Israelite. . . . God has not rejected his people whom he foreknew." As in Romans 8:29, the objects of foreknowledge are people themselves rather than historical events or a particular person's faith.

And Paul contrasts foreknowledge in Romans 11:1–2 with rejection and the breaking of a prior commitment; the issue is not ignorance versus previous cognition of them, but divorce versus a prior, personal commitment to them. Hence, we can paraphrase the passage:

> God has not totally rejected all Jews, has he? No! As proof, I too am an Israelite, and thus a member of the remnant he still knows. So he has not abandoned his commitment made to Israel with whom he previously had a covenant relation [foreknew] for so long."

The Arminian notion of "foreseen faith" is impossible as an interpretation of God's foreknowledge in Romans 11:1–2, and, consequently, in the earlier passage, Romans 8:29, as well. The latter explains that God initiated a committed relationship from eternity with certain individuals whom he predestined for grace.

Foreknowledge in 1 Peter 1:1–2

The Greek noun *prognōsis* (foreknowledge) occurs in a passage distinctly similar to Romans 8:29. Peter opens his epistle by addressing his readers as the diaspora church, who are "elect people . . . according to the foreknowledge of God the Father, by sanctification of the Spirit, for obedience and sprinkling with the blood of Jesus Christ" (1 Pet. 1:1–2). Note the trinitarian structure of this opening: Father, Spirit, and (Son) Jesus Christ.

One Arminian interpretation of 1 Peter 1:1–2 takes Peter's phrase *elect according to foreknowledge* to mean that God's choice of an individual is predicated upon his foresight of that person's faith. Hence God's choice is reduced to a ratification of the individual's autonomous decision. This is the same line of interpretation that imports foreseen faith as the basis of predestination in Romans 8:29.

If 1 Peter 1:1–2 were an isolated fragment, the only defense against this Arminian interpretation would be by analogy with the correct interpretation of Romans 8:29—which still makes a strong case—and the fact that the Arminian must import faith into the passage as the object of God's foreknowledge. Faith is in view here not as the object of prescience, but as the goal of the Father's foreknowledge and of the Spirit's operation when Peter says "for obedience" to Christ.

But 1 Peter 1:1–2 is not an isolated fragment. In verse 20 of the same chapter, Peter uses the verb *proginōskō* in an important reference to indicate how he conceives of God's foreknowledge. And in this passage, there can be no doubt that the idea of previous commitment is the only possible meaning of foreknowledge:

> You were not redeemed with corruptible things, silver or gold, . . . but with the priceless blood as of an unblemished and spotless lamb, Christ, who was, on the one hand foreknown before the world was created, but was in the last days manifested for your sakes who believe in God through him. . . . (1 Pet. 1:18–21)

Here neither Christ's faith nor any other action or attribute of his is the object of foreknowledge; rather, it was Christ himself foreknown. And just as it was specifically the Father's foreknowledge of us in verse 2, so here it must be the Father who foreknew Christ, because he was foreknown from all eternity. This foreknowledge expresses a loving, committed relationship between the members of the Trinity, and is given in verse 20 to emphasize the precious character of the redeeming blood and its efficacy to bring us to faith. Again, faith is the goal of God's foreknowledge, not its object, source, or basis.

Therefore, we can be confident from 1 Peter 1:1–2, as we were from Romans 8:29, that speaking about God's foreknowledge may be a way of expressing his eternal commitment to individuals as part of his determination to bring them to faith and to all the glories and benefits of Christ's work.[49] God does foresee our faith, but this is not the point in these passages.

To summarize our discussion of the relevant New Testament passages, we saw how reference to God's foreknowledge in Acts 2:23 speaks of his prescience of historic events, but that those events occur precisely because God willed, planned, and predestined them, including all the free human decisions that contributed to their occurrence. In four places in Romans and 1 Peter, we saw that to say that God foreknows persons means not prescience per se, but expresses his previous (in three places eternal), personal commitment to them.

---

49. See commentaries on 1 Peter by Best, Goppelt, Grudem, Kelly, Selwyn, and others for "foreknowledge" as "God's electing predetermination" (Goppelt) or "his fatherly love for his own people" (Grudem).

Arminian and Socinian Answers

In the face of the foregoing biblical evidence, how do the Arminian and neo-Socinian views of God's foreknowledge stand up? I have already reviewed the position and failings of classic Arminianism's interpretation of foreknowledge as prescience of faith in Romans 8:29 and 1 Peter 1:1–2.

But how would an Arminian account for God's foreknowledge of Christ's work in Acts 2:23 or of predictive prophecies such as those about Cyrus in Isaiah? Can their libertarian definition of free will coexist with the infallibility of divine foreknowledge? Evidently not, for Jack Cottrell explains that in cases of prophecy and works of redemption like this, through "subtle manipulation," sometimes "God intervenes in history in a way that violates natural law and even free will if necessary."[50] This answer begs the question loudly and undermines the whole edifice of Arminianism. To say that God occasionally "violates" human nature makes him out to be an unpredictable tyrant (ironically, the very thing mistakenly charged to Calvinism), and we can know nothing of his nature and actions now that the biblical revelation is full of divine eccentricity as assumed. Such whimsy is foreign to God's very being (Mal. 3:6; James 1:17).

Neo-Socinianism, on the other hand, denies God's ability to know historical events or human decisions in advance. Predictive prophecies in the Bible are mere probabilities: "Since God knows the present exhaustively, he also knows everything that will happen as the *inevitable consequence* of past and present factors. This would be particularly applicable where the predicted event lay in the relatively near future."[51]

"The best seer is the best guesser," said Euripides.[52] Although Rice mentions "inevitable consequences," nothing would be inevitable in a world governed by libertarian human wills and chance. Such a world, like that described by the ancient atomists, would consist of myriads of capricious decisions bouncing mindlessly about under the (non-)guidance of Lady Luck (Greek *Tyche;* Latin *Fortuna*).[53]

To his credit, Rice does try to account for the predictive prophecy of Cyrus. He flirts with the Arminian idea that God occasionally "violates" human freedom[54] but is really not satisfied with this solution. He still prefers to base God's foreknowledge on good hunches: "God may have perceived factors that indicated the decline of Babylon and the rise of Persia a hundred

---

50. Cottrell, "Nature of Divine Sovereignty," 113.
51. Rice, "Divine Foreknowledge," 135 (italics added).
52. In Plutarch *De defectu oraculorum* 432C; *De Pythiae oraculis* 399A; cf. Cicero *De divinatione* 2.5.
53. The atomist philosophy of Democritus and Leucippus is best seen, with certain modifications, in Lucretius *De rerum natura*.
54. Rice, "Divine Foreknowledge," 136.

years ahead. He also must have known the ancestors of Cyrus and foreseen the *possibility* of his birth."[55]

God foreknows nothing for certain, only possibilities. And given the capriciousness of libertarian volition, how could God have known with any certainty that Cyrus's ancestors would successively marry and eventually produce him? It would take only one break in the infinitely complex chain of human decisions to have dissolved Cyrus's existence. Yet God reveals through Isaiah that he knows Cyrus's name—that is, his person—long before he came to be. How could this be unless God has complete, perfect foreknowledge?

And God, according to Rice, would be taking a tremendous risk by venturing his prediction of Cyrus's existence and decision to restore the exiles (a decision that is inherently "unknowable") since Jehovah stakes his claim to be the true God upon his certain knowledge of Cyrus's actions. Undaunted, Professor Rice believes that a god who is uncertain of the future is "genuinely personal and lovable." "It presents us with a God who is vulnerable, who can take risks and make sacrifices, a God who is momentarily delighted and disappointed, depending on our response to his love."[56] I find this description more appropriate for Homer's Zeus[57] than for Israel's God.

Thus declares Yahweh, the Holy One of Israel, its Potter: "With regard to future events, do you question me about my sons and do you command me regarding the work of my hands?" (Isa. 45:11; cf. NIV).

It is Cyrus who is vulnerable: "I am the One who will say to Cyrus, 'My Shepherd!' and he will carry out my will!" (Isa. 44:28).

Neo-Socinianism has similar problems with the New Testament evidence bearing on God's foreknowledge. When discussing Romans 8:29, 1 Peter 1:2, and other passages, Rice tells us again that God cannot foreknow individuals, for this proposition "excludes genuine (i.e., non-biblical, libertarian) freedom." Instead, he continues, "The biblical references to people as objects

---

55. Rice, *God's Foreknowledge*, 78–79 (italics added). Regarding the same prophecy in his other essay, Rice concedes that his position is out of accord with the Bible and says: "At any rate, it is not necessary to provide a precise explanation for each particular prophecy. That would be known only to God. It is sufficient to show that prophecy is compatible with the view that future free decisions are not knowable in advance" ("Divine Foreknowledge," 136). This is question begging on a grand scale, for he does not demonstrate this point; instead he merely asserts that he does not need to bring his position into harmony with all of God's revelation.
56. Rice, "Divine Foreknowledge," 136.
57. For instance, Zeus the Vulnerable wrings his hands over the impending death of Hector and deliberates over whether to defy the cruel fates by saving him (*Iliad* 22.167–76; cf. 16.426–38). He does not. Not even Zeus the Savior can defy the fates.

of God's foreknowledge or predestination are typically concerned with corporate election. They do not refer to personal salvation."[58]

Let us say in passing that "corporate election" substitutes a divine, hypothetical theorizing for the personal, committed knowledge of God in the Scripture passages that we have carefully examined. It is like saying that I foreknow and choose as my heirs my great-great-grandchildren whose very existence I have no way of accurately ascertaining given the vicissitudes of libertarian wills and the chance universe implied by Socinianism.

The biblical picture shows us that God formed us in the womb in accordance with that intimate knowledge he has had of us from eternity, and such knowledge is wedded to his sovereign, gracious purposes. In the case of all whom he has chosen out of his sheer grace, God's foreknowledge represents his personal commitment to us as individuals before our existence. God's foreknowledge extends to all of our free actions as well, which erases neither human liberty nor moral responsibility; rather, they are confirmed.

Conclusion

As a Calvinist, or better, an Augustinian, it appears to me that the naturalistic theology germinal in Arminianism comes to its logical fruition in Socinianism. For the Arminian, the world operates on its own volitional rules. God may fiddle with it here and there to try to get his programs accomplished, but it is essentially an autonomous system. Divine foreknowledge of human decisions is the key for the Arminian to give God a foot in the back door. God foresees that someone will exercise his or her autonomous will, without any divine interference, and God responds by choosing and predestining that one. We have seen that God's role in our lives is more active, formative, and personal.

As a consciously more consistent Arminianism, Socinianism has closed the door of foreknowledge to God. This closed world is by itself, isolated and defiant, denying to God even the possibility of peeking ahead at human choice. "God knows a great deal about the future," they say.[59] Does he? How? What can God know if future human choices are by nature unknowable to him?

In all the phenomenally interconnected chain of human choices, God knows none of them for certain. He knows only possibilities. He knows not the names recorded in the Lamb's book of life before the world's foundation, for he cannot be certain which parents will decide to abort that precious, pos-

58. Rice, *God's Foreknowledge*, 87. Corporate election is the main thesis of Shank's *Elect in the Son*. Interestingly, Cottrell finds Shank's position "puzzling" ("Conditional Election," 71–72 n. 23).

59. Rice, "Divine Foreknowledge," 121.

sible saint whom God says he foreknew by name but had, in fact, only vainly hoped to know.

For the neo-Socinian, the most pressing question is: "What must God know in order not to seem 'stupid'?"[60] It is my prayer that those who are going down this road will stop and reconsider the biblical teaching. May they join us whose only question is an expression of joyful wonder: "Who has known the mind of the Lord? Or what counselor has he consulted? Oh, the bottomless riches of God's wisdom and knowledge!" (Rom. 11:34, 33).

---

60. Sontag, "Omnipotence," 508.

Part 2
Theological Issues

8

Effectual Calling
and Grace

BRUCE A. WARE

All those whom God hath predestinated unto life, and those only, he is pleased, in his appointed and accepted time, effectually to call, by his Word and Spirit, out of that state of sin and death, in which they are by nature, to grace and salvation, by Jesus Christ; enlightening their minds spiritually and savingly to understand the things of God, taking away their heart of stone, and giving unto them a heart of flesh; renewing their wills, and, by his almighty power, determining them to that which is good, and effectually drawing them to Jesus Christ: yet so, as they come most freely, being made willing by his grace.[1]

The purpose of this chapter is to explain the contribution made to Calvinism by the doctrine of God's effectual calling of sinners to saving faith through the provision of irresistible grace (indicated hereafter as the ECG doctrine, the doctrine of effectual calling and grace), and to defend the ECG doctrine as expressive of clear biblical teaching. As such, this doctrine provides strong evidence against an Arminian, and in favor of a Calvinist, soteriology. Furthermore, the strength of the ECG doctrine is greater for Calvinism than might be thought at first. Since the ECG doctrine both entails the Calvinist doctrine of unconditional election and precludes the Arminian doctrine of prevenient grace, establishing the ECG doctrine adds strength to the broader structure of a Calvinist soteriology.

1. The Westminster Confession of Faith, "Of Effectual Calling," 10.1.

It should be mentioned that I am holding together in a unity (i.e., the ECG doctrine) what is commonly expressed under two doctrinal headings. The twin Calvinist doctrines of God's *effectual call* to saving faith extended to the elect (as distinct from the general gospel call extended to all), and of the provision of *irresistible grace,* leading necessarily to the saving-faith response of the elect, are two aspects of one reality. Both doctrines may rightly be used to speak of the work of God's Spirit, through the word of the gospel, by which he opens the blind eyes and enlivens the hardened hearts of those dead in sin. For the first time, they then understand and embrace the gospel for what it is, namely, good news of God's salvation through faith in Christ. This saving work may be described variously as the Spirit's call to sinners to hear and to believe the gospel, rendered effectual by his supernatural enlivening work, or as the Spirit's provision of grace resulting in saving faith, rendered irresistible against all blindness, hardness, and unbelief. The Spirit supernaturally liberates the human heart from sin's clutches to turn from sin and joyfully accept God's gracious provision of salvation in Christ. For our purposes, then, these twin doctrines will be treated as a unity (i.e., the ECG doctrine) and understood as the doctrine of God's effectual calling of sinners to saving faith, by the word of the gospel and through the provision of irresistible grace.[2]

One other introductory comment is in order. I wish to affirm that my goal in this defense is primarily to contribute to the formulation of a biblically responsible soteriology; only secondarily do I hope to support Calvinism, and this insofar as a proper biblical and theological understanding requires it. Calvinists and Arminians share, in principle, the same mindset: that theological systems must not be permitted to rule over the best and most responsible biblical understandings and theological formulations. But the theological system that grows out of and makes the best sense of those most compelling and responsible biblical understandings ought, then, to be upheld and commended. Calvinism ought to be defended not because of its inherent logic, symmetry, or comprehensive structure per se, but because the substance of its biblical understanding is more compelling than that of its rivals.

Arminian and Calvinist Structures of Soteriology

Calvinists and Arminians have more points of agreement than disagreement in their respective soteriologies. They agree on the doctrines of salvation by

---

2. See also John Murray, *Redemption—Accomplished and Applied* (Grand Rapids: Eerdmans, 1955), 96: "God's call, since it is effectual, carries with it the operative grace whereby the person called is enabled to answer the call and to embrace Jesus Christ as he is freely offered in the gospel."

grace through faith, justification by faith, adoption, union with Christ, sanctification as the outworking of one's justification and union with Christ, and the full and final salvation—glorification—of all who truly believe. In these shared convictions, we are evangelical allies.

In other areas significant disagreement arises. The two most critical differences between Arminian and Calvinist soteriologies concern the doctrines of divine election and of God's calling of sinners to saving faith through grace. That is, both on the question of how, in eternity past, the composition of the elect occurs, and of how, in the time-space medium of human history, sinners come to express saving faith in Christ, there is fundamental disagreement.

Arminian Soteriological Structure

Arminians hold the view that God's election of sinners to salvation is really his election of Christ to be Savior, so that all who place their faith in Christ thereby constitute the elect insofar as they are placed in Christ, God's elect One.[3] How, then, can God be said to elect certain *people* in Christ before the foundation of the world (Eph. 1:4)? According to classic Arminianism, God has exhaustive knowledge of all things, including exhaustive knowledge of the future. He knows from eternity past those who will in fact freely come. On the basis of this advance knowledge, God is said to "elect" in Christ those whom he knows will believe in Christ.[4] For the Arminian, election is primarily God's election of Christ, such that all who believe in Christ—whom God knows from

3. Arminius states: "The first precise and absolute decree of God for effecting the salvation of sinful man is that he has determined to appoint his Son, Jesus Christ, as a Mediator, Redeemer, Savior, Priest, and King, to nullify sin by his death, to obtain the lost salvation through his obedience, and to communicate it by his power. . . . The second precise and absolute decree of God is that he has determined graciously to receive in favor those who repent and believe, and, the same persevering, to effect their salvation in Christ, for Christ's sake, and through Christ, and to leave the unrepentant and unbelieving in sin and under wrath, and to damn them as strangers to Christ" (quoted in Carl Bangs, *Arminius: A Study in the Dutch Reformation* [Grand Rapids: Zondervan, [2]1985], 350–51). See also, for example, Robert Shank, *Elect in the Son* (Springfield, Mo.: Westcott, 1970); William W. Klein, *The New Chosen People: A Corporate View of Election* (Grand Rapids: Zondervan, 1990); and William G. MacDonald, "The Biblical Doctrine of Election," in *The Grace of God, the Will of Man: A Case for Arminianism*, ed. Clark H. Pinnock (Grand Rapids: Zondervan, 1989), 207–29.

4. Arminius states: "From this follows the fourth decree to save certain particular persons and to damn others, which decree rests upon the foreknowledge of God, by which he has known from eternity which persons should believe according to such an administration of the means serving to repentance and faith through his preceding grace and which should persevere through subsequent grace, and also who should not believe and persevere" (quoted in Bangs, *Arminius*, 352). Some contemporary Arminians are departing from this classic doctrine of God's exhaustive knowledge of the future. See, for example, Clark H. Pinnock, "From Augustine to Arminius: A Pilgrimage in Theology," in *The Grace of God, the Will of Man*, 25–27; and Richard

eternity past as part of his exhaustive knowledge of the future (in the classic Arminian view)—constitute those elect in Christ.[5]

Since God's election is of Christ primarily, and all who freely believe in Christ are thereby constituted the elect, it follows that all people must be able to accept or to reject Christ. That is, the moral responsibility and volitional freedom necessary to believe freely in Christ and so to be placed in Christ as the elect must be present with all humans, some of whom believe and thereby become part of the elect in Christ, and some of whom reject God's offer of salvation in Christ. But the point is, in whatever response, whether belief or rejection, each person must be able to act freely, apart from any causal determination that necessitated one response or the other. What enables this free human response?

If this doctrine of corporate election is accepted, one of three possible positions is required regarding the question of how, in the time-space medium of human history, sinners come to express saving faith in Christ. First, one may be morally and volitionally free in the Pelagian sense of being unaffected by Adam's sin and so able by nature to perform moral actions in one way or another, as one chooses. Second, one may retain, as the semi-Pelagian argued, the vestiges of a weakened, although still vital, moral will enabling one to choose for either good or evil, assisted only by the presence of divine grace. Arminius and those in the classic Arminian tradition have rejected both of these theological options. Sin has caused a "bondage of the will" (to use Luther's phrase and concept, which Arminius affirmed) such that, apart from grace, human nature cannot choose to act in ways that please God or honor the gospel of Christ.[6] So third, in Arminius's understanding, God provides commonly to all people his prevenient grace, a grace sufficient to overcome

Rice, "Divine Foreknowledge and Free-Will Theism," in ibid., 121–39. But for a staunch Arminian defense of God's exhaustive knowledge of the future, see William Lane Craig, *The Only Wise God* (Grand Rapids: Baker, 1987); and "Middle Knowledge, A Calvinist-Arminian Rapprochement?" in *The Grace of God, the Will of Man,* 141–64.

5. In the argument I develop, I purposely focus attention on the classic Arminian view, which holds to God's exhaustive knowledge of the future. I do so because this is a stronger Arminian view than the more recent and distressing neo-Arminian view advocated by Pinnock, Rice, and others, in which God knows all things past and present, but nothing (i.e., no real knowledge) of the future. This view is weaker than the classic Arminian view because it has no satisfactory answer to the question of how people could be spoken of as God's eternally elect ones. In the neo-Arminian view, surely God can have elected Christ in eternity past, but it is inconceivable how he would elect us in Christ before the foundation of the world (Eph. 1:4), since he had no way of knowing whether any people would in fact come to Christ, much less who those people would be who constitute the "elect" of eternity past.

6. Arminius states: "In this [sinful] state, the free will of man towards the true good is not only wounded, maimed, infirm, bent, and weakened; but it is also imprisoned, destroyed, and lost. And its powers are not only debilitated and useless unless they be assisted by grace, but it has no powers whatsoever except such as are excited by divine grace. For Christ has said, 'Without me ye can do nothing'" (quoted in Bangs, *Arminius,* 341). Regarding Arminius's position on the effects of sin on the human will, Bangs comments: "There is nothing here of grace as an *assistance* given to a man who is only weakened by sin" (ibid., 341).

the effects of sin, such that every person is made able either to accept in saving faith or to reject in disbelief the gospel of Christ.[7]

These temporal poles form the structure of an Arminian soteriology. In eternity past, God first elects Christ, and secondarily he elects in Christ the corporate body of those whom he knows (i.e., foresees) will freely respond in saving faith to the gospel. Then, in human history, he provides prevenient grace, commonly distributed to all, enabling all to believe while actually effecting the salvation only of those whom he previously knew would freely come.

Given this understanding, it should be clear how the doctrine of corporate election in the one elect Man, Christ, depends for its credibility on the corresponding doctrine of prevenient grace.[8] If God's election is of certain people to be saved (albeit those whom he foreknows will freely come), then there must be the provision of grace, sufficient to overcome the deadening effects of sin while not necessitating a believing response, in order for God to be said truly to know and to choose in eternity past those who would freely come. If there were to be either a lack of sufficient prevenient grace given to all (i.e., the absence of or insufficient distribution of prevenient grace as Arminians conceive it), or the presence of grace that necessarily brings about a saving response in the elect (i.e., the presence of irresistible grace as Calvinists conceive it), the doctrine of corporate election would fail along with the doctrine of prevenient grace.[9] An Arminian soteriology, then, depends greatly on its

---

7. Arminius states: "The third decree of God is that by which he has predetermined to administer the necessary, sufficient, and powerful means of repentance and faith, which administration occurs according to the wisdom of God, by which he knows what becomes his mercy and his severity, and according to his justice, by which he is prepared to follow what his wisdom has carried out" (quoted in ibid., 351–52).

8. It should be noted that even for the neo-Arminian position (called free-will theism by Pinnock and Rice [see Pinnock, *The Grace of God, the Will of Man,* chaps. 1, 6] in which God is said not to have exhaustive knowledge of the future and, therefore, cannot be said to elect those whom he knows will freely accept Christ), the doctrine of prevenient grace is essential. The neo-Arminian soteriology is still committed to the notion that God gives commonly to all a bestowal of grace that enables a positive response to revelation given, such that people either may or may not seek the salvation offered.

9. The point being made here is an instance of the valid type of argumentation called *modus tollens,* which argues as follows:
1. If A, then B
2. Not B
3. Therefore, not A
The point being made is that the doctrine of conditional election of classic Arminianism entails and depends on its doctrine of prevenient grace. So, if the doctrine of prevenient grace fails, likewise does its doctrine of conditional election. That is:
1. If conditional election, then prevenient grace
2. Not prevenient grace
3. Therefore, not conditional election
For a discussion of *modus tollens* and other valid forms of argumentation, see, e.g., Douglas N. Walton, *Informal Logic: A Handbook for Critical Argumentation* (Cambridge: Cambridge University Press, 1989), 108–33.

doctrine of prevenient grace, both as an explanation of how those dead in their sin exercise saving faith and of how God may rightly be said to know and to choose those who freely respond in saving faith.

Calvinist Soteriological Structure

For Calvinists, their complementary doctrines of God's unconditional election of those whom he will save and the effectual calling of those elect ones through the provision of irresistible grace (i.e., the ECG doctrine) are closely related. In fact, even more so than with the corresponding Arminian doctrines, the Calvinist doctrines are mutually dependent and mutually entailing.

If God in eternity past has elected some to salvation, and this election is without respect to any qualities, actions, behavior, virtues, vices, or choices of those individuals themselves (i.e., God's election is not conditioned on their characteristics or actions),[10] then his calling of them to salvation must necessarily be effectual through the means of the bestowal of grace that is irresistible, bringing just those and no others to salvation whom he had in eternity past unconditionally elected to salvation. More simply put, an election that is unconditional requires God to be the one to bring to salvation those whom he has chosen through the means of effectual calling and irresistible grace. In a similar manner, if the ECG doctrine can be maintained, it follows that his effectual calling was of those and only those whom he previously and unconditionally chose to save.[11] Hence, the doctrine of unconditional election both entails and is entailed by the ECG doctrine.

The Outcome for Arminian and Calvinist Soteriologies

It should be evident that Arminian and Calvinist soteriologies stand or fall on their respective doctrines of saving grace. For the Arminian, the doctrine of prevenient grace is not an optional luxury that may be either included or

10. When Calvinists refer to God's election as unconditional, they have in mind conditions pertaining to the elect, not God. That is, God's election is unconditioned with respect to any and all qualities and behavior of elect persons in comparison to nonelect persons; but of course his election is conditioned on something in God: his wise counsel and perfect will resulting in the praise of the glory of his grace (Eph. 1:11–12). Therefore it is a caricature and a false representation of Calvinism to say that its doctrine of unconditional election requires that God's choice be arbitrary or capricious. For a recent enlightening treatment of this issue, see John Piper, *The Pleasures of God* (Portland, Ore.: Multnomah, 1991), 126–39.

11. See also John Calvin, *Institutes of the Christian Religion*, Library of Christian Classics, 2 vols., ed. John T. McNeill, trans. Ford Lewis Battles (Philadelphia: Westminster, 1960), 2.964 (3.24), where the chapter title reads, in part, "Election Is Confirmed By God's Call," and is followed by the section heading (3.24.1) that reads: "The call is dependent upon election and accordingly is solely a work of grace."

discarded; it is a necessary element without which an Arminian soteriology, and hence Arminianism, would collapse. Likewise, the ECG doctrine of Calvinism is a necessary complement to its doctrine of unconditional election, each of which entails and is entailed by the other, and both of which are necessary to its soteriology.

Given this understanding, it is important to see what Calvinists are claiming regarding Arminian and Calvinist soteriologies respectively. The reader must examine for himself or herself the biblical teaching and the argumentation presented on both sides of the issue, but we must be clear on what the Calvinist argumentation claims to yield. To see this, several comments are in order:

1. Calvinists claim that the Arminian doctrine of prevenient grace is not rightly supported by biblical teaching.[12]

2. Calvinists also claim that the Arminian doctrine of corporate election is unfounded.[13]

3. It is clear that if this Calvinist critique succeeds, an Arminian soteriology collapses.

4. The case against Arminianism is strengthened when positive support is forthcoming for both Calvinist soteriological doctrines of unconditional election and the ECG doctrine. Elsewhere in this work and beyond, Calvinists have endeavored to explain and to commend the biblical support for the doctrine of unconditional election.[14] If God's unconditional election of some to be saved can be successfully defended biblically, this doctrine not only supports a Calvinist soteriology, but also refutes its Arminian counterpart, because the two competing doctrines are mutually exclusive. Either God chooses those whom he knows will freely choose him (in which case the logical priority is given to human choice, and divine choice echoes human determination), or God chooses apart from external considerations those whom he will save (in which case the logical priority is given to God's choice, and human choosing reflects precisely what God previously and unconditionally determined). It cannot be both ways; one position is correct, or neither is correct, but both cannot be correct. It is the Calvinist contention that the doctrine of unconditional election reflects clear biblical teaching. As such, it supports a Calvinist soteriology while at the same time rendering impossible an Arminian soteriology.

12. See chapter 9 by Thomas R. Schreiner.
13. See chapter 4 by Thomas R. Schreiner; and see also John Piper, *The Justification of God* (Grand Rapids: Baker, ²1993).
14. See chapters 2, 3, and 7 by Robert Yarbrough, Donald J. Westblade, and S. M. Baugh. See also Paul K. Jewett, *Election and Predestination* (Grand Rapids: Eerdmans, 1985); C. Samuel Storms, *Chosen for Life* (Grand Rapids: Baker, 1987); R. C. Sproul, *Chosen by God* (Wheaton: Tyndale, 1986); and Piper, *Pleasures of God*, 123–58.

5. Likewise, the ECG doctrine of Calvinism is at direct odds with the Arminian doctrine of prevenient grace. They are mutually exclusive doctrines. Calvinists claim not only that the argumentation for prevenient grace is unconvincing, but also that the ECG doctrine is demanded by a careful understanding of biblical teaching. If the Calvinist ECG doctrine can be successfully argued, it then simultaneously supports Calvinism while it refutes Arminianism.

This summary explains the contribution that the ECG doctrine makes within a Calvinist soteriology. As the necessary complement and entailment of the doctrine of unconditional election, the ECG doctrine must be shown to be biblically and rationally supported if Calvinism is to succeed. And when support is given to establish the ECG doctrine as biblically correct, not only is a Calvinist soteriology supported but also its Arminian rival is rendered impossible. This leads us to examine the case for the ECG doctrine. Can it be successfully defended as a biblically correct doctrine?

Support for the ECG Doctrine
Preliminary Definitions and Distinctions

The means by which God brings sinners to saving faith involves his effectual calling through the word of the gospel and the provision of irresistible grace. What is meant by the terms *effectual calling* and *irresistible grace* as understood in a Calvinist soteriology?

The doctrine of effectual calling does not propose that each and every calling, by God to sinners, is effectual. In fact, Calvinists are careful to distinguish the general call from the effectual call. They make this distinction because they believe biblical teaching supports both kinds of calls. The *general call* (sometimes referred to as the *vocatio externa*) refers to God's revelation made known to all people, calling them to recognize that revelation as truth and to respond accordingly. There are, then, two expressions of the general call. The *vocatio realis,* the call from things (i.e., nature), is extended to all people through general revelation (expressed in the natural world and conscience), calling them to acknowledge and honor God as their Creator (Ps. 19:1–4; Acts 17:27; Rom. 1:19–21; 2:14–15). The *vocatio verbalis,* the call from words (i.e., the word of the gospel), is also extended throughout the world, through the proclamation of the gospel, telling all sinners everywhere that through faith in Christ they may receive forgiveness of their sins and have eternal life (Matt. 28:18–20; Acts 1:6–8; 26:16–23; Rom. 10:8–15;

1 Cor. 15:1–8).[15] But, because this call goes out to all people, and because not all are saved, clearly the general call is not effectual. That is, people may and do resist this twofold general call to honor God and to turn to Christ to be saved.

The doctrine of the *effectual call* (or the *vocatio interna*)[16] refers more specifically to God's inward and ultimately persuasive summons to repent of sin and to turn to Christ for salvation. Because it is always effectual or ultimately persuasive, and because not all are saved, not all are given this call; it is extended only to the elect, those whom God has unconditionally chosen to save (Rom. 8:28–30; 1 Cor. 1:22–24).[17]

In like manner, the doctrine of *irresistible grace* does not propose that each and every gracious work or influence of the Holy Spirit is irresistible. Clearly, there is biblical warrant for affirming a doctrine of resistible grace, if by this one means that people may resist certain gracious influences of the Spirit. The grieving and quenching of the Spirit (Eph. 4:30 and 1 Thess. 5:19 respectively) are examples of such resistance, as is the explicit statement by Stephen that the Jewish leaders "always resist[ed] the Holy Spirit," just as their fathers did (Acts 7:51). And when believers are admonished to "live by the Spirit, and you will not gratify the desires of the sinful nature" (Gal. 5:16), clearly the implication is that they may choose not to live by the Spirit's power, thus resisting the gracious and transforming work he wishes to accomplish in their lives. Not all grace, then, is irresistible.

When Calvinists refer to irresistible grace, they mean to say that the Holy Spirit is able, when he so chooses, to overcome all human resistance and so cause his gracious work to be utterly effective and ultimately irresistible. In soteriology, the doctrine of irresistible grace refers to the Spirit's work to overcome all sin-induced resistance and rebellion, opening blind eyes and enlivening hardened hearts so that sinners understand and embrace the gospel of salvation through faith in Christ (Acts 16:14; 2 Cor. 4:4–6; 2 Tim. 2:24–25). Such is the grace by which we are saved. May all honor and glory be given to God alone for such a wondrous salvation!

Biblical Support for the ECG Doctrine

In this section, I will endeavor to demonstrate how each of three central passages teaches the ECG doctrine, and how they form a strong cumulative

15. For the distinction between the *vocatio realis* and the *vocatio verbalis*, see Louis Berkhof, *Systematic Theology* (London: Banner of Truth, 1939), 457–58.

16. For the distinction between the *vocatio externa* and the *vocatio interna*, see Heinrich Heppe, *Reformed Dogmatics*, trans. G. T. Thomson (reprint, Grand Rapids: Baker, 1978), 512–13.

17. Discussion of these supporting biblical texts will be given shortly.

Bruce A. Ware

case for this Calvinist doctrine. Although each of these texts is discussed elsewhere in this work, special note is made of the particular implications they have toward the ECG doctrine.

John 6:22–65. In this text, we find Jesus in the midst of a striking confrontation with the multitudes, among whom were many disbelieving Jews. The multitudes had requested a sign from Jesus in order to believe in him, just as God in the past had performed the miracle of giving to ancient Israel manna out of heaven (6:30–31).[18] Jesus' response is startling. He claims that the Father is the one who gave bread out of heaven in the past, and now, in their very presence, he is again providing bread that gives life to the world. And when they ask that he give them this bread (6:34), Jesus declares, "I am the bread of life. He who comes to me will never go hungry, and he who believes in me will never be thirsty. But as I told you, you have seen me and still you do not believe" (6:35–36). In other words, God has indeed performed the sign that the multitudes were seeking. Jesus, the bread out of heaven, is here in their midst! All that is required of them is that they believe in him, and yet they remain in their unbelief.

It is here in the narrative that one of the main issues of the following section arises (that runs throughout 6:35–65). How is it that some, having seen the sign or revelation given by God, choose to believe in Christ and so gain eternal life, while others, presented with the same sign, continue in their disbelief, challenging Christ's claims and resisting the truth made known to them? Notice that both believers and unbelievers are presented with the same revelation, so the difference between the two groups cannot be a matter of requisite knowledge; both have seen the sign of Christ. What, then, accounts for belief by some and disbelief by others?

One might think at first blush that the answer to this question is found by appeal to differences in the respective groupings of people themselves. Some believe because they choose to believe, while others disbelieve because they choose to disbelieve. Despite its tautological structure, one might attempt to argue for the acceptance of this conclusion because it may appear that the text encourages it. After all, it is Jesus who says, "He who comes to me will never go hungry, and he who believes in me will never be thirsty" (6:35); "whoever comes to me I will never drive away" (6:37); "everyone who looks to the Son and believes in him shall have eternal life" (6:40); "he who believes has everlasting life" (6:47); and "I am the living bread that came down from heaven. If

18. This request is particularly difficult to account for in light of the immediately preceding miracle whereby Jesus fed the five thousand (presumably those of the multitude who ask for the sign were among this group—see Jesus' discussion with them about this earlier feeding [John 6:22–29]) from five loaves and two fish. In all likelihood this reveals the hardness of the sinful heart, that even after such a display of miraculous power, this same multitude wants to see a sign in order to believe.

anyone eats of this bread, he will live forever" (6:51). Surely, so the argument goes, these statements must indicate that anyone and everyone can believe. For indeed, what sense does it make to say generally to the multitudes that everyone who does believe may have eternal life unless everyone first is able so to believe? The "ought" of believing in Christ to be saved implies the "can" of common human ability to believe. Therefore, the answer to why some believe and others disbelieve is that some choose to believe while others choose to disbelieve. We are left with our tautology, but we are content in this, because of our conviction that ought implies can.

Our text devastates the logic of this position. The notion that the ought of believing to be saved implies the can of common human ability to believe is nowhere to be found in this text. Having said this, we must be clear on what is being argued. It is undeniable that the ought of believing to be saved is throughout this text. That is, Jesus explains in no uncertain terms that he is the bread of life, and that only as people believe in him will they have eternal life. All must believe in Christ to be saved; the ought or the necessity of belief in Christ for salvation is undeniable.

What is deniable is that this ought of belief implies the can of common human ability to believe. Our text never explicitly makes this logical inference upon which so much of Arminian soteriology rests, nor is it implied by anything said by Jesus here. What our text does tell us precludes the possibility of this ought-implies-can view.

Notice the development from 6:35–36 to 6:37. In 6:35–36 Jesus tells the multitudes that he is the bread of life and that anyone who believes in him will be saved. But they do not believe, although they have seen him. In Jesus' following statement we hear something of startling significance. He continues, "All that the Father gives me will come to me, and whoever comes to me I will never drive away" (6:37).[19] Jesus' point to the disbelieving multitudes might be paraphrased as follows: "Though you have seen me, the Father's sign of life-giving bread sent from heaven, even so you have not believed. But how different it is with those whom the Father gives me to save! All the Father gives to me, these, without fail, come to me. And because the Father gives them to me that I may save them, and because they, therefore, come to me to be saved, I certainly will not fail in my purpose to save them. Because all the Father gives me come, and because of your refusal to come even

19. It should be noted that in John 6:35–37 "coming" to Christ and "believing" in Christ are synonymous and interchangeable concepts. This understanding is made especially clear in 6:35, where Christ says that those who come to him shall not hunger and those who believe in him shall not thirst. Just as hungering and thirsting are parallel expressions of the destitute and desperate condition of those outside of Christ, so too, coming to Christ and believing in Christ are parallel expressions of what such destitute sinners must do to be saved.

213

though you have been shown the sign, it is evident that you have not been given to me by the Father."[20]

Implicit is the idea that only those given by the Father can come (an idea made explicit by Jesus), while explicit is the idea that all those given by the Father do come. The multitudes' disbelief is evidence that they are not among those given to Christ by the Father. They do not believe because they are not given to the Son.[21] As such, Jesus' teaching in John 6:35–37 parallels exactly his words to disbelieving Jews on another occasion: "But you do not believe because you are not my sheep" (John 10:26; cf. 8:47).[22] The point is not that they are not his sheep because of their disbelief, but their disbelief is owing to the fact they are not his sheep. Coming to Christ is causally linked by Jesus to having been given by the Father; all those who come do so precisely because the Father has given them to the Son.

And the point continues in 6:38–39. After making clear that he has come to do only the will of the Father, Jesus says, "And this is the will of him who sent me, that I shall lose none of all that he has given me, but raise them up at the last day" (6:39).[23] As if to make his point unmistakably clear, Jesus essentially repeats what he had just told the unbelieving multitudes: that he surely will save (i.e., raise up) all the Father gives him to save. That is, none that the Father gives to the Son will fail to come (6:37), and none that the Father gives the Son will be lost (6:37, 39).

What is the message to the unbelieving multitudes? Their disbelief indicates not only their personal rejection of the revelatory sign given from the Father (6:36), but even more profoundly, that they have not been given to the Son by the Father, because all of those that the Father gives the Son do not fail to come to him (6:37a), and all those given the Son, who then come,

---

20. See also D. A. Carson, *The Gospel According to John* (Grand Rapids: Eerdmans, 1991), 290, where he writes regarding 6:37: "The flow of the verse is then as follows: All that (a singular neuter is used to refer to the elect collectively) the Father gives to Jesus, as his gift to the Son, will surely come to him; and whoever in fact comes (by virtue of being given by the Father to the Son), Jesus undertakes to keep in, to preserve."

21. See Leon Morris, *The Gospel According to John* (Grand Rapids: Eerdmans, 1971), 367: "Before men can come to Christ it is necessary that the Father give them to Him. This is the explanation of the disconcerting fact that those who followed Jesus to hear Him, and who at the beginning wanted to make Him a king, were nevertheless not His followers in the true sense. They did not belong to the people of God. They were not among those whom God gives Him."

22. It is evident that John Calvin (*Commentary on the Gospel According to John*, vol. 1 [Grand Rapids: Eerdmans, 1948]) likewise saw this parallel. Commenting on John 6:37, he writes (251): "That their unbelief may not detract anything from his doctrine, he says, that the cause of so great obstinacy is, that they are reprobate, and do not belong to the flock of God."

23. Jesus' statement in 6:39 might be restated as: all the Father gives are saved. This being the case, this statement is a conflation of Jesus' previous statements, showing it to be their logical complement. Consider this sequence:
1. All the Father gives come (6:37a)
2. All who come are saved (6:35, 37b)
3. Therefore, all the Father gives are saved (6:39)

are saved (6:37b, 39b). Their ongoing disbelief is clear indication, for Jesus, that the Father has not given them to the Son to save. This seems the most compelling understanding of the meaning of Jesus' statements in 6:37–39 in light of his observation in 6:36 that the multitudes remain in disbelief though they have been faced with the Father's saving revelation in Jesus himself.

Thus far, we have seen that all the Father gives to the Son believe in him and are saved. The multitudes' disbelief is evidence, therefore, that they have not been given to the Son. Implicit in Jesus' understanding of their disbelief is the notion that only those given by the Father can come. But is there evidence that this notion, implicit in Jesus' teaching in John 6:35–39, is also explicitly taught? Is it possible for someone to come to the Son to be saved if the Father has not given that one to the Son? That is, it is one thing to claim (as Jesus explicitly does) that all those given by the Father come to the Son to be saved. But it is another question whether any not given by the Father may nonetheless come. Is it necessary, then, that one be given by the Father to the Son in order for that person to come to Christ and so be saved? Jesus addresses this question in his ongoing discussion with the disbelieving Jews (John 6:41–45).

In response to the Jews who grumbled over Jesus' claim to be the bread that came from heaven, Jesus answers, "Stop grumbling among yourselves. No one can come to me unless the Father who sent me draws him, and I will raise him up at the last day" (6:43–44). Here is Jesus' answer to the question of whether it is necessary that the Father gives to the Son those who will believe and so be saved. It is also Jesus' answer to the question of why some believe and others disbelieve. According to Jesus, those who come to him (i.e., believe in him) do so because they have previously been drawn by the Father to him. In other words, although all ought to believe in Christ, only those drawn by the Father can believe and be saved.

Of course, the nature of the drawing of the Father becomes the central concern. Those who insist on the ought-implies-can logic, and who accept the classic Reformation notion of total depravity affirmed also by Arminius, would be quick to assert that no people, in their deadened sinful state, are able on their own to believe in Christ. Anyone who comes must be drawn previously by the Father. All who come must have God's grace administered to their hearts, giving them the ability they otherwise would have lacked of believing in Christ. But, whether they believe or not is their doing, not God's. God must draw, to be sure; his drawing, however, only makes possible but not actual (or effectual) a believing response. This is the essence of the Arminian doctrine of prevenient grace. It affirms without question what the Pelagians and semi-Pelagians denied, namely, that as Christ himself says, "no one can come to me unless the Father who sent me draws him" (6:44a).

But, is the drawing of the Father (John 6:44) the type of drawing affirmed by Arminians? Is it an expression of prevenient grace, commonly distributed to all people, overcoming the effects of sin such that people can (but not must) believe in Christ? It will become clear that this cannot be the case, and that instead this text teaches that the drawing of the Father is both effectual (i.e., people not only are made able to believe, but also are drawn unfailingly and irresistibly to such belief) and selective (i.e., he draws those whom he chooses to give to the Son).[24] Notice the following points concerning John 6:44.

1. The drawing of the Father precedes the coming to Christ. When Christ says that no one can come (*dunatai elthein*) unless the Father draws him, it is clear that anyone's coming to Christ is preceded by being drawn by the Father. There is, then, a gracious and necessary drawing work of the Father without which no one is able to come to Christ.

2. The drawing of the Father results in the full and final salvation of those drawn. That is, the drawing of the Father does not result in the mere possibility of being saved, which possibility becomes an actuality only when the one drawn chooses to assent to that drawing; rather, it results in the actual salvation of all those drawn. This point is easily missed if 6:44a is permitted to stand without the remainder of Jesus' statement in 6:44b. Jesus' claim, "No one can come to me unless the Father who sent me draws him" (6:44a), is directly followed by, "and I will raise him up at the last day" (6:44b). It is clear that the one drawn is raised up on the last day; that is, the one drawn is saved.

3. Still, the question may arise whether being saved (or being raised up) is the result of the Father's drawing or of coming to Christ. That is, is Jesus saying that he will raise up all who come to him? Or is it that he will raise up all whom the Father draws? The answer is that both are true. As we observed, Jesus makes several references to the fact that everyone who comes to him or believes in him will be saved (see 6:35, 40, 47, 51). There is no doubt concerning this. But the question is, how do they come? Or, why do they believe?

Consider again the point of these statements: "All that the Father gives me will come to me, and whoever comes to me I will never drive away" (6:37); "And this is the will of him who sent me, that I shall lose none of all that he has given me, but raise them up at the last day" (6:39); and "Everyone who listens to the Father and learns from him comes to me" (6:45). As we saw, sinners come to be saved because they have been given to Christ by the Father. They believe because they are drawn, and all who are drawn, so believe.

---

24. Regarding John 6:44, Grant R. Osborne ("Soteriology in the Gospel of John," in Pinnock, *The Grace of God, the Will of Man,* 248–49) argues against the irresistibility of the drawing unto sure and certain salvation for all those drawn. He suggests that if the drawing here is irresistible, this leads to universalism, because in John 12:32 Jesus says he will draw all men to himself. It is not at all certain that the drawing of John 12:32 is universal. The context indicates it rather to be a drawing without distinction, not a drawing without exception (see Carson, *Gospel According to John,* 293, 444; and in this work, Schreiner, "Prevenient Grace," 241–42). Surely the individual contexts of the two passages must regulate the sort of drawing that is meant in each case. Putting John 12:32 aside, the issue we here are addressing is what is meant by the drawing of the Father in John 6:44 in light of its own context.

Therefore, it appears that it is true both that everyone who comes to Christ is saved and that all whom the Father draws are saved. In John 6:44, when Jesus says, "and I will raise him up at the last day," he has in mind the future salvation of all of those drawn to Christ by the Father, without which none would ever come.

The drawing of the Father has two results. First, it enables sinners to come to Christ (6:44a). Second, because of Christ's commitment to raise up those drawn (see 6:39 with 6:44), it ensures the final salvation of all those whom the Father has so drawn (6:44b).

4. Since the Father's drawing precedes belief in Christ, and since that drawing results in the salvation of those drawn, it follows that this drawing is effectual.[25] That this cannot be a general drawing merely making possible belief in Christ is evident in that the drawing produces both belief and actual salvation.

5. Because the drawing of the Father is effectual, it is clear that it cannot be a universal or commonly bestowed drawing to Christ, exerted on all people, but rather a selective drawing of those whom the Father chose to give to the Son.[26] Jesus spoke earlier in John's Gospel of the ultimate destinies of two peoples. For example, in John 5:27–29, Jesus referred to the day when the Son of man will exert his authority over all people, resulting in a resurrection of life for those who do good and a resurrection of judgment for those who do evil. Because it is clear that Jesus affirms the reality of heaven and hell and so denies the ultimate salvation of all people, the effectual drawing the Father performs must be selective. But of course, this is no surprise since Jesus has made clear throughout his discussion with the Jews in John 6 that all that the Father gives to him, he will not lose but will surely raise up at the last day (see 6:37, 39, 44–45, 65).

Jesus' statement in 6:45 ("Everyone who listens to the Father and learns from him comes to me") only reinforces his point in 6:44 by stating again its complementary truth. As 6:44 had stressed that no one can come apart from the drawing of the Father, 6:45 reaffirms the truth Jesus already presented in 6:37, namely, that all those given by the Father do come. As Augustine puts it:

> What is the meaning of "Every man who has heard and learned from the Father comes unto me" [John 6:45] except that there is none who hears from the Father,

25. Calvin, *John*, 257: "it follows that all are not drawn, but that God bestows this grace on those whom he has elected."

26. Carson, *Gospel According John*, 293, comments: "The thought of v[erse] 44 is the negative counterpart to v[erse] 37a. The latter tells us that all that the Father gives to the Son will come to him; here we are told that no-one can come to him unless the Father draws him. . . . The combination of v[erse] 37a and v[erse] 44 prove that this 'drawing' activity of the Father cannot be reduced to what theologians sometimes call 'prevenient grace' dispensed to every individual, for this 'drawing' is selective, or else the negative note in v[erse] 44 is meaningless."

217

and learns, who comes not to me? For if everyone who has heard from the Father, and has learned, comes, certainly everyone who does not come has not heard from the Father or learned; for if he had heard and learned, he would come. . . . [27]

These two truths (i.e., only those drawn can come, and all those drawn do come) serve together to require the ECG doctrine of Calvinism. Jesus' repeated affirmations of both truths, along with his rejection of universalism, make this doctrine undeniable.

Finally, Jesus' continued confrontation with these unbelievers comes to a climax in 6:60–65. Jesus acknowledges publicly the fact that some among his listeners do not believe, despite seeing and hearing all that has been presented to them (6:61–64). And then, as if to summarize again the reason why persistent disbelief continues on the part of these who have been with him, Jesus repeats and reinforces his earlier claim, saying, "This is why I told you that no one can come to me unless the Father has enabled him" (6:65). At this, we are told, many of those listening departed from Jesus and quit following him.

The substance of Jesus' response in the presence of persistent unbelief is significant.[28] He did not encourage these unbelievers to overcome the internal obstacles to belief in their own hearts as if it were up to them whether they would believe or not. Rather, Jesus' point here, just as it was in 6:44, is that the Father's enablement, the Father's drawing, is necessary for them to believe.

But what of the Arminian proposal that this drawing of the Father, although necessary, is in fact resistible? Could this be a reference to the common drawing that the Father exerts on all people, enabling but not rendering certain a response of saving faith? To the great detriment of an Arminian soteriology, this cannot be. If this enablement or drawing is distributed commonly to all, as Arminians hold, enabling any and all to believe, then Jesus' response makes no sense. In the Arminian view, what separates belief and unbelief is not the drawing of the Father; the Father draws all. Belief and unbelief, rather, is owing to what particular individuals (all of whom are drawn by the Father and so enabled to believe) freely choose to do. They may come, or they may refuse to come. God has drawn all, so it is up to them.

Jesus' analysis is quite different. When faced with persistent disbelief, Jesus affirms again unequivocally that only those drawn by the Father can come (6:65). But if all are drawn, what is the significance of this point to those re-

27. Augustine *On the Predestination of the Saints* 7.13, as quoted by Calvin, *Institutes*, 2.965 (3.24.1).
28. See also C. K. Barrett, *The Gospel According to St John* (London: SPCK, 1955), 252: "Because of the emergence of unbelief Jesus had explained the divine initiative which underlies faith. . . . There is no difference in meaning between the two clauses [v. 44 and v. 65] and they illuminate each other. Faith in Christ is not merely difficult; apart from God it is impossible (cf. Mark 10:27). Coming to Jesus is not a matter of free human decision."

maining in their disbelief? Clearly there would be no point to it, and it certainly would not prompt those listening to Jesus to depart permanently from him.

The Arminian view, that Jesus speaks in 6:65 (as he does also in 6:44) of God's prevenient grace, given to all, which is necessary for everyone to come but not rendering certain that any in fact comes, is akin to the following situation. Suppose a medical doctor diagnosed each of the members of a group of people as having the same disease. He prescribed two medications (call them RXA and RXB), both of which must be taken by each person in the group in order for each to get well. Some weeks later he meets with the group of patients and discovers that some remain sick while others are noticeably better. After inquiring further, he also discovers that all of the patients in the group have taken RXA but only those now doing better have taken, in addition, RXB. In response to this situation, the doctor declares to those still sick, "No one can get well without taking *RXA!*" While it is true that RXA is necessary to bring about these patients' healing (so the doctor is not technically incorrect in what he says), the doctor's response misses the point. Since all have been taking RXA, the necessity of their taking RXA is irrelevant. The doctor's statement, although it is true, does nothing to explain why some remain sick while others are now well.

The only point that Jesus can sensibly be making by his statement in 6:65 is that those resistant to him do not believe because they are not so drawn by the Father. He surely is not saying to people who are drawn by the Father that only those drawn by the Father can come. This would do nothing to explain what the context of this passage demands: why his opponents remain in their unbelief.[29] Rather, Jesus' point is this: no one can come who is not drawn by the Father (6:44, 65); all of those drawn by the Father do come (6:37, 45); those speaking with Jesus remain in their unbelief (6:36, 64); and therefore, the logical conclusion must be that their continued unbelief indicates that they are not drawn by the Father. That is, they do not believe because they are not drawn. The drawing of the Father, then, is both necessary and effectual.[30]

Let me bring the discussion on John 6 to a close by summarizing the main

29. Calvin, *John*, 276: "If this grace were bestowed on all without exception, it would have been unseasonable and inappropriate to have mentioned it in this passage; for we must understand that it was Christ's design to show that not many believe the Gospel, because faith proceeds only from the secret revelation of the Spirit."

30. The case for Arminianism is not made any easier by appealing to the fact that Jesus knew from the beginning who would believe and who would not (6:64), as if this is about the Arminian conception of foreknowledge, which somehow explains why some come and others do not. The point of 6:64 with 6:65 rather is this: because Jesus knew who would not believe, therefore this is why he had said to these unbelievers that no one can come unless the Father grants it. Jesus' knowledge of those who would not believe explains not why they remain unbelieving; rather, it explains why Jesus tells them (i.e., these particular disbelieving opponents) what he does: that only those whom the Father grants may in fact come. Because Jesus knew who the unbelievers were, he explains to them the reason for their continued disbelief despite the signs and revelation that has been presented to them.

ideas as they relate to our discussion.[31] In his dialogue with those persistent in their unbelief, Jesus makes two main points. Together, these points establish what the ECG doctrine affirms, namely, that God calls effectually and irresistibly his elect to saving faith in Christ.

First, all of those drawn to Christ by the Father do in fact come and are in fact saved (6:37, 39, 45). Second, only those drawn to Christ by the Father can in fact come (6:44, 65). Both of these points are derived directly from Jesus' own teaching within the context of continued unbelief (6:36, 64). Now, if all of those drawn do come (first point), the drawing that causes them to come must be effectual. If it were not effectual, Jesus could not rightly and explicitly say, as he does say, that all those drawn (i.e., given to the Son) come and that all those drawn will be raised up. Furthermore, if only those drawn can come (second point), then surely the drawing of God is selective. There is no point in telling disbelieving people who supposedly already are drawn by the Father that they must be drawn in order to come. Rather, to make sense of Jesus' analysis of the persistent disbelief surrounding him, his affirmations that only those drawn by the Father can come (6:44, 65) must signify the selective nature of the Father's drawing. Apart from this selective drawing, belief is impossible and the continued unbelief faced by Jesus is thereby explained. The calling of God on individuals' lives to salvation is effectual, thwarting all unbelieving resistance and drawing them irresistibly to belief in the Christ who will not fail to save them utterly.

1 Corinthians 1:18–31. First Corinthians 1:24 presents to us a powerful and God-honoring instance of God's calling that is at once effectual, irresistible, and selective. It reads: "but to those whom God has called, both Jews and Greeks, Christ the power of God and the wisdom of God." How does this text support the ECG doctrine?

Beginning in 1:17, Paul makes a temporary transition from discussing his own preaching of the gospel and baptism of others to centering on the nature of the gospel itself. That gospel or "message of the cross" (1:18), which he purposely refused to preach in clever, human wisdom (1:17), is, at one and the same time, God's power and wisdom for those being saved (1:18, 21, 24; cf. Rom. 1:16), while it is weakness and foolishness to those perishing (1:18, 23, 25). It is the same gospel in both cases, but some regard it as wise, powerful, and life-giving while others see it as mere folly.[32]

---

31. The theme of God's choosing and effectual drawing to saving belief continues through the rest of chapter 6, focusing now on the disciples themselves. In other words, Jesus' teachings more generally (6:22–65) are applied specifically with his own. See Carson, *Gospel According to John*, 303–4.

32. Notice the parallel thought in 2 Corinthians 2:15–16, where Paul likens the gospel to a fragrance or an aroma of Christ. To those being saved (2:15) it is an aroma of life (2:16); to those perishing (2:15), an aroma of death (2:16). The gospel, or aroma, is the same! The difference is in those smelling the fragrance and not in the fragrance itself.

The burning question, for our purposes, is why some consider it God's power and wisdom while others reject it as weakness and foolishness. That both responses to the same gospel occur is not disputed. What we must see is whether Paul gives any indication as to why such contrary responses occur.

Paul gives two answers to this question. First, he says that although the world in its wisdom did not come to know God, God was pleased to use the gospel to "save those who believe" (1:21). So what accounts for these two conflicting responses to the gospel? Answer: Some resist the message and some believe it. Paul affirms what Jesus had likewise taught in John 6 (see 6:35, 40, 47), namely, that all who believe the gospel of the Christ will be saved.

What must one believe to be saved? According to Paul, the object of a true and saving belief does not reside in a show of miraculous signs (1:22a; and note the parallel to Jesus' discussion with the disbelieving Jews in John 6:30–36), or in rhetorically wise human knowledge (1:22b), but is centered on the gospel affirmation of Christ crucified (1:23a). This is precisely why the gospel is for Jews a stumbling block and for Gentiles foolishness (1:23b). There is in the cross no outward display of the divinely spectacular or the humanly sagacious. And as such, there is no basis for human boasting when one's dependence is on the cross (see 1:29). The cross calls Jews and Greeks alike to humble acceptance of their own weakness and folly and of Christ crucified as the only true expression of real (i.e., God's!) power and wisdom (1:24) and hence as the only basis of their salvation.[33]

Still, the question lingers. When asked why the same gospel elicits two opposite responses, Paul says that the message preached saves those who believe. But, we wonder, is there any accounting for why some believe and others do not? By asking this question I am not suggesting that anything thus far presented by the apostle is wrong or misplaced. He is right to make clear that salvation comes to those who believe. So my question inquires whether he might be saying more than this, not something that would be corrective or contrary. And indeed, a close look at our text indicates that he offers another reason why some consider the message of the cross God's power and wisdom, while others reject it as weakness and foolishness.

Second, then, the gospel elicits conflicting responses because God calls some from among Jews and Gentiles who, as a group, reject the gospel, so that these (i.e., the called) accept the cross as God's power and wisdom while others (i.e., Jews and Gentiles generally, who are not called) remain in their prideful un-

33. See Gordon D. Fee, *The First Epistle to the Corinthians* (Grand Rapids: Eerdmans, 1987), 67, for a superb summary statement of 1:18–2:5: "[Paul] says in effect, 'So you think the gospel is a form of *sophia*? How foolish can you get? Look at its *message*: it is based on the story of a crucified Messiah. Who in the name of wisdom would have dreamed that up? Only God is so wise as to be so foolish' (1:18–25); 'Furthermore, look at its *recipients*. Yourselves! Who in the name of wisdom would have chosen you to be the new people of God?' (1:26–31); 'Finally, remember my *preaching*. Who in the name of wisdom would have come in such weakness? Yet look at its results' (2:1–5)."

belief and resistance. Look again for the development of thought in 1 Corinthians 1:23–24: "But we preach Christ crucified: a stumbling block to Jews and foolishness to Gentiles, but to those whom God has called, both Jews and Greeks, Christ the power of God and the wisdom of God." Consider the following paraphrase of these verses: "When Christ crucified is preached among Jews and Greeks generally, Jews stumble over it for its apparent weakness and ignobility while Gentiles ridicule it as the height of human folly. But amazingly, some among these very same Jews and Greeks, who otherwise flatly reject the gospel, are savingly called by God out of their resistant frame of mind regarding the gospel, to understand and embrace it now as God's marvelous good news! Here, they now see, in the cross, is found real power and wisdom. In Christ and Christ alone, they now understand, there resides the power of God and the wisdom of God that leads to salvation."

Why is it that the calling of 1 Corinthians 1:24 must be viewed as effectual (or, as stated in the preceding paraphrase, a "saving" call)? Or negatively, why cannot the call here be a call to all urging them to believe and so be saved? Consider the following two points:

1. The wording of 1:24 does not permit the notion of a general call given to all unbelieving Jews and Greeks, calling all to believe in Christ. Very specifically, Paul says, *autois de tois klētois, Ioudaiois te kai Hellesin*, literally, "but to those ones, to the called ones, both Jews and Greeks," or more naturally, "but to those who are the called, both Jews and Greeks" (NASB). The call is issued to a specific group, referred to here as *tois klētois*, the called ones, and it is clear that this group of the called ones comes out of the broader, general group of all the Jews and Gentiles. Therefore, the wording of the text precludes the notion that this is a call to all; it is a call to some from among all the Jews and Gentiles, to "the called."

2. It makes no sense to contrast Jews and Greeks generally with those Jews and Greeks who are called (as 1:23–24 does) if the difference between believing Jews and Greeks and disbelieving Jews and Greeks is in their respective choices only. In such a case, all are called, and some choose to believe while some disbelieve. It is true that other texts speak clearly of the gospel going to all so that whoever believes may come and be saved (e.g., Rom. 10:12–13), but this clearly cannot be what our present text is about.

The contrast is made between those called from disbelieving Jews and Greeks and, by implication, those not called, making up the general class of Jews and Greeks who regard the gospel as weakness and folly. The point is that Jews and Greeks generally reject the gospel. But God intervenes, and toward some of these otherwise disbelieving Jews and Gentiles, he extends his saving call. This cannot be a call to all; it must be a call to some.

The Arminian view of the general call extended with prevenient grace will not work here. Again, similarly to John 6:65, it makes no sense to say regarding Jews and Greeks, if all are called (as Arminians claim), that God called from Jews and

Greeks those who were then saved. A calling in such a case does not explain the contrary responses to the gospel. Consider again the illustration of the two medications. To explain why some are still sick and others well, it will not do to appeal to the medication they take in common. So, if 1:24 refers to the general call, it is then irrelevant to why some believe and others reject the gospel, since by definition both groups received in common the benefit of the call.

Furthermore, this cannot be a resistible call, making merely possible but not certain a saving response. Why must the call here be seen as irresistible? Because the called are not described as those who hear and may (or may not) believe, but as those who hear and do believe. That is, the called actually see and believe in Christ as God's power and wisdom. It results in their actual salvation.[34] In short, then, the call of 1 Corinthians 1:24 is, of necessity, selective, effectual, and ultimately irresistible against all previous rejection and disbelief.

The remaining verses (1:26–31) only serve to strengthen the conclusion just arrived at by providing for us the reason God's call to salvation must be seen as his work of effectually bringing sinners to salvation. Paul states two reasons in the following verses, which actually merge into one comprehensive and glorious divine purpose for our salvation. First, since any and all are saved, not because of their wisdom or power but because God has chosen them (note: this is stated three times in 1:27–28) out of their weakness, impotence, and baseness (1:26–28), it follows that "no one may boast before him" (1:29). And second, because those who are saved are in Christ "because of him" (1:30), it follows that any who boast must boast solely "in the Lord" (1:31). That God has so called us to see Christ as his wisdom and power that leads to salvation means, then, that all human boasting is deemed utterly unfounded and that rightful boasting belongs only in the Lord. To God alone belongs all honor and glory![35]

34. Fee, *First Epistle to the Corinthians*, 76–77: "Those who are 'being saved' (v. 18), the 'believing ones' (v. 21), are so because of God's prior action; they are 'those whom God has called' (see 1:1–2, 9). For them the preaching of 'Christ crucified' is effectual. . . . Paul's concern here is not so much on their being able to *perceive* the cross as wisdom . . . , but on the actual *effective work* of the cross in the world."

35. This insistence, that all glory be given to God alone for our salvation, leads many Calvinists to demean and reject the Arminian notion that, ultimately, we are responsible for whether we are saved or not. Yes, for the Arminian, God provides in Christ a substitute sacrifice for our sins, and yes, he gives prevenient grace enabling belief; but ultimately it is up to us whether to believe or not. That is, God does all he can do, commonly and universally, so the difference between those who believe and those who do not rests in what we humans do, not in what God does. How, then, can the Arminian contend all the credit for our salvation is owing to God alone? Consider these words from Loraine Boettner, *The Reformed Doctrine of Predestination* (Grand Rapids: Eerdmans, [7]1951), 170: "[Arminianism] has insisted upon 'free will,' 'the power of contrary choice,' etc., and has taught that ultimately the sinner determines his own destiny. In its more consistent forms it makes man a co-savior with Christ, as if the glory in redemption was to be divided between the grace of Christ and the will of man, the latter dividing the spoils with the former."

Notice that the point is not that God deserves such honor because he provided Christ as the way of salvation, or because he commissioned the proclamation of the gospel to all the world, or because he extends the offer of salvation generally to any who will believe. These are all good and right bases for giving honor to God, but they are not, either individually or collectively, the basis for honoring God stated in our text. Rather, God alone is to be honored because he chose the foolish, the weak, and the lowly (1:26–28), and it is because of him that we are in Christ (1:30). In other words, the basis for boasting in the Lord is not that he made our salvation possible but that he saved us by his calling (1:24, 26) and his choosing (1:27–28, 30). Therefore any and all human basis for boasting is eliminated (1:29), and all honor and glory is owing solely to him (1:31)!

One final point. Notice Paul's use of "calling" to link his more general discussion of God's salvation of unnamed Jews and Greeks (1:18–25) with his very personal references to God's salvation of these particular Corinthian Christians (1:26–31). Verse 26 provides the link when it says, "Brothers, think of what you were when you were called" (lit., "consider your calling"). The point is this: what Paul taught generally in 1:24 about God's calling of otherwise disbelieving Jews and Greeks to see in Christ God's wisdom and power, he now, in 1:26, applies to the Corinthians themselves.[36] Just as Jews and Greeks as a general class reject the gospel, so that God must call some out of their hardness and resistance to see and to embrace the glory of the cross of Christ, in like manner he has called you! The calling of 1:24, which we argued can only rightly be seen as effectual, must likewise, in 1:26, refer to the effectual calling to salvation of these weak and lowly Corinthians. Only then is the usage of "calling" in 1:24 and 1:26 parallel, as it surely must be, and only then does the emphasis in the following verses (1:27–31) on God's glory owing to his choosing and saving make good sense and rightly follow.

The word of the cross is repulsive to sinners. It rebukes our humanly crafted idols of wisdom and power, and it calls us to bow humbly and destitute before a cross on which hangs one who is himself destitute, beaten, bleeding, and dying. But why do this? Why exchange the pinnacles of human glory for this cross, this symbol of sheer impotence and utter folly? Indeed, it makes no sense, until—until, that is, God opens eyes blinded to the beauty and glory of the truth and softens hearts hardened with prideful and sinful resistance. Among the hosts of these blind and resistant, God calls! And when that call is extended, a transformation occurs (not that it may occur, but it does occur). That ignoble cross now is seen as the most magnificent

36. For the relation of "call" in 1:24 and 1:26, see Fee, *First Epistle to the Corinthians*, 79; and John Calvin, *Commentary on the Epistles of Paul the Apostle to the Corinthians*, vol. 1 (Grand Rapids: Eerdmans, 1948), 90.

symbol of glory! Here, and here alone, is the epitome of true power and wisdom! Here, and here alone, is God's saving grace manifest. May praise, therefore, be given to God *alone*, not only for the provision of Christ, and not only for the proclamation of the gospel, but also for his saving and effectual calling by which we now see Christ for who he is, nothing less than the power of God and the wisdom of God. To offer such humble and solitary praise to God is to give living expression to the command of 1 Corinthians 1:31: "Let him who boasts boast in the Lord"!

Romans 8:28–30. We come now to the last, and perhaps the most straightforward, expression of God's effectual call we will examine in this chapter. The statement of greatest importance for our present concerns is found in 8:30: "those he predestined, he also called; those he called, he also justified; those he justified, he also glorified." We might paraphrase it in this way: "All[37] of those whom God has predestined to become conformed to the likeness of Christ (from 8:29), to all of these so predestined, he extends his call. And just as all the predestined are also called, so too all those whom he calls heed the call to believe and so are justified. And just as all the predestined are called and all the called are justified, so too all those justified are also glorified."

The calling spoken of here cannot be the general gospel call to repent and believe in Christ to be saved.[38] Rather, the calling of 8:30 must refer to God's effectual call, that is, a call that cannot fail to lead people to exercise saving faith and so be justified. Why is this? The general call is extended to everyone indiscriminately, some of whom believe and others of whom disbelieve. There are two categories of people who receive the general call: those who hear and accept the gospel and those who hear and reject it. But such is not the case with those spoken of as "called" in 8:30.

One category of people is described in 8:29–30. Those foreknown[39] are the same individuals as those predestined, those predestined are the same as those called, those called the same as those justified, and those justified the same as those glorified. That is, all the individuals spoken of in 8:29–30 are foreknown,

37. That it is precisely the same people who are predestined as are called, justified, and glorified, see Douglas J. Moo, *Romans 1–8*, WEC (Chicago: Moody, 1991), 572: "The exact correspondence between those who are the objects of predestining and those who experience this calling is emphasized by the demonstrative pronoun (*toutous*, "these"): 'it was precisely those who were predestined who also (*kai*) were called.'"

38. Regarding *ekalesen* of 8:30, see James D. G. Dunn, *Romans 1–8* (Dallas: Word, 1988), 485: "The thought is not of an invitation which might be rejected; God does not leave his purpose to chance but puts it into effect himself. Paul looks at the whole process from the perspective of its successful outcome, where the redeemed gladly affirm that their coming to faith was wholly God's doing."

39. On "foreknowledge" here as expressive of God's prior loving and elective purposes, see chapter 7 by S. M. Baugh. And for a careful and thorough discussion of "foreknowledge" in Romans 8:29, see Moo, *Romans 1–8*, 568–71.

predestined, called, justified, and glorified. None is foreknown that is not predestined. None is predestined that is not called. And none is called that is not both justified and glorified. So then, if in Romans 8:30 all those called are justified and glorified, but if many who hear God's general gospel call to believe instead resist and so are neither justified nor glorified, then it follows that the "call" of 8:30 is the effectual call (which effects the justification of all those so called) and not the general call (which does not effect the justification of all those so called because it can be—and is—resisted).

Of what benefit is this teaching to those who are the called of God? In the flow of thought of Romans 8, verses 29–30 are meant to provide the theological basis or undergirding for the promise articulated in verse 28. God works in all things for the good of those who love him, those who are called according to his purpose. What relation does being called by God have to this stated assurance of God working good? Simply this: since all whom God calls he also justifies and glorifies, it is clear that God will permit nothing to hinder his ultimate and good purposes for his called ones from coming to fruition. It is a sovereign God who saves sinners, and the same sovereign God works all things for the good of his own—those whom he has called and who, then, love him—guaranteeing their salvation now as well as their future glory and joy! Because God calls to salvation, and because God's calling is effectual to save both now and forever, we can be confident that nothing can hinder God's good purposes. He will fulfill them, for his own, to the end.

Conclusion

If a Calvinist soteriology is to commend itself as coherent, viable, and sound, establishing the ECG doctrine is essential. As the necessary complement and entailment of the doctrine of unconditional election, the case for the ECG doctrine must succeed. Furthermore, if a Calvinist soteriology is to commend itself to those committed fully and unreservedly to biblical authority, the ECG doctrine must be shown to be expressive of clear biblical teaching. For the purposes of this study, it is hoped that sufficient biblical warrant has been offered for concluding that the ECG doctrine of Calvinism is scripturally justified and that, therefore, the case for the ECG doctrine succeeds.

In addition, to the extent that the case for the ECG doctrine of Calvinism succeeds, its Arminian rival doctrine of prevenient grace falters. Since evidence for the ECG doctrine is evidence against the doctrine of prevenient grace, we conclude as well that an Arminian soteriology is correspondingly harmed.

The focus of this chapter has been, of necessity, on one significant aspect of a Calvinist soteriology. Not everything for Calvinism or against Arminianism can here be shown. But when the case for the ECG doctrine is put alongside the case against the doctrine of prevenient grace (as demonstrated elsewhere in this work), one gains a fuller picture of the relative strengths and weaknesses of the two rival soteriologies. Furthermore, one's ability in such an evaluation is again enlarged when the case for unconditional election is set alongside the case against conditional (or corporate) election (which are also dealt with in this work). The result of this cumulative case must be judged by each thoughtful Christian. The judgment of this writer is that, when all is considered, the evidence overwhelmingly supports a Calvinist soteriology while rendering its Arminian counterpart untenable.

Although the case made here for the ECG doctrine is only part of a much bigger picture, the result has been to show the place effectual calling and irresistible grace have in a broader Calvinist soteriology. Everything about this doctrine elicits our humble amazement at a gracious God who would call undeserving and blind sinners out of darkness into his marvelous light. To God alone belongs all glory and honor! Praise be to his great and gracious name!

9

Does Scripture Teach
Prevenient Grace
in the Wesleyan Sense?

THOMAS R. SCHREINER

The Nature of Fallen Humanity

This chapter explores whether the Wesleyan concept of prevenient grace can be supported from the Scriptures. Before examining this question, I want to emphasize that there is a significant area of common ground between Wesleyans and Calvinists. The disagreements that we have in some areas can cause us to overlook the extent to which we agree on major doctrines. In one arena of theology, namely, anthropology, the harmony between Wesleyans and Calvinists is of the utmost importance and our harmony in this area should be celebrated. Both camps acknowledge that fallen human beings are born with a corrupt nature that is in bondage to sin, and that human beings can do no good apart from the grace of God.

To sketch in the biblical data on the human condition since the fall is helpful. Thereby we will see the extent to which Wesleyans and Calvinists agree, and the gulf that the Wesleyan understanding of prevenient grace creates between Arminians and Calvinists will also be illuminated. Paul teaches that all human beings are born with a corrupt nature inherited from Adam (Rom. 5:12–19). Without specifying the precise connection between Adam's sin and our condemnation—which is itself the subject of a long theological controversy—it is clear from the text that we are sinners because of Adam's sin.[1] Through Adam's sin we died (Rom. 5:15, 17), are condemned (Rom. 5:16, 18), and are constituted as sinners (Rom. 5:19).[2]

Harmonizing with this portrait of humanity in Romans 5 is Ephesians 2:3, which says we are by nature "objects of wrath." Human beings by nature (*physei*) are deserving of wrath, indicating that they are all born with a nature that is sinful. The near context in Ephesians 2 confirms the depth of human depravity. Human beings are "dead in transgressions and sins" (Eph. 2:1; cf. 2:5 and Col. 2:13). The deadness of fallen humanity indicates that we are devoid of life upon our entrance into the world. We have no inclination toward genuine righteousness or goodness. Paul proceeds to say in Ephesians 2:2–3 that we lived under the sway of the world, the devil, and the flesh before conversion.

What is in the consciousness of those who are under the control of the "flesh"? There is not necessarily a conscious awareness of rebellion against God. Life in the flesh consists in "gratifying the cravings of our sinful nature and following its desires and thoughts" (Eph. 2:3). The desires of people who are "by nature objects of wrath" are naturally and instinctively sinful desires. In other words, unregenerate people sin by merely doing what they wish to do, by carrying out the motivations that are in their hearts. Sinful desires dominate those who are in the flesh.

Is there biblical warrant for saying that the desires of the unregenerate are dominated by sin? Ephesians 2:3 suggests such a conclusion in saying that people are dead in trespasses and sins and that they are "by nature objects of wrath." The trespasses and sins flow from a nature that is sinful and warrants God's wrath. Titus 3:3 confirms such a conclusion. "At one time we too were foolish, disobedient, deceived and enslaved by all kinds of passions and pleasures. We lived in malice and envy, being hated and hating one another." Note here that Paul says that we were "*enslaved* by all kinds of passions and pleasures" (italics added). It is fair to conclude that people who are enslaved by their own desires are under the domination and tyranny of sin. This kind of tyranny is not externally coerced. People do what they want to do, in that they pursue their own pleasures and desires. Nonetheless, to describe this pursuit of their own desires as slavery because they have no desire, inclination, or aspiration to do good is appropriate.

The bondage of the will, then, is a slavery to our own desires. Unregenerate human beings are captivated by what they want to do! Jesus himself diagnosed sinning as an indication of slavery. "Everyone who sins is a slave to sin" (John

---

1. For two insightful treatments of this text see Douglas J. Moo, *Romans 1–8*, WEC (Chicago: Moody, 1991), 325–59; C. E. B. Cranfield, *A Critical and Exegetical Commentary on the Epistle to the Romans*, 2 vols., ICC (Edinburgh: T. and T. Clark, 1975, 1979), 269–91.

2. Arthur Skevington Wood ("The Contribution of John Wesley to the Theology of Grace," in *Grace Unlimited*, ed. Clark H. Pinnock [Minneapolis: Bethany Fellowship, 1975], 212) demonstrates that Wesley interpreted our participation in Adam's sin similarly.

8:34; cf. 2 Pet. 2:19). Paul confirms that unregenerate people are slaves of sin. He reminds the Romans that "you are slaves to sin" (Rom. 6:17) and speaks of the time "when you were slaves to sin" (Rom. 6:20). They had presented "the parts of [their] bod[ies] in slavery to impurity and ever-increasing wickedness" (Rom. 6:19). Believers have been crucified with Christ "so that the body of sin might be done away with, that we should no longer be slaves to sin" (Rom. 6:6). If Christ died so that we should no longer be slaves to sin, the clear implication is that we were formerly slaves to sin. Sin is described in Romans 6 as a power that holds its captives in thralldom. Unbelievers are enslaved to sin in the sense that all they want to do is sin. They are free to do what is good in the sense that they have opportunities to do so. They fail to avail themselves of these opportunities, however, because they do not desire to do what is good. The captivity of sin is so powerful that they always desire to sin.

Do unregenerate human beings always sin? Is there not some good in their lives? We are not saying that they are as evil as they can possibly be. Jesus says, ". . . you then, though you are evil, know how to give good gifts to your children" (Luke 11:13). If people were as evil as they possibly could be, they would not desire to give good things to their children. They would presumably find ways to inflict only evil upon their children. Unbelieving parents often love their children and their friends (cf. Matt. 5:46–47). They also may do much that is good for society. It should be noted that Jesus still says that they are evil. Evil people still give good gifts to their children and do kind things for other people.

If people are not as sinful as they can possibly be, then in what sense are they slaves to sin? It is crucial to establish a biblical definition of sin. Of course, sin consists in disobeying the law (1 John 3:4). But the root of sin is much deeper than this. Romans 1:21–25 clarifies that the heart of sin is failing to glorify God as God. The heart of sin is a belittling of God and a scorning of his glory, which involves a failure to glorify and thank him (Rom. 1:21). As Romans 3:23 says, "All have sinned and fall short of the glory of God." Sinners do not give God the supreme place in their lives but exchange "the glory of the immortal God for images made to look like mortal man and birds and animals and reptiles" (Rom. 1:23). In other words, people "served created things rather than the Creator" (Rom. 1:25). Sin is not first and foremost the practice of evil deeds but an attitude that gives glory to something other than God. People may be loving to their children and kind to their neighbors and never give a thought to God. The essence of sin is self-worship rather than God-worship. The serpent persuaded Eve and Adam to eat the fruit of the tree by promising them that they would "be like God" (Gen. 3:5). They could dispense with God and worship themselves; they would worship the creature rather than the Creator.

Such a conception of sin helps us understand how people can perform actions that externally conform with righteousness yet remain slaves of sin. These actions are not motivated by a desire to honor and glorify God as God.

They are not done out of an attitude of faith, which brings glory to God (Rom. 4:20). Faith brings glory to God because he is seen to be the all-powerful one who supplies our every good, and thus is deserving of praise and honor. Actions that externally conform with righteousness may still be sin, in that they are not done for God's glory and by faith. The necessity of faith is underscored by Romans 14:23, where Paul notes that "everything that does not come from faith is sin." Slavery to sin does not mean that people always engage in reprehensible behavior. It means that the unregenerate never desire to bring glory to God, but are passionately committed to upholding their own glory and honor.

Of course, the power of sin is such that all have fallen short of conformity with God's law (Rom. 1:18–3:20). No one has perfectly done all that the law requires. The extent of our slavery to sin is, however, even deeper than this. It is not merely that the "sinful mind is hostile to God" (Rom. 8:7). It is also true that it "does not submit to God's law, nor can it do so" (Rom. 8:7). Those in the flesh have an intense hatred of God burning within them, whether they are conscious of this or not. Moreover, they have no ability to keep God's law. Paul is not saying that there is no opportunity to keep the law. Nor is he saying that people want to keep the law, but God prevents them from keeping it. His point is that those in the flesh have no moral ability to keep the law perfectly or to glorify God. The power of sin is so great that they "cannot please God" (Rom. 8:8) and do his will. They are slaves to sin.

The Wesleyan View of Fallen Humanity

It is notable that John Wesley would agree with the preceding diagnosis. He writes,

> I believe that Adam, before his fall, had such freedom of will, that he might choose either good or evil; but that, since the fall, no child of man has a natural power to choose anything that is truly good. Yet I know (and who does not?) that man has still freedom of will in things of indifferent nature.[3]

Human beings since the fall are so enmeshed in the power of sin that apart from divine grace they cannot choose what is spiritually good.[4] This point is

---

3. *The Works of John Wesley*, ed. T. Jackson, 14 vols. (1831; reprint, Grand Rapids: Baker, 1979), 10:350. Hereafter designated as *Works*.

4. Wesleyan theology differs from that of Charles Finney in that Finney believed that all people possess the ability, apart from grace, to choose what is good. Contrary to Wesleyans he rejects the idea that people are born morally depraved because of Adam's sin. Thus, it is not surprising to learn that Finney repudiated the doctrine of prevenient grace. See J. E. Smith, "The Theology of Charles Finney: A System of Self-Reformation," *Trin J* 13 (1992): 75–77, 82–84.

often acknowledged by Wesley scholars.[5] Harald Lindström rightly remarks that "Wesley maintains that natural man is totally corrupt."[6] He is "sinful through and through, has no knowledge of God and no power to turn to him of his own free will."[7] Robert V. Rakestraw says that in Wesley's theology "men and women are born in sin and unable in themselves to make the least move toward God."[8] Colin W. Williams affirms the same point: "Because of original sin, the natural man is 'dead to God' and unable to move toward God or respond to him."[9] Leo G. Cox says, "By nature man receives nothing that is good. . . . He is free but free only to do evil and to follow on in the way of sin."[10] Wesley did not believe that the will of fallen humanity was free. He says, "Such is the freedom of the will; free only to evil; free to 'drink iniquity like water;' to wander farther and farther from the living God, and do more 'despite to the Spirit of grace!'"[11] The Wesleyan analysis of the human condition does not differ fundamentally from the Calvinistic one.[12] Indeed, in 1745 John Wesley said that his theology was "within a hair's breadth" of Calvinism "(1) In ascribing all good to the free grace of God. (2) *In denying all natural free-will*, and all power antecedent to grace. And, (3) In excluding all merit from man; even for what he has or does by the grace of God."[13] Wesley's analysis of the human condition and his bold proclamation of divine grace should warm the heart of any evangelical Calvinist.

Prevenient Grace in the Wesleyan System

If Wesleyans and Calvinists concur on the human condition, wherein do they differ? One major place that Wesleyans break with Calvinists is through their doctrine of prevenient grace. Elton Hendricks says that this doctrine "played a more important role in Wesley's theological thought

5. See Wood, "Theology of Grace," 212–13; Charles A. Rogers, *The Concept of Prevenient Grace in the Theology of John Wesley* (Ph.D. dissertation, Duke University, 1967), 107–13, 156–58, 194–98, 200–2.
6. Harald Lindström, *Wesley and Sanctification: A Study in the Doctrine of Salvation* (London: Epworth, 1950), 45.
7. Ibid.
8. Robert V. Rakestraw, "John Wesley as a Theologian of Grace," *JETS* 27 (1984): 196.
9. Colin W. Williams, *John Wesley's Theology Today* (Nashville: Abingdon, 1960), 41.
10. Leo G. Cox, "Prevenient Grace—A Wesleyan View," *JETS* 12 (1969): 147.
11. *Works*, 5:104.
12. So also Melvin E. Dieter, "The Wesleyan Perspective," in *Five Views on Sanctification* (Grand Rapids: Zondervan, 1987), 21–23; M. Elton Hendricks, "John Wesley and Natural Theology," *Wesley Th J* 18 (1983): 9; J. Weldon Smith III, "Some Notes on Wesley's Doctrine of Prevenient Grace," *Religion in Life* 34 (1964–65): 70–74. The extent of the agreement should be qualified, according to H. Orton Wiley, *Christian Theology* (Kansas City, Mo.: Beacon Hill, 1952), 2:353.
13. *Works*, 8:284–85. Italics added.

than in that of any other Protestant theologian."[14] Williams affirms that it "has very great significance in his theology."[15] Even though Calvinists and Arminians hold much in common, H. Ray Dunning rightly says that "the truth that holds them but a hair's breadth apart at the point of the watershed is the doctrine of *prevenient grace.*"[16] The differences between Calvinists and Arminians on this point should not be minimized. William Ragsdale Cannon is correct in saying that "though Wesleyanism and Calvinism come in this instance so close together, they are in reality worlds apart."[17] How crucial is prevenient grace to the Wesleyan system? Wesleyans themselves seem to concur that their theology hinges on the doctrine. Robert E. Chiles says that "without it, the Calvinist logic is irrefutable."[18] Williams asserts that Wesley's theology of prevenient grace "broke the chain of logical necessity by which the Calvinist doctrine of predestination seems to flow from the doctrine of original sin."[19] It seems fair to conclude that if prevenient grace is not taught in Scripture, then the credibility of Wesleyan theology is seriously undermined.

Before probing to see whether Scripture teaches prevenient grace, it is necessary to explore what Wesleyans mean by the term. We need to recall that Wesley himself was not a systematic theologian but a pastoral theologian who developed his theology in the course of his ministry. Thus, no systematic treatment of the theme of prevenient grace is found in his writings.[20] In Wesleyan theology there are various conceptions of prevenient grace that we do not need to specify here since, as we shall see, there is common ground within the various positions on the issue that concerns us.[21]

---

14. Hendricks, "Natural Theology," 8.

15. Williams, *Wesley's Theology,* 41.

16. H. Ray Dunning, *Grace, Faith, and Holiness: A Wesleyan Systematic Theology* (Kansas City, Mo.: Beacon Hill, 1988), 49.

17. William Ragsdale Cannon, *The Theology of John Wesley: With Special Reference to the Doctrine of Justification* (New York: University Press of America, 1974), 102.

18. Robert E. Chiles, *Theological Transition in American Methodism: 1790–1935* (Nashville: Abingdon, 1965), 50.

19. Williams, *Wesley's Theology,* 44. See also his comments on 46. In agreement with Williams are Rakestraw ("John Wesley," 197) and Wood ("Theology of Grace," 215).

20. For a survey of the positions of Wesley and John Fletcher see Mark Royster, *John Wesley's Doctrine of Prevenient Grace in Missiological Perspective* (D.Miss. dissertation, Asbury Theological Seminary, 1989), 30–72.

21. Rogers in his dissertation (see n. 5) has provided the most comprehensive analysis of Wesley's doctrine. See particularly his distinction between the early (*Prevenient Grace,* 127–35) and later Wesley (159–263) on prevenient grace. For the purposes of this chapter only Wesley's later theology of prevenient grace is in view. Rogers also includes a survey (5–16) of Wesleyan scholarship on prevenient grace; see also Royster (*Missiological Perspective,* 73–93). For three different understandings of prevenient grace in the Wesleyan tradition see Thomas A. Langford, *Practical Divinity: Theology in the Wesleyan Tradition* (Nashville: Abingdon, 1983), 33. Chiles (*American Methodism,* 150–51) specifies two strands of prevenient grace among Wesleyans.

In some respects Wesleyans use the term *prevenient grace* in a way that matches with the Calvinist term *common grace*.[22] The conscience, according to Wesley, is to be ascribed to prevenient grace.[23] It is not to be understood as a natural gift but is supernaturally given by God.[24] In addition, some moral excellence and virtue in the world exists even among those who are unregenerate.[25] Prevenient grace is responsible for the goodness that is present to some extent in every society, even in cultures that are largely non-Christian.[26] We are not surprised to learn, then, that the relationship between prevenient grace and natural theology has been explored by some, with a close connection being suggested.[27]

The Wesleyan understanding of prevenient grace differs from the Calvinistic conception of common grace in one important area. In the Calvinistic scheme common grace does not and cannot lead to salvation. It functions to restrain evil in the world but does not lead unbelievers to faith. For Wesleyans, prevenient grace may lead one to salvation. Cox rightly says, "The Wesleyan teaches that the prevenient grace leads on to saving grace, prepares for it, enables a person to enter into it."[28] Indeed, in Wesley's theology it seems that a proper response to prevenient grace could lead to the salvation of those who have not heard the gospel.[29] What we are interested in exploring, however, is not how prevenient grace affects those who have never heard the gospel. The distinctive aspect of prevenient grace that is relevant for our discussion is that it provides the ability to choose salvation, an ability that was surrendered by Adam's sin. Wesley describes it as follows:

> Salvation begins with what is usually termed (and very properly) *preventing grace;* including the first wish to please God, the first dawn of light concerning his will, and the first slight transient conviction of having sinned against him. All these imply some tendency toward life; some degree of salvation; the beginning of a deliverance from a blind, unfeeling heart, quite insensible of God and the things of God.[30]

22. So Dunning, *Grace, Faith, and Holiness*, 296; cf. Cox, "Prevenient Grace," 143–44. In fact, Wiley (*Christian Theology*, 2:357) thinks that the Wesleyan conception of prevenient grace precludes any need for "common grace."

23. *Works*, 7:187–88. For Wesley's understanding of the role of prevenient grace in relationship to the conscience see Rogers, *Prevenient Grace*, 184–89.

24. So Rakestraw, "John Wesley," 197; Lindström, *Wesley and Sanctification*, 48. Wesley (*Works*, 7:187; see also 6:512) specifically says it is "a supernatural gift."

25. Wesley, *Works*, 7:345; see also 7:374.

26. So John Miley, *Systematic Theology* (New York: Eaton and Mains, 1894), 2:244, 246.

27. See Hendricks, "Natural Theology," 7–17; Smith, "Prevenient Grace," 77–80; Lindström, *Wesley and Sanctification*, 46–47.

28. Cox, "Prevenient Grace," 144.

29. See Dunning (*Grace, Faith, and Holiness*, 161–70) for a helpful discussion. See also Rogers, *Prevenient Grace*, 243–47.

30. *Works*, 6:509.

235

What separates Calvinists from Wesleyans is that the former see electing grace as given only to some (the elect) and insist that this grace cannot ultimately be resisted. The latter argue that prevenient grace is given to all people and that it can be resisted.

What is common in all Wesleyan theories of prevenient grace is that the freedom, which was lost in Adam's sin, is sufficiently restored to enable people to choose salvation.[31] Prevenient grace provides people with the ability to choose or reject God. As sinners born in Adam, they had no ability to do good or to choose what is right. But as recipients of prevenient grace they can once again choose the good. Wesley said, "Natural free-will, in the present state of mankind, I do not understand: I only assert, that

---

31. The description of prevenient grace in this paragraph is supported by Langford, *Practical Divinity*, 33; Dunning, *Grace, Faith, and Holiness*, 339; Rakestraw, "John Wesley," 196; Williams, *Wesley's Theology*, 41, 46; Chiles, *American Methodism*, 149; Cox, "Prevenient Grace," 147–49; Lindström, *Wesley and Sanctification*, 45–46; Hendricks, "Natural Theology," 9–11; Smith, "Prevenient Grace," 75; Henry C. Thiessen, *Lectures in Systematic Theology*, rev. Vernon D. Doerksen (Grand Rapids: Eerdmans, 1979), 106, 259; William B. Pope, *A Compendium of Christian Theology* (London: Wesleyan Conference Office, 1880), 2:358–67.

Rogers's own conclusions regarding Wesley's understanding of prevenient grace, on first glance, seem to be radically different from that suggested by the other scholars. Further analysis, however, reveals that the difference is one of degree, not one of kind. Rogers argues (*Prevenient Grace*, 217–19) that prevenient grace, according to Wesley, does not provide people with the ability to choose salvation. Prevenient grace in Wesley's thought is a gift given, not a gift that is offered and can be rejected. People are passive in the reception of faith, and there is no emphasis on the role of human decision in receiving faith. Thus faith is irresistible at the moment given. Rogers's explanation may lead one to think that Wesley was a Calvinist! But this is not the whole story. Rogers contends that prevenient grace (*Prevenient Grace*, 228–30, 237, 271, 282–83, 288) in Wesley's thought plays a decisive role before one comes to faith. Prevenient grace operates through the law and conscience to bring conviction of sin and despair of ever pleasing God. People have the freedom to resist the conviction of sin that comes from the law and conscience. If they do not respond appropriately to the conviction of sin mediated by the law and conscience, then they will not be saved. Prevenient grace leads one to the very brink of salvation if one responds positively to the "means of grace" that precede saving faith. Thus, prevenient grace is irresistible at the moment one exercises faith, but long before one receives faith the grace of God can be resisted. Only those who satisfactorily respond to prevenient grace come to the point where saving faith can be exercised. It seems that Rogers is in harmony with other Wesleyans in his conception of prevenient grace, for the grace God gives can still be resisted. Human beings may choose to respond to or resist the influence of the law and conscience. The final and ultimate determination lies with human choice. Rogers differs from other Wesleyans in locating the point of resistance in another place in Wesley's theology, namely, one's response to the means of grace before conversion.

For views that are quite similar to Rogers's see Royster (*Missiological Perspective*, 90–91) and Robert E. Cushman, "Salvation for All: Wesley and Calvinism," in *Methodism*, ed. W. K. Anderson (Nashville: Methodist Publishing House, 1947). It is clear from Royster's concluding definition that ability to choose what is good is included in his understanding of prevenient grace, for he says (92) that prevenient grace provides "the freedom/power to respond positively to subsequent directions from God."

there is a measure of free-will supernaturally restored to every man, together with that supernatural light which 'enlightens every man that cometh into the world.'"[32] Prevenient grace does not guarantee that the good will be chosen. It simply provides the opportunity or liberty to choose salvation. People may stifle the grace given and turn away from God, or they may respond to God's grace and turn to him in order to be saved.

Obviously, prevenient grace fixes a large gulf between Calvinism and Wesleyanism. Calvinists contend that the unregenerate have no ability or desire to choose God. God's election of some is what brings them from darkness to light, from Satan's kingdom to God's. Wesleyans believe that God has given prevenient grace to all people. As descendants of Adam they were born with no ability or desire to choose God, but God has counteracted this inability by the gift of prevenient grace. Now all people have the ability to choose God. The ultimate determination of salvation is the human decision to say no or yes to God.[33]

Wesleyan Arguments in Favor of Prevenient Grace

For all Bible-believing Christians, the most important question in matters of doctrinal dispute is this: what is the Bible's teaching as it pertains to the issue at hand? Calvinists and Arminians likewise must turn to the Bible. The critical question is whether or not the doctrine of prevenient grace is supported by Scripture. We cannot examine this issue until we see the arguments that are put forward to defend the doctrine. Wesleyans use at least four arguments to support the idea that prevenient grace is a doctrine rooted in Scripture.

First, the Scripture text that is appealed to quite often is John 1:9.[34] "The true light that gives light to every man was coming into the world." The meaning of this text is not analyzed in detail by Wesleyan scholars, but their understanding seems clear enough. The coming of Jesus Christ into the world brought enough light to all people so that they are now able to reject or accept the message of the gospel. The illumination *(phōtizei)* refers to the granting of grace that overcomes the darkness that penetrated human hearts as a result of Adam's sin. This illumination does not guarantee salvation; it simply makes it possible for men and women to choose salvation.

---

32. *Works*, 10:229–30.

33. Rakestraw ("John Wesley," 199) rightly says that in Wesley's theology "that one is ultimately the determining factor in the decision of his or her justification. Faith is offered as God's free gift, but the sinner must then actively respond to that offer and reach out with the arms of true repentance to receive the gift."

34. E.g., Wesley, *Works*, 10:230, 7:188; Lindström, *Wesley and Sanctification*, 45.

Such an understanding of the verse may be confirmed in the subsequent context. Some rejected the light and "did not receive him" (John 1:11), while others responded to the light and "received him" (John 1:12). It should also be noted that this illumination is not restricted to a few. It is granted to "every person" *(panta anthrōpon)*. This would support the Wesleyan view that prevenient grace is given to all people.

A second argument employed by Wesleyans is that prevenient grace is granted in the atonement of Christ (e.g., Tit. 2:11; John 12:32).[35] This argument is bound up with the universality of Christ's atonement. His death for all necessarily implies that grace is given to some extent to all. The argument is that Christ would not die for all unless all were granted the opportunity to accept or reject him. John 12:32 can be understood as supporting this theory. Jesus says, "But I, when I am lifted up from the earth, will draw all men to myself." Henry Thiessen says about this verse, "There issues a power from the cross of Christ that goes out to all men, though many continue to resist that power."[36] In the death of Christ grace is operative so that all people are "drawn" *(helkuō)* to him. The drawing does not guarantee salvation but makes it possible,[37] supporting the idea that grace is given in the atonement that reverses the total inability of people to choose God. In addition, it should be pointed out that John 12:32 refers to "all people" *(pantas)*. The grace given in the atonement is not limited to some but is universally distributed, giving all people everywhere the opportunity to respond or reject it.

The third Wesleyan argument in favor of prevenient grace has a theological cast. God must have granted the power to choose him because otherwise the warnings, invitations, and commands in Scripture are meaningless.[38] Why would God give commands to people if they are unable to put them into practice? There are numerous texts in Scripture in which commands, invitations, and warnings are employed. Perhaps Romans 2:4 is a particularly appropriate verse to cite in support.[39] "Or do you show contempt for the riches of his kindness, tolerance and patience, not realizing that God's kindness leads you toward repentance?" God would not command people to repent and be waiting for them to repent if he knew that they could not do so. His kindness is such that he has provided the means

---

35. So, e.g., Miley, *Systematic Theology*, 2:247; Wiley, *Christian Theology*, 2:353; Adam Clarke, *Christian Theology* (New York: Eaton and Mains, 1835), 117; Wood, "Theology of Grace," 216; Langford, *Practical Divinity*, 34; Smith, "Prevenient Grace," 75; Lindström, *Wesley and Sanctification*, 49; Dunning, *Grace, Faith, and Holiness*, 339.

36. Thiessen, *Systematic Theology*, 261.

37. Cf. Grant R. Osborne, "Soteriology in the Gospel of John," in *The Grace of God, the Will of Man: A Case for Arminianism*, ed. Clark H. Pinnock (Grand Rapids: Zondervan, 1989), 249.

38. Cf. Clarke, *Christian Theology*, 130, 132; Miley, *Systematic Theology*, 2:245–46.

39. Cf. Thiessen, *Systematic Theology*, 106.

for every person to repent if they would only avail themselves of that means.

Fourth, prevenient grace is supported by the very nature of God.[40] A God of mercy, wisdom, justice, and love would not leave human beings without an opportunity to repent and choose salvation. A God of love and mercy who desires all to be saved (1 Tim. 2:4) would see to it that all have the chance to partake of salvation. If God elects only a few, he is guilty of partiality.[41]

A Critique of the Wesleyan Arguments for Prevenient Grace

We now proceed to analyze the four arguments for prevenient grace advanced by Wesleyans. I will argue that their case is unpersuasive and that their doctrine of prevenient grace is not found in Scripture. Wesleyans, however, advance some exegetical and theological arguments in defense of prevenient grace that will be considered here.

We turn first of all to John 1:9. The crucial phrase for our purposes is *phōtizei panta anthrōpon* (enlightens every person), which enlightening is ascribed to "the true light." Wesleyans understand this enlightenment to refer to prevenient grace, which is given to all people, but there are serious reasons for doubting that this is the meaning of the verse. In fact, the verse can be understood in three other ways that do not yield the Wesleyan interpretation. First, the illumination could refer to general revelation, which is granted to all people through the created order.[42] This shifts the debate to different ground, for some argue that general revelation is sufficient for salvation.[43] Such a view is unpersuasive given Paul's estimation of general revelation in Romans 1:18–32.[44] In any case, D. A. Carson is correct in dismissing a reference to general revelation since this would have been more appropriately dealt with earlier in the prologue (i.e., John 1:3–4).[45] The

40. So Wesley, *Works*, 10:36ff; Wood, "Theology of Grace," 211–12; Lindström, *Wesley and Sanctification*, 46.

41. Cf. Thiessen, *Systematic Theology*, 260.

42. So Leon Morris, *The Gospel According to John*, NICNT (Grand Rapids: Eerdmans, 1971), 95.

43. In fact, in Wesleyan theology there is not a clear line of demarcation between general revelation and special revelation with respect to prevenient grace. See 235.

44. See Moo's (*Romans 1–8*, 91–124) thorough exegesis in defense of this conclusion. Neither does Romans 2:14–15 suggest the possibility of salvation through obeying one's conscience. See Thomas R. Schreiner, "Does Paul Believe in Justification by Works? Another Look at Romans 2," *The Bulletin for Biblical Research* 3 (1993): 131–58. Wesley believed that this passage taught the doctrine of prevenient grace. See John Wesley, *Explanatory Notes Upon the New Testament*, 2 vols. (reprint, Grand Rapids: Baker, 1981), comment on Romans 2:14 in volume 2.

45. D. A. Carson, *The Gospel According to John* (Grand Rapids: Eerdmans, 1991), 123.

specific context is not general revelation but the response of people to the incarnate Word of God, Jesus Christ.

Second, the illumination may refer to an inward illumination that leads to conversion.[46] In this case, John would not be saying that illumination is given to all people "without exception" but to all "without distinction."[47] The light is not confined to the Jews, but also has an effect among the Gentiles. Other sheep that are not of the fold of the Jews will be brought in (John 10:16). Jesus died not only for the Jews but also for the children of God scattered throughout the world (John 11:51–52).

The context of John 1:9–13, however, suggests that another interpretation is the most probable.[48] The word *enlighten (phōtizō)* refers not to inward illumination but to the exposure that comes when light is shed upon something. Some are shown to be evil because they did not know or receive Jesus (John 1:10–11), while others are revealed to be righteous because they have received Jesus and have been born of God (John 1:12–13). John 3:19–21 confirms this interpretation. Those who are evil shrink from coming to the light because they do not want their works to be exposed (v. 20). But those who practice the truth gladly come to the light so that it might be manifest that their works are wrought in God (v. 21). The light that enlightens every person does not entail the bestowment of grace, nor does it refer to the inward illumination of the heart by the Spirit of God. Rather, the light exposes and reveals the moral and spiritual state of one's heart. C. K. Barrett rightly says that "the light shines upon every man for judgement, to reveal what he is."[49] Or, as Carson remarks, "Inner illumination is then not in view" but "the objective revelation" that occurs at the coming of the "true light."[50] John 1:9 is not, therefore, suggesting that through Christ's coming each person is given the ability to choose salvation. The purpose of the verse is to say that the coming of the true light exposes and reveals where people are in their relationship to God.[51]

46. The word *phōtizō* has the meaning of inward illumination in, e.g., Psalm 18:9 (LXX); Ephesians 1:18; 3:9.
47. So Carson, *John*, 123.
48. For the interpretation suggested here see C. K. Barrett, *The Gospel According to St. John* (Philadelphia: Westminster, ²1978), 161; Carson, *John*, 124.
49. Barrett, *John*, 161.
50. Carson, *John*, 124.
51. John emphasizes that the light, Jesus, has come into the world so that people might believe in him (1:6–8; 12:35–36) or follow him (8:12). The call to believe in the light, though, is a far cry from saying that all have been given the ability to do so. Indeed, John, speaking of those who did not believe, says they "could not believe" because God "has blinded their eyes" (12:39–40). This judicial hardening by God does not lessen human responsibility in John's eyes (cf. 12:43). Jesus has come into the world as light so that people would believe in him and they should do so! For some wise comments on how God's judicial hardening is compatible with other biblical themes see Carson, *John*, 448–49.

Wesleyans appeal to grace given in the atonement and Christ's death for all as an indication of prevenient grace. I shall not examine the question of the extent of the atonement since that is treated elsewhere in this work.[52] Indeed, Calvinists have typically seen grace as bestowed upon the elect in the atonement, but in this case the grace bestowed is effective and guarantees salvation. The question is whether in the atonement of Christ the Wesleyan conception of prevenient grace is taught; that is, does Scripture teach that people are given the ability to choose or to reject God by virtue of the atonement? Doubtless grace is manifested in the atonement. For instance, Titus 2:11 says that "the grace of God that brings salvation has appeared to all men." Calvinists usually argue that this text teaches that the atonement secures and accomplishes redemption for the elect. It is not my purpose to defend or refute that interpretation. Even if the text were suggesting that salvation is potentially available for all people (cf. 1 Tim. 4:10), that is a far cry from saying that through the atonement God has counteracted the effects of Adam's sin so that all people have the opportunity to accept or reject him. Titus 2:11 says that God's grace has been manifested through Christ's work on the cross, but it does not say that God has thereby supplied the ability to believe to all people. Wesleyans conclude from the atonement effected by Christ that enough grace has been imparted to all people so that they can now choose whether or not to believe. But it is precisely this point that is not taught explicitly in the verse. It does not necessarily follow that since grace was manifested in the death of Christ that all people as a result have the ability to believe in him. Specific exegetical support for this conclusion is lacking.

A text that might lead to the Wesleyan conclusion is John 12:32. But this involves a misreading of the text. In John 6:37 Jesus says, "All that the Father gives me will come to me, and whoever comes to me I will never drive away." Note that this text specifically teaches that only some will come to Jesus, namely, those who have been given by the Father to the Son. In other words, the Father has not given all to the Son; he has selected only some, and it is they who will come to the Son and believe in him (cf. John 6:35).[53] The teaching of John 6:37 is reaffirmed in 6:44. "No one can come to me unless the Father who sent me draws him, and I will raise him at the last day." The word *draw (helkuō)*, which is used in John 12:32, is also used in John 6:37. The point of John 6:44 is that the Father does not draw all people, only some. Carson rightly remarks, "The combination of v[erse] 37a

---

52. See chapter 11 by J. I. Packer.
53. For more detailed support of divine election in John see Robert W. Yarbrough, "Divine Election in the Gospel of John," in chapter 2 of this work; see also D. A. Carson, *Divine Sovereignty and Human Responsibility: Biblical Perspectives in Tension* (Atlanta: John Knox, 1981), 125–98.

and v[erse] 44 prove that this 'drawing' activity of the Father cannot be reduced to what theologians sometimes call 'prevenient grace' dispensed to every individual, for this 'drawing' is selective, or else the negative note of v[erse] 44 is meaningless."[54] The Johannine conception of drawing is not that it makes salvation possible, but that it makes salvation effectual. Those who are drawn will come to Jesus and believe in him.

Does this definition of drawing mean that John teaches universalism, since 12:32 says that Jesus will draw all to himself by virtue of the cross? The context of John 12:20–33 helps us answer that question. Greeks, that is, Gentiles, approached Philip because they wanted to see Jesus (vv. 20–23). Jesus ignores the request and instead speaks of the need for a grain of wheat to die in order to bear fruit (vv. 24–26), and of his commitment to carry out his commission (vv. 27–28). Jesus' death is the means by which God's judgment of the world and his triumph over Satan will be accomplished (v. 31). He concludes by saying that if he is lifted up he will draw all people to himself (v. 32).

The context is of paramount importance for understanding John 12:32. Jesus appears to ignore the request from his disciples to meet with the Greeks who wanted to see him. But the point Jesus makes is that the only way Gentiles will come to him is through his death. He must die in order to bear much fruit and bring Gentiles to himself. The power of Satan as the ruler of the world will be broken only by the cross. Thus, when Jesus speaks of drawing all people to himself by virtue of the cross, the issue in the context is how Gentiles can come to Jesus. The drawing of all does not refer to all people individually but the means by which Gentiles will be included in the people of God. Carson again rightly interprets the verse. "Here 'all men' reminds the reader of what triggered these statements, [namely,] the arrival of the Greeks, and means 'all people without distinction, Jews and Gentiles alike', not all individuals without exception."[55] The Wesleyan theory that prevenient grace is provided in the atonement so that people are given ability to choose salvation cannot be supported from the context of John 12.

The third Wesleyan argument for prevenient grace is probably the most powerful one. Why would God give commands unless people were given some ability to obey them? Romans 2:4 says that his kindness is intended to lead people to repentance. Does this not imply that people have the ability to repent if they would only choose to do so?

It should be acknowledged that Wesleyan logic is coherent here, and one can see why Wesleyans would deduce human ability from the giving of commands. Nonetheless, even though their logic is impeccable, it does not necessarily follow that their conclusion is true. An argument may be logically co-

54. Carson, *John*, 293.
55. Ibid., 444.

herent and not fit with the state of affairs in the world because the answer given is not comprehensive. To put it another way, one of the premises in the Wesleyan argument is not in accord with the reality of life as it is portrayed in the Scriptures. They are incorrect in deducing that God would not give commands without giving the moral ability to obey them. The distinction between physical and moral ability is crucial.[56] For instance, human beings are physically able (in most cases) to walk up steps, but they are physically unable to jump over houses. In a similar way, God gives commands to unbelievers that they can physically obey; that is, they could observe his commandments if they desired to do so. Unbelievers are morally unable to keep God's commands in the sense that they have no desire to obey all of his commandments. God commands all people (Gal. 3:10; Rom. 1:18–3:20) to obey his law perfectly, but no one is morally able to do this. Because all people are born with a sin nature inherited from Adam, they will inevitably sin. Even though people cannot morally obey God's commands, biblical authors assume that they should keep his commandments. They should keep his commandments because they are right and good (Rom. 7:12) and are not physically impossible to keep. People could observe the commandments if they wanted to do so. The biblical view, however, is that unbelievers as slaves of sin have no desire to keep God's law.[57]

The state of affairs that obtains under the law remains when Christ comes. That is, all people should come to Jesus in order to have life (John 5:40). Jesus upbraids those who do not believe despite all his works (Matt. 11:20–24), and he invites all to come to him (Matt. 11:28–30). Yet he also teaches that no one can come to him unless drawn by the Father (John 6:44), and only those to whom the Father and Son reveal themselves will come to know him (Matt. 11:25–27). All people are summoned to believe in Jesus and are censured for not believing. Nonetheless, the Scriptures also teach that they have no moral ability to believe, and that the only way they will believe is if they are given by the Father to the Son. This revelation is not vouchsafed to all people but only to the elect. Jesus commands believers to be perfect (Matt. 5:48), but the need for forgiveness (Matt. 6:14–15) demonstrates that perfection is impossible to attain.

The problem with Wesleyanism at this point is that it is guided by human logic and rationality rather than the Scriptures. Their view that commands would not be given that people could not morally obey is certainly attractive. But our counterargument is that such a notion is not taught in the Scriptures. The doctrine of original sin and human inability is

---

56. For a recent explanation of this distinction which is a model of clarity see David M. Ciocchi, "Understanding Our Ability to Endure Temptation: A Theological Watershed," *JETS* 35 (1992): 463–68.

57. It should be pointed out that Adam was created with both physical and moral ability to obey God's commands. We cannot here pursue the difficult question as to why Adam sinned.

an offense to reason.[58] This is not to say that it is irrational. The distinction between physical and moral ability goes a long way toward resolving the difficulties. Nonetheless, not all the difficulties are resolved by the Calvinist view, for ultimately we do not fully understand how people can be responsible for sin when they are born with an inclination that will inevitably lead them to sin.

An example from another area of life might help. Robert Wright in an article on alcoholism was musing on the theory that it might be determined by one's genes.[59] If so, could we conclude that people are not responsible for alcoholism? Wright correctly says no. If we draw this conclusion, then the reality of human responsibility will be slowly whittled away as we discover the impact of genetics on human behavior. Even if alcoholism is determined genetically, people are still responsible for their behavior.[60] We may not fully understand how both determinism and human responsibility can be true, but both are necessary to account for the nature of humanity and genetic research. So too, sinners who have inherited a sin nature from Adam and who have no moral ability to obey God's law and no inclination to respond to him are still responsible for their failure to respond to God's grace.

The preceding comments prepare us for understanding Romans 2:4. The wording of this text should be taken seriously, but our own philosophical presuppositions should not be read into it. It is the case that the kindness of God should lead people to repentance.[61] God's kindness is not a charade but is profoundly present in that he spares people and does not immediately destroy them for their sin. The kindness and patience of God should induce people to seek him and to confess their sin. But this text does not say that people have the moral ability to repent and turn to God. It simply says that they should repent and turn to him. Wesleyans read into this verse their theology of prevenient grace, thereby squeezing more out of the verse than it says.[62]

---

58. This is the title of Bernard Ramm's book on original sin, *Offense to Reason* (New York: Harper and Row, 1985).

59. Robert Wright, "Alcohol and Free Will: The Supreme Court Reopens an Old Question," *The New Republic* 197, 24 (14 December 1987): 14–16.

60. Wright himself seems to fall prey to rationalism insofar as he subordinates human responsibility to determinism. Nonetheless, he insists that life will not make sense unless we hold people to be responsible.

61. The present indicative *agei* is understood here as conative. So C. F. D. Moule, *An Idiom Book of New Testament Greek*, 2d ed. (Cambridge: Cambridge University Press, 1959), 8. *Agei* should not be pressed as a present indicative to say that God's kindness is actually leading the Jews to repent. The point of the verse is that God's kindness should lead them to repent.

62. Another text that could be used to support prevenient grace is Acts 7:51, where Stephen says to his adversaries, "you always resist the Holy Spirit." It is true that there is a work of the Spirit that is resisted by unbelievers. This should be distinguished, however, from saying that God has granted all people the ability to respond to his grace. In fact, the text seems to suggest the opposite. People resist the Holy Spirit because of their bondage to sin. Scripture teaches that for the elect God graciously overcomes their resistance and brings them to repentance (2 Tim. 2:25–26).

What we have said about Romans 2:4 leads us naturally to the fourth argument used for prevenient grace, that is, the justice, wisdom, mercy, and love of God. What I have been arguing is that the fundamental problem with the Wesleyan understanding of prevenient grace is that it is not taught in the Scriptures. It is a philosophical imposition of a certain world view upon the Scriptures. This world view is attractive because it neatly solves, to some extent, issues such as the problem of evil and why human beings are held responsible for sin. But the Scriptures do not yield such neat solutions.[63] God is wholly just in condemning sinners who have no ability to obey his law (Rom. 8:7–8). They fail to keep the law because they do not want to obey it. In sinning they carry out the desires of their hearts. God is merciful and loving in not destroying them immediately and offering them salvation. It is a mistake, however, to say that God's love and mercy will provide every person an equal chance to believe. God would be just in sending all to hell since all have sinned. The love and mercy extended to the elect is undeserved. God is obligated to save no one, but out of a heart of mercy he saves some (Eph. 2:4–7). Those who believe that God must extend mercy equally to all are subtly falling into the trap of believing that God would not be good without showing mercy equally to all. This comes perilously close to the conclusion that God should show mercy to all to the same extent, and that such mercy is obligatory. But if God should show equal mercy to all, then mercy is no longer viewed as undeserved. In this view mercy extended to all is demanded by justice. This kind of reasoning should be rejected because the Scriptures make it clear that no one deserves to be saved, that all people could be justly sent to hell, and that God's mercy is so stunning because it is undeserved.

The scandal of the Calvinist system is that ultimately the logical problems posed cannot be fully resolved. The final resolution of the problem of human responsibility and divine justice is beyond our rational capacity. The doctrine of prevenient grace in the Wesleyan sense is read into the Scriptures because it solves so many logical problems and attempts to clarify how God is just and loving. Calvinists also affirm God's mercy, wisdom, justice, and love. We trust that he is good, and that no one will perish who does not deserve judgment. There is significant evidence to vindicate the justice, mercy, and love of God. Nonetheless, we cannot comprehensively explain how these attributes of God fit the reality portrayed in the Scriptures. There are finally some mysteries that we cannot unravel.

63. For a semipopular treatment that is a more detailed explanation of the biblical view see D. A. Carson, *How Long O Lord? Reflections on Suffering and Evil* (Grand Rapids: Baker, 1990).

Conclusion

The doctrine of prevenient grace should be accepted only if it can be sustained from a careful exegesis of the Scriptures. What was most striking to me in my research was how little scriptural exegesis has been done by Wesleyans in defense of prevenient grace. It is vital to their system of theology, for even Wesleyans admit that without it "Calvinist logic is irrefutable."[64] Nonetheless, not much exegetical work has been done in support of the doctrine. This is particularly astonishing when one compares the biblical data for prevenient grace to Calvinist texts that support unconditional election. The Calvinist case has been promulgated, rightly or wrongly, via a detailed exegesis of numerous texts. The plight of humanity due to Adam's sin (which we investigated) is reversed only by the electing grace of God, according to the Calvinist. Wesleyans contend that prevenient grace counteracts the inability of humanity due to Adam's sin, but firm biblical evidence seems to be lacking. One can be pardoned, then, for wondering whether this theory is based on scriptural exegesis. Millard Erickson rightly says about it, "The problem is that there is no clear and adequate basis in Scripture for this concept of universal enablement. The theory, appealing though it is in many ways, simply is not taught explicitly in the Bible."[65]

Prevenient grace is attractive because it solves so many problems, but it should be rejected because it cannot be exegetically vindicated. But if prevenient grace is rejected, then all people are in bondage to sin. They will never turn to God because they are so enslaved by sin that they will never desire to turn to him. How then can any be saved? The Scriptures teach that the effectual calling of God is what persuades those who are chosen to turn to him. God's grace effectively works in the heart of the elect so that they see the beauty and glory of Christ and put their faith in him (2 Cor. 4:6). Because God's choice lies behind our salvation, we cannot boast before him that we were noble or wise enough to choose him. We can only boast in the Lord who chose us to be his own (1 Cor. 1:29, 31).

64. See note 18.
65. Millard J. Erickson, *Christian Theology* (Grand Rapids: Baker, 1985), 925.

10

Reflections on Assurance

D. A. Carson

Introduction

So far as I know, there has been no English-language, full-scale treatment of the biblical theology of Christian assurance for more than fifty years. There have been numerous dictionary articles and the like, along with occasional discussions in journals. There have also been sophisticated studies of assurance as found in the theology of some notable Christian thinker or period, such as the book by Arthur S. Yates that examines assurance with special reference to John Wesley,[1] or the discussion of assurance that pervades R. T. Kendall's treatment of the move from Calvin to English Calvinism,[2] or the dissertation by Joel R. Beeke that studies personal assurance from Westminster to Alexander Comrie.[3] There have been countless studies of related biblical themes: perseverance, apostasy, the nature of covenant, the nature of faith, justification, and much more—too many to itemize; and there have

From D. A. Carson, "Reflections on Christian Assurance," *WTJ* 54 (1992): 1–29. Reprinted by permission. This chapter includes some minor changes from the original.

1. Arthur S. Yates, *The Doctrine of Assurance with Special Reference to John Wesley* (London: Epworth, 1952).

2. R. T. Kendall, *Calvin and English Calvinism to 1649* (Oxford: Oxford University Press, 1979). Similarly, there is more limited but still important discussion of the theme in Alan C. Clifford, *Atonement and Justification: English Evangelical Theology 1640–1790—An Evaluation* (Oxford: Oxford University Press, 1990).

3. Joel R. Beeke, "Personal Assurance of Faith: English Puritanism and the Dutch 'Nadere Reformatie': From Westminster to Alexander Comrie (1640–1760)" (Ph.D. dissertation, Westminster Theological Seminary, 1988).

been numerous popular treatments of Christian assurance. But although at one time assurance was not only a question of pressing pastoral importance but in certain respects a test of theological systems, in recent decades it has not received the attention it deserves.

This chapter makes no pretensions of redressing the balance. My aim is far more modest. First, I shall identify a number of tendencies in contemporary literature that bear on Christian assurance. Then I shall offer a number of biblical and theological reflections—really not much more than pump-priming—designed to set out the contours in which a biblical theology of Christian assurance might be constructed.

Some Contemporary Tendencies

By "Christian assurance," I refer to a Christian believer's confidence that he or she is already in a right standing with God, and that this will issue in ultimate salvation. This definition of assurance maintains the future orientation that has dominated much of the discussion in past centuries, but there are two entailments: (1) This is a far narrower definition than might have been deployed. For instance, the Epistle to the Hebrews speaks of the boldness Christians enjoy in coming before God, now that their high priest has entered into the heavenly tabernacle to intercede on their behalf. John writes of the confidence believers enjoy when they approach God in prayer. These, too, are dimensions of Christian assurance, important dimensions—but not the assurance that is the focal point of this study. (2) It should be immediately obvious that no single word gives us access to the theme. Some studies have begun by analyzing *pistis* or *parrēsia* or some other word, but questions about Christian assurance rise from the pages of the New Testament wherever believers are promised consummated salvation, or are warned of apostasy, or are assured of eternal life conditional on some factor; and so we must probe, however superficially, a representative number of such themes and passages. Ideally, we should begin with inductive study of each corpus; pragmatically, the limitations of this study dictate that we attempt no more than brief explorations.

Before embarking on such explorations, however, it is important to grasp the dominant parameters of the discussion today. What, then, are some of the more important tendencies in contemporary biblical and theological literature that bear on the subject? I begin with the most narrowly academic tendencies, and work down to the most popular.

Not only is there a tendency to stress the diverse emphases in many biblical texts, but there are even more diverse interpretations of them. Certainly the question of Christian assurance is raised by what appear to be tensions within the biblical documents themselves. On the one hand, Paul insists that all those who are foreknown, predestined, called, and justified will one day be glorified (Rom. 8:30); on the other, he tells the Corinthians to examine themselves to see if they are in the faith (2 Cor. 13:5). Christians are given "very great and precious promises" (2 Pet. 1:4), but such promises properly function to enable them to make their calling and election sure (1:10). If the fourth Gospel repeatedly assures us that Jesus, and then the Father himself, preserve all those the Father has given to the Son (e.g., John 6:37–40; 17:6–17), Jesus' interlocutors nevertheless are told that only those who hold to his teaching are truly his disciples (8:31). On the face of it, passages such as Hebrews 6:4–6 envisage the possibility of apostasy from which there is no reprieve. If so, how can believers be finally certain that they will not fall into such abysmal loss? John writes his first epistle in order that those who believe in the name of the Son of God might know that they have eternal life: this certainly sounds as if it is possible to believe in the name of the Son of God without knowing that one has eternal life.

Many scholars attempt no synthesis; indeed, they judge any attempt at synthesis to be illegitimate. But even among less skeptical scholars, these and many more passages are variously interpreted. One need only read the published form of I. Howard Marshall's dissertation,[4] and the recent dissertation by Judith M. Gundry Volf,[5] to appreciate how differently many of the same texts can be read. Meanwhile, the voluminous writings of E. P. Sanders,[6] and the growing number of responses to them, have shifted the center of discussion on Paul from justification and freedom from law to "covenantal nomism," thereby giving rise to notions of "getting in" and "staying in" that are quite different from those historically assumed by much of Protestantism, especially Lutheran Protestantism. At the risk of simplification, "getting in" turns on God's grace; "staying in" turns on the believer's obedience. The texts that can be lined up to defend this reading of Paul are substantial. If they are accepted without qualification, the implications for Christian assurance are stunning: Christian assurance becomes entirely hostage to Christian obedience, and is not established as a constituent element of saving faith itself.

4. I. Howard Marshall, *Kept by the Power of God: A Study of Perseverance and Falling Away* (Minneapolis: Bethany, 1975). See also his essay, "The Problem of Apostasy in New Testament Theology," now most accessible in his recently published book of essays, *Jesus the Saviour: Studies in New Testament Theology* (London: SPCK, 1990), 306–24.

5. Judith M. Gundry Volf, *Paul and Perseverance: Staying In and Falling Away*, WUNT 37 (Tübingen: J. C. B. Mohr [Paul Siebeck], 1990).

6. Especially *Paul and Palestinian Judaism: A Comparison of Patterns of Religion* (Philadelphia: Fortress, 1977); idem, *Paul, the Law, and the Jewish People* (Philadelphia: Fortress, 1983).

Or again, one need only compare Protestant and Catholic commentaries on 1 John to observe a chasm between their approaches. With but rare exceptions, the former treat 1 John as a treatise that provides criteria or tests (understood and arranged rather differently from commentator to commentator) to foster assurance among believers; the latter largely bypass the theme of assurance and see in this book a depiction of proper Christian communal life.

A major reexamination of relevant Reformation arguments is currently underway. Although some pre-Reformation Christian thinkers had treated the possibility of Christian assurance (e.g., Augustine, Duns Scotus), the consensus in the period leading up to the Reformation treated such assurance as conjectural, since knowledge of God's saving grace depended on good works and penance that "tied forgiveness to ecclesiastical authority."[7] Not only did the Reformation, by emphasizing Scripture, reduce the intermediary authority of the church, and therefore its role in binding and loosing the Christian conscience—its virulent emphasis on *sola fide* led Luther to see assurance as an element of saving faith. If one truly trusts Christ for the forgiveness of sins and full justification, so far also is one assured of his forgiveness. The same connection can be found in Calvin (*Institutes* 3.2.7); ultimately, he grounds assurance on Christ himself (*Institutes* 3.24.5). It is disputed just what place Calvin allows for works in Christian assurance; certainly in his thought they do not enjoy more than a subsidiary role. By contrast, the English Puritans, greatly dependent on the transitional figure of William Perkins,[8] himself deeply indebted to Beza and others, placed much more emphasis on the role of a transformed life in lending assurance to the Christian mind and conscience.[9]

Most scholars would not demur from this potted history. Debate has become heated, however, owing to the work of Kendall and those who have rushed to support him or to detract from his argument that English Calvinism owes far less to Calvin and far more to Beza than is commonly recognized, and to the work of M. Charles Bell, who argues that

7. R. W. A. Letham, "Assurance," in *New Dictionary of Theology*, ed. Sinclair B. Ferguson et al. (Leicester: InterVarsity, 1988), 51.
8. Cf. especially Ian Breward, ed., *The Work of William Perkins* (Abingdon: Marcham, 1970).
9. Despite the best efforts of R. M. Hawkes ("The Logic of Assurance in English Puritan Theology," *WTJ* 52 [1990]: 247–61) to minimize the conceptual distance between the magisterial reformers and the English Puritans on the matter of assurance, his own evidence admits more of a distance than he acknowledges. For instance, he argues that for Thomas Brooks "assurance is, somehow, a necessary part of faith" (250). The authenticating citation from Brooks reads, "Faith, in time, will of its own accord raise and advance itself to assurance" (*Heaven on Earth* [1654; reprint, London: Banner of Truth, 1961], 21). But that is simply another way of saying that *mature* ("in time") faith brings with it assurance. The issue is whether saving faith entails assurance in all who at any time are exercising such faith.

whereas Calvin taught that faith is fundamentally passive in nature, is centred in the mind or understanding, is primarily to be viewed in terms of certain knowledge, such that assurance of salvation is of the essence of faith, and is grounded *extra nos*, that is, outside ourselves in the person and work of Jesus Christ, Scottish theology, on the other hand, gradually came to teach that faith is primarily active, centred within the will or heart, and that assurance is *not* of the essence of faith, but is a fruit of faith, and is to be gathered through self-examination and syllogistic deduction, thereby placing the grounds of assurance *intra nos*, within ourselves.[10]

For Kendall, the challenge is not merely one of naming the right heroes, but of returning to the pristine Calvinism of Calvin, over against what he judges to be the scholastic Calvinism of many of his successors. There are important (and disputed) entailments in Kendall's study for the doctrine of definite atonement—and for understanding Christian assurance. Positions are sufficiently entrenched, and the topic sufficiently current, that in the second volume of the biography of Martyn Lloyd-Jones, Iain Murray devotes six pages to refuting Kendall.[11] Murray concludes that if Kendall is right and "full assurance" inheres in saving faith, there are "devastating practical consequences":

> If it were true then it would follow: (1) that anyone lacking "full assurance" has to be treated as not being a Christian at all; (2) that all converts can be told that their assurance is complete, contrary to the New Testament directions to converts to press on to fuller assurance (Hebrews 6:11; 2 Peter 1:5–10; 1 John 1:4); and (3) that if faith means full assurance then the many warnings of Scripture on the need to observe that true faith is always accompanied by holiness of life become needless.[12]

Of course, Kendall might well reply that Murray makes assurance dependent not on justification but on sanctification (understanding the latter term in its use in Reformed dogmatics, not in its more flexible use in the Pauline corpus), and ultimately fosters an unhealthy introspection that functions not unlike Arminianism or semi-Pelagianism. For his part, Beeke[13] argues that the differences between Calvin and the (later) Calvinists on the relations between faith and assurance are largely quantitative, not qualitative. Faced with changing pastoral contexts, Beeke argues, Calvinists allotted greater sensitivity to the degree of assurance that a Christian might experience, but nevertheless in their "meticulous argumentation" adhered to the fundamen-

---

10. M. Charles Bell, *Calvin and Scottish Theology: The Doctrine of Assurance* (Edinburgh: Handsel, 1985), 8.
11. Iain H. Murray, *D. Martyn Lloyd-Jones*, vol. 2, *The Fight of Faith: 1939–1981* (Edinburgh: Banner of Truth, 1990), 721–26.
12. Ibid., 726.
13. "Personal Assurance of Faith."

tal principles of the early Reformation. Within this framework they could argue that assurance of faith has more complex grounds than a simple resting on God's objective promises. On the whole, Beeke is correct for the notable figures he treats. Unfortunately, he writes history as if the "Annales" school of historiography had never developed, and makes no attempt either to limit his conclusions to those he studies or to probe how faith and assurance were handled in the lives of ordinary Christians in both English Puritanism and the Calvinist infiltration of the Dutch Reformation.

Certainly both sides of this essentially historical debate have full arsenals by which to take on the other's positions. For our purposes, however, it is worth observing that both sides recognize that the debate is not merely a historical one—What did Calvin (or Beza, or Perkins, or Comrie) actually teach?—but a doctrinal one with substantial theological and pastoral implications. We may range from the experience of many Scottish highlanders who habitually refuse to receive the communion elements on the ground that they lack personal assurance (and this lack stems from their own estimate of unsatisfactory evidences of grace in their lives), to the wretched "easy believism" of many in the western world who, having professed faith, feel no pull toward holiness and no shame when they take the elements. A thousand variations of experience dot the landscape between these two extremes.

In America, the basis of Christian assurance has erupted as the distinguishing banner of a small but vociferous segment of evangelicalism. The movement is strong enough to have formed its own organization, the Grace Evangelical Society, complete with its own journal.[14] All of the publications that have emerged so far are at the popular or semipopular level; but that ensures wider circulation, not less. Doubtless the most influential of these writings is a book by Zane Hodges, *The Gospel under Siege.*[15] The popular preacher John F. MacArthur Jr. has responded at about the same level,[16] but with so large a number of unguarded statements or overstatements that his work has spawned more controversy than healing.[17]

The concern of Hodges and his colleagues is to make Christian assurance absolutely certain. To accomplish this, they tie assurance exclusively to saving faith and divorce it from any support in a transformed life. The countless passages that tie genuine discipleship to obedience are handled by making a

14. *Journal of the Grace Evangelical Society.*
15. Zane C. Hodges, *The Gospel under Siege: A Study on Faith and Works* (Dallas: Redencion Viva, 1981). See also his *Grace in Eclipse* (Dallas: Redencion Viva, 1985), and his *Absolutely Free* (Dallas: Redencion Viva; Grand Rapids: Zondervan, 1989).
16. John F. MacArthur Jr., *The Gospel according to Jesus* (Grand Rapids: Zondervan, 1988).
17. One of the better reviews is by Darrell F. Bock, "A Review of *The Gospel according to Jesus,*" *BibSac* 141 (1989): 21–40.

disjunction between "discipleship" passages and those that promise eternal life. Eternal life turns on faith in the saving Son of God; discipleship turns on obedience; and Christian assurance is tied only to the former. To link assurance in any way to the latter, it is argued, is to corrupt a salvation of free grace and turn it into a salvation partly dependent on works. If my salvation depends only on free grace, then the basis of my assurance is as steadfast as the freedom of that grace. But if my assurance depends on observing certain changes in conduct in my life, themselves the fruit of obedience, then implicitly I am saying that, since I cannot be assured of salvation without seeing obedience, salvation itself depends on some mixture of faith plus obedience—and free grace is thereby destroyed. Hence the name of this new evangelical society. Its members are persuaded that the purity of the gospel of grace is at stake.

There are numerous entailments to this analysis. Those who disagree with them are dismissed as supporters of "lordship salvation," understood to mean that these opponents insist that part of the requirement for becoming a Christian, for receiving salvation, is the confession of Jesus as Lord. In the view of Hodges and his colleagues, trusting Jesus as Savior is all that is required for salvation. "Repentance," in their view, must be understood in a narrowly etymological sense: it is the mental "change of mind" that accepts Jesus as the Savior, but entails no necessary sorrow over sin or turning away from it. That is the fruit of confessing Jesus as Lord; it is the fruit of obedience, and properly emerges from the confidence of knowing that one's sins are already forgiven. In some of the writings of this camp, this analysis is justified by referring to 1 Corinthians 3 and Paul's division of the race into the natural man, the carnal man, and the spiritual man. The natural man is unredeemed; the carnal man enjoys salvation, but lives like the world, and is finally saved "only as one escaping through the flames" (3:15), while his works are burned up. The spiritual man knows Jesus as Lord and is walking in growing obedience.

Hodges would feel offended to have his view branded as "easy believism" or "cheap grace" or "greasy grace" or the like. He insists that Christians who do not constantly commit themselves to obedience pay high prices for their rebellion. But the price, he says, is never loss of salvation, nor (assuming the initial trust was genuine) a post facto discovery that the initial trust was not genuine, for that would tie assurance, and therefore salvation itself, to works.

Apart from these movements, there is a tendency to say very little about Christian assurance in most of our churches. Indeed, one might reasonably argue that a major reason why so many aberrant views are being so widely circulated is that there is a vacuum that cries out to be filled. I have not conducted a scientific poll to establish changing patterns over the last few decades. My impression, however, is that in many churches Christian assurance is not a major topic for sermons or discussion groups, largely because popular eschatology has become so realized that there is very little futurist element left, except at the merely creedal level. If we do not long for the consummation of our salvation in the new heaven and the new earth, for the *visio Dei* that is the believer's inheritance, then there is little point in talking about our assurance of gaining it.

In what follows, I shall sometimes engage one or more of these tendencies directly; but my principal aim is to offer some biblical and theological observations that may help us to cut a swath through the debates and refocus them a little. For instance, whatever the rights and wrongs of the historical arguments over the influence of Calvin, it is arguable that some of the lines of the debate are seriously askew because they too quickly press toward atemporal *dogmatic* questions without pausing adequately to reflect on *redemptive-historical* matters lodged in Scripture itself. I shall also argue that one major biblical-theological motif has largely been overlooked in these debates, a motif that has the potential for orienting the discussions, both academic and popular, in fresh directions.

Biblical and Theological Reflections

The New Testament writers admit no qualitative, absolute disjunction between genuine believers who display obedience to Jesus in their lives, and genuine believers who do not. Limitations of time and space require that I restrict my comments to one passage and one theme.

1 Corinthians 3. All of 1 Corinthians 1:10–4:20 is devoted to Paul's handling of the divisiveness of the Corinthians (see esp. 1:10–11; 3:5–6, 21–23; 4:6ff.), itself tied to their conviction that they are preeminently wise and spiritual (see 1:18ff.; 2:6ff.; 3:18ff.). Meanwhile, their thinking and their conduct are so spiritually immature—they are "mere infants in Christ" (3:1)—that Paul could not address them as "spiritual" *(pneumatikos),* as they thought themselves to be, but as "worldly." This last word is perhaps better rendered more literally as "fleshly" *(sarkinos),* that is, made of flesh. The charge has extra bite, since the Corinthians think themselves so "spiritual" that they are not even sure there is a resurrection body still to be gained (1 Cor. 15). They were certainly "fleshly," "made of flesh," when Paul was among them (v. 1); the tragedy is that they are still "fleshly" (v. 3): here Paul changes to *(sarkikos)* (in the best reading), that is, having the characteristics of flesh, clearly with ethical overtones.[18] They are "acting like mere men"

18. So, rightly, Gordon D. Fee, *The First Epistle to the Corinthians*, NICNT (Grand Rapids: Eerdmans, 1987), 123–24.

(*anthrōpoi*, v. 3). The evidence for this is found in their "jealousy and quarreling," in their determination to lionize this or that human leader. The crucial question, then, is whether Paul is introducing a new ontological level of Christian existence. He does not place the Corinthians among all whom he dismisses as *psychikoi* (2:14), those who are "natural" and therefore without the Spirit. Not only has he already noted their spiritual endowments (1:4–9), but Paul elsewhere repeatedly insists that one cannot be utterly devoid of the Spirit and be a Christian (Rom. 8:9; Gal. 3:2–3; Tit. 3:5–7). Yet by saying that the Corinthians are acting and thinking not like "spiritual" but "fleshly" people, like "mere men," he is charging them with the thoughts and conduct of those who do not have the Spirit. The tension is palpable, and the result is centuries of debate and misunderstanding. But the most obvious way to take Paul's words is that he is using strong language to force his readers to face up to the inherent inconsistency of their position. They have the Spirit, but at this junction they are neither thinking nor acting as if they do.

This is a more believable approach than those that suppose Paul himself is introducing an ontological distinction in the congregation. That is surely intrinsically unlikely, given the concern of the first four chapters to establish unity. Others try to find a shift in meaning in *pneumatikos* (spiritual) from chapter 2 to chapter 3,[19] or base a massive tripartite division of humankind (natural/carnal [KJV]/spiritual) on these verses. But apart from the fact that the same division cannot be found clearly drawn out elsewhere in Paul, such a reading flies in the face of one of the principal emphases in Pauline ethics, namely, the appeal "to be what you are."

Thus, when Paul says that he could not address the Corinthians as "spiritual," there is a sense in which he is admitting that there are "unspiritual" believers. He does not mean the Corinthian believers do not have the Spirit—there are no "unspiritual" believers in that sense—but that they are displaying a great deal of "unspiritual" behavior, which must stop.

Three observations must be entered. (1) If this is a fair reading of the passage, nothing here introduces an absolute, qualitative disjunction between those who are "fleshly" ("carnal" if you prefer) and those who are spiritual. All apart from perfectionists will admit that at the level of behavior, all Christians, insofar as they too participate in jealousy and quarreling, are sometimes "carnal." There is no attempt to tie the distinctions here to a theoretical disjunction between those who accept Jesus as Savior and those who accept him as Lord. (2) The sins in view are not of the sort that make us think the Corinthians are distancing themselves from their baptismal vows. This is not the case of someone who made a profession of faith at an evangelistic rally, followed

19. E.g., P. J. Du Plessis, ΤΕΛΕΙΟΣ: *The Idea of Perfection in the New Testament* (Kampen: Kok, 1959), 183–85.

the way of Christ for a few months, and then lived in a manner indistinguishable from that of any pagan for the next fifteen years, despite conscientious pastoral interest. Nor is it the case of a person who indulges in gross sexual immorality and who will not repent, like the man described in 1 Corinthians 5, of whose spiritual state not even the apostle seems to be sure, let alone confident. This is not to minimize the sins of jealousy and quarreling; it is to place them within the context of Christians who at many levels do display the presence and power of the Spirit (1:3–8), even though in this regard they are thinking and acting in ways that are out of step with the Spirit. (3) Above all, there is nothing in this chapter to connect these "carnal" Christians to the person described in verses 14–15. To justify this point, we must press on to the contribution of the next two paragraphs in the text.

Because the Corinthians' carnality is displayed in their propensity to form parties attached to particular leaders, Paul finds it necessary to explain the limited contribution such leaders have made. He develops two extended metaphors. The first is agricultural (3:5–9): Paul planted the seed, Apollos watered it, but God alone made it grow. Both the sower and the one who waters the seed have one purpose. Each "will be rewarded according to his own labor" (3:8). In this metaphor, the Corinthians do not figure as laborers. Paul and Apollos are "God's fellow workers"; the Corinthians are "God's field" (v. 9).

Then the metaphor changes, but with the same distinctions firmly in place. The Corinthians are "God's building" (v. 9); Paul is the contractor who has laid the foundation, Jesus Christ himself, with others building on the foundation that he laid. Within the constraints of this metaphor, it is the *builder* whose work will be shown up for what it is on the last day; the fire will test the quality of each *builder's* work.[20] "If what he has *built* survives, he will receive his reward. If it is burned up, he will suffer loss; he himself will be saved, but only as one escaping through the flames" (3:14–15). It is slightly misfocused to conclude, with Hans Conzelmann and many other commentators, that "unsatisfactory works performed by the Christian *as a Christian* do not cause his damnation."[21] Doubtless there is some sense in which that is true, but Paul's concern in this context is not to make application to the ordinary Christian, and certainly not to those whom he thinks are still "mere infants" (3:1), but to raise a standard that holds Christian leaders to account. In short, we are not here dealing with perennial backsliding or utter moral indifference, but shoddy workmanship among those who are accounted the leaders of the Christian church.

20. We need not decide here if this "work" is the Christian church, or professing Christians, or some abstraction of the builder's labor. That question is important in its own right, but irrelevant to our present concerns.
21. Hans Conzelmann, *1 Corinthians*, Hermeneia (Philadelphia: Fortress, 1975), 77.

Only in verses 16–17 is there a hint of a broader application, and it is no more than a hint. Maintaining the metaphor drawn from the building industry, Paul specifies that the Corinthians are not merely a building, but God's temple, his dwelling. If "anyone destroys God's temple, God will destroy him; for God's temple is sacred, and you are that temple." It is possible to read these verses as nothing more than a forceful reiteration of the lesson drawn in verses 10–15. Nevertheless, because Paul now speaks of "anyone" and not simply the builders, it suggests, in the context of the first four chapters, that those given to division, jealousy, and quarreling in the church are also in danger of doing damage to the church, God's temple. Since they are that temple, they are simultaneously doing damage to themselves and courting God's judgment.

It appears, then, that in this chapter Paul acknowledges that Christians do not always live up to what they are called to be, that every such failure is a serious breech, that those who do damage to the church are particularly threatened by God's judgment, and that some who are viewed as leaders in the church, although they will themselves be saved on the day of judgment, will have nothing to show for their labor. It does not encourage us to think that it is possible to accept Jesus as Savior, and thus be promoted from the "natural" to the "carnal" level, in transit, as it were, to the "spiritual" stage, at which point one has accepted Jesus as Lord. Still less does it encourage us to think of the "carnal" Christian as someone who once made a profession of faith and who now lives in every respect like the surrounding pagan world.

The new covenant. New covenant language is fairly pervasive in the New Testament, its themes far more so. Both Luke (Luke 22:20) and Paul (1 Cor. 11:25) report that Jesus, on the night he was betrayed, took such language on his own lips and tied the theme to his impending death. If Matthew and Mark omit "new," the implication is present anyway, since it is difficult to discover any sense in which Jesus' impending death signaled or ratified the old covenant. Hebrews 8 and 10 specifically tie the prophecy of Jeremiah 31:31–34 to the substance of Christian faith; 2 Corinthians 3 and Galatians 4 are no less insistent on setting forth the significance of the (new) covenant. Beyond such explicit language lies a large array of New Testament themes that presuppose the Old Testament promises of the new covenant (e.g., Jer. 31:29ff.; 32:36–41; Ezek. 36:25–27; Mal. 3:1), not least the "new birth" language of John 3.[22]

The point to be observed is that these Old Testament promises foresee a time when God's law is written on the heart of his people. Teachers will no longer say, "Know the Lord," for they will all know him (Jer. 31): the outlook is not of a time when there will be no teachers, but no *mediating* teach-

---

22. See D. A. Carson, *The Gospel according to John* (Grand Rapids: Eerdmans, 1991), 185–203.

ers, no *mediators,* whose very office ensures them that they have an endowment not enjoyed by others. The new covenant will not be like the tribal covenant associated with Moses' name, when the fathers ate sour grapes and their children's teeth were set on edge. Rather, it is characterized by the removal of the heart of stone among all of God's covenantal people.[23] To use the language of Ezekiel 36, the new covenant will be characterized by cleansing (sprinkling with water) and spiritual renewal (a new heart and a new spirit).

Add to this the many Old Testament passages that anticipate the time when God's Spirit is poured out on his people (e.g., Isa. 44:3–5; Ezek. 11:19–20; 36:25–27; Joel 2:28–32), along with the fulfillment of these passages in the New Testament, and another important part of what is characteristic of the new covenant age is dropped into place. The Spirit is bequeathed by the glorified Christ (John's Gospel), the Spirit is given as the *arrabōn* of the ultimate inheritance (Paul), the Spirit vivifies, empowers, and directs the church (Acts). The period between Pentecost and Christ's return is supremely the age of the Spirit, the powerful Spirit who renews, convicts, cleanses, empowers. Doubtless we "groan inwardly as we wait eagerly for our adoption as sons, the redemption of our bodies" (Rom. 8:23), but meanwhile God has sent his own Son in the likeness of sinful man, "in order that the righteous requirements of the law might be fully met in us, who do not live according to the sinful nature but according to the Spirit" (Rom. 8:4).

It appears that a great deal of the debate over assurance has been controlled by forensic categories associated with justification and faith, but has largely ignored the categories of power and transformation associated with the Spirit and new covenant. A fundamental component of such themes is that the people of the new covenant are *by definition* granted a new heart and empowered by the Spirit to walk in holiness, to love righteousness, to prove pleasing to the Lord. This means that, insofar as the writers of the New Testament thought of themselves as new covenant heirs, they could not think of themselves as other than Spirit-endowed, regenerate, transformed. The New Testament does not preserve the old covenant distinction between the locus of the covenant community and the locus of the remnant, or between the locus of the covenant community and the locus of the leaders on whom special endowment had fallen. It is of the essence of the new covenant that those who are in it have been given a new heart, have been cleansed, have received the Holy Spirit. Moreover, this theme cannot rightly be divorced from the entailments of justification and of salvation through faith. The gift of the Spirit is tied to justification (Rom. 5–8); salvation by grace through faith (Eph.

23. Thus the explicit eschatological focus of Jeremiah's use of the "sour grapes" proverb makes it function rather differently from the formal parallel in Ezekiel 18:2. Cf. Robert P. Carroll, *Jeremiah: A Commentary* (Philadelphia: Westminster, 1986), 608–9.

2:8), "not by works so that no one can boast" (Eph. 2:9), is tied to the fact that we are "God's workmanship, created in Christ Jesus to do good works, which God prepared in advance for us to do" (Eph. 2:10).

One must not conclude from this line of reasoning that new covenant believers are anywhere promised moral and spiritual perfection this side of the new heaven and the new earth. Nevertheless, both the Old Testament prophecies regarding the new covenant and the age of the Spirit, and the New Testament claims regarding their fulfillment, lead us to expect transformed lives. Indeed, it is precisely this unequivocal expectation that authorizes Paul to set up the tension we have already noted: the exhortations to live up to what we are in Christ are predicated on the assumption that what we are in Christ *necessarily* brings transformation, so that moral failure is *theologically* shocking, however pragmatically realistic it may be. Indeed, it might be argued that this accounts for some of the tension in 1 John. The setting that calls forth that epistle I shall briefly discuss a little farther on. For the moment, it is worth recalling John's insistence that believers do sin, and people who claim they do not are liars, self-deluded, and guilty of charging God with falsehood (1 John 1:6–10). At the same time, he repeatedly insists that sinning is not done among Christians. Various explanations have been advanced, but the most obvious is still the best: although both our experience and our location between the "already" and the "not yet" teach us that we do sin and we will sin, yet every single instance of sin is shocking, inexcusable, forbidden, appalling, out of line with what we are as Christians.[24]

It would take too much space to treat all the passages that are adduced to justify the counterclaim, or to demonstrate the methodological flaws inherent in Hodges' treatment of repentance. But even on the basis of the brief probings here, especially into the nature of the new covenant, it appears justified to claim that the New Testament writers nowhere admit an absolute, qualitative disjunction between genuine believers who in their conduct display obedience to the Lord Jesus and genuine believers who do not. This at least raises the possibility that some forms of Christian assurance might be validly based on observably transformed conduct, without in any way suggesting that such conduct wins or earns or gains salvation. How that might be related to other themes—the grounding of Christian assurance in the object of faith, Jesus Christ himself—is still to be explored. But ignoring the covenantal aspects of Christianity in favor of narrowly forensic categories has been one of the chief reasons for confusion in this area.

24. On Paul's view of some of the tensions experienced by Christians living under the aegis of the kingdom while still living in the old creation, see David Wenham, "The Christian Life: A Life of Tension? A Consideration of the Nature of Christian Experience in Paul," in *Pauline Studies: Essays Presented to Professor F. F. Bruce on His Seventieth Birthday*, ed. Donald A. Hagner and Murray J. Harris (Exeter: Paternoster, 1980), 80–94.

Several New Testament writers recognize the existence of spurious or transitory faith, and this recognition must be factored into any responsible doctrine of Christian assurance. This subject is exceedingly complex, for it is tied to the nature of apostasy and to protracted debates over the security of the believer in the New Testament. For the sake of clarity, I shall proceed in seven steps.

1. Discussion of a figure like Judas Iscariot is extremely problematic. Frequently comparisons and contrasts are drawn between his "defection" and that of Peter (I use "defection" in an attempt to find a word that can reasonably refer to the actions of both men). But quite apart from the intrinsic value of the exercise, it is doubtful if the apostasy of Judas is to be construed as apostasy from full-blown Christian faith. To put the matter another way, the experiences of "coming to faith" of men and women in the four Gospels is in certain respects unique, unrepeatable in any generation after the resurrection and Pentecost. Their coming to faith required the lapse of time until the One they came to confess as Messiah was crucified and rose again. Doubtless they struggled with doubts and sins and selfishness, and therefore in certain respects they may serve as paradigms for our own spiritual pilgrimages. Nevertheless, none of us today, in our own coming to faith, had to wait for the next major redemptive-historical appointment, the death and resurrection of God's Son, before our fledgling faith could become fully Christian. Nor did we have to tarry in Jerusalem until the day of Pentecost had come.[25] But if the first disciples' coming to faith was not exactly like ours, then Judas Iscariot's apostasy from whatever level he had attained before the crucifixion was not exactly like apostasy in Hebrews 6 or 10. This is not to minimize his sin in the slightest; it is to argue that no substantial view of what apostasy might mean under the new covenant can begin with Iscariot, still less with, say, Korah.

2. Little help on the nature of apostasy is to be gained by simple word studies. The word *apostasia*, for instance, occurs only twice in the New Testament, once to refer to turning away from Moses on the part of Jews (Acts 21:21), the other to refer to the great rebellion that takes place when the man of lawlessness is revealed (2 Thess. 2:3).

We may perhaps adopt a working definition of "apostasy," independent of any Greek word, along such lines as these: it is the decisive turning away from a religious position and stance once firmly held. It differs from ordinary unbelief in that it involves turning away from a position of belief; it differs from backsliding in that it is calculated, decisive, and irrevocable; it differs from merely changing one's mind over some relatively minor theological point in that it involves the rejection of an entire position and stance.

---

25. Incidentally, this is one of the reasons why studies that seek to use the Gospels as first and foremost guides to the nature of Christian discipleship, on the basis of the first followers' experiences and reactions, are deeply flawed.

3. It is disputed how many passages in the New Testament describe or refer to such apostasy. Was Demas an apostate (2 Tim. 4:10)? Did the immoral man of 1 Corinthians 5 die an apostate? But however many or few, some passages cannot easily be circumvented. It must be strenuously insisted that attempts to reduce the shock and power of severe warnings like those in Hebrews 6:4–6 and 2 Corinthians 13:5, by arguing that the warnings are merely hypothetical, or that the turning aside of those described in Hebrews 6:4–6 and 1 John 2:19 is from useful service but not from salvation, are desperate expedients that responsible exegesis will happily avoid.

4. The real question is whether, with Marshall[26] and others who follow him, we shall say that in these instances genuine believers have fallen away, or that although they were believers in some sense they were not genuine believers at all. There are genuine difficulties both ways.

One of the most competent treatments of some of the issues is the study by Volf, which examines the theme of perseverance in the seven Pauline Epistles over which there is least dispute as to their authenticity.[27] In the first section, she describes what it is like to "stay in." "A continuity in the divine work of salvation emerges in which a particular aspect of salvation is seen to imply the succeeding ones."[28] Paul repeatedly draws attention to the "eternal divine initiatives in salvation: divine election, foreknowledge and predestination"[29] (Rom. 8:23, 29–30; 2 Cor. 1:22; 5:5; Phil. 1:6; 1 Thess. 5:9; 2 Thess. 2:13–14). On the other hand, for Paul "the process of consummating the work of salvation is more like an obstacle course than a downhill ride to the finishline"[30] (Rom. 5:1–11; 8:28, 31–39; 1 Cor. 1:8–9; 10:13; 1 Thess. 5:23–24; 2 Thess. 3:3). God's faithfulness is manifested in strengthening and protecting and preserving his people.

> Paul gives clear and ample evidence of his view that Christians' salvation is certain to reach completion. This thought is integral to his understanding of individual salvation. Though threats to the consummation of Christians' salvation may and will appear, they cannot successfully challenge it. God's faithfulness and love make divine triumph the unquestionable outcome. For Paul, certainty of final salvation rests on God's continued intervention to that end.[31]

In the second section of her book, Volf examines an array of passages (Rom. 14:1–23; 1 Cor. 5:1–5; 6:9–11; 8:7–13; 10:12; 11:27–34; Gal. 5:9–11) to argue that for Paul "continuity in salvation does not make Christian

---

26. *Kept by the Power of God;* "The Problem of Apostasy."
27. *Paul and Perseverance.*
28. Ibid., 80.
29. Ibid.
30. Ibid., 81.
31. Ibid., 82.

conduct irrelevant."[32] Against Sanders, Volf argues that although morality and integrity and obedience matter enormously to Paul, and although Paul envisages punishment falling on some believers who disobey, "Paul does not make Christians' final salvation dependent on their repentance from post-conversion sins."[33] Then she makes one of the few false steps in her book: she argues that it is possible to lose one's membership in the "in-group" by "falsifying one's Christian profession by one's behavior. . . . But when this happens, continuity in actual salvation is not interrupted."[34] In other words, at this point she agrees with Sanders that staying in the "in-group" is conditional on good behavior, but she qualifies Sanders by arguing that this is not the same as remaining in salvation. Her exegesis is to be questioned at a number of points, and she has not adequately come to grips with the significance of what belonging to the new covenant community entails; for as we have seen, the nature of the new covenant drives us to the conclusion that there is a certain sense in which *extra ecclesiam nulla salus.*

In part 3, Volf examines Romans 9–11, 2 Corinthians 13:5; and Galatians 5:1–4 in order to discover what unbelief signifies among those who profess to be Christians. In 2 Corinthians 13:5, for instance, she argues that Paul cannot be warning against loss of salvation, since the context "shows that ἀδόκιμος can only mean rejection as a nonconvert, and that the exhortation to self-testing has the main purpose of pointing out Paul's own provenness as an apostle and possibly the subordinate purpose of exposing some Corinthians to be falsely professing Christians."[35] She holds that the election of Israel does not entail automatic participation in salvation *"apart from faith in Christ."*[36] She might have done a little more work on the diverse ways Paul thinks of "election"; but that is perhaps a picky point. In her final section, Volf examines Paul's reflections on the final outcome of his own apostolic mission (1 Cor. 9:23–27; 15:2; 2 Cor. 6:1; Gal. 2:2; 4:11; 1 Thess. 3:5; Phil. 2:16). If he fears that his labor might prove to be "in vain" (Phil. 2:16; 1 Thess. 3:5; Gal. 2:2; 4:11), it can only be because he fears that some of "his seeming converts would have no salvation. Whether failure in the eschatological test should be traced to his converts' false profession or their apostasy from salvation is a question not answered by Paul in these texts."[37] But Volf notes that Paul, while distrusting his own success, seems to give way to confidence "when he views the situation from the perspective of God's faithful-

32. Ibid., 155.
33. Ibid., 157.
34. Ibid.
35. Ibid., 226.
36. Ibid.
37. Ibid., 282.

ness to professing Christians in whom he sees the divine work of salvation taking place."[38] I shall argue that this is an extremely important observation.

5. Apart from points of exegetical detail, the methodological difference between those who hold that genuine believers fall away and those who hold that those who fall away are not genuine believers seems to turn on two issues.

How strong are the passages that seem to affirm the ultimate preservation and perseverance of God's people? This is something that Marshall, for instance, does not directly address. He fairly expounds some of the passages that affirm that God's people continue in salvation to the end, but then diminishes their weight by setting over against them those passages that emphasize human responsibility to persevere, or those passages that refer to apostasy (however defined). The resulting formulation always makes the preservation of God's people unto consummated salvation absolutely contingent: God is the one who faithfully preserves his people, provided they do not defect. But what warrants such diminution of the apparent weight of the perseverance passages?

For example, John refers to the elect as all that the Father gives Jesus (John 6:37a), and by a litotes insists that Jesus will keep in or preserve all of these people (i.e., he will not drive them away, 6:37b),[39] on the ground that the Son came to do his Father's will, which is none other than that he should preserve all those whom the Father has given him (6:38–40). It is exceedingly difficult to diminish the finality of this statement without implying that Jesus proves unwilling to preserve or incapable of preserving all those the Father has given him. Most Christians would be aghast to use texts that affirm or assume Jesus' humanity to diminish those that affirm his deity, and vice versa. We have come to accept some mystery in our christological formulations; we seek interpretations that allow complementary texts to have their full vigor without permitting diminution of their most obvious meaning by some form of mutual annihilation. Can a case be mounted that in this area, too, there is a definable mystery that should not be allowed to be diminished by such mutual annihilation? I shall shortly argue that there is. But meanwhile, it seems that the strong New Testament emphases on the security of the believer should not be qualified by mere subtraction, unless there is the strongest exegetical warrant for doing so.

More positively, is there warrant for thinking the New Testament writers have categories for transitory faith, spurious faith—in short, for faith that seems like saving faith, but which proves to be spurious? If there is, then the

38. Ibid.
39. The litotes cannot possibly mean that Jesus will welcome in those who come to him. In context it must mean that he will keep in those who have been given to him. See Carson, *John*, 290.

passages that speak of falling away do not force us to conclude that the defection is from *genuine* faith.

In fact, in every major New Testament corpus, there are numerous warnings against or descriptions of spurious faith. For instance, in Matthew Jesus envisages that some who have addressed him as "Lord, Lord," and who have prophesied in his name and driven out demons in his name and performed many miracles in his name, will be excluded from the kingdom of heaven: "I will tell them plainly, 'I never knew you. Away from me, you evildoers!'" (Matt. 7:21–23). The one who enters the kingdom is "he who does the will of my Father who is in heaven" (7:21). John (2:23–25) testifies that when Jesus attended the first Passover feast of his ministry, "many people saw the miraculous signs he was doing and believed in his name,"[40] but Jesus would not entrust himself to them: he knew what was in their heart. A little later (John 8:31), to "the Jews who had believed him,"[41] Jesus gives a criterion that establishes who are genuine disciples: "If you hold to my teaching, you are really my disciples." The same stance is reflected in 1 John 2:19. Those who have seceded from the church are described in telling terms: "They went out from us, but they did not really belong to us. For if they had belonged to us, they would have remained with us; but their going showed that none of them belonged to us." In other words, genuine faith, by definition, perseveres; where there is no perseverance, by definition the faith cannot be genuine. Again, "anyone who runs ahead and does not continue in the teaching of Christ does not have God; whoever continues in the teaching has both the Father and the Son" (2 John 9). Paul says as much: he informs the Colossians that God has reconciled them by Christ's physical body through death, to present them holy in his sight, without blemish and free from accusation— "if," he writes, "you continue in your faith, established and firm, not moved from the hope held out in the gospel" (Col. 1:22-23). In short, genuine faith is tied to perseverance; transitory faith is spurious. We find similar emphases in 2 Peter 1:10–11. Before we come across the "apostasy" passages in the Epistle to the Hebrews, we read (in Heb. 3:14), "We have come to share in Christ if we hold firmly till the end the confidence we had at first" (see also 3:6; 4:14; 6:11; etc.).

40. It is important to recognize that the expression here is *pisteuō eis* plus the accusative, thereby providing a critical counterexample to those who think this expression always signals saving faith in the Fourth Gospel, while *pisteuō* plus the dative denotes unreliable faith. In reality, the small variation in form is typical of the Fourth Evangelist, who is well known for his slight variations without clear-cut semantic distinction.

41. Because the expression in 8:31 is *pisteuō* plus the dative, while in 8:30 *pisteuō eis* plus the accusative lies behind "those who put their faith in him," some have argued that the Jews in 8:31 constitute a separate group with distinguishably inferior faith. This is wholly unlikely; see note 40.

The range and diversity of these sorts of passages (I have cited only a small percentage of them) utterly preclude the possibility that they all refer to persevering in discipleship that goes beyond "mere" salvation. Whereas a few of these passages, taken alone, might suggest that continuing in salvation to the end depends absolutely on our own efforts at perseverance, responsible biblical theology must seek to integrate them with the promises of God's preserving initiative, not less rich in each major New Testament corpus, and with the passages in this list that make perseverance a criterion of genuine faith. For example, those who had seceded had once belonged to the church (1 John 2:19); otherwise John could not say that "they went out from us."[42] To all observers, for all practical purposes, the seceders were once baptized members of the church, fully accepted as Christians. Nevertheless, John insists, they were never really "of us," for if they had been "they would have remained with us." In other words, John presupposes that spurious faith is possible, but that genuine faith, by definition, perseveres.

In short, the methodological point of division between the two principal interpretations—the one that argues genuine believers can fall away, and the one that argues that those who fall away are necessarily spurious or transitory believers—turns on the two issues I have just defined.

6. If the tack I have taken is largely correct, the doctrinal area where we must become a little more sophisticated is in the theology of conversion. The question could be put several ways, but perhaps this will do: Is there New Testament warrant for thinking that there is some third alternative to being clearly "in" or "out"? To simplify the discussion, let us grant that God knows precisely who is "in" or "out." The question then becomes, Is there New Testament warrant for thinking that, as far as Christian observers are concerned, some people are not clearly either "in" or "out," that the step of conversion is not always luminously clear?

Implicitly, of course, we have already answered this question by listing a few of the New Testament passages where apparent conversions proved spurious (e.g., 1 John 2:19), or where the genuineness of the profession is irrefragably tied to perseverance (thereby implying that transitory faith is under a cloud). The parable of the sower—or, better, of the soils (Mark 4 par.)—illustrates the same point. In addition to the receptive soil that enables the seed to produce fruit in varying measure, there are three other kinds. The hard pathway stops the seed from embedding itself in dirt, and the birds of the air eat it: the picture is of people who hear the word of God, but from whom it is snatched away by Satan before it can germinate. The seed that falls "on rocky places" lodges in a thin layer of topsoil that covers limestone bedrock.

42. The attempt to avoid this by Hodges (*Gospel under Siege*, 54), who rather implausibly takes the "us" to refer to the apostolic communion, or perhaps the initial Palestinian church, does not solve the problem, but merely changes the location of the church.

Because it is so shallow, this topsoil heats up quickly, encourages the seed to germinate, and therefore initially produces what seems to be the most promising crop. Unfortunately, as the sun burns throughout the long, hot summer, these plants are scorched: their roots search for moisture, but come up against the bedrock, and the plant dies. The explanation tells us that this pictures those who receive the word with joy. Sadly, because they have no root, "they last only a short time." When trouble or persecution comes, they fall away. And finally, some seed falls on thorny ground. Here, too, the seed germinates and sends up tendrils, but the competition exerted by the more robust thorns chokes the young plants, so that they bear no grain. Here we are to think of those who hear the word, but whose hearing faces the competition of worries, the deceitfulness of wealth, and desires for other things. These distractions "choke the word, making it unfruitful."

The important thing to observe is that two of the three fruitless soils sprout life, but do not bear fruit This is not bleeding the parable for more than it is worth: recall that in the case of the seed that falls on rocky soil, the interpretation of the parable provided in the text itself describes the reality pictured by the parable as people who "hear the word and at once receive it with joy," but who "last only a short time." To all observers save God himself, this seed promises the best harvest, but this spiritual life proves transitory.

Several popular interpreters associated with the Grace Evangelical Society find this so uncomfortable that they reinterpret the parable. They say that instead of having three soils that are viewed negatively and one that is viewed positively, the alignment should go another way: there are two soils that are viewed negatively (the pathway and the thorns), and two that produce life (the rocky soil and the good soil), one of which also produces fruit. This will not do: the seed scattered on thorny soil also produces plants, but these plants never bear grain (Mark 4:7): the thorns choke the plants, not the ungerminated seeds. I suppose they could respond by suggesting that there is only one soil treated negatively (the pathway), and three treated positively, only one of which bears fruit. But the narrative parable does not read that way: such an interpretation is being imported from an alien theological structure; it would be strange in the context of a Gospel tradition that repeatedly insists people are known by their fruit, not by their life without fruit; and in its context the parable of the soils, especially in Mark and Matthew, joins other parables in elucidating the nature of the kingdom that has already dawned but is not yet consummated. Its purpose is to show that the kingdom is not now dawning with apocalyptic suddenness and clarity, but in the lives of those who hear the gospel of the kingdom and produce fruit. To argue that it is also introducing a category for spiritual life that is nevertheless fruitless is simply alien to the concerns of the chapter, and contrary to one of the driving motifs of all three synoptic Gospels.

Ideally, it would be helpful at this point to offer a detailed exegesis of Hebrews 6:4–6, and of similar passages in the New Testament, but we must limit ourselves to some focal observations. Too often the challenge raised by Hebrews 6 is cast in a simple alternative: Are those who are so warned Christians or not? If one argues for the "not," one is hard-pressed to explain the string of descriptions: "those who have once been enlightened, who have tasted the Holy Spirit, who have tasted the goodness of the word of God and the powers of the coming age." If one argues they are Christians, the dominant alternatives in the commentaries are that the warning is merely hypothetical—which is utterly at odds with the driving repetition of the theme in the book, and the seriousness with which it is presented; that the falling away is not from salvation—which simply will not square with 6:6 and especially with 10:26ff.; or that genuine believers may lose their salvation—which resurrects the problems of reconciling this view with the many passages that urge us to trust the certain, preserving work of the grace of God, not least in this epistle, where God offers comfort and incentive to his people by promising, "Never will I leave you; never will I forsake you" (13:5).

But there is a better alternative, once we have recognized that our theology of conversion is too simplistic. We have already seen that three chapters earlier Hebrews virtually defines true believers as those who hold firmly to the end the confidence they had at first (3:6, 14). In other words, like other New Testament books the Epistle to the Hebrews allows for a kind of transitory faith, a form of conversion which, like the seed sown on rocky soil, has all the signs of life, but which does not persevere. The Spirit brings initial enlightenment; the person enjoys the word of God (like the one in Mark 4 who hears the word and immediately receives it with joy), and tastes something of the power of the coming age: perhaps old habits fall away, and a new love for holiness and for God and his reign emerge. But according to the description of genuine Christianity already provided by the book, none of this is enough: there must also be perseverance.

Against the background of the theology of the epistle, the reasons for such warnings are clear enough. The incarnate Son of God is God's last word to humankind (1:1–4). Therefore those who neglect the great salvation that only he brings cannot escape (2:1ff.). The sacrifice the Son offered was "once for all." There is therefore no more offering for sin (10:18, 26), still less a repetition of this one sacrifice (9:25–28). This one sacrifice, offered once for all, is forever entirely sufficient for all of God's people (10:10–14). Therefore any who taste of its fruit, recognize its origin, ally themselves with its significance, and then deliberately reject this gospel, have no place left to turn: there is no more forgiveness of sins. This is apostasy: it is turning away from a religious position and stance once firmly held. But that is still shy of saying that the faith so exercised was necessarily saving faith in some ultimate sense, if part of the definition of saving faith includes the criterion of perseverance.

7. What is the essence of the difference, then, so far as assurance is concerned, between the person who holds that all genuine believers will be preserved to the end, and that those who fall away from apparent faith only enjoy spurious, transitory faith, and the person who holds that genuine believers may fall away? Marshall's analysis, using "Calvinist" and "non-Calvinist" to denote the two groups respectively, runs like this:

> If a person is in the former group, he has still to heed the warning: only by so doing can he show that he is one of the elect. In other words, the Calvinist 'believer' cannot fall away from 'true' faith, but he can 'fall away' from what proves in the end to be only seeming faith. The possibility of falling away remains. But in neither case does the person know for certain whether he is a true or a seeming disciple. All that he knows is that Christ alone can save and that he must trust in Christ, and that he sees signs in his life which may give him some assurance that he is a true disciple. But these signs may be misleading.
>
> It comes down to a question of assurance. Whoever said, 'The Calvinist knows that he cannot fall from salvation but does not know whether he has got it', had it summed up nicely. But this can be counterfeit and misleading. The non-Calvinist knows that he has salvation—because he trusts in the promises of God—but is aware that, left to himself, he could lose it. So he holds to Christ. It seems to me the practical effect is the same.[43]

At a merely mechanistic level, I think this analysis is largely correct. But three caveats must be added. Even if at certain levels the practical effect is the same, that does not mean the underlying structures are the same. One must still decide which approach is most faithful to most texts. In my view, Marshall does not adequately handle the numerous passages and themes that do promise the security of the believer. Psychologically, the focus is not the same. Historically, of course, it is a commonplace that some branches of Calvinism have developed their own forms of introversion, believers constantly examining themselves to see if they were displaying sufficient fruit to justify their conclusion that they were among the elect—thus strangely mirroring their Arminian counterparts who sometimes gave themselves to worrying if they were truly holding on to the promises of God. Thus at their worst, the two approaches meet in strange and sad ways. But at their best, the focus of the two systems is nonetheless quite different. Despite Marshall's salutary emphasis on the promises of God, at the end of the day the security of the believer finally rests with the believer. For those from the opposite camp, the security of the believer finally rests with God—and that, I suggest, rightly taught and applied, draws the believer back to God himself, to trust in God, to renewed faith that is of a piece with trusting him in the first place. In any case, this analysis entirely neglects to wrestle with the way we are to think of

43. Marshall, "The Problem of Apostasy," 313.

God's sovereign preservation of his people, and our responsibility to persevere; and so to that subject we now turn.

The biblical writers either presuppose or explicitly teach what might be called compatibilism, and this has an important, and neglected, bearing on the subject of Christian assurance. I have written on this subject at some length elsewhere,[44] and must restrict myself to a few potted explanations. Compatibilism is the view that the following two statements are, despite superficial evidence to the contrary, mutually compatible: God is absolutely sovereign but his sovereignty does not in any way mitigate human responsibility; human beings are responsible creatures (i.e., they choose, decide, obey, disobey, believe, rebel, and so forth), but their responsibility never serves to make God absolutely contingent.

The compatibilist, then, believes that both of these statements are true, that they are mutually compatible. That does not mean compatibilists claim they can show exactly how both of these statements can be simultaneously true. Rather, if they are rigorous thinkers, they think that there is enough reasonable evidence to demonstrate that nothing proves the pair of statements incompatible. Therefore other evidence that seems to justify the statements individually cannot be ruled out of court on the grounds that the two statements contradict each other.

My contention is that the biblical writers, insofar as they reveal themselves on this subject, are without exception compatibilists. When Joseph responds to his brothers' alarm by saying that when they sold him to the Midianites they meant it for evil, while God meant it for good (Gen. 50:19–20), the thinking is compatibilistic. Joseph does not say that God had initiated a lovely plan to send Joseph down to Egypt by first-class chariot, but the brothers corrupted the plan by their evil machinations. Nor does he say that the brothers hatched an evil plot, but God rushed in to the rescue by turning their evil into good (though some passages portray God in precisely such categories). Rather, in one and the same event, God and the brothers were working, the one with good intent, the others with evil intent. God's sovereign, unseen sway does not mitigate the brothers' evil; their malice does not catch God by surprise and make him utterly contingent.

In the same way, the Assyrians can be described as mere tools in Yahweh's hands as he disciplines his people (Isa. 10:5ff.). But that does not reduce their responsibility. In their foolish pride they think they are achieving these military victories on their own. Therefore God will hold them accountable for

---

44. D. A. Carson, *Divine Sovereignty and Human Responsibility: Biblical Themes in Tension* (Atlanta: John Knox, 1981); idem, *How Long, O Lord? Reflection on Suffering and Evil* (Grand Rapids: Baker, 1991), chaps. 11 and 12.

their arrogance, and, after using them the way a workman wields a saw or an axe, will turn again to rend them.

When the Philippians are told to work out their own salvation with fear and trembling,[45] on the ground that it is God who is working in them both to will and to act according to his good purpose, it is important to observe what is not said. The Philippians are not told to work out their salvation since God has done his bit and now it is their turn; nor are they told that they should simply "let go and let God," since salvation is all of grace. Rather, they are encouraged to work out their salvation precisely because it is God who is at work in them, both at the level of their wills and at the level of their actions. God's sovereignty functions as an incentive to work, not a disincentive. Similarly, when in a night vision the Lord encourages Paul to preach on in Corinth (Acts 18:9–10), the ground is that the Lord has many people in this place. In other words, election here functions as an incentive to evangelism, not a disincentive.

Nowhere, perhaps, are such compatibilistic tendencies more starkly presupposed than in Acts 4, when the church turns to prayer after the first whiff of persecution. The Christians invoke the "Sovereign Lord" who made the heaven and earth, and cite Psalm 2 as they remember that all the rage and plotting of the nations against the Lord and against his anointed One are futile: the Lord will have them in derision. Small wonder these believers saw the deepest fulfillment of Psalm 2 in the death of their Master: "Indeed Herod and Pontius Pilate met together with the Gentiles and the people of Israel in this city to conspire against your holy servant Jesus, whom you anointed" (4:27). Then they add, "They did what your power and will had decided beforehand should happen" (4:28).

A moment's reflection discloses that anything other than a compatibilist approach to these events destroys the gospel itself. Christians cannot possibly believe that the cross began as a nasty conspiracy by wicked politicians, with God riding in on a white charger at the last moment to turn their evil into good: that would mean that the plan of redemption was not a plan after all. Nor can they believe that God's sovereign control of the events excused all the human players: if Herod, Judas, Pontius Pilate, and other leaders were not involved in a conspiracy of which they were wretchedly culpable, it is hard to imagine how any human being in God's world could be thought culpable of anything—and in that case, why offer an atoning sacrifice for actions for which there could be no guilt?

---

45. I do not accept the interpretations of these verses advanced by O. Glombitza ("Mit Furcht und Zittern. Zum Verständnis von Phil.2.12," *NovT* 3 [1959]: 100–106) and R. P. Martin (*Philippians*, NCB [London: Oliphants, 1976], 102–3) respectively, but detailed discussion would be out of place here. Cf. now Peter T. O'Brien, *The Epistle to the Philippians: A Commentary on the Greek Text*, NIGTC (Grand Rapids: Eerdmans, 1991).

Before turning to the bearing of compatibilism on Christian assurance, it is necessary to take three steps.

1. If we accept, on the admittedly scanty evidence marshalled here, that biblical writers in every major corpus espouse compatibilism, we should perhaps pause to allay suspicions that compatibilism surreptitiously embraces sheer logical contradiction, and should forthwith be abandoned, regardless of what biblical writers think.[46] Modern compatibilists, I have said, do not try to show exactly how the two crucial propositions hold together. Rather, they elucidate the considerable unknowns that nullify most of the counterarguments. In particular: We do not know how an eternal God operates in time. We scarcely know what time is; it is not at all clear what eternity is (Does God know sequence?), still less how he relates to our time. The question is critical in debates over foreordination and predestination. Similarly, we do not know how a sovereign God operates through secondary agents who nevertheless are held accountable for their deeds. The definition of freedom that enters almost all discussions of human responsibility is far more problematic than people think. If freedom entails absolute power to contrary, then God is necessarily contingent, and compatibilism is destroyed. But if, for instance, freedom turns on voluntarism, that is, human beings are responsible and accountable because they do what they want to do, there is no necessary infringement on the sovereignty of God—as Jonathan Edwards demonstrated more than two centuries ago. Above all, we have almost no idea how God can be simultaneously sovereign and personal—yet the Scriptures insist on both. Virtually all of the elements that go into our thinking as to what personal relationships are about are based on our experience of relations with other human beings—and we are finite. We talk with one another, ask questions, hear answers, respond with love or wrath, cherish friendships, and so forth—and all of these elements demand the passage of time and presuppose finite actors. Similarly, in Scripture God can be portrayed asking questions, hearing answers, responding with love or wrath, cherishing friendships, and so forth; yet other texts insist he is also sovereign, the one "who works out everything in conformity with the purpose of his will" (Eph. 1:11). I have no idea how to conceptualize a God who is both sovereign and personal, but I perceive that if both are not simultaneously true, the God of the Bible disappears, and Christianity, indeed theism itself, is destroyed. In short, the mystery of compatibilism is traceable to the mystery of God, to what we do not know about God.

2. Along with the Bible's insistence on compatibilism is its insistence on the goodness of God. Elsewhere I have argued at length[47] that the enormous biblical evidence for this duality leads to an unavoidable conclusion: al-

---

46. Many philosophers adopt exactly that stance. Nevertheless, compatibilism enjoys respectable support in some philosophical circles. See the bibliography in the works already cited.

47. *How Long, O Lord?*

though God, by virtue of the fact that he is sovereign, stands behind both good and evil (e.g., God can be portrayed as the one who incites David to number the people, the one who sends a strong delusion so that people will believe the lie, the one who sends nations to war, the one of whom Romans 8:28 is predicated), he stands behind good and evil asymmetrically. He stands behind evil in such a way that none of it takes place outside the limits of his sovereign sway, but so that no evil is chargeable to him; he stands behind good in such a way that all of it is credited to him. Do not ask me to explain *how* this can be so: these are components of the biblical "givens," perspectives that the biblical writers teach or assume.

3. This means that we are locked into mystery. That should not be surprising: we are thinking about God. If there were nothing mysterious about him, I suppose he would not be God: he would be too small, too easily tamed, too domesticated. But if we respect the mystery of compatibilism, precisely because it is tied to what we do not know about God himself, then the most important thing we can do to foster personal and corporate fidelity to the portrait of God disclosed in Scripture, is to observe how the complementary truths of compatibilism *function in Scripture, and insist that in our hands they will function in the same ways, and in no other.*

For example, election, an element in the biblical portrayal of God's sovereignty, never functions so as to destroy human responsibility, to limit the urgency of preaching the gospel, to foster fatalism, or the like. It frequently functions to tie salvation to grace and to engender humility (Rom. 9), to encourage evangelism (Acts 18:9–10), and much more. Invitations to believe or to obey the gospel never function to make God absolutely contingent; rather, they function to bring people to saving faith, increase human responsibility, magnify the forbearance of God, and so forth. If we allow the components of compatibilism to function in ways much removed from the biblical constraints, we will end up implicitly disowning the compatibilism that is everywhere assumed, and is, finally, nothing more than a corollary of the doctrine of God. We will end up tarnishing the biblical witness to who God is and what he is like.

Most Christians have become used to other facets of Christian doctrine that involve mystery, and if they are reasonably informed they will be fairly careful both to locate the mystery in the right place and not to destroy the mystery by drawing inferences that destroy some essential component elsewhere in the structure. Perhaps the best example is Christology. Most of us want to be careful enough about our affirmation of Jesus' deity that we do not unwittingly derogate his humanity, and vice versa. We acknowledge the mystery, and we take some pains, along with believers in every era, to try to incorporate all the biblical evidence on this subject into the formulations of our doctrinal affirmations. We may not be completely successful; but that is our commitment. In the area of compatibilism, however, too few have adequately recognized that there is a mystery at stake, and that laying profane hands on the biblical evidence too quickly, without recognizing the nature and location of the mystery, ends up with tragic loss to the doctrine of God. For example, if human responsibility is made to depend on a definition of freedom that involves absolute power to contrary, then God becomes absolutely contingent. One of the poles of combatibilism is destroyed; we are left, not with mystery, but with logical contradiction.

Clearly, compatibilism touches many subjects: election, the problem of suffering, the nature of prayer, and much else. What is not often recognized is that it bears directly on the nature of Christian assurance. For, on the one hand, we are dealing with a plethora of texts that promise God's sovereign commitment to preserve his own elect; on the other, believers are enjoined to persevere in faithfulness to the new covenant and the Lord of the covenant, to the calling by which they were called. This is nothing other than God's sovereignty and human responsibility dressed up in another form.

So we will always have some mystery. The important thing will be to locate the mystery in the right place. It will not do to affirm God's sovereign protection of his elect, and then make such preservation absolutely contingent on human faithfulness: that is not mystery, but logical contradiction. But if our articulation of the doctrine of assurance leaves no loose ends, there is every reason to think that we have denied compatibilism somewhere—in exactly the same way that some treatments of election remove all difficulties but leave the texts behind. Moreover, the same safeguard that we apply in other areas where mystery intrudes into Christian doctrine must be applied here: let the various passages relevant to Christian assurance function in our lives and theological systems the way they do in Scripture. Do warnings against apostasy function to annul the promises of God? Of course not. They are designed to promote perseverance. Do the promises of God serve to engender lethargy? Of course not. They are designed to promote zeal, gratitude, and appreciation of God's fidelity.

But this discussion of function leads us to the final reflection.

The biblical writers do not deal with only one sort of doubt, and therefore they do not mete out only one kind of assurance. This rather obvious fact is sometimes overlooked. The magisterial Reformers rebelled against the sale of indulgences, the location of absolution within the hands of a priestly minority, the loss of confidence in the finished work of Christ, the lack of Christian assurance. By tying assurance to justification, they successfully met this challenge, prompting the Tridentine standards to pronounce the *anathema sit* on those who claimed such assurance.[48]

48. See the excellent discussion by Klaas Runia, "Justification and Roman Catholicism," in *Right with God: Justification in the Bible and the World,* ed. D. A. Carson (Exeter: Paternoster; Grand Rapids: Baker, 1992).

But there are many different kinds of doubt. Even if we narrowly focus on those elements of doubt that can jeopardize the Christian's assurance that the salvation now begun will finally be brought to victorious consummation, the diversity is nevertheless remarkable. Doubtless the solution to much of it is to focus attention on the exclusive finality of Christ and his death and resurrection on our behalf, to magnify God's unfailing promises and his love (e.g., John 5:24; 6:37ff.; 10 passim; Rom. 8:15–17, 29–30, 38–39; Phil. 1:6; 2 Tim. 1:12). But lack of assurance may be prompted by secret sin. Worse, a Christian may stumble into prolonged sin and not feel any lack of assurance—just like the Israelites in Deuteronomy and elsewhere who are warned against relying on election and feel no fear or shame when they sin. In that case, James 2 may call into question the reality of the "faith" that is exercised, if it is not accompanied by works; for the assumption in the New Testament is that saving faith, tied as it is to the new covenant and the power of the Spirit, necessarily issues in good works. Although works cannot save and cannot be the primary ground of one's assurance (that, surely, is Christ and his work and promises), they may serve as corroborating evidence. More accurately, in James 2 and 2 Corinthians 13:10, the lack of corroborating evidence may call in question the reality of the putative faith; in 2 Peter 1:10 the desirability of persevering corroboration functions as an incentive to enduring fidelity and fruitfulness. Here, then, the English Puritans have some justification for their emphases, if not always for their overemphases.

Still more interesting is the argument of 1 John. Many Protestant commentators follow the classic treatment of Robert Law in detecting "tests of life" in this epistle. These are usually thought to be three, sometimes four: appropriate allegiance to certain truth, in this case the confession that the Christ, the Son of God, is Jesus; principial obedience; love for other believers; and, in some analyses, the witness of the Spirit (though some think this witness is not a private experience but a way of summarizing the other "tests").

But a more refined analysis is possible if we observe more carefully the likely background and observable function of these so-called tests. Despite many counterproposals, I remain persuaded that John is confronting a crisis precipitated by the secession of some members who have been powerfully influenced by some form of protognosticism. Their departure left behind believers who were, spiritually speaking, badly bruised. The raw triumphalism of most forms of gnosticism dented the confidence of those who refused to go along with the movement. In this light, the so-called tests are not primarily given to exclude certain people on the grounds that they failed to meet the challenges, but to reassure believers that their fidelity to the gospel, along the lines indicated, was itself reason enough to enable them to regain their quiet Christian assurance. The very places where the seceders failed or made outrageous counterclaims, thereby threatening the Christians and jolting their assurance, were the places where the Christians were proving faithful and reliable—in doctrine, obedience, and love. Such faithfulness and reliability constituted evidence of God's work in their lives, and therefore could legitimately be taken by those who believed in the name of the Son of God as corroborating grounds that they truly enjoyed eternal life. Such restored confidence before God had other practical ramifications: in particular, it also issued in renewed confidence in prayer (3:21–22; 5:14–16).[49]

What we learn from these observations is that there is a pastoral dimension to the biblical witness on Christian assurance. We should have known it all along. No one can long serve as a pastor without coming across, say, a young woman who doubts that she is good enough to be forgiven by Christ, an aging man who wonders if he will be transported to glory when he dies, a church member who is having doubts about his salvation and who (it is discovered) is sleeping with his secretary, some nominal believers who display nothing of the promised fruit of the new covenant but who are convinced by the slogan "Once saved, always saved" that they are in no danger, and a gaggle of young people who are unsure of their spiritual status because they have been confronted by those who claim to have the "full gospel." Anyone who applies exactly the same spiritual remedy to these diverse ailments ought to have his license as a spiritual physician immediately rescinded.

Some Conclusions

If we appreciate the undergirding mystery that stands behind Christian assurance, we will let the various complementary biblical statements stand in their naked power and function without endless reductionism.[50]

Close observation of the functions of the various biblical statements in their immediate and canonical contexts will do much to safeguard our theology against dangerous reductionism and pastoral malpractice. Zane Hodges is happy to speak of Christians ceasing to name the name of Christ and denying the faith completely, even though (he insists) God keeps such people "saved," that is, in the faith. From a pastoral point of view, what is one to say to these unbelieving believers, these Christ-denying Christians? If the way

49. Of course, virtually everything I have said about 1 John is disputed. I shall seek to offer detailed defense of these judgments in a forthcoming commentary (NIGTC).

50. I should point out that in many classic treatments on assurance there is a threefold focus: the objective work of Christ grounded in the plan of God, the demonstrable transformation of the believer that is the new birth's inevitable result, and the inner witness of the Spirit (so, for instance, Richard Sibbes: see the discussion in Mark E. Dever, "Richard Sibbes and the 'Truly Evangelicall Church of England': A Study in Reformed Divinity and Early Stuart Conformity" [Ph.D. dissertation, Cambridge University, 1992]). This third leg, tied to such passages as Romans 8:15–17, I have not discussed here, but it needs and deserves serious reflection. It is connected in important ways to the subject of revival. All three legs must be set out in biblical array and pastorally wise proportion in any comprehensive treatment of assurance.

the Scriptures function in such cases is borne in mind, both our theology and our counsel will grow in maturity and biblical balance.

The sort of approach that makes absolute, epistemologically tight, Christian assurance the sine qua non of theological systems and proceeds to engage in a massive rereading of the rest of Scripture, rereadings that are too clever by half, in order to justify this a priori, are ill-conceived. Indeed, granted the proper location of the underlying tension between God's sovereignty and human responsibility, they are as methodologically ill-conceived as, say, J. A. T. Robinson's attempt to develop a Christology grounded exclusively in Jesus' humanity, that humanity serving as a grid that filters out complementary evidence.[51]

Because every part of Christian doctrine is tied, one way or another, to every other part, doubtless a case can be made for beginning with the doctrine of assurance. It is odd, however, that a few contemporary studies have made personal assurance, or some peculiar understanding of it, the touchstone for the entire structure of Christian theology. The result has been truly astonishing distortions. On balance, this is a strange place to begin and end the study of theology. One might have begun with God, with Christ, with redemption, with revelation.

It is important to insist that the view of perseverance and assurance outlined in this chapter does not make perseverance the basis of assurance—as if to say that no one is entitled to any form of assurance until ultimate perseverance has been demonstrated. I have not argued that perseverance is the basis for assurance; rather, I have argued that failure to persevere serves to undermine assurance. The basis of assurance is Christ and his work and its entailments.

In short, the biblical writers offer believers all the assurance they could ever want, grounding such assurance in the character of God, the nature of the new covenant, the finality of election, the love of God, and much more beside. But they never allow such assurance to become a sop for spiritual indifference; indeed, the same vision is what drives them to insist that the God who has called them to his new covenant works powerfully in them to conform them to the likeness of his Son, to the fruitfulness the Spirit empowers us to produce. This becomes both an incentive to press on to the mark of the upward call in Christ Jesus, and an implicit challenge to those who cry "Lord, Lord" but do not do what he commands.

---

51. *The Human Face of God* (London: SCM, 1973).

11

The Love of God:
Universal and Particular

J. I. PACKER

On Knowing Love

It was, I think, Voltaire who first observed that ever since God made man in his own image man has been trying to return the compliment. Whoever said it, it is true, and many theological mistakes have been made through likening the God of infinite power, holiness, goodness, and wisdom to finite and fallen humanity.

The KISS formula—"keep it simple, stupid!"—is current wisecracking wisdom. But the idea behind the formula, namely, that the notion that seems simplest will always be soundest, has been around in theology since at least the third century, when Sabellians and Arians "simplified" the truth of the Trinity in a way that actually denied it (the former turning God into a quick-change artist playing three roles, the latter turning the divine Son and Spirit into two high-class creatures). Many more theological mistakes have come from embracing simplistic naiveties that at the time felt comfortable to the mind.

The idea of the grace of God that prompts this chapter seems to involve error of both kinds, as we shall see. Since however my goal here is positive exposition with the minimum of controversy, I focus first not on disputable opinions, but on basic questions of definition and method.

My title affirms that God's love is a reality. All Christian teaching says this. But what is love? Asking that question must be our starting point, for "love," both as a noun and as a verb, is among the most misused words in the English language. And although God's love is our prime concern we must begin by noting how modern Westerners use the word of each other, for it is here that the worst confusions arise.

"Love" is a term that, because of its historic Christian associations, still carries in what was once Christendom glowing overtones of nobility and grandeur. Certainly, the mutual devotion of lovers, and the self-sacrificing paths of parenthood and friendship, can be noble indeed. But in current use "love" has become virtually synonymous with liking and wanting something or someone, and there is nothing necessarily noble or grand about that. "I love chocolate," "I love sunsets," "I love jazz," "I love redheads," "I love sex"—such states of liking and wanting are so many egocentric highroads to self-gratifying self-indulgence. When persons are the objects of our likes and wants, then manipulation, exploitation, and abuse are likely to result, alternating with unprincipled indulgence of the other person's whims on the principle, it seems, of doing to others as you would like them to do to you. Parents "loving" their children by giving them everything they ever want is an obvious example. Thus, what we call our love for people often does them harm. Sometimes it is assumed that God's love, if real, would itself take the form of unprincipled indulgence of our whims, and then the fact that comforts we pray for are not always given is treated as proving a lack either of love or of power on God's part. Such are the confusions that have to be sorted out.

In *The Four Loves* C. S. Lewis distinguished *agape* (the New Testament Greek word for God's love and Christian love) from *storge* (the feeling of affection or fondness); *eros* (the feeling of desire and need for some person or thing that is felt to be attractive, especially in sexual or aesthetic contexts); and *philia* (the attitude of friendliness to one who is friendly to you). Each of these three is a blend of animal instinct, personal taste, appreciative awareness, and self-gratifying impulse, and in this all three differ radically from *agape*.

What is *agape*? Human *agape* is a way (1 Cor. 13:1)—that is, a path of action—of which four things are true. First, it is a purpose of doing good to others, and so in some sense making those others great. *Agape* Godward, triggered by gratitude for grace, makes God great by exalting him in praise, thanksgiving, and obedience. *Agape* manward, neighbor love as Scripture calls it, makes fellow humans great by serving not their professed wants, but their observed real needs. Thus, marital *agape* seeks fulfillment for the spouse and parental *agape* seeks maturity for the children. Second, *agape* is measured not by sweetness of talk or strength of feeling, but by what it does, and more specifically by what of its own it gives, for the fulfilling of its purpose. Third, *agape* does not wait to be courted, nor does it limit itself to those who at once appreciate it, but it takes the initiative in giving help where help is required, and finds its joy in bringing others benefit. The question of who deserves to be helped is not raised; *agape* means doing good to the needy, not to the meritorious, and to the needy however undeserving they might be. Fourth, *agape* is precise about its object. The famous *Peanuts* quote, "I love the human race—it's people I can't stand," is precisely not *agape*. *Agape* focuses on particular people with particular needs, and prays and works to deliver them from evil. In all of this it is directly modeled on the love of God revealed in the gospel.

Knowing God's Love: The Method

Basic to Christianity is the conviction that we learn what love is from watching God in action—supremely, from watching God in the person of the Father's incarnate Son, Jesus Christ, as he lives, gives, suffers, and dies to achieve our redemption. We do the watching through Bible study, following the narratives of the Gospels and the explanations in the Epistles. The point is often made that before Christianity arrived the *agape* word-group was unspecific, was rarely used, and signified no more than contentment with something, so that by defining it in terms of the love shown forth in Christ the apostles made it a new thing—love of a kind that the world never dreamed of before. This is right, and we must never let ourselves think of *agape* in any terms not validated by the redemptive work of Jesus.

But to understand correctly what the New Testament says about this love of God we must set it in the frame of the total biblical witness to God, and that means observing the following perspectival guidelines.

Remember *the sovereignty of the divine Creator*. Older Reformed theology, organizing the teaching of the canonical Scriptures, called the different aspects of God's being his attributes, some communicable and others incommunicable. The former, so called because in our sanctification they begin to be reproduced in us, were commonly listed as wisdom, truth, goodness (meaning grace, mercy, and longsuffering love), holiness, and righteousness; highlighting God's personhood, they together answered the question How does God behave? The latter, commonly listed as self-existence (aseity), immutability, infinity, eternity, and simplicity (meaning inner integration), highlighted God's transcendence; combining as an answer to the question How does God exist? They underlined at every point the contrast between the majestic self-sustaining omnipotence of the divine life and the creaturely dependence, weakness, and sinful disorder of ours. God's sovereignty, in which the perfection of his powers operates to express the perfection of his moral character, straddles this classification, for it is essentially personal action on an altogether transcendent plane. God "rules in the world and his will is the final cause of all things, including specifically creation and preservation (Ps. 95:6; Rev. 4:11), human government (Pr. 21:1; Dn. 4:35), the salvation of God's people (Rom. 8:29f.; Eph. 1:4, 11), the sufferings of Christ (Lk. 22:42; Acts 2:23), man's life and destiny (Acts 18:21; Rom. 15:32), and even the smallest details of life (Mt. 10:29). God reigns in his universe. . . ."[1] The love of God is thus sovereign love, and must always be acknowledged as such.

Remember *the triunity of the divine Lord*. Within the one God's complex being are three personal centers ("centers" is not perhaps an ideal word, but we have none better). Each is "I" to himself and "you" to the other two. By God's own naming they are the Father, the Son, and the Holy Spirit. God is a society, a community of mutual love, and a team: he is they and they are he, if such language may be allowed. (See Matt. 28:19; John 14:15–26; 2 Cor. 13:14; Eph. 1:3–14; 2:18–22; Rev. 1:4–5; etc. Though the apostles developed no trinitarian vocabulary, trinitarian thinking pervades the entire New Testament.) Speaking epistemologically, the truth of the Trinity became known only through the life and words of the incarnate Son who came from the Father and prayed to the Father, and who when returning to the Father promised that the Spirit would be sent as his deputy; but speaking ontologically, the fact of God's triunity is eternal. The love of God is thus triune love, and should always be thought of in that way.

Remember *the unity of the divine character*. God in Scripture regularly uses the word *holy* with a global meaning, to bring together and hold together in our minds both the metaphysical perfections and the moral glories characterizing the triune Lord, who in all his words and deeds is unchangeably wise, just, pure, good, and true. Every time he says he is holy or calls himself the Holy One of Israel, the adjective carries this full weight of meaning. In this broad sense, therefore, holiness is the attribute displayed in all God's attributes; and thus the love of God is holy love, and must ever be viewed so, in explicit relation to the other aspects of God's being.

Remember *the analogy of the divine self-description*. This point follows from the last. God who gave us language prompted his penmen in Scripture to speak of him in nouns, verbs, and adjectives taken from the common human stock of language, just as he did himself when speaking through the prophets and through his Son, Jesus Christ. But because all these words ordinarily refer to finite and fallen human beings, when they are used of God they must be partially redefined: the core of the meaning will remain, but all associations or implications that suggest human finitude and fallenness must be eliminated, and the core meaning must be set in the frame of God's perfection and purity. It is evident that the Bible writers were mentally doing this all the time, in a way that had become second nature to them, and in interpreting their writings we must follow this out. So the love of God is not identical with, but analogous to, what is noblest in human love, and the precise

1. Bruce Milne, *Know the Truth* (Downers Grove: InterVarsity, 1982), 66.

terms of the analogical adjustment our minds must make at this point have to be learned from the rest of the teaching about God that the Bible gives. What was said about *agape* has already alerted us to the major difference there is between God's love and man's.

Remember *the epistemology of the divine instruction*. God through his Spirit interprets the Bible to us, that is, enables us to understand the writers' meaning and apply their points to ourselves, and so to apprehend what he, the divine Author, wishes to teach us from the inspired text. But the Bible is a set of more or less occasional writings, in which things dealt with in detail are clearer than those to which only passing reference is made. Knowing that sin has twisted our minds, just as it has twisted our moral sensibilities, and both at a deeper level than we can track, we should not let ourselves speculate beyond what Scripture clearly teaches, and should be willing to settle for ignorance (*docta ignorantia,* well-taught ignorance, as it has been called) rather than indulge our theological fancies.

Also, we should take "what Scripture clearly teaches" to mean "what exegesis shows that the Bible writers wanted their readers to gather from their words"—not what those words might seem to be saying when recontextualized in a latter-day dogmatic frame. So our understanding of the love of God must be limited by what the Bible's homiletical flowings of thought actually yield. We should confine ourselves to this, and eschew extrapolations beyond it.

A model of this kind of conscientious theological discretion, and one that bears directly on our present subject, is Anglican Article 17 (1571), "Of Predestination and Election." In Reformation days, as since, treatments of God's love in election were often given shape, overshadowed, and indeed preempted by wrangles of an abstract sort about God's sovereignty in reprobation. But in the New Testament, most notably in Romans 8:28–11:36 and Ephesians 1:3–14, election is a pastoral theme, spelled out for believers' encouragement, reassurance, support, and worship. That is exactly how Article 17 treats it, by drawing out in direct echoes of Scripture the comfort of election, by bypassing debates about reprobation, and by directing unbelievers, seekers, and saints alike to the "whosoever will" promises and mandates of the gospel, which chart the way of life. Because methodologically the article is such a good example of observing biblical parameters, and also because its contents bear directly on what we must deal with next, it is here reproduced in full, in hope that the quaintness of the wording will not obscure the quality of the thinking.

17 *Of Predestination and Election*

Predestination to Life is the everlasting purpose of God, whereby (before the foundations of the world were laid) he hath constantly [firmly] decreed by his counsel secret to us, to deliver from curse and damnation those whom he hath chosen in Christ out of mankind, and to bring them by Christ to everlasting salvation, as vessels made to honour. Wherefore, they which be endued with so excellent a benefit of God be called according to God's purpose by his Spirit working in due season: they through Grace obey the calling: they be justified freely: they be made sons of God by adoption: they be made like the image of his only-begotten Son Jesus Christ: they walk religiously in good works, and at length, by God's mercy, they attain to everlasting felicity.

As the godly consideration of Predestination, and our Election in Christ, is full of sweet, pleasant, and unspeakable comfort to godly persons, and such as feel in themselves the working of the Spirit of Christ, mortifying the works of the flesh, and their earthly members, and drawing up their mind to high and heavenly things, as well because it doth greatly establish and confirm their faith of eternal Salvation to be enjoyed through Christ, as because it doth fervently kindle their love towards God: So, for curious and carnal persons, lacking the Spirit of Christ, to have continually before their eyes the sentence of God's predestination [i.e., the thought of it] is a most dangerous downfall, whereby the Devil doth thrust them either into desperation, or into wretchlessness [recklessness] of most unclean living, no less perilous than desperation.

Furthermore, we must receive God's promises in such wise, as they be generally set forth to us in holy Scripture: and, in our doings, that Will of God is to be followed, which we have expressly declared unto us in the Word of God.

Calvinism, like Arminianism, is a word that means somewhat different things to different people. The present chapter has its place in an anti-Arminian symposium to which writers from various Christian traditions have contributed. I should like to observe here that the essence of my Calvinism, so-called (I do not refuse the label), is found in Anglican Article 17.

Knowing God's Love: The Biblical Witness

The love of God is a great and wide-ranging biblical theme on which one could dilate at length, but for our purposes the scriptural testimony may be summarized as follows.

God's love is spoken of by means of a varied and overlapping vocabulary. Goodness (glorious generosity), love itself (generous goodness in active expression), mercy (generous goodness relieving the needy), grace (mercy contrary to merit and despite demerit), and loving-kindness (KJV) or steadfast love (RSV) (generous goodness in covenantal faithfulness), are the main terms used. The often-echoed self-description whereby God expounds his name (Yahweh, the LORD) to Moses on Sinai crystallizes these ideas: "The LORD, the LORD, the compassionate and gracious God, slow to anger, abounding in love and faithfulness, maintaining love to thousands, and forgiving wickedness, rebellion and sin. . ." (Exod. 34:6–7). The New Testament gauges divine *agape* by the staggering gift of God's Son to suffer for mankind's salvation (see Rom. 5:7–8), and thus deepens all these ideas beyond what Old Testament minds could conceive.

God's love is revealed in his providential care for the creatures he made. "The LORD is good to all; he has compassion on all he has made. . . . The eyes of all look to you, and you give them their food at the proper time. You open your hand and satisfy the desires of every living thing" (Ps. 145:9, 15–16; and see also Ps. 104:21; Matt. 5:45; 6:26; Acts 14:17).

God's love is revealed in the universal invitations of the gospel, whereby sinful humans are invited to turn in faith and repentance to the living Christ who died for sins and are promised pardon and life if they do. "God so loved the world that he gave his one and only Son, that whoever believes in him shall not perish but have eternal life" (John 3:16; see also Rom. 10:11–13; Rev. 22:17). "God is love (*agape*). This is how God showed his love among us: He sent his one and only Son into the world that we might live through him. This is love: not that we loved God, but that he loved us and sent his Son as an atoning sacrifice for our sins" (1 John 4:8–10). And God in the gospel expresses a bona fide wish that all may hear, and that all who hear may believe and be saved (1 Tim. 2:3–6; cf. 4:9–10). This is love in active expression.

God's love is revealed when "because of his great love for us" (1 John 4:8) he brings the spiritually dead to life in Christ and with Christ under the ministry of the gospel (Eph. 2:1, 4–5), uniting us to Christ in co-resurrection for everlasting life and joy (vv. 6–7). "Dead" evidently signifies total unresponsiveness to God, total unawareness of his love, and total lack of the life he gives: no metaphor for spiritual inability and destitution could be stronger. What Paul speaks of here is the work of grace that elsewhere he describes as God "calling"—that is, actually bringing unbelievers to faith by his Spirit so that they respond to the invitation given and trust in Christ to save them. "Those he called, he also justified" (Rom. 8:30)—and no one is justified who has not come to faith. (For further instances of this Pauline usage see Rom. 9:24; 1 Cor. 1:9, 26; Gal. 1:15; 1 Thess. 2:12; 2 Thess. 2:14; 2 Tim. 1:9.) Other New Testament passages designate this same work of grace, whereby God makes us Christians, as new creation (2 Cor. 5:17; Gal. 6:15), and as regeneration or new birth (John 1:12–13; 3:3–8; Tit. 3:5; James 1:18; 1 Pet. 1:23; 1 John 2:28; 3:9; 4:7; 5:1, 4). No declarations that we do not become Christians without creative prevenient grace could be clearer. Passages like John 6:37–39; 17:2, 6, 9, 24; Romans 8:29; Ephesians 1:3–12; 2 Thessalonians 2:13 show that this grace is given according to a pretemporal divine plan, whereby its present recipients were chosen as sinners to be saved.

So it appears, first, that God loves all in some ways (everyone whom he creates, sinners though they are, receives many undeserved good gifts in daily providence), and, second, that he loves some in all ways (that is, in addition to the gifts of daily providence he brings them to faith, to new life, and to glory according to his predestinating purpose). This is the clear witness of the entire Bible.

Knowing God's Love: The Theological Models

The Reformation was an Augustinian revival. Its great discovery, the doctrine of justification by faith, was fitted into a robust Augustinian and Pauline doctrine of grace, according to which fallen humans are totally unable to respond in repentance, faith, and love to God, until prevenient grace—that is, the regenerating Holy Spirit—inwardly renews them. That is, God "calls" them in Paul's special sense of the word. The doctrine that the God who calls thereby shows love to the called that goes beyond the love he shows to others, and that this love is gratuitous and as such amazing, being the opposite of what they deserved, was taken in stride. But such teaching is strong meat, too strong for some stomachs, and as in Augustine's day it produced the reaction of semi-Pelagianism, so in the late sixteenth century it produced the reaction of Arminianism, an adjustment of the Calvinist thesis about God's saving love and man's moral responsibility. Our next task is to compare these two models of the saving love of God.

Historically, Arminianism has affirmed, in the words of W. R. Bagnall, "conditional in opposition to absolute predestination, and general in opposition to particular redemption."[2] This verbal antithesis is not in fact as simple or as clear as it sounds, for changing the adjective involves redefining the noun. What Bagnall should have said is that Calvinism affirms a predestination from which conditionality is excluded and a redemption to which particularity is essential, and Arminianism denies both. To Calvinism predestination is essentially God's unconditional decision about the destiny of individual sinners; to Arminianism it is essentially God's unconditional decision to provide means of grace to sinners, decisions about individuals' destiny being secondary and consequent upon foresight (or as Clark H. Pinnock, who denies God's foresight, would presumably say, discovery) of what use they make of those means of grace. To mainstream Calvinism, predestination of persons means the foreordaining of both their doings, including their response to the gospel, and their consequent destinies; to mainstream Arminianism, it means a foreordaining of destinies based on doings foreseen or discerned but not foreordained. Arminianism affirms that God predestined Christ to be the world's Savior, and repentance and faith to be the way of salvation, and the gift of universal sufficient grace to make saving response

2. W. R. Bagnall, in *Writings of Arminius*, trans. James Nichols and W. R. Bagnall (Grand Rapids: Baker, 1956), 1.3.

to Christ possible for everyone everywhere, but denies that any person is predestined to believe.

On the generic Calvinist view, election, which is a predestinating act on God's part, means the sovereign choice of particular sinners to be saved by Jesus Christ through faith, and redemption, the first step in working out God's predestining purpose, is an achievement that actually guarantees salvation—calling, pardon, adoption, preservation, final glory—for all the elect. In the generic Arminian view, however, what the death of Christ secured was a possibility of salvation for sinners generally, a possibility that, so far as God is concerned, might never have been actualized in a single case; and the electing of individuals to salvation is God noting in advance who will believe and so qualify for glory, as a matter of contingent (not foreordained) fact. Whereas to Calvinism election is God's resolve to save, for Arminianism salvation rests neither on God's election nor on Christ's cross, but on each person's own cooperation with grace, which is something that God does not himself guarantee.

Biblically, the difference between these two conceptions of how God in love relates to fallen human beings may be pinpointed thus. Arminianism characteristically treats our Lord's parable of the supper to which further guests were invited in place of those who never came (Luke 14:16–24; cf. Matt. 22:1–10) as picturing the whole truth about the love of God in the gospel. On this view, when you have compared God's relation to fallen humans with that of a dignitary who urges needy folk to come and enjoy his bounty, you have said it all. Calvinism, however, does not stop here, but characteristically links the picture of the supper with that of the Shepherd (John 10:11–18, 24–29) who has his sheep given to him to care for (vv. 14, 16, 27; cf. 6:37–40), who lays down his life for them (10:15), and who guarantees that all of them will hear his voice, follow him (vv. 16, 27), and be kept by him from perishing forever (v. 28). In other words, Calvinism holds that divine love does not stop short at graciously inviting, but that the triune God takes gracious action to ensure that the elect respond. On this view, both the Christ who saves and the faith that embraces him as Savior are God's gifts, and the latter is as much a foreordained reality as is the former. Arminians praise God for his love in providing a Savior to whom all may come to find life; Calvinists do that too, and then go on to praise God for actually bringing them to the Savior's feet.

So the basic difference between the two positions is not, as is sometimes thought, that Arminianism follows Scripture while Calvinism follows logic, nor that Arminianism knows the compassionate love of God while Calvinists know only his sovereign power; nor that Arminianism affirms a connection between persevering in faith and obedience as a means and reaching heaven as an end that Calvinism's "once saved—always saved" slogan actually denies; nor that Arminianism discerns a bona fide free offer of

Christ in the gospel that Calvinism fails to discern and take seriously; nor that Arminianism acknowledges human moral responsibility before God while Calvinism reduces our race to robots. No, the difference is this: that Calvinism recognizes a dimension of the saving love of God against which Arminianism has reacted and which it now denies, namely, God's sovereignty in bringing to faith and keeping in faith all those who are actually saved. Arminianism gives Christians much to thank God for, but Calvinism gives them more.

Arminians appear in public as persons supremely concerned to do justice to the love of God, the glory of Christ, the moral responsibility of man, and the call to Christian holiness. The reason why they maintain universal redemption; human ability, whether by nature or by grace, for independent response to the gospel; and the conditional character of election is that they think these assertions necessary as means to their avowed end. What they rarely see is that in all this they are not affirming what Calvinism denies so much as denying what Calvinism affirms. Everyone in the Reformed mainstream will insist that Christ the Savior is freely offered—indeed, freely offers himself—to sinners in and through the gospel; and that since God gives us all free agency (that is, voluntary decision-making power) we are indeed answerable to him for what we do, first, about universal general revelation, and then about the law and the gospel when and as these are presented to us; and that only those who persevere in their Christian pilgrimage ever reach the heavenly city. But Calvinism at the same time affirms the total perversity, depravity, and inability of fallen human beings, which results in them naturally and continually using their free agency to say no to God, and the absolute sovereignty of the regenerating God who effectually calls and draws them into newness of life in Christ. Calvinism magnifies the Augustinian principle that God himself graciously gives all that in the gospel he requires and commands, and the reactive rationalism of Arminianism in all its forms denies this to a degree. The Arminian idea is simpler, for it does not involve so full or radical an acknowledgment of the mystery of God's ways, and it assimilates God more closely to the image of man, making him appear like a gentle giant who is also a great persuader and a resourceful maneuverer, although he is sometimes frustrated and disappointed. But if the measure of love is what it really gives to the really needy and undeserving, then the love of God as Calvinists know it is a much greater thing than the Arminians imagine, and is much diminished by the Arminian model of God and his ways with mankind.[3]

3. Some of the material in this paragraph is adapted from J. I. Packer, "Arminianisms," in *Through Christ's Word: A Festschrift for Dr. Philip E. Hughes*, ed. W. Robert Godfrey and Jesse L. Boyd III (Phillipsburg, N.J.: Presbyterian and Reformed, 1985), 121–48.

Knowing God's Love: The Nature and the Extent of the Atonement

That the atoning death of Jesus Christ is the supreme achievement and demonstration of God's love is Christian common ground, on which both Calvinists and Arminians take their stand. Disagreement begins, however, when the cross is fitted into the larger theological frame that each embraces. The Reformed way, as marked out by Luther and Calvin (who, be it said, not all Calvinists think spoke the last word about the cross), was to celebrate the atonement in an inclusive rhetoric that aimed to highlight the availability to all of pardon through Calvary, and the sufficiency of Christ's blood to cleanse the foulest from sin. The Reformers then highlighted the particularity of God's love to his elect in their treatment of the calling, justifying, preserving, and glorifying of Christians. As we have already seen that both the universal availability of Christ and his benefits and the particularity of effectual calling are set forth in Scripture as expressions of God's love, the Reformers cannot at this point be seriously faulted. Later, however, when Lutheran and Arminian revisionists began to turn the apparent universality of the atonement against the idea of personal salvation as a fruit of God's sovereign election, Reformed theologians searched the Scriptures again; and, facing the view that Christ died for everyone equally, thus making salvation possible for all though guaranteeing it for none, they focused the question that Louis Berkhof with his unfailing pedestrian clarity states in the following way:

> The question . . . is not (a) whether the satisfaction rendered by Christ was in itself sufficient for the salvation of all men, since this is admitted by all; (b) whether the saving benefits are actually applied to every man, for the great majority of those who teach a universal atonement do not believe that all are actually saved; (c) whether the *bona fide* offer of salvation is made to all who hear the gospel, on the condition of repentance and faith, since the Reformed Church does not call this in question; nor (d) whether any of the fruits of the death of Christ accrue to the benefit of the non-elect in virtue of their close association with the people of God, since this is explicitly taught by many Reformed scholars. On the other hand, the question does relate to the design of the atonement. Did the Father in sending Christ, and did Christ in coming into the world, to make atonement for sin, *do this with the design or for the purpose of saving only the elect or all men?*[4]

And their answer, in brief, was that Scripture, when searched, shows clearly enough that Christ died at the Father's will with a specific purpose of saving the elect.

4. Louis Berkhof, *Systematic Theology*, 4th ed. (Grand Rapids: Eerdmans, 1949), 393–94.

John Owen's *The Death of Death in the Death of Christ* (Latin title, *Sanguis Jesu Salus Electorum*, the blood of Jesus the salvation of the elect), a polemical work published in 1648,[5] seems to show conclusively that biblical statements about the cross, viewed in context, are characteristically particularist. Christ is said to have died for his sheep (John 10:11, 15), his church (Eph. 5:25), God's elect (Rom. 8:32–35), "many" (Matt. 20:28), his own people (Matt. 1:21), "us" who now believe (Tit. 2:14, etc.), and among them "me" (Gal. 2:20); and the language of Christ "dying for" others (*hyper* or *anti* in the Greek) proves on examination regularly to imply that those others are or will be saved. The atonement thus appears as an effective propitiatory transaction that actually redeemed—that is, secured redemption for—those particular persons for whom Jesus on the cross became the God-appointed substitute (see Gal. 3:13; Eph. 1:7; Col. 2:14). Since the Bible rules out all thought of universal salvation, yet depicts the cross as effective for the salvation of those for whom it was endured, "particular" or "definite" redemption must be the true concept. Sometimes, for the sake of the T-U-L-I-P acronym,[6] Calvinists have spoken of limited atonement, but Roger Nicole counsels against this.

> The language of limited atonement describes inadequately and unfairly the view which is held by Reformed people. The problem is that it seems to place emphasis upon limits. It seems to take away from the beauty, glory and fullness of the work of Christ. We seem to say that it does not go quite as far as it could or should go . . . what we need to say is that the atonement is definite, that it is related to a particular people whom God has chosen. This helps us psychologically. Because if you say, "I believe in limited atonement," the one who disagrees with you will say, "I believe in *unlimited* atonement." He appears to be the one who exalts the greatness of the grace of Christ . . . Why put ourselves at a disadvantage? On that account, I will gladly send the tulips flying! You see, I am not Dutch; I am Swiss, and I do not care so much about the tulips. I do not care about acronyms. I care about the precious faith of the Reformed church . . . and I do not think that "limited atonement" represents me. I want to say "definite atonement" or "particular redemption," and I would encourage other people to do so also.[7]

Surely this is wise advice. I wish I had taken it earlier in life.

In 1959 I wrote a longish introduction to a reprint of Owen's treatise, as a kind of hors d'oeuvres to the study of the work itself. Though the essay was not originally intended to be read apart from Owen, I let it be reprinted as a

---

5. John Owen, *Works* (Edinburgh: Banner of Truth, 1967), 10.193–428.
6. T(otal Depravity)—U(nconditional election)—L(imited atonement)—I(rresistible grace)—P(erseverance of the saints). It works only in English.
7. Roger Nicole, "Particular Redemption," in *Our Savior God*, ed. James Montgomery Boice (Grand Rapids: Baker, 1980), 168–69.

separate pamphlet, and eventually reprinted it separately myself as a chapter in *A Quest for Godliness*.[8] (When you can't beat 'em, join 'em.) Terry Miethe, discussing it,[9] evidently did not think it necessary to read Owen's treatise, where the actual argumentation is contained, and faulted me for outlining in my introduction assertions about Calvinism that it would take a book or two to make good.[10] Miethe's whole discussion is unsatisfying; he regularly confuses his readers by not distinguishing his own idea of divine sovereignty and election, and of human freedom, from that of Calvinists generally and myself in particular; he fails to engage with the best exponents of the position he controverts; he presents arguments inexactly; he writes constantly as if what is at issue is the availability of Christ to all who turn to him, something that was never in dispute; he treats echoes of biblical phraseology in sixteenth-century Anglican formularies as the Church of England taking sides in a seventeenth-century debate; and he claims to be defending the view that "the redemptive events in the life of Jesus provided a salvation so extensive and so broad as to potentially include the whole of humanity past, present and future!"[11] But he never tells us how this salvation might reach humanity past, or persons who do not encounter the gospel in the present. Again, he writes: "Man's natural inability to believe, (it has been shown) is not taught, at least in Ephesians 2:8 [who ever thought it was?], and (I would argue) not in the rest of Scripture either"[12]—which makes one wonder how he would handle John 6:43–44; Romans 8:7–8; and 1 Corinthians 2:14. Understanding is not advanced by such discussions.

Knowing God's Love: Gratitude and Joy

We have seen that the measure of *agape* is its giving, and that our holy, sovereign, triune, self-revealed Creator-God shows *agape* to all his rational creatures in some ways and to some in all ways; that is, not only in providential

---

8. (Wheaton: Crossway, 1990), 125–48.

9. Terry Miethe, "The Universal Power of the Atonement," in *The Grace of God, the Will of Man: A Case for Arminianism*, ed. Clark H. Pinnock (Grand Rapids: Zondervan, 1989), 71–96. "I was asked by my editor and publisher to 'address' Packer's introduction," 95 n. 44.

10. Ibid., 87–88. "This is a clear example of a simple assertion, which in logic amounts to nothing more than the fallacy of *petitio principii* (begging the question)." The same might with equal justice, or injustice, be said of Miethe's own statement. Miethe adduces a professional logician, Irving M. Copi, to explain what begging the question means (see 95 n. 43). From the Copi quote it is clear that when no inferential argument is being attempted, as in the Packer passage that Miethe is discussing, no question is or can be begged.

11. Ibid., 72; quoting from Donald Lake, "He Died for All: The Universal Dimensions of the Atonement," in *Grace Unlimited*, ed. Clark H. Pinnock (Minneapolis: Bethany Fellowship, 1975), 31.

12. Ibid., 86.

provision but also in saving them from sin for eternal glory. We have seen that there is a gospel addressed to all, which the church is charged to take to all, that proclaims a Savior who is there for all in the power of his atoning death and risen life; and we have seen that through this gospel a pattern of sovereign grace in effectual calling, justification, sanctification, and glorification is being worked out in life after life. We may now say that to know that nothing ever "will be able to separate us from the love of God that is in Christ Jesus our Lord" (Rom. 8:39) is the height of Christian assurance, and to that "to know this love that surpasses knowledge—that you may be filled to the measure of all the fullness of God" (Eph. 3:18–19) is the acme of Christian progress, and that these are the twin peaks of true Christian living in this world.

In all the Christian's knowledge of God's gracious giving Luther's *pro me*—the "for me" of Galatians 2:20—is central. To know that from eternity my Maker, foreseeing my sin, foreloved me and resolved to save me, though it would be at the cost of Cavalry; to know that the divine Son was appointed from eternity to be my Savior, and that in love he became man for me and died for me and now lives to intercede for me and will one day come in person to take me home; to know that the Lord "who loved me and gave himself for me" (Gal. 2:20) and who "came and preached peace" to me through his messengers (Eph. 2:17) has by his Spirit raised me from spiritual death to life-giving union and communion with himself, and has promised to hold me fast and never let me go—this is knowledge that brings overwhelming gratitude and joy. As Luther himself put it in his answer to Erasmus, "now that God has taken my salvation out of the control of my own will, and put it under the control of His, and promised to save me, not according to my working or running, but according to his own grace and mercy, I have the comfortable certainty that he is faithful and will not lie to me, and that He is also great and powerful, so that no devils or opposition can break Him or pluck me from Him. 'No one', He says, 'shall pluck them out of my hand, because my Father which gave them to me is greater than all' (John 10:28–29). Thus it is that, if not all, yet some, indeed many, are saved . . . Furthermore, I have the comfortable certainty that I please God, not by reason of the merit of my works, but by reason of His merciful favour promised to me; so that, if I work too little, or badly, He does not impute it to me, but with fatherly compassion pardons me and makes me better. This is the glorying of all the saints in their God."[13] Such glorying is in truth mainstream biblical Christianity—an immeasurably richer reality than can ever emerge from any account of the love of God that stops short at general goodwill and that drops the personal, individualizing *pro me* of sovereign grace.

13. Martin Luther, *The Bondage of the Will*, trans. J. I. Packer and O. R. Johnston (London: James Clarke; Old Tappan, N.J.: Revell, 1957), 314.

"Thank God for his gift that is too wonderful for words!" (2 Cor. 9:15 CEV). May all God's people come to appreciate it! In heaven we all most certainly will, and it is a sad thing that any in this world should take up with a theology that in any measure deprives them of this cognitive foretaste of heaven here and now. I pray that our loving God will show the full glory of his love, in its particularity as well as its universality, to us all.

Part 3
Pastoral Reflections

12

Does Divine Sovereignty Make a Difference in Everyday Life?

JERRY BRIDGES

Few things are more ordinary or mundane than planning. We plan to go shopping tomorrow, or to take a trip next week, or to have a family picnic on the Fourth of July. Most people's calendars are full of appointments and things they plan to do. Turning to Scripture, we find the apostle Paul planning to visit the believers at Rome on his way to Spain (Rom. 15:24). Even God has plans. Job acknowledged to God that "no plan of yours can be thwarted" (Job 42:2).

Yet a certain type of planning is condemned in Scripture. It is planning that fails to take into account the sovereignty of God. James describes it this way:

> Now listen, you who say, "Today or tomorrow we will go to this or that city, spend a year there, carry on business and make money." Why, you do not even know what will happen tomorrow. What is your life? You are a mist that appears for a little while and then vanishes. Instead, you ought to say, "If it is the Lord's will, we will live and do this or that." As it is, you boast and brag. All such boasting is evil. (4:13–16)

James was addressing people who tend to make ordinary business plans. In a modern setting he was addressing business people who might plan to open a new store or to introduce a new product line, or even in principle, a church congregation that might plan to start a building program. James does not condemn such planning. He does not even condemn the plans to make money. What he condemns is presumptuous planning; that is, plans that ignore the purposes of God and the sovereignty of God to prosper or to frustrate our plans.

Yet this is the type of planning most people, including believers, do every day. We make plans without acknowledging that God is sovereign in all the affairs and circumstances of our lives. In former generations it was common for believers to include in their statement of plans the phrase *the Lord willing*. Although that phrase undoubtedly became a meaningless cliché for many, it was nevertheless intended to express a heartfelt awareness that all of life is lived under the absolute sovereignty of God.

James is not advocating a certain manner of speaking. Rather he is teaching an attitude of the heart, an attitude that springs from a belief in and a submission to the sovereign control of God in all the affairs of life. Furthermore, James is not teaching a doctrine of irresponsible fatalism, that is, "what will be, will be," so why make any plans or exert any effort to execute them? He encourages us to make plans (v. 15), but to make those plans in an attitude of submission to and dependence on the sovereign will of God.

We are not forced to choose between the extremes of irresponsible fatalism and presumptuous planning. Rather the Bible provides us a safe course to steer of responsible yet dependent and submissive planning. It is beyond the scope of this chapter to attempt to define or describe responsible planning other than to observe that it should be consistent with scriptural principles and should aim to glorify God. For now we are focusing on the attitude of dependence and submission with which biblically responsible planning must be carried out. By dependence we acknowledge our reliance on God to guide us in our planning, even though we will want to use all human means at our disposal as we make our plans. We also acknowledge that we are ultimately dependent on him to enable us through his divine providence to accomplish those plans.[1]

By submission we acknowledge that all our plans should aim for the glory of God. "So whether you eat or drink or whatever you do, do it all for the glory of God" (1 Cor. 10:31). But we also acknowledge that when we have exhausted every reasonable effort to execute those plans, God may for his own good reasons thwart our efforts. In that case, we submit in humility and trust to him believing that he does all things well.

Randall G. Basinger, writing from an Arminian viewpoint, denies God's complete sovereignty over the world and instead maintains, "that what actually occurs in the world is, to an extent, consequent on the human will"

---

1. Elsewhere I have defined God's providence as "his constant care for and his absolute rule over all his creation for his own glory and the good of his people." Jerry Bridges, *Trusting God Even When Life Hurts* (Colorado Springs: NavPress, 1988), 25.

and "that things can occur that God does not will or want."[2] He then draws the application that our responsibility is to work with God to bring about a better world.

Those of us who affirm God's complete sovereignty over the world would agree with Basinger that we have a responsibility to work together with God, for God indeed has ordained to carry out a significant portion of his eternal plan through human instruments. We would also affirm that our working together with God involves wise planning and avoidance of an irresponsible attitude of fatalism. So, Basinger asks, if both Arminians and Calvinists approach planning and decision making in the same way, that is, as responsible moral agents, what difference does divine sovereignty make?

It makes a considerable difference. Calvinists recognize that when they have done their best to plan and make wise decisions, their planning is at best imperfect and their decisions may sometimes turn out to be bad decisions. But they also believe that God is in control of even their bad decisions and will, through his infinite wisdom, work out the results of those decisions in such a way as to accomplish his sovereign will. In other words, they believe that God cannot be thwarted or frustrated by their bad decisions. They do not use this as an excuse for irresponsibility, but they do take courage in the fact that God's will and God's plan are not finally dependent on their coming through for God.

Of course it does not finally matter what either Arminians or Calvinists believe. The only issue is, what is the truth? What is in accordance with the reality of things? Our only definitive resource for determining the answer is Scripture. And the Bible is replete with references to the sovereignty of God in the affairs of this world. The passage from James is only one of many that could be cited.

Exhaustive Divine Sovereignty

Of course James 4:13–16 does not address the issue of what Basinger calls "exhaustive divine sovereignty." By that expression Basinger refers to the belief that "God has . . . decreed—down to the very last detail—the actual course this world will take" and that "all events are consequent and hence subservient to the will of God."[3] To address this issue we must turn elsewhere in the Bible. Of the several passages we could turn to, one of the most explicit is Jesus' statement in Matthew 10:28–31:

2. Randall G. Basinger, "Exhaustive Divine Sovereignty: A Practical Critique," in *The Grace of God, the Will of Man: A Case for Arminianism*, ed. Clark H. Pinnock (Grand Rapids: Zondervan, 1989), 196.
3. Ibid., 191.

"Do not be afraid of those who kill the body but cannot kill the soul. Rather, be afraid of the One who can destroy both soul and body in hell. Are not two sparrows sold for a penny? Yet not one of them will fall to the ground apart from the will of your Father. And even the very hairs of your head are all numbered. So don't be afraid; you are worth more than many sparrows."

In turning to this passage, however, we leave the subject of our own planning and enter into what may be, for purposes of considering the effect of divine sovereignty in our lives, a more pertinent aspect of this issue, namely, the effects on us of other people's often malicious plans and actions. This is undoubtedly the issue Jesus was addressing, for in verse 28 he says, "Do not be afraid of those who kill the body but cannot kill the soul." His reference to God's care over the sparrows and his numbering the hairs of our heads is clearly in regard to the evil actions of other people toward us.

Jesus' words are so familiar to us that we can easily fail to grasp the significance of what he said. The word translated as "penny" was often used to denote a trifling amount. Yet Jesus said not one of those birds, worth only a trifle, could fall to the ground (i.e., lose its life) without the will and permission of God our Father. But Jesus extends our Father's care to a yet finer detail: "even the very hairs of your head are all numbered." The average human head has about 140,000 hairs. Jesus said that each individual hair is numbered; that is, has its own identity. The obvious inference is that each hair is important to God.

God does not exercise his sovereignty in only a broad way, leaving the smaller details of our lives to "chance" or "luck." That is precisely Jesus' point. God our Father, who exercises his sovereignty in such minute detail as to control the destiny of a little bird, will certainly exercise his sovereignty to control even the most insignificant details of our lives.

Sometimes the Scriptures affirm the sovereignty of God in an almost incidental way. One such instance occurs in Isaiah 5, where the prophet is predicting the invasion of the Assyrian army in response to God's summoning "whistle" (v. 26). Isaiah describes the battle-ready condition of this army: "They come, swiftly and speedily! Not one of them grows tired or stumbles, not one slumbers or sleeps" (vv. 26–27). Then he adds a rather amazing statement: "not a sandal thong is broken" (v. 27). In a modern setting we would say, "Not a single shoelace [of any soldier] is broken."

We see in this statement not only an affirmation of the absoluteness of God's sovereignty, but also the thoroughness with which his sovereignty penetrates. Nothing is left to chance, not even the brokenness of a sandal thong. We all know the old saying, "for want of a nail, the shoe was lost; for want of a shoe, the horse was lost; for want of a horse, the rider was lost; for want of a rider, the battle was lost." That saying reminds us that details are important. And God is just as sovereign over the details as he is over the great matters of the world. Every major event of history consists of a mosaic of details. The happening by "chance" of any one of those details could significantly affect the outcome of the event itself.

So Jesus assures us that God does not leave the details of our lives to chance. Every hair on our heads is numbered and is under the watchful eye of our Father. That is why Jesus can say so assuredly, "So don't be afraid; you are worth more than many sparrows" (Matt. 10:31). There are innumerable events and circumstances of our lives that, considered in themselves, are calculated to make us afraid. If God were not in sovereign control of those situations, Jesus' words would be meaningless. If God is not in control, then I ought to be afraid. It is of little comfort to me to know that God loves me if he is not in control of the events of my life.

Basinger asks, "What difference does [a belief in exhaustive divine sovereignty] make?"[4] This is one of the crucial differences. It enables us to trust God. It enables us to obey Jesus' command, "Don't be afraid," because we know that our lives are not subject to chance or luck, to the whims of nature, or the malevolent actions of other people.

God's Sovereignty over People

One of the more difficult areas in the discussion of God's sovereignty is his sovereignty over people. Many people are prepared to grant God's sovereignty over nature and impersonal circumstances such as a mechanical failure in an airplane, or a broken shoelace on a soldier's boot. After all, nature does not have a will of its own. God is free to operate through his physical laws as he pleases. But the concept of divine sovereignty over people seems to destroy the free will of humans and make them no more than puppets on God's stage.

Yet the Bible repeatedly affirms God's sovereignty over people. It speaks of God making the Egyptians favorably disposed toward the Israelites (Exod. 12:35–36), of his moving the heart of Cyrus, king of Persia, to fulfill his word (Ezra 1:1), and of his causing King Nebuchadnezzar's official to show favor and sympathy to Daniel (Dan. 1:9).

One of the strongest assertions of God's sovereignty over people is Proverbs 21:1: "The king's heart is in the hand of the LORD; he directs it like a watercourse wherever he pleases." Charles Bridges comments on this verse, "The general truth [of God's sovereignty over the hearts of all people] is taught by the strongest illustration—his uncontrollable sway upon the most absolute of all wills—the *king's heart.*"[5]

---

4. Ibid., 204.
5. Charles Bridges, *An Exposition of the Book of Proverbs* (Evansville: Sovereign Grace Book Club, 1959), 364.

In our day of limited monarchies and figurehead kings and queens it may be difficult for us to appreciate fully the force of what Bridges is saying when he speaks of the king's heart as the most absolute of all wills. But in Solomon's time the king was an absolute monarch. There was no legislature to pass laws he did not like or a Supreme Court to restrain his actions. The king's word was the last word. His authority over his realm was unconditional and unrestrained.

Yet this Scripture teaches that God controls the king's heart. The stubborn will of the most powerful monarch on earth is directed by God as easily as the farmer directs the flow of water in his irrigation canals. The argument, then, is from the greater to the lesser—if God controls the king's heart surely he controls everyone else's. All must move before his sovereign influence.

All of us at times find ourselves and our future, be it immediate or long range, in the hands of other people. Their decisions can determine the success or failure of our plans. A government official can approve or deny a visa to enter a country. A professor can determine the academic success of a graduate student. A supervisor can block or promote a career. I do not overlook our own responsibility for diligent and prudent efforts in these areas, but when we have done our best, we are often still at the mercy of other people and their decisions or actions.

In reality, though, we are not at their mercy, because God sovereignly rules over those decisions and actions. God moves people to do his will and he restrains people from accomplishing the evil they would normally carry out. A striking illustration of this is found in what appears to be an almost passing comment in Exodus 34:23–24:

> Three times a year *all your men* are to appear before the Sovereign LORD, the God of Israel. I will drive out nations before you and enlarge your territory, and *no one will covet your land* when you go up three times each year to appear before the LORD your God. (italics added)

To grasp the significance of this passage, let us recast it in our present setting. What God commanded Israel to do was equivalent to commanding our nation to shut down all its commerce, close all its educational institutions, and furlough all its military personnel simultaneously, and gather all those people into one giant Christian assembly three times a year. Think how vulnerable our nation would be during those three occasions each year.

Yet that is what God commanded Israel to do. But along with the command, he promised them that no one would covet their land during those times, let alone invade to take it over. God could make that promise because in his sovereignty, he had the power to restrain people from even desiring to harm them. God is sovereign over not only our actions; he is sovereign even over our desires.

Obviously God does not always restrain the wicked desires or actions of sinful people. We have only to read our daily newspaper to see that. But God can do so when he chooses. And he does do so when it is his will. Therefore, as his children we can be sure that all evil intended against us by other people passes through his sovereign control and is either permitted or restrained as he chooses.

No doubt all of us have at times been the victim of some other person's malicious behavior. In fact, some of that behavior has come from other believers in the form of gossip, or slander, or other hurtful actions. But what we do not know is how much evil behavior has been restrained by God quite apart from our knowing about it. God has restrained not only the other person's behavior but sometimes even his or her desires to harm us.

God's sovereignty over the hearts of people does not mean that their decisions or actions always work out the way we desire. God often allows malicious and spiteful people to act in ways that frustrate our plans and desires, or are in some way harmful to us. Such was the case with Joseph. There is no question that his brothers acted spitefully and maliciously in selling him into slavery. And there is no question that Potiphar's wife acted viciously in falsely accusing Joseph so that he was cast into prison. Furthermore, there is no question that each of them acted of his or her own free will. None of them was coerced by God to do something he or she did not want to do. Joseph said to his brothers, "You intended to harm me" (Gen. 50:20).

Yet there is also no question that God was sovereignly controlling all their actions so as to accomplish his plan in and through Joseph. Joseph could later say to his brothers, "So then, it was not you who sent me here, but God" (Gen. 45:8). God used their evil actions to accomplish his good purpose, as Joseph said to his brothers: "You intended to harm me, but God intended it for good to accomplish what is now being done, the saving of many lives" (Gen. 50:20).

God's sovereignty over people does not mean we do not experience pain and suffering. It means that God is in control of our pain and suffering, and that he has in mind a beneficial purpose for it. There is no such thing as pain without a purpose for the child of God. We may be sure that however irrational and inexplicable it seems to us, all pain has a purpose. As Margaret Clarkson has so beautifully written:

> The sovereignty of God is the one impregnable rock to which the suffering human heart must cling. The circumstances surrounding our lives are no accident: they may be the work of evil, but that evil is held firmly within the mighty hand of our sovereign God. . . . All evil is subject to Him, and evil cannot touch His children unless He permits it. God is the Lord of human history and of the personal history of every member of His redeemed family.[6]

6. Margaret Clarkson, *Grace Grows Best in Winter* (Grand Rapids: Eerdmans, 1984), 40–41.

So we see once again that divine sovereignty does make a difference in everyday life. Its reality does make an objective difference. We are not at the mercy of people who intend to harm us, even though from our human perspective it may seem so. God is sovereign in their actions whether we believe it or not. Our belief does not make it so. But the comfort God intends for us to derive from his sovereignty is dependent upon our believing it. Those who do not believe God is sovereign over the intents and actions of others do not enjoy this comfort. They often struggle unduly with the sinful actions of other people and, in many instances, allow bitterness to ruin their lives. Those who do believe God is in control can take courage in the fact that God is working in and through their pain and suffering for their ultimate good.

A belief in the sovereignty of God over people does not mean we should not act prudently with respect to those who may wish to harm us. Jesus himself is a good example to us. John tells us that "Jesus went around in Galilee, purposely staying away from Judea because the Jews there were waiting to take his life" (John 7:1). Jesus acted prudently despite the fact that no one could lay a hand on him, "because his time had not yet come" (John 7:30). No one could have been more confident of the sovereignty of God over his life than Jesus. Yet he did not act carelessly. He took steps to avoid danger when he needed to.

We must do the same, for again it must be emphasized that belief in divine sovereignty in the everyday affairs of our lives should never cause us to act imprudently or irresponsibly. The Scriptures repeatedly teach us our responsibility for prudent actions. The Book of Proverbs, for example, is filled with this type of teaching. What we are addressing is our response to the harmful actions of other people over which we have no control. It is in those instances that we can repose quietly in the sovereignty of God in all the details of our lives.

God Is Sovereign over Nature

Another major area in which we struggle over God's sovereignty is the area of physical affliction or infirmities. The evil actions of other people are oftentimes temporary in their consequences, but physical infirmities may be with us for life. Children are born with permanent birth defects. Accidents leave people who were previously healthy and vigorous with lifelong limitations. Others suffer for years with major chronic diseases. Is God then in control of birth defects, major accidents, and crippling diseases?

When God called Moses to lead the nation of Israel out of Egypt, Moses protested his inadequacy, primarily because he was slow of speech. God's reply to Moses is instructive to us in this area of physical affliction, for God said, "Who gave man his mouth? Who makes him deaf or mute? Who gives him sight or makes him blind? Is it not I, the LORD?" (Exod. 4:11). Here God specifically assumes the responsibility for the physical afflictions of deafness, muteness, and blindness. These physical defects are not merely the product of defective genes or birth accidents. Those things may indeed be the immediate cause, but behind them is the sovereign purpose of God. As Donald Grey Barnhouse once said, "No person in this world was ever blind that God had not planned for him to be blind; no person was ever deaf in this world that God had not planned for him to be deaf—If you do not believe that, you have a strange God who has a universe which has gone out of gear and He cannot control it."[7]

This God who is the God of deafness, muteness, and blindness is also the God of cancer, arthritis, Down's syndrome, and all other afflictions that come to us or our loved ones. None of these afflictions just happen. They are all within the sovereign will of God.

Obviously God does work in nature and our physical bodies through a complex sequence of cause-and-effect relationships. The doctrine of the sovereignty of God in the physical adversities we encounter does not deny this causal system. Rather it teaches that God so superintends the actions of the system that all cause-and-effect relationships are under his direct control.

Those who deny the total sovereignty of God do not believe God so controls all such details. Rather they believe that God has so established the laws of nature (including the laws of genetics and disease) that the causal system operates quite apart from any immediate direction or control from God. This view is ably expressed by Jon Tal Murphree, who wrote, "The method we observe operating in the world reflects the arrangement of nature to run itself with little divine tampering," and "because the system was given the ability to run itself once it was begun, the specific purpose of God is not immediately and directly behind every natural event."[8]

Yet Scripture speaks of God's direct, immediate control over nature. Consider the following passage;

> He unleashes his lightning beneath the whole heaven and sends it to the ends of the earth. . . . He says to the snow, "Fall on the earth," and to the rain shower, "Be a mighty downpour." . . . The breath of God produces ice, and the broad waters become frozen. He loads the clouds with moisture; he scatters his lightning through them. At his direction they swirl around over the face of the whole earth *to do whatever he commands them.* He brings the clouds to punish men, or to water his earth and show his love. (Job 37:3, 6, 10–13, italics added)

7. Quoted from a printed copy of a message, "The Sovereignty of God," preached by Dr. Donald G. Barnhouse, n.d., 2.
8. Jon Tal Murphree, *A Loving God and a Suffering World* (Downers Grove: InterVarsity, 1981), 106, 101.

It could be argued that these Scriptures are simply metaphorical expressions to denote the laws of nature that God established. But note the phrase *to do whatever he commands them.* This seems to indicate immediate control. Then note his twofold purpose to punish men, or to water the earth and show his love. Such discriminating action with the motive either to punish or to bless could not be attributed to the laws of nature that are established and left to run their course with little or no direct intervention.

For Murphree, divine causal input into the natural cause-and-effect system constitutes a miracle, which he defines "as the occurrence of any event from a non-natural cause." According to him, a divine miracle "is the occurrence of an event from a divine cause."[9] There does not appear to be any room in his system for divine providence whereby God guides and governs all events, circumstances, and acts of human beings in ways consonant with the laws that he has established and, in the case of human beings, through the often unconscious concurrence of their free wills.

God Is Sovereign over the Evil and the Good

Scripture not only affirms God's controlling sovereignty over the physical laws he has established, and over the actions and even desires of people; it also affirms his sovereignty over evil events as well as good ones. This is another dimension of his sovereignty that is sometimes difficult for us to accept. We are quite happy to ascribe the apparent blessings of life to God (at least we should be), but we are reluctant to ascribe calamities and disasters to him. This reluctance is well articulated by Harold S. Kushner, who wrote:

> Insurance companies refer to earthquakes, hurricanes, and other natural disasters as "acts of God." I consider that a case of using God's name in vain. I don't believe that an earthquake that kills thousands of innocent victims without reason is an act of God. It is an act of nature. Nature is morally blind, without values. It churns along, following its own laws, not caring who or what gets in the way.[10]

Again, however, we must turn from what we might like to believe to the Scriptures to determine what they actually tell us. Two passages of Scripture are explicit and definitive:

9. Ibid., 101.
10. Harold S. Kushner, *When Bad Things Happen to Good People* (New York: Avon, 1981), 59. I realize Kushner is not a Christian and that those of the Arminian position would likely not own him as one of their spokesmen. However, I have quoted from Kushner because I believe he sets forth in an able manner the essence of the Arminian position in denying the total sovereignty of God.

I form the light and create darkness, I bring prosperity and create disaster; I, the Lord, do all these things. (Isa. 45:7)

Who can speak and have it happen if the Lord has not decreed it? Is it not from the mouth of the Most High that both calamities and good things come? (Lam. 3:37–38)

In these passages God expressly says that he brings both prosperity and disaster, and that from him come both calamities and good things. We may not like that idea, but we should not seek to minimize the force of those statements. Rather, we must allow the Bible to say what it says, not what we think it ought to say.

The question naturally arises, though, that if God is a good, loving God, how can he allow, or ever cause such disasters or calamities? But we could perhaps better ask, if God is holy and just, why does he not punish all the ungodliness and wickedness on earth by even greater calamities? The answer to both questions is, we do not know. God has not chosen to reveal to us his reasons for his sovereign actions in the world. What we do know, however, is that God will work out everything, both the good and the bad, in conformity with the purpose of his will (Eph. 1:11), and will cause all things, both the good and the bad, to work together for the good of those who love him (Rom. 8:28).

This is where belief in exhaustive divine sovereignty makes a significant difference. Both Arminians and Calvinists can be battered by a similar set of circumstances. Arminians apparently believe that the most God can do is to pick up the pieces of a disastrous situation and try to bring about some good from it. Calvinists believe that God was in control of the disaster from start to finish and that he knew from all eternity how he would use the disaster to bring glory to himself and good to his aching child.

Of course a belief in the absolute sovereignty of God is of little comfort if we do not also believe just as strongly in the infinite love and unfathomable wisdom of God. But it is also of little comfort to believe in the love of God if we do not believe in his sovereignty. Paul assures us that nothing can separate us from the love of God (Rom. 8:35–39). Yet, if God is not in control of every circumstance of our lives, then we can effectively be separated from his love. If my son is drowning, my love to him is of little value if I cannot swim. But God can swim, so to speak.

Therefore divine sovereignty ought to make a difference in our lives. It ought to give us courage when we encounter adversity of any sort. It ought to help us to obey Jesus' command, "don't be afraid," and even Paul's command to "give thanks in all circumstances" (1 Thess. 5:18). It ought to cause us to live our lives and make our plans in all humility, knowing that only "if the Lord wills" can we do even the most mundane things of life. Above all, it will give us the confidence that no plan of God's can be thwarted by either human actions or acts of nature and that, therefore, God is indeed working out all things in conformity with the purpose of his will—for his glory and the good of his people.

13

Prayer and Evangelism under God's Sovereignty

C. Samuel Storms

Are divine sovereignty and human responsibility contradictory or compatible? Is only one true and the other a concoction of clever theologians who stubbornly refuse to acquiesce to the biblical portrayal of reality? This work is dedicated to the belief that both are biblical verities, neither of which can be ignored without serious theological and practical consequences.

But if divine sovereignty is true, how should it influence the way we pray and preach? Indeed, if divine sovereignty is true, should we do either? Is the sovereignty of God a disincentive to evangelism? Does election reduce prayer to a pious recital of inane religious clichés? These are not easy questions, and the answers are slippery. But the issues at stake are too important to ignore. So let us proceed.

The Antecedence of Divine Sovereignty: Another Look at Philippians 2:12–13

> Therefore, my dear friends, as you have always obeyed—not only in my presence, but now much more in my absence—continue to work out your salvation with fear and trembling, for it is God who works in you to will and to act according to his good pleasure.

One often hears the accusation that Calvinism is less a product of reasoned exegesis than of philosophical deduction.[1] Arminians, we are told, de-

---

1. Such is the charge of Clark H. Pinnock, who argues that the defense of both divine sovereignty and human freedom is the "result of Calvinian logic, not scriptural dictates" ("From Augustine to Arminius: A Pilgrimage in Theology," in *The Grace of God, the Will of Man: A Case for Arminianism* [Grand Rapids: Zondervan, 1989], 21).

rive their view from Scripture whereas Calvinists impose theirs upon it. If anything, the opposite is true. This can be seen when we identify the presupposition underlying the Arminian response to the assertions of this work. Arminians assume that the antecedence of divine sovereignty empties subsequent human effort of any spiritual significance. If foreknowledge or predestination or foreordination or any other act of God is causally antecedent to human activity, the latter is morally vacuous.

The obvious trouble with this view is that it lacks biblical warrant. No text of which I am aware says any such thing. This philosophical assumption is based on what the Arminian considers "intellectually reasonable." It is brought to the text as a pre-exegetical criterion to be used in deciding what a passage will be allowed to say. When confronted with texts that simultaneously assert the antecedence of divine sovereignty and the significance of human behavior, Arminians recoil, insisting that such is at best theologically contradictory and at worst morally devastating.

Interestingly, neither God nor the authors of Scripture seem bothered by what agitates Arminians. A case in point is the comment by Paul in Philippians 2:12–13. This text does not directly address the issue of divine election or that of prayer or evangelism. Nevertheless, in it Paul articulates a principle that will go a long way in clarifying the relationship between God's sovereignty and the responsibility of the church to pray for and witness to the lost.

Moreover, this passage is an explicit denial of the aforementioned Arminian assumption. Here Paul asserts the urgency of responsible human behavior based on the antecedence of divine causality. This textual declaration will enable us to understand the place of prayer and evangelism under the sovereignty of God.

Not everyone, however, believes this passage may be used in the way that I propose. Gerald Hawthorne, for example, in his otherwise excellent commentary on Philippians, argues that "Paul is not here concerned with the eternal welfare of the soul *of the individual.* . . . Rather the context suggests that this command is to be understood in a corporate sense. The entire church, which had grown spiritually ill (2:3–4), is charged now with taking whatever steps are necessary to restore itself to health and wholeness."[2] In other words, the focus of Paul's exhortation is more sociological than theological.[3]

Hawthorne bases his view on four points. First, Paul's rebuke of the Philippians for their selfish disregard of others (2:3–4) makes it unlikely that he would reverse himself by urging them to focus on their individual salvation.

2. Gerald F. Hawthorne, *Philippians,* Word Biblical Commentary (Waco: Word, 1983), 98.
3. For a lengthy and persuasive refutation of this view, see Peter T. O'Brien, *The Epistle to the Philippians: A Commentary on the Greek Text* (Grand Rapids: Eerdmans, 1991), 276–80; Moisés Silva, *Philippians* (Grand Rapids: Baker, 1992), 135–40.

The error here is in thinking that concern for salvation is tantamount to self-ishness.[4] Verses 12–13 do not contradict the call to cultivate those virtues of service and humility urged on the readers in verses 1–4. An exhortation to be diligent in holiness (vv. 12–13) is hardly a reversal of a prohibition against selfishness (vv. 3–4). Indeed, one can hardly think of a better way of re-sponding to the rebuke of verses 3–4 than by obeying the exhortation of verses 12–13.

Second, by means of the verb translated "work out," Paul "in effect com-mands the Philippians to keep working and never let up until their 'salvation' is achieved."[5] This is compatible with the view I am defending, so long as we remember that the effort encouraged in verse 12 is energized by the promise of verse 13.

Third, Hawthorne contends that since both the verb and the reflexive pro-noun are plural, Paul has in view a corporate responsibility. But a plural verb does not preclude reference to individual obligation. Virtually every com-mand in the New Testament is plural (cf. Phil. 2:14, 16, 18) because the epis-tles are addressed to the entire church. And what is the corporate church if not a collection of individuals on each of whom the obligation falls? And what is "corporate responsibility" if not each Christian, in his or her mutual relationship with and dependence on every other Christian, working out his or her salvation with fear and trembling? Therefore, I agree with Peter T. O'Brien that the plurals *work out* and *your own* indicate "that *all* the believ-ers in Philippi are to heed this apostolic admonition; it is *common* action that is in view rather than corporate."[6]

Fourth, Hawthorne defines "salvation" as "health" or "wholeness," that is, the spiritual well-being of the church at Philippi in which selfishness and dissension are eliminated. Aside from the fact that *sōtēria* more readily means spiritual salvation in the traditional Pauline sense (cf. 1:28),[7] what is "health" or "wholeness" if not another way of describing the sanctification of individual believers in their mutual relationships with others in the body of Christ? And is not sanctification one among the many elements in our sal-vation through faith in the Son of God?

I see no reason, then, to doubt that Paul's exhortation is "to common ac-tion, urging the Philippians to show forth the graces of Christ in their lives,

4. Silva (*Philippians*, 137) insightfully responds to the objection that verses 12–13 contradict verses 3–4. "The difficulty with this argument is its suggestion that concern for one's soul is tan-tamount to selfishness (what is forbidden in 2:4). On the contrary, Gal[atians] 6:1–5 shows how easily Paul can move from the need for spiritual self-concern ('looking to yourselves,' v. 1) to con-cern for others ('bear one another's burdens,' v. 2) and back again ('let each one examine his own work,' v. 4)."
5. Hawthorne, *Philippians*, 98.
6. O'Brien, *Epistle to the Philippians*, 279; Silva, *Philippians*, 136.
7. In support of this see I. Howard Marshall, *Kept by the Power of God* (Minneapolis: Be-thany Fellowship, 1969), 124–25; Silva, *Philippians*, 136.

to make their eternal salvation fruitful in the here and now as they fulfill their responsibilities to one another as well as to non-Christians."[8]

Of primary concern to us is the basis on which Paul issues his command. "Work out your salvation," says Paul, "for *(gar)* it is God who works in you" to provide both the incentive and the strength to do that which is eminently pleasing to him. Far from undermining the responsible activity of the believer, God's sovereignty is its inspiration!

Paul unashamedly asserts that antecedent divine causality is the foundation on which Christian men and women actively and responsibly build the superstructure of holiness. He does not believe that the causal priority of divine power enervates the decision making of man. Far from undermining human volition, God's sovereign power inspires it by reassuring us that our efforts, if undertaken in the strength that the Spirit supplies, will not prove vain. The hope for working out our salvation in all its varied dimensions is grounded in the help of God's working in us the will and the wherewithal to pursue his good pleasure.

Again, the causal priority of divine in-working in no way precludes the moral significance of human out-working. The former makes the latter possible. Each impulse and act of the human heart may be traced to the prior operation of divine power without in any way diminishing its moral value. The urgent call for responsible human "doing" follows and flows out of the assurance of a divine "done."

A closer look at Paul's language supports this understanding. The theological foundation and explanation for what we do in the flowering of our salvation is the dynamic activity of God (*ho energōn*, the One who powerfully works) in us. Thus "there is no suggestion of any division of labour between God and the Philippians, and so it is inappropriate to speak of synergism."[9]

The present infinitive *thelein* (to will, v. 13) denotes a volitional resolve on the part of the Christian. God energizes the mind and heart of the believer to want to do his will. Paul does not explain how this transformation occurs, but we may reasonably assume that the Holy Spirit creates in us a desire and a love for that which, prior to regeneration, we spurned and hated.

God also energizes the believer to do what he wills. The present infinitive *energein* (to do, v. 13) indicates that God's work in us brings to effectual fruition the behavioral end toward which one's will is inclined. In other words, the continuous and sustained working out of the Christian is the gracious product of the continuous and sustained working in of God. We not only desire but actually do by virtue of the dynamic, antecedent activity of God in our souls.

8. O'Brien, *Epistle to the Philippians*, 280.
9. Ibid., 285–86.

There is obviously no room for synergism in Paul's thinking. But neither is there a place for human passivity, for as J. I. Packer reminds us, "the Holy Spirit's ordinary way of working in us is through the working of our own minds and wills. He moves us to act by causing us to see reasons for moving ourselves to act. Thus our conscious, rational selfhood, so far from being annihilated, is strengthened, and in reverent, resolute obedience we work out our salvation, knowing that God is at work in us to make us '. . . both . . . will and . . . work for his good pleasure.'"[10]

Any suggestion, then, that the precedence of divine causality nullifies the moral urgency of human behavior is not biblical. Paul certainly did not believe it. Neither should we.

This theological principle, exegetically derived, may be applied in our attempt to understand the place of prayer and evangelism in the sovereign purpose of God. What we see in Paul and other biblical authors is an energetic and zealous commitment to prayer and proclamation based on the antecedent elective and regenerating action of God. The pretemporal choice of sinners to salvation does not eliminate the urgent need to bring them the gospel and to pray for their conversion. We may not fully know why that is true, but our duty is first to imitate Paul in this regard and only afterward, if possible, to make harmonious sense of both truths.

How, then, did evangelism and prayer function in the ministry of this man who so unashamedly avowed the sovereignty of God? Do we see a decreasing emphasis on evangelistic work? Did his conviction concerning the antecedent causality of divine sovereignty diminish his zeal for the lost? Did Paul ever use the doctrine of election as a way of excusing himself from the rigorous demands of missionary outreach? Did Paul's commitment to prayer wane while his Calvinism waxed? As he taught more on the sovereignty of God did he teach less on the prayers of people?

A cursory reading of Paul's letters and a glimpse at his life reveal that prayer and preaching were a vital element in the working out of his own salvation. The fact that he believed such responsible and morally accountable actions were themselves the fruit of an antecedent working in by God in no way diminished the urgency with which he worked them out in his own life and ministry and encouraged others to do likewise.

Prayer, Proclamation, and the Purpose of God in 2 Thessalonians 2:13–14 and 3:1

One text in particular demonstrates this truth. In 2 Thessalonians 2:13–14; 3:1, we see both the Pauline affirmation of sovereign election and the indispensable place of prayer and proclamation in the salvation of those whom

---

10. J. I. Packer, *Keep in Step with the Spirit* (Old Tappan, N.J.: Revell, 1984), 156.

God has ordained to life. A careful examination of what Paul says not only enlightens us theologically but also provides us with an example of how we should minister under the sovereignty of God.

> But we ought always to thank God for you, brothers loved by the Lord, because from the beginning God chose you to be saved by the sanctifying work of the Spirit and through belief in the truth. He called you to this through our gospel, that you might share in the glory of our Lord Jesus Christ. . . . Finally, brothers, pray for us that the message of the Lord may spread rapidly and be honored, just as it was with you.

As is the case in other texts dealing with election, Paul begins by thanking God. In Ephesians 1:3–4 he declares God "blessed" for having chosen us in Christ. In 1 Thessalonians 1:2–5 he again thanks God for the Thessalonians because he knows they are chosen to life. In brief, election evokes gratitude. It is God's gracious and loving action to which we contribute nothing and for which, therefore, God receives all the glory.

The apostle says that God chose the Thessalonians "from the beginning." There is some manuscript evidence for the reading *first fruits* (an idea that in itself is certainly biblical; see Rom. 16:5; 1 Cor. 16:15; James 1:18). But this is unlikely for at least two reasons. In the first place, nowhere else when he discusses election does Paul use this term. This verse could be the exception, but then that is precisely what it would be: exceptional.[11] Second, and more important, the Thessalonian Christians were not, in point of historical fact, the first fruits in Macedonia. The Christians in Philippi were.

But if the correct reading is "from the beginning," the question remains, from the beginning of what? Some scholars suggest Paul means "from the beginning of the preaching of the gospel in Thessalonica." What might this mean? I suppose it would imply that God's elective choice in some sense emerges from within history rather than predating it. However, if Paul had intended to direct our attention to the inception of the gospel proclamation he would probably have been more explicit (see, for example, Phil. 4:15).

Furthermore, even if this were true, it would not help the Arminian case. To say that God elects when the gospel is first preached is not the same as saying he elects only after and because of a person's faith. Also, if God's choice of the Thessalonians occurred when the gospel was first preached, what becomes of those who did not believe until some time subsequent to the initial proclamation? When did God choose them? Are we to conceive

11. Then again, as Charles A. Wanamaker points out, "Paul nowhere else uses *ap' archēs* to denote 'from the beginning of time,' which is what it would have to mean here (cf. 1 Cor. 2:7; Col. 1:26; Eph. 1:4), and only on one occasion does he employ *archē* in a temporal sense at all (cf. Phil. 4:15)." *The Epistles to the Thessalonians: A Commentary on the Greek Text* (Grand Rapids: Eerdmans, 1990), 266.

of election not as a singular decree, but as a series of isolated and independent choices scattered throughout history, coincident with every proclamation of the gospel in every age? Is this what the Bible teaches? I am more convinced from Paul's language that God's election antedates faith. And
elsewhere he explicitly places that moment in the pretemporal, which is to
say "eternal," counsel of God (see Eph. 1:4; 2 Tim. 1:9; cf. Rom. 9:11; Rev.
13:8; 17:8).[12]

Although it is pretemporal, election must take effect in history, in the experience of those who are its objects. Thus, Paul says that God has chosen
them from the beginning for salvation "through the sanctifying work of the
Spirit and through belief in the truth." Here we see the means by which that
salvation to which they were destined is secured or comes to pass in their
hearts. Paul may even be describing the shape or form that their salvation assumes when they come into the experiential possession of it.

In any case, Paul is not saying the Thessalonians (or we) were chosen to
salvation on account of sanctification and faith. The two phrases are governed by the single preposition *en* and are related to the salvation for which
one has been chosen, and cannot be construed as positing the condition on
which election itself is based. In other words, Paul is not describing what
happens before election (its cause), but what happens after election (its effect). His point of emphasis is on not the condition but the consequence of
God's elective decision.

It is important to remember that even if it could be shown that election
is conditional, perhaps based on God's foresight of human faith and repentance, Arminians are a long way from proving their thesis. After all,
God foresees and foreknows everything. Consequently, we would need to
determine how a person comes to the faith that God foresees in him or
her. Numerous texts assert that such faith is God's own gracious gift (see
especially Eph. 2:8–10; Phil. 1:29; 2 Pet. 1:1; 2 Tim. 2:24–26; Acts 5:31;
11:18).

Someone once said to Charles Spurgeon, "God foresaw that you would
have faith, and therefore He loved you." To which Spurgeon replied:

What did He foresee about my faith? Did he foresee that I should get that faith
myself, and that I should believe on Him of myself? No; Christ could not foresee that, because no Christian man will ever say that faith came of itself without
the gift and without the working of the Holy Spirit. I have met with a great
many believers, and talked with them about this matter; but I never knew one

12. We should also note that this election is unto "salvation" and not merely external privi-
leges, historical tasks, prominence, or other notions, as is often suggested by Arminian scholars.
For more on this see my *Chosen for Life: An Introductory Guide to the Doctrine of Divine Election* (Grand Rapids: Baker, 1987).

who could put his hand on his heart, and say, "I believed in Jesus without the assistance of the Holy Spirit."[13]

It is this that accounts for Paul's placing sanctification by the Spirit prior to faith in the truth. It is his way of asserting that belief in Christ is possible only after and because of the regenerating work of the Holy Spirit in our hearts. Or, if not, perhaps "faith" in this context refers not so much to that initial act of saving belief as to the continuous habit and daily experience of dependent trust on God.

This affirmation of divine sovereignty in human salvation has a profound impact on Paul's view of the gospel, but not in the way an Arminian might think. Those whom God has chosen do not come to faith willy-nilly, no matter what, as some mockingly suggest. Rather, they are called through the preaching of the good news (v. 14). The elect are not saved irrespective of faith, but always through the Spirit-induced response of repentant trust in the Son of God.

In virtually the same breath that he asserts divine election Paul requests prayer for the success of the gospel (3:1–2). The philosophical certainty inherent in the former truth did not, in Paul's mind, reduce the moral urgency or the practical necessity of the latter. Let us look more closely at Paul's request.

He exhorts the Thessalonian believers to "pray for us that the message of the Lord may spread rapidly and be honored" (v. 1). The imagery is to the point: "The Thessalonians are asked to pray that the gospel may run well, run fast, and that, wherever it goes, it may have a glorious reception."[14] When the gospel came to Thessalonica it was happily received in the midst of much tribulation (1 Thess. 1:5–6). Paul asks that the believers pray such would be the case elsewhere as he proclaims the offense of the cross.

The word of God is glorified or "honored" (v. 1) when people not only hear it but also believe it. One example of this is the response of the Gentiles at Pisidian Antioch. Whereas the Jews dishonored the gospel, the Gentiles "honored the word of the Lord; and all who were appointed for eternal life believed" (Acts 13:48).

Paul and Barnabas preached to the Gentiles, universally and indiscriminately. Those who responded were they who had been "appointed for eternal life." Neither more nor less believed than the number of those whom God had appointed (elected)[15] to life. Were they appointed to life because they be-

13. Charles H. Spurgeon, *Autobiography*, vol. 1, *The Early Years, 1834–1859* (reprint; Edinburgh: Banner of Truth Trust, 1973), 167.

14. John R. Stott, *The Gospel and the End of Time* (Downers Grove: InterVarsity, 1991), 185.

15. F. F. Bruce has suggested that the word *appointed* might be taken in the sense of "inscribed" or "enrolled." See *The Acts of the Apostles: The Greek Text with Introduction and Commentary* (Grand Rapids: Eerdmans, 1975), 275. If so, the idea would be akin to that which we find in Revelation 13:8 and 17:8, where reference is made to those whose names were inscribed or written down in the book of life in eternity past.

lieved? Or did they believe because they were appointed to life? Was their belief in Jesus the condition in view of which God chose them? Or was their belief the instrument whereby the Spirit brought them into experiential possession of what God had decreed in eternity past should be theirs?

Luke does not say, "and as many as believed, God appointed to eternal life," as if to suggest that their belief was the volitional condition on which their election was suspended. On the contrary, he asserts that "all who were appointed for eternal life believed." Faith or belief is the fruit of God's gracious appointment. The appointment to eternal life precedes believing. Yet neither Paul nor Barnabas preached any less fervently or urgently. God's eternal appointment energized their evangelistic outreach and inspired confidence to proclaim the gospel notwithstanding the hostility of an unbelieving Jewish mob.

Neither on the occasion of his evangelistic endeavors in Pisidian Antioch nor in his request for prayer from the church in Thessalonica did Paul display the slightest indication that such evangelical duties were inconsistent with the sovereignty of God.

An identical approach is taken in the advice Paul gives to young Timothy concerning how he should respond to those who oppose him. "And the Lord's bond-servant must not be quarrelsome, but be kind to all, able to teach, patient when wronged, with gentleness correcting those who are in opposition, if perhaps God may grant them repentance leading to the knowledge of the truth, and they may come to their senses and escape from the snare of the devil, having been held captive by him to do his will" (2 Tim. 2:24–26 NASB).

If people are to repent they must be equipped by God to do so. They must be granted repentance as a gift. Ultimately it rests with God and his sovereign good pleasure to give or to withhold that which leads "to the knowledge of the truth." That God does not bestow this gift universally is self-evident. Were repentance something that God gives to all, Paul would hardly have said "if perhaps" God may grant repentance. Clearly he envisions the real possibility that God may not so grant.

It is important to note that in Paul's mind God's sovereignty in no way minimizes Timothy's ethical obligation or the urgency with which he fulfills it. Paul does not say, "Relax, Timothy; do not worry about how you act. After all, whether or not these people repent is in God's hands, not yours. So ease up and do as you please." Paul knew that Timothy's patient love may well be one means utilized by God in the gracious bestowal of repentance. Thus, once again we see that the antecedence of divine sovereignty does not undermine the moral significance or necessity of human volition.

Do not be misled by distortions of Calvinism. It is not as though contrite and sorrowful sinners stand before God pleading that he grant them repentance, but God, locked in by his cruel decree, refuses to heed their request.

315

No, there is "no one righteous," says Paul, there is "no one who seeks God" (Rom. 3:10–11). If any should repent, he will be saved. But none will repent, because none want to repent, unless God graciously brings life to their otherwise spiritually dead hearts.

This doctrine undeniably has a significant impact on our motives and methods in evangelism. Packer has explained how:

> While we must always remember that it is our responsibility to proclaim salvation, we must never forget that it is God who saves. It is God who brings men and women under the sound of the gospel, and it is God who brings them to faith in Christ. Our evangelistic work is the instrument that He uses for this purpose, but the power that saves is not the instrument: it is in the hand of the One who uses the instrument. We must not at any stage forget that. For if we forget that it is God's prerogative to give results when the gospel is preached, we shall start to think that it is our responsibility to secure them. And if we forget that only God can give faith, we shall start to think that the making of converts depends, in the last analysis, not on God, but on us, and that the decisive factor is the way in which we evangelize.[16]

Once people begin to think that faith and repentance are in a man's power to produce, they adopt those methods and contrived devices by which to extract them. Knowing what the gospel is becomes only half the task, for one must also develop an irresistible technique for evoking a response. Sinful pragmatism of this sort measures the validity of an evangelistic method based principally on the fruit it bears. It reduces evangelism to a war of wills, "a battle in which victory depends on our firing off a heavy enough barrage of calculated effects. Thus our philosophy of evangelism would become terrifyingly similar to the philosophy of brainwashing."[17]

That Paul should speak with perfect ease of both sovereign election and prayer for successful evangelistic outreach requires that we view them as theologically (and logically) compatible. Divine sovereignty does not preempt prayer, nor does prayer render God's choice contingent. The God who is pleased to ordain the salvation of sinners, based solely on his good pleasure, is no less pleased to ordain that he will save them in response to the prayers of others whom he has previously saved via the same means.

We assert, therefore, that the success of the gospel depends on God's elective decree. But we also assert, with no less conviction, that its success depends on the prayers of Christian people like the Thessalonians. Were this not the case, the Holy Spirit who inspired the biblical text would have revealed as much to Paul who in turn would have communicated the same to us.

---

16. J. I. Packer, *Evangelism and the Sovereignty of God* (Downers Grove: InterVarsity, 1961), 27.

17. Ibid., 28.

One of the problems we face is that theologians often have a way of "resolving" apparent conflicts that God is happy to let lie. They feel driven either to inflate the power of prayer, thereby making God contingent, or to exalt divine sovereignty so as to make prayer superfluous.

Paul's handling of the problem is of a different order. He does not conclude from divine sovereignty that the Thessalonians need not bother interceding on his behalf. He declines to suggest that the certainty of the end precludes the necessity of means. Were you to have asked him, "Has God's elective purpose guaranteed the salvation of its objects?" he would have happily said, "Yes." Were you to have then suggested that certainty of this sort reduces prayer and evangelism to a religious charade, nice but not at all necessary, I can almost hear his angry *mē̄ genoito!* "May it never be!"

The apostle was following the example of his Lord, who on more than one occasion juxtaposed the certainty of eternal election with the urgency of gospel proclamation. In Matthew 11 Jesus extols divine sovereignty in determining who shall be the recipients of a saving knowledge of the Son virtually simultaneous with his urgent plea for sinners to seek their soul's rest in him (vv. 25–30). Again, in John 10, Jesus openly invited belief in himself as the Messiah while declaring that those who rejected him did so because they "are not my sheep" (v. 26).

Jesus was not being theologically dishonest with his audience and neither was Paul with his. Divine sovereignty and human responsibility are not mutually exclusive propositions, except in the minds of those theologians who bristle at the thought of God ultimately deciding which, if any, hell-deserving sinners are saved.

What, then, did Paul expect the prayers of these Christians to achieve? Wherein is found their moral and theological significance? Be it noted first that Paul is not suggesting prayer can alter the pretemporal divine choice described in 1 Thessalonians 2:13. Our prayers do not increase the number of the elect nor does our disobedience to the command of 1 Thessalonians 3:1 deprive God's kingdom of those whom he otherwise wished to save.

Paul asks the Thessalonians to pray because he is persuaded that God does not will the salvific end apart from the specified means. Our mistake is in thinking that the divine decree makes an event certain irrespective of the causes and conditions (such as prayer) on which it depends. But the latter are encompassed in God's sovereign purpose no less than the former.

A closer look at this principle as it pertains to preaching and prayer is warranted.

Prayer, Evangelism, and the Sovereignty of God

The question is often phrased with brutal honesty: "If the spiritual destiny of all men is fixed and certain from eternity past, why preach, why pray?" This sort of inquiry prompted A. A. Hodge to ask another series of questions:

> If God has eternally decreed that you should live, what is the use of your breathing? If God has eternally decreed that you should talk, what is the use of your opening your mouth? If God has eternally decreed that you should reap a crop, what is the use of your sowing the seed? If God has eternally decreed that your stomach should contain food, what is the use of your eating?[18]

Hodge does not leave us without an answer:

> In order to educate us, [God] demands that we should use the means, or go without the ends which depend upon them. There are plenty of fools who make the transcendental nature of eternity and of the relation of the eternal life of God to the time-life of man an excuse for neglecting prayer. But of all the many fools in the United States, there is not one absurd enough to make the same eternal decree an excuse for not chewing his food or for not voluntarily inflating his lungs.[19]

If God has graciously decreed that a certain soul shall in due course believe in Jesus Christ, we may be assured that he has also decreed that the gospel shall be presented to that person, either through preaching or in print or by some other medium (such as the Thessalonians in the first century or you in the twentieth). One must not assume that the ordained end (the salvation of the soul) will occur apart from the prescribed means (the preaching of the good news, which, I might add, is likewise ordained by God).

We must also remember that our responsibility to preach fervently, urgently, and universally is dependent neither upon our speculations as to who may or may not be elect nor upon our ability to comprehend the relationship between preaching and predestination. God's command, not our curiosity, is the measure of duty.

Much to our chagrin, it is not a part of God's revealed will in Holy Scripture to indicate who is and who is not elect. The names of those written in the Lamb's book of life cannot be found by reading between the lines of Scripture. No such information is to be found nestled between Malachi and Matthew, or is tucked away in the notes of certain study Bibles, or is listed under the heading *Elect* in a concordance.

---

18. A. A. Hodge, *Evangelical Theology* (1890; reprint, Edinburgh: Banner of Truth Trust, 1976), 92–93.
19. Ibid., 93.

In Acts 18:9–10 we again see Paul's approach to ministry based on this truth. There we read how the Lord appeared to Paul in a vision to encourage and fortify him for continued work in Corinth, notwithstanding heated opposition. "Do not be afraid; keep on speaking, do not be silent. For I am with you, and no one is going to attack and harm you, because I have many people in this city."

Paul might have responded to this information in several ways. He could have said to himself: "Well, now, I think I shall ask God for the names and addresses of his elect people so that it will save me the time and effort of having to preach to everyone." Or perhaps he might have said: "It is good to know this, for it frees me to go elsewhere. After all, if they are God's elect people, they will eventually come to faith whether I evangelize the city or not."

But Paul did nothing of the sort. Far from being discouraged or dissuaded from his evangelistic zeal, far from being reduced to passive reliance on a secret sovereign decree, he immediately returned to the city and stayed for a year and a half (v. 11). Precisely because he knew that God had sheep in Corinth, he labored there diligently.

Nothing is more of a stimulus to evangelistic zeal and effort than the assurance of success, which the truth of sovereign election alone can give. "So far from making evangelism pointless," observes Packer, "the sovereignty of God in grace is the one thing that prevents evangelism from being pointless. For it creates the possibility—indeed, the certainty—that evangelism will be fruitful. Apart from it, there is not even a possibility of evangelism being fruitful. Were it not for the sovereign grace of God, evangelism would be the most futile and useless enterprise that the world has ever seen, and there would be no more complete waste of time under the sun than to preach the Christian gospel."[20]

Why? Because were it not for sovereign grace regenerating hearts and enabling the unbelieving to believe, heaven would remain forever barren of life. Apart from sovereign grace that makes us alive, we would do as well screaming at a corpse in the county morgue, "Rise up and live!" Evangelism is possible and will bear fruit for one reason: God in sovereign grace is in the business of making alive and renewing hearts that they might love him whom they formerly despised.

We may choose to exhaust ourselves preaching fluently, cogently, unceasingly, and sincerely, handing out tracts, organizing revival services, and availing ourselves of every conceivable opportunity to reach the lost. But "unless there is some other factor in the situation," says Packer, "over and above our own endeavors, all evangelistic action is foredoomed to failure. This is the fact, the brute, rock-bottom fact, that we have to face."[21]

20. Packer, *Evangelism*, 106.
21. Ibid., 109.

Of course, that "over-and-above" factor is God's electing grace. Evangelism is successful because God does what we cannot do. Paul returned to preach in Corinth because the sovereignty of God gave him "hope of success as he preached to deaf ears, and held up Christ before blind eyes, and sought to move stony hearts. His confidence was that where Christ sends the gospel there Christ has His people—fast bound at present in the chains of sin, but due for release at the appointed moment through a mighty renewing of their hearts as the light of the gospel shines into their darkness, and the Saviour draws them to Himself."[22]

Let us take one hypothetical example as a way of illustrating the relation of sovereignty to prayer. Let us suppose that, unbeknownst to me, God has decreed that Gary should come to saving faith in Christ on August 8, 1997. Suppose also, again without my knowledge, that God wills to regenerate Gary and bring him to faith on the eighth only in response to my prayer for him on the seventh. (Of course, my prayers for Gary should not be restricted to one day of the year. I am using these two specific days for the sake of illustration.) Apart from my prayer on August 7 that Gary be saved, he will remain in unbelief. Does this mean that God's will for Gary's salvation on the eighth might fail should I forget or refuse to pray on the seventh (perhaps because of some misguided notion about divine sovereignty)? No.

We must remember that God has decreed or willed my praying on the seventh for Gary's salvation, which he intends to effect on the eighth. God does not will the end, that is, Gary's salvation on the eighth, apart from the means, that is, my prayer on the seventh. God ordains or wills that Gary come to faith on August 8 in response to my prayer for his salvation on August 7. If I do not pray on the seventh, he will not be saved on the eighth. But I most certainly shall pray on the seventh because God, determined to save Gary on the eighth, has ordained that on the seventh I should pray for him. Thus, from the human perspective, it may rightly be said that God's will for Gary is dependent upon me and my prayers, as long as it is understood that God, by an infallible decree, has secured and guaranteed my prayers as an instrument with no less certainty than he has secured and guaranteed Gary's faith as an end.

Someone may object at this stage by saying: "But if your prayer on August 7 is ordained/willed by God, why bother?" I bother because I do not know what God has ordained relative to my prayer life. I do not know what he has determined to accomplish by means of it. And it is inexcusably arrogant, presumptuous, and disobedient to suspend my prayers on the basis of a will that God has declined to disclose. What I do know is that he has commanded me to pray for this lost soul. Whether or not he has willed for Gary to believe in consequence of my prayer is not mine to know until after the fact (and per-

22. Ibid., 116–17.

haps not even then). But it must not, indeed cannot, be made the reason for praying or not praying before the fact.

Often when God wants to pour out his blessings he begins by awakening in his people an awareness of their great need, thereby provoking them to ask him for what he longs to give. Or, as Jonathan Edwards put it, "God has been pleased to constitute prayer to be antecedent to the bestowment of mercy; and he is pleased to bestow mercy in consequence of prayer, as though he were prevailed upon by prayer. When the people of God are stirred up to prayer, it is the effect of his intention to show mercy."[23] Thus prayer becomes an effective way to obtain those blessings from God that God himself has foreordained to give to those who pray for them.

D. A. Carson has expressed the same point in somewhat different terms:

> If I pray aright, God is graciously working out his purposes in me and through me, and the praying, though mine, is simultaneously the fruit of God's powerful work in me through his Spirit. By this God-appointed means I become an instrument to bring about a God-appointed end. If I do not pray, it is not as if the God-appointed end fails, leaving God somewhat frustrated. Instead, the entire situation has now changed, and my prayerlessness, for which I am entirely responsible, cannot itself escape the reaches of God's sovereignty, forcing me to conclude that in that case there are other God-appointed ends in view, possibly including judgment on me and on those for whom I should have been interceding![24]

I have argued that Paul unequivocally affirmed the sovereignty of God in human affairs. I have also argued that he viewed prayer, particularly for the success of the evangelistic enterprise, as crucial. An excellent example of this is found in Romans 15:30–32. There Paul makes this request: "I urge you, brothers, by our Lord Jesus Christ and by the love of the Spirit, to join me in my struggle by praying to God for me. Pray that I may be rescued from the unbelievers in Judea and that my service in Jerusalem may be acceptable to the saints there; so that by God's will I may come to you with joy and together with you be refreshed."

Such a statement may seem incongruous to some, appearing as it does in an epistle known principally for its emphasis on divine sovereignty (see especially Rom. 8–9). Paul, however, felt no discomfort in arguing that God had suspended the success of his journeys and mission on the prayers of his people. Without those prayers Paul was at a loss. His concern over a threat from the unbelieving Jews in Judea was well-founded (Acts 20–21). So, "his re-

---

23. Jonathan Edwards, "The Most High a Prayer-Hearing God," in *The Works of Jonathan Edwards*, vol. 2 (Edinburgh: Banner of Truth, 1979), 116.

24. D. A. Carson, *A Call to Spiritual Reformation: Priorities from Paul and His Prayers* (Grand Rapids: Baker, 1992), 165.

quest for continued prayers was not merely a tactical maneuver to engage their sympathy, but a call for help in what he knew to be a matter of life and death."[25]

Paul also believed that the approval of his ministry was dependent, at least in part, on the prayers of these believers. Although it may at first appear odd that he feared his service might prove unacceptable, he had ample evidence that many regarded with suspicion his ministry to the Gentiles. So his request in understandable.

His plans to visit Rome and enjoy the fellowship of these saints were also dependent on prayer (1 Thess. 3:10–13). Important here is Paul's reference to the will of God (v. 32). He does not presume to know if it was God's determinate purpose to bring him to Rome in response to the Christians' petitions. Subsequent history proved that it was, though his arrival there was not in the manner he had intended (see Acts 21:17–28:16). But clearly the apostle believed in prayer as a means employed by God in the effectual fulfillment of his will (see also, in this regard, Philem. 22; Phil. 1:19; 2 Cor. 1:8–11).

Praying for the Lost: Should We? Can We?

The charge has been leveled that Calvinism undermines prayer. In this chapter we have seen that nothing could be further from the truth. In point of fact, it is Arminians who cannot pray for God to transform a lost soul, bringing him to faith and repentance, and remain consistent with their system.

Why? Those who deny divine sovereignty, explains John Piper, "do not believe that God has the right to intrude upon a person's rebellion, and overcome it, and draw that person effectually to faith and salvation. They do not believe that God has the right to exert himself so powerfully in grace as to overcome all the resistance of a hardened sinner. Instead they believe that man himself has the sole right of final determination in the choices and affections of his heart toward God. Every person, they say, has final self-determination in whether they will overcome the hardness of their hearts and come to Christ."[26]

The most that God can do is restore in fallen men a measure of enabling grace (which is what most Arminians insist he does). This being the case, the ultimate reason one person repents and another does not is to be found in them, not God. Thus "if the only [ultimate] cause of difference is in the men, it follows that we ought to pray for men to convert themselves, i.e., to make

25. Gordon P. Wiles, *Paul's Intercessory Prayers: The Significance of the Intercessory Prayer Passages in the Letters of St. Paul* (Cambridge: Cambridge University Press, 1974), 269.
26. John Piper, *The Pleasures of God* (Portland, Ore.: Multnomah, 1991), 224–25.

322

themselves to differ."[27] In which case one must ask, "Who gets the glory?" . . . the God who can go only so far in saving a soul or the man who is the self-determining cause of his own conversion?

But could one not pray that God would plant in the lost soul an inner unrest and longing for Christ? Yes. But then one must answer this question:

> If it is legitimate for God to "plant a longing" in a person's heart, how strong can the longing be that God chooses to plant? There are two kinds of longings God could plant in an unbeliever's heart. One kind of longing is so strong that it leads the person to pursue and embrace Christ. The other kind of longing is not strong enough to lead a person to embrace Christ. Which should he pray for? If we pray for the strong longing, then we are praying that the Lord would work effectually and get that person saved. If you pray for the weak longing, then we are praying for an ineffectual longing that leaves the person in sin (but preserves his self-determination).[28]

This can mean only one thing:

> People who really believe that man must have the ultimate power of self-determination, can't consistently pray that God would convert unbelieving sinners. Why? Because if they pray for divine influence in a sinner's life they are either praying for a successful influence (which takes away the sinner's ultimate *self*-determination), or they are praying for an unsuccessful influence (which is not praying for *God* to convert the sinner). So either you give up praying for God to convert sinners or you give up ultimate human self-determination.[29]

What a joy it is, knowing sovereign election to be true, that we have the privilege and duty of proclaiming the gospel to lost sinners while praying that God would effectually, and for eternity, bring them to saving faith. Paul was right: "How beautiful are the feet of those who bring good news" (Rom. 10:15).

27. A. A. Hodge, *Outlines of Theology* (1860; Edinburgh: Banner of Truth Trust, 1972), 221.
28. Piper, *Pleasures*, 226.
29. Ibid.

14

Preaching and the Sovereignty of God

EDMUND P. CLOWNEY

Are preachers, after all, hucksters who need market research to discover what people want to hear? Or are they entertainers, variety-show hosts, emceeing the performance of singers, dancers, and actors? Must we choose between charm-school personalities and ranting television evangelists? Will preaching that is recognizably biblical survive into the next millennium?

The last question raises a more basic one. If preachers are being cast in a mold drawn from the media, so, too, is the God of preaching being remodeled to accommodate contemporary sensibilities. The more drastic renovators have called up goddesses from the millennia of heathen darkness. Against this repristinated worship of Astarte the polemic of the Old Testament prophets speaks with fresh force. But they warn us too against any scaling down of the glory of almighty God. The prophets proclaimed the word of the Lord in the presence of the Lord of the word.

Underlying the so-called culture war in the United States is the most basic of issues: Does the God of the Bible exist? That is the determinative question for the future of preaching as well. The mind of modernity despises the gospel that is preached as well as the church that preaches it. "Question authority" reads the bumper sticker. The final question is always, "Sez who?" Intellectuals have no defense against the question, much as they may fear the nihilism to which it leads.[1]

---

1. See Philip E. Johnson, "The Modernist Impasse in Law," in *God and Culture: Essays in Honor of Carl F. H. Henry*, ed. D. A. Carson and John D. Woodbridge (Grand Rapids: Eerdmans, 1993), 180–94.

The answer of the Bible is clear enough. Who says? God says. The living God does exist, has ultimate authority, and calls to account those who rebel against him and his revealed will. No humanist is safe, for the King of heaven has no plans to abdicate in favor of cosmic egalitarianism.

Biblical preaching cannot compromise the sovereignty of the Lord. By the power of God's own word, preaching must proclaim God's own plan of salvation through God's own servants, those whom he has called and appointed to that task.

The Sovereignty of God's Word

To understand how God's sovereignty is the rock on which preaching is grounded, we must understand how the Bible views the word of God. That view differs remarkably from our own thinking about words. Inundated with phone-in talk shows and junk mail, we have no need of literary deconstruction to persuade us that words are cheap. A newspaper will serve to light a fire or wrap a fish; talk shows are even more disposable—they can be clicked off without the trouble of recycling.

The Bible does not view words that way. Scripture links thought, word, and deed to represent the whole of human life. Jesus reminded us that in the day of judgment we will be accountable for every idle word we have spoken (Matt. 12:36). To speak against others is not "just talk"; to speak against God is the grave sin of blasphemy. The tongue can set the whole course of life on fire, and is itself set on fire by hell (James 3:6).

If human words have enduring meaning, how much more are the words of God filled with significance and power! The word for "breath" in both Hebrew and Greek is also the word for "spirit." The spoken word is vocalized breath: By that model God's word is linked with his Spirit. When God speaks, his life-breath goes forth with all the power of his Spirit. God creates by his spoken word. He speaks and it is done, he commands and it stands fast. "By the word of the LORD were the heavens made, their starry host by the breath of his mouth" (Ps. 33:6). "And God said, 'Let there be light,' and there was light" (Gen. 1:3).

The power of God's declarative word in creation continues in his word of direction. The celestial luminaries were created by his command and he set them in place by a decree that will never pass away (Ps. 148:5–6). The seasons turn at his command: "He sends his word and melts them; he stirs up his breezes, and the waters flow" (Ps. 147:18). The storms come at his bidding (Ps. 148:8).

What is true of nature is equally true of history. "Nations are in uproar, kingdoms fall; he lifts his voice, the earth melts" (Ps. 46:6). "The LORD foils the plans of the nations; he thwarts the purposes of the peoples. But the plans of the LORD stand firm forever, the purposes of his heart through all generations" (Ps. 33:10–11).

The sovereign power of God's word is not the power of a magic spell, as in tales in which a mere mortal is given a word of power and utters it to his own consternation. Rather, God's declarative and directive utterances are always deliberate. Indeed, that is the point of saying that God exercises his power by speaking. His word expresses the thought of his heart, thought that follows the wisdom of his sovereign plan. He can assure his people of the destruction of Assyria, as he has purposed:

> The LORD Almighty has sworn,
> "Surely, as I have planned, so it will be,
>   and as I have purposed, so it will stand.
> I will crush the Assyrian in my land;
>   on my mountains I will trample him down. . . .
> This is the plan determined for the whole world;
>   this is the hand stretched out over all nations.
> For the LORD Almighty has purposed, and who can thwart him?
>   His hand is stretched out, and who can turn it back?" (Isa. 14:24–27)

The Old Testament does not present the deterministic universe of fatalism; unlike the gods of the Greeks, the Almighty is not subject to the fates. Neither mechanistic necessity nor the laws of chance determine the future. Rather, the purpose of God determines the future. He is personal, and he will accomplish his purpose, his design. That he does so in the word of his decree reveals the absoluteness of his control. He does not have to struggle with unforeseen difficulties or overcome taxing obstacles. It is enough that he speak. That his power is expressed in his word, and not in the abracadabras of magic, shows that his power is intelligent and wise. The living God is not an impersonal blind force. He is the all-wise Sovereign, the holy Lord, the righteous King.

The same power of God's word that formed creation and governs history will accomplish the redemption of his people:

> "As the heavens are higher than the earth,
>   so are my ways higher than your ways
>   and my thoughts than your thoughts.
> As the rain and the snow come down from heaven,
> and do not return to it without watering the earth
> and making it bud and flourish, . . .
> so is my word that goes out from my mouth:
>   It will not return to me empty,
> but will accomplish what I desire
>   and achieve the purpose for which I sent it." (Isa. 55:9–11)

327

God's prophets can announce his purposes as certain of accomplishment because God can speak his word of power in the future tense as easily as in the present. He can say, "I will put enmity" (Gen. 3:15) as surely as "Let there be light." His power over history is no less than his power over creation; he is not bound by space or time. All things are ordered by his decree, who has determined the end from the beginning.

The Lord shows his good purposes for his people by addressing them in words of promise. His promises disclose what his purposes are, purposes that exceed the range of our thoughts and surpass our imagination. He who plans all things to accomplish them calls on his people to call on him, and promises to show them high mysteries, inaccessible wonders, treasures of his design that will overwhelm their minds and melt their hearts to praise (Jer. 33:2–3, 9).

We cannot of ourselves conceive of his purposes, nor can we understand how he will accomplish them. We have his word that he will make all things work together for good to them that love him, that are the called according to his purpose (Rom. 8:28), but we are often baffled in our weakness. We do not understand how he is working. We do not even know what to pray for according to his will. For that reason, the Spirit of God prays for us with groaning that bears with our weakness, but intercedes according to that will of God, well known to him (Rom. 8:26–27).

God's promises to his people are sure. To seal his promises to Abraham, the Lord used an oath-taking ceremony, passing between the pieces of divided carcasses (Gen. 15; Jer. 34:18–20). God swore to Abraham that he would be faithful to his covenant with his descendants, would take them down to Egypt and then bring them up again to possess the land he had promised (Gen. 15:7–21). God kept the promise when he called to Moses at the burning bush in the desert. He gave assurance that he had heard their cry in Egypt, knew their suffering, and had come to deliver them as he had promised (Exod. 3:7–8, 17).

To Israel the words of God's covenant were themselves a seal, for they were written first by the Lord himself on tablets of stone. These were tablets of witness; that is, the engraved words served to attest God's covenant bond and promise. Another symbol of God's faithfulness, also kept in the ark of the covenant, was an almond branch. It was Aaron's rod that had budded and blossomed to certify God's word in calling him (Num. 17:8); later, the explanation of the symbol was given to Jeremiah: God said, "I watch over my word to perform it" (Jer. 1:11–12).[2]

The epochs of the history of redemption are marked out by God's watching over his word. In the interval between promise and fulfillment, the promise often seemed impossible of realization. Both Abraham and Sarah had

---

2. There is a play on words between the noun *shaqedh*, "almond," and the verbal form *shoqedh*, "watch"—the early blossoming almond is the "watcher" tree, heralding spring.

laughed at the absurdity of God's promise that Sarah would have a child. She was ninety years old. But the Lord put her laughter on record, for in the season of the Lord's promise, the son was born, bearing the name God gave him: *Isaac,* "Laughter" (Gen. 17:15–19; 18:10–15; 21:1–7).

That beautiful account in Genesis is given to demonstrate what the angel of the Lord said to Sarah: "No word is too wonderful for God" (Gen. 18:14, literal translation). There is no promise God cannot keep, and the time that he will keep it is the time of his appointment, of his own plan. When Mary demurred at the promise given her by the angel Gabriel, the angel repeated the word given to Sarah: "No word is impossible for God" (Luke 1:37).[3]

We cannot take this to mean that the eternal God is rather better at reaching his goals than a captain of industry, or that he can predict cosmic events better than our local forecaster. It must mean that beyond all our imagining God works his will through all the universe that he has formed. He can speak any word he chooses, and its fulfillment is sure.

Time and time again, indeed, epoch and epoch again, God carries forward his purpose, and the impossibilities that stagger our minds are made tributary to his plan, for they are included in his purpose. In Deuteronomy 30 we have a divinely inspired overview of the history of promise and fulfillment. God will make good on his promises, giving Israel the land and blessing them by dwelling with them in the place where he would put his name. That fulfillment is acknowledged by Solomon when the temple is dedicated. He declares that God has kept all the promises he made to Moses (1 Kings 8:56). But the outline of covenantal history in Deuteronomy goes on to present the dark side of rebellion: The people will apostatize and bring upon themselves the sanctions of the covenant, the curses that the Lord pronounced against those who despise his goodness.[4] The history of the Old Testament records the fulfillment of those judgments as well. Then, after the blessings and the curses have been visited on Israel, the Lord promises a new time of blessing. In the latter days he will circumcise the hearts of his people: They will at last be his people and he will be their God.

God's Word Incarnate

This saving plan of God is brought to fruition in the New Testament with the incarnation and the saving work of Jesus Christ. New Testament believers

---

3. The Greek term *rhema* may mean "thing" but primarily "word." In the context it is the *word* of God's promise that is in view.

4. Words of blessings and cursing, even when spoken by men, are taken with full seriousness in the Old Testament because they are uttered before God, whose will and power may enforce them. See Jerome Murphy-O'Connor, O.P., *La prédication selon Saint Paul* (Paris: Gabalda, 1966), 94–95.

are those upon whom the "fulfillment of the ages has come" (1 Cor. 10:11). God's plans did not miscarry, "for no matter how many promises God has made, they are 'Yes' in Christ" (2 Cor. 1:20).

The ultimate glory of the word of God comes when the Lord speaks his own Name. That is the word above all words, revealing not only the will of God, but the very presence of God. The Name of God, God's word of his presence, came in Jesus Christ, not in syllables merely but in human flesh. "The Word became flesh and made his dwelling among us" (John 1:14). For God's promises to be fulfilled, God himself must come. Only he could fulfill the plan that goes beyond all plans, the eternal wisdom of divine love. No one else could meet the need. Our doom was sealed by the guilt of our sin; our situation was hopeless. God's people were seen by Ezekiel as a cemetery of unburied dead: dry bones scattered on the valley floor. "Son of man, can these bones live?" (Ezek. 37:3). Only God's Spirit can breathe life into the valley of death. The situation is so desperate that only God can remedy it, and the promises of God are so great that only God can keep them. He promises not only a new covenant, but also a new creation (Jer. 31:31–34; Isa. 34:4; 35:5–10; 65:17). Zechariah must assure those returned from exile that there is much more to come: a Jerusalem so holy that every washpot will be like a temple vessel, horses' bridles like the golden plate in the tiara of the high priest, the weakest inhabitant of Jerusalem like King David, and the King?—as God himself, the angel of the Lord before them (Zech. 14:20–21; 12:8). God's thoughts are not ours, his ways are not ours; praise his name!

John's proclamation of Jesus as the Word reminds us of the promise that God himself must come. "The Word became flesh and dwelt among us, and we beheld His glory, the glory as of the only begotten of the Father, full of grace and truth" (NKJV). The verb *dwelt* (literally, tabernacled) reminds us of the symbolic dwelling of God in the midst of Israel in the desert, and of Moses' prayer to see God's glory. The Lord proclaimed his name to Moses as the one full of grace and truth (Exod. 34:6). The law was given by Moses, and in that law, Moses wrote of Christ (John 5:46). But the grace and truth declared to Moses came with God the Son (John 1:18 mg). The fullness of God's own name is revealed in him who said to Philip, "Anyone who has seen me has seen the Father. How can you say, 'Show us the Father'? Don't you believe that I am in the Father, and that the Father is in me?" (John 14:8–10).

That which is an offense to the Jews and foolishness to the Gentiles is the plan of God for our salvation. By the unthinkable reality of the incarnation, heightened to the scandal of the cross, it is God's will to save sinners.

The Gospel of the Sovereign Savior

Jesus Christ is Lord. The demand of faith is that we trust him absolutely, that we forsake all other hope and rest in him alone. Paul is God's commissioned servant to "fulfill" the word of God, that is, to bring the promise of God to its completion by proclaiming to the Gentiles the mystery of Christ (Col. 1:25–27). That which was hidden from ages and generations has now been revealed: God's plan to save sinners through the person and work of his Son, through whom all things were created, and in whom all things hold together (Col. 1:16–17).

The sovereign plan of God has been executed in the sovereign will of God by the sovereign Son of God.

God's plan is understood and executed by the only One who could do so. The witness of Jesus is to himself, for in him the plan of God is accomplished. He claimed to be the very wisdom of God, calling the weary and burdened to him that they might find rest (Matt. 11:28–30). Using the wisdom language of the son of Sirach (Ecclus. 51:24–27), Jesus radically changes its thrust. He calls men to him not to learn about wisdom, but to receive him as God's wisdom, for the yoke of wisdom is his yoke, and the lesson of wisdom is to know him. He makes that claim because he is the Son of God. "No one knows the Son except the Father, and no one knows the Father except the Son and those to whom the Son chooses to reveal him" (Matt. 11:27b).

The Jewish leaders found his claim outrageous and blasphemous, but Jesus did not back down before their rage. Rather, he confronted them yet more pointedly with the sovereignty of his Father. They could not come to him or believe in him without the heart-changing work of the Father. Only those who are drawn by the Father will come to the Son (John 6:44, 65). The new birth is the work of the Spirit of God, who moves as he wills (John 3:3). Jesus knows his sheep, those who were given to him by the Father (John 10:27–30). He prays for them, not for the world; he came to save them, and to lose none of them (John 17:9–12). His own chosen disciples were of that number, with one exception: Judas, who fulfilled the plan of the Father by betraying Jesus and so realized the Scripture that foretold his treachery (Acts 1:16–17).

In every respect Jesus labored to accomplish the plan of his Father. As a child he was surprised that his parents did not know where to find him: He was already in his Father's house and about his Father's business. On the cross he cried "I thirst!" not simply out of the agony of his suffering, but also that the Scripture might be fulfilled (John 19:28). His whole life followed his Father's plan; when he said at last, "It is finished," he spoke not only of his passion, but of his whole life as the faithful Servant and the obedient Son.

His submission to the will of the Father is seen especially in Jesus' going to the cross. When Peter rebuked him for this intention, he called his disciple "Satan," for he heard in his words the assault of the evil one. When Gentiles came, seeking Jesus, he saw in their coming the beginning of the hour of his glory and, therefore, the hour of the cross. He cried out, "Now my heart is troubled, and what shall I say? 'Father, save me from this hour'? No, it was for this very reason I came to this hour. Father, glorify your name!" (John 12:27–28). He might well ask to be saved from that hour. The cry for deliverance is the constant prayer of the psalmists, whose writings pointed to him, the true King of Israel. But he will not seek to be delivered; it was for this that he came. The cross is the Father's will. Later, as the hour drew near when he must be abandoned to the wrath of the Father, he could not but ask if there were another way; yet his final prayer was, "Not as I will, but as you will" (Matt. 26:39). He would not call for twelve legions of angels, but he would fulfill his Father's will, revealed in Scripture.

The cross was not a divine afterthought, an expedient undertaken when unforeseen circumstances arose. Rather, the cross was God's chosen means of displaying love that could be seen in no other way. Jesus is the Lamb of God, "slain from the creation of the world" (Rev. 13:8).[5] The Christ who was foreknown in God's loving choice before the foundation of the world was the Lamb without blemish or spot, God's Lamb by whose blood (so precious to the Father) the price of redemption would be paid (1 Pet. 1:18–20).

Through the life, death, resurrection, and ascension of Jesus Christ, the plan of God was realized. Psalm 22, anticipating the sufferings and the triumph of Christ, ends with the cry, "He has done it." This is the message of the gospel. God has accomplished what only he could, and he has done it through the work of his incarnate Son.

The Apostolic Gospel

What was central for the Savior—that he should accomplish his Father's will—became central for his apostles. That conviction shaped the apostolic gospel. The disciples had resisted the teaching of Jesus about his coming death. As they accompanied the sorrowing Savior to Jerusalem for his last Passover, they could only argue among themselves about who would have the places of greatest honor in his kingdom. Peter proudly claimed the greatest loyalty to Christ: he would follow him to death. Jesus predicted that Peter's boasts would become denials before the cock would crow on that dark morning (Luke 23:31–34). The prediction came true; Peter, shamed before a

5. The last phrase in Revelation 13:8, "from the creation of the world," may be taken with "written in the book of life" rather than with "the Lamb was slain," although the position of the phrase makes that less likely. The import of the statement would not be substantially changed, however, for the verse would then speak of the writing, before the foundation of the world, of the names of God's elect in the book of the Lamb that was slain. On either reading, Christ is already the sacrificial Lamb of God before creation.

servant girl in the courtyard of the high priest's house, swore that he did not know Jesus, then fled out into the blackness, weeping in remorse.

Jesus had prayed that Peter's faith not fail, and that prayer was heard. After the resurrection, Jesus appeared to Peter personally; then, as cocks were crowing on another morning by the Lake of Galilee, Jesus examined Peter's heart and renewed his commission (John 21:15–19). Yet we must not miss the upheaval that was necessary in Peter's understanding, for we need the same if we are to confess Christ as Lord. Peter well knew the offense of the cross. Christ's shameful death had no place in Peter's view of the kingdom. He was quick to draw the sword to fight for Christ; as a warrior for the kingdom his courage would not fail. But to take up a cross and follow Jesus was another matter. Jesus had to bring Peter back to the way of the cross. "And when you have turned back," Jesus had said, "strengthen your brothers" (Luke 22:32). That is what Peter did.

In his preaching after Pentecost Peter bore witness to the resurrection, the act of God's power that not only reversed the effect of the cross, but also established its necessity. Fearlessly he told the astonished crowds in Jerusalem that they by the hand of Gentiles had crucified the Messiah, the Prince of life. But he also testified that they did it "by God's set purpose and foreknowledge" (Acts 2:23). Peter had come to know that determined purpose of God. He said to the people: "Now, brothers, I know that you acted in ignorance, as did your leaders. But this is how God fulfilled what he had foretold through all the prophets, saying that his Christ would suffer" (Acts 3:17–18). Peter's conviction with respect to the sovereign purpose of God is not peripheral to his preaching. It is the heart of his message, as it was of his experience. In God's plan the cross was not ultimate disaster, but the ultimate victory. Peter and the other apostles had learned from Jesus the same lesson he had taught to the two disciples on the road to Emmaus (Luke 24:25–27, 44–47). The apostles understood that the sufferings and the glory of Christ had been promised by all the prophets. Peter's messages were drawn from the Old Testament passages that Christ has fulfilled: the prophecy of Joel, the psalms of David, Moses' writing in Deuteronomy. "Indeed, all the prophets from Samuel on, as many as have spoken, have foretold these days" (Acts 3:24). The Scriptures all bear witness to the coming of Christ, because, as Peter wrote later, it was the Spirit of Christ in the prophets who was predicting "the sufferings of Christ and the glories that would follow" (1 Pet. 1:11).

The apostolic witness to the resurrection was not merely their testimony to a strange event, or just their sharing the thrilling conviction that Jesus was, after all, alive. It was their knowledge that the cross was no accident. God had not been defeated, nor had he only later remedied by the resurrection what he had been unable to prevent at the crucifixion. It was God's will and purpose all along, and had been promised by all the prophets. God's kingdom was not destroyed, but established at Calvary.

What was true of Peter was equally true of Paul. He had been sure that Jesus was a false Messiah and had poured his life into an effort to stamp out Christianity. Jesus could not be the Messiah because he had died on a cross. As Saul the Pharisee, Paul had well known the Scripture that said, "Cursed is everyone who is hung on a tree" (Gal. 3:13; Deut. 21:23). The Messiah was the blessed one; Jesus had died as one accursed; therefore, Jesus was not the Messiah. On the road to Damascus, blinded by the glory of the risen Lord, Paul learned his mistake. He discovered that Jesus was the Christ, not in spite of the fact that he was crucified, but because of the fact that he was crucified: "Christ redeemed us from the curse of the law by becoming a curse for us, for it is written, 'Cursed is everyone who is hung on a tree'" (Gal. 3:13).

Paul's conversion brought a radical reversal of his pride. He learned to count as loss the very things in which he had boasted, and to boast in that which he had despised.

> For the message of the cross is foolishness to those who are perishing, but to us who are being saved it is the power of God. . . . Jews demand miraculous signs and Greeks look for wisdom, but we preach Christ crucified: a stumbling block to Jews and foolishness to Gentiles, but to those whom God has called, both Jews and Greeks, Christ the power of God and the wisdom of God. (1 Cor. 1:18, 22–24)

Paul had learned that God's foolishness is wiser than man's wisdom, and that God's weakness is stronger than man's strength (1 Cor. 1:25). His glorying in the cross is glorying in Christ; his glorying in Christ is glorying in God. God has nullified the things that are and chosen nullities so that no one may boast before him, but only in him. This is only to say that God is totally sovereign in salvation, as in all things.

Paul learned to apply the lesson of the cross to all his missionary preaching. He found divine comfort in the fact that when he was weak, then he was strong, for the power was God's, not his. When he faced discouragement at Corinth, Christ appeared to him in a dream, assuring him that he had many of his people in that city (Acts 18:9). Paul could speak boldly, knowing that his efforts were not in vain: There were many in Corinth who would hear the gospel and believe because they had been chosen in Christ. He knew that the Lord who had chosen them had also chosen him and sent him. "And how can they hear without someone preaching to them? And how can they preach, unless they are sent? As it is written, 'How beautiful are the feet of those who bring good news!'" (Rom. 10:14b–15; Isa. 52:7). Paul's own mission was fulfilling the prophecy of Isaiah. He came as the servant of the Lord preaching the good news of God's salvation (Acts 13:47). None knew better than Paul that the task of proclaiming salvation was God's calling, and effective only through his power. His ministry was a savor of life to life or of death to death (2 Cor. 2:16); some would reject, but those who were ordained to eternal life would believe (Acts 13:48).

Most urgently, Paul had to apply the sovereignty of God's calling in Christ to the great sorrow of his life. In synagogue after synagogue across the Roman world he preached Christ from the Scriptures, only to have the majority of the Jewish community reject his message and turn against him, often with violent persecution. How could it be possible that his own brothers, his kinsmen, would refuse their promised Messiah? They are the people of Israel, adopted as children of God. They had received the divine glory, the covenants, the law, the temple worship, and the promises. The patriarchs were their ancestors, and of them Christ was born, who is God over all, blessed forever (Rom. 9:1–5).

Paul's concern about the Jews' rejection of the gospel became an overwhelming grief. He would be willing to be accursed from Christ if by that doom his own nation could be saved (Rom. 9:3).

What can he say? Shall he declare, as more than one American evangelist has, that God has done all he can, that his hands are now tied, and it is up to those who hear to choose or reject Christ? Certainly Paul made clear to synagogue audiences that they bore responsibility for their response. He was ready to pronounce judgment against them before turning to the Gentiles (Acts 13:46, 51). Yet Paul's answer to the deepest agony of his ministry is to affirm again the sovereignty of God that is the heart of the gospel. The reason that many in Israel reject their Messiah is that "not all who are descended from Israel are Israel" (Rom. 9:6). God's word did not fail, for his purpose stands in those whom he has chosen. Not all the descendants of Abraham are heirs of the promise of God, but only those whom God has raised up. God chose Isaac, not Ishmael; Jacob, not Esau. In the latter case the Scripture is especially clear, for as Paul points out, before the twins were born or had any opportunity to do anything good or bad, God said, "The older will serve the younger." That choosing of Jacob is expressed even more strongly in the prophecy of Malachi, "Jacob I loved, but Esau I hated" (Rom. 9:13; Mal. 1:2–3).

It is not just some contemporary evangelical theologians that find Paul's teaching difficult. Paul anticipates possible objections from the Roman Christians to whom his letter is addressed. The objections that Paul anticipates show us that we have not misunderstood his meaning, for they are the objections we would be likely to make, too. In fact, my own accepting of the apostle's teaching came more than a half century ago when I was a student at Wheaton College and heard the dean, in a chapel talk, use one of these objections as his refutation of Calvinism. "If God's will determines who will be saved," he said, "unbelievers could stand in the day of judgment and claim acquittal on the ground that they had done God's will."

The dean's argument had a familiar sound, and after chapel in my dorm room I found the passage in my King James Bible: "Thou wilt say then unto me, why doth he yet find fault? For who hath resisted his will?" (Rom. 9:19). Since the apostle had anticipated the dean's objection, it was clear to me that he was teaching what the dean was objecting to. Once the two sides were clear in my mind, I had no choice!

Often Paul's affirmation of the sovereignty of God's grace in Romans 9–11 is passed over as a troublesome parenthesis in the magnificent theology of the epistle. Certainly the apostle himself did not so view it. Without the deep foundation of those chapters, the glorious assurance of Romans 8 is cut away. It is the sovereign grace of God that forges the unbreakable golden chain of salvation described in that chapter. All things work together for good to those who are called according to God's purpose. Those whom God foreknew in his electing love[6] he predestined, called, justified, and glorified.

It is the gospel of God's grace that Paul expounds in Romans 9–11 as in the rest of the epistle. The doxology at the end of the section invites us to join the apostle in adoring worship. God's judgments are untraceable, his ways past tracing out, but they are ways of mercy beyond all our imagining. The apostle sometimes gives answers to our questions that seem most unsatisfying. When we ask if in election God is unjust, Paul answers that he has mercy on whom he will have mercy: he owes mercy to no rebellious sinner. We cannot earn it; he freely gives it. There the mystery rests. When we come up with the dean's objection, Paul answers, "But who are you, O man, to talk back to God? 'Shall what is formed say to him who formed it, "Why did you make me like this?"'" (Rom. 9:20; Isa. 29:16; 45:9).

Here, as at the beginning of his epistle, Paul emphasizes the hardening judgments of God as he gives men up to the unbelief of their hearts. There he spoke of the Gentiles who gave up on God and were given up by God to their own lusts. Here he speaks of Israel who heard and did not understand or heed. Yet God's mercy is still shown: "All day long I have held out my hands to a disobedient and obstinate people" (Rom. 10:21; Isa. 65:2). Indeed, through his very judgments God shows mercy. The abandoned Gentiles were neither destroyed nor forgotten, and now God calls them to repent (Acts 14:16; 17:30–31; Rom. 9:23–24). Israel has not submitted to God's righteousness, but the Gentiles are obtaining it by faith (Rom. 9:30–32). For Israel, too, Paul sees mercy in God's judgment. This is his hope as the apostle to the Gentiles. If through judgment on Israel, blessing has gone out to the Gentiles, then the blessing the Gentiles receive will stimulate the Jews to jeal-

6. For this understanding of "foreknowledge" see chapter 7 in this work by S. M. Baugh.

ousy. They will begin to realize that they are the natural branches of God's olive tree, and understand that by faith they may be grafted back into that tree. Paul therefore sees two great sweeping waves in God's plan of salvation. First there is the wave that he is riding as he carries the gospel to the nations. His role is unique. There are other apostles, but his distinctive calling is to be God's servant as a light to the Gentiles (Acts 13:47).[7] Yet as he calls the Gentiles into the people of God, he looks for another wave drawn on and following behind him: the wave of Israel according to the flesh. His ministry has not abandoned Israel. Even when he turns from them, his trust is in the plan of God in which the "fullness" of both the Gentiles and Israel will be gathered in (Rom. 11:12, 25). As the disobedience of the Gentiles provided for the display of God's mercy to Israel, so the disobedience of Israel now provides for the display of God's mercy to the Gentiles. All is in God's hands, and all disobedience will also provide for his showing mercy.[8]

Paul would never dream of seeing God's sovereign saving power as an obstacle to evangelism. On the contrary, only God's royal grace can draw in Gentiles and Jews to the Lord Jesus Christ. God is rich in mercy to all who call upon him (Rom. 10:12), and whoever calls on the name of the Lord will be saved (Rom. 10:13). Salvation is by faith, not works. But for Paul there is no contradiction between the "whoever" of the gospel offer and divine election, for the opposite of works is not only faith, but grace: "So too, at the present time there is a remnant chosen by grace. And if by grace, then it is no longer by works; if it were, grace would no longer be grace" (Rom. 11:5–6).

Paul, the herald of God's grace, gathers in from the Jews first and also from the Gentiles a remnant according to the election of grace. He labors toward the "fullness" of the Gentiles receiving the word of God, and beyond that, the "fullness" of Israel, moved by jealousy as they see the Gentiles receiving the blessings of their inheritance. This is his inspired understanding of the purpose of God, fulfilled in a foundational way by his own apostolic ministry.

Luke traveled with Paul and describes the spreading of the church in the same terms. It is the word of God that grows and prevails. The first volume of Luke's work instructed Theophilus in what Jesus began to do and to teach.

---

7. Although Isaiah 49:6 has reference to the ultimate Servant who fulfills the calling of Israel, Paul, knowing that he shares in the calling of the true Israel, can apply the words to his own mission. He characteristically thinks of Jesus Christ as the Lord, and himself as the servant of the Lord (2 Cor. 3:12–13; 4:1; Gal. 2:8; 1 Cor. 15:8–10; 1 Tim. 2:7). See Peter Jones, "1 Corinthians 15:8: Paul the Last Apostle," *TynBul* 36 (1985): 3–34.

8. It may be necessary to note that "mercy on . . . all" in Romans 11:32 cannot be used to support universalism. Paul seeks by his efforts to save some (v. 14). He teaches both the goodness and the severity of God (vv. 21–22). Not all branches are grafted into the tree. The "all" of 11:32 describes Jews and Gentiles as such, not every person.

Volume 2, the Book of Acts, carries on the story by telling us what Jesus continued to do and teach through his Spirit and through the Spirit-filled apostles and those who believed through their word. The connection between the spread of the church and the spread of the word is so close that Luke can describe the first in terms of the second (Acts 6:7; 12:24; 19:20). From the start, those who believe are those who have received the word (Acts 2:41; 4:4; 8:14). The prayer of the disciples is that they may speak the word of God with boldness (Acts 4:29–31). The apostles see the ministry of the word and prayer as their primary function, and the seven are appointed to relieve them of administrative duties (Acts 6:2–4). Yet the seven, filled with the Spirit as they are, also engage in proclaiming the word. When the church was scattered by persecution, the word was spread with them, for "they preached the word wherever they went" (Acts 8:4). The spread of the word to the Jews of the dispersion, to the Samaritans, to the Gentiles is the substance of the Book of Acts. When Cornelius seeks the Lord and is made the evidence of God's admission of the Gentiles to the kingdom, Peter is brought by the Spirit so that he may speak the words of truth, and as Peter is speaking, the Spirit falls on the Gentiles. When this is reported to the church in Jerusalem, the disciples conclude, "So then, God has granted even the Gentiles repentance unto life" (Acts 11:18). As they hear and believe, Gentiles glorify the word of the Lord (Acts 13:48).

In their preaching, the apostles witness to the work of God in sending Jesus as the Christ, in displaying wonders through his words and deeds, leading him to the cross for our sins, and raising him from the dead to the throne of glory. Their preaching is witness, not in the current evangelical sense of describing a conversion experience, but in the sense of attesting from their own observation the work that God did to bring salvation to a lost world. Paul's witness does include his experience on the Damascus road, but we must remember that he was the last to be made an eyewitness of the resurrection body of the Lord who had been crucified.

The apostles were earwitnesses as well as eyewitnesses. The Spirit aided them to recall the teaching of Jesus and revealed to them more of the mysteries of Christ. Further, as they explained the meaning of what they had seen and heard, they were also witnesses to the Old Testament promises. They could certify from their own knowledge that Jesus had done what the prophets had spoken.

In short, the message that the apostles proclaimed was that God's plan and purpose had been fulfilled far beyond what they or anyone else could have imagined. It was a message giving all praise and glory to God, a message proclaiming the sovereign grace of God, and a message that called sinners to turn to God and receive from him the gift of eternal life. They well understood the "musts" of Christ's teaching: that the Son of man must suffer these things and enter into his glory (Luke 24:26), that the Scripture must be fulfilled (Luke 24:44). They preached the "whole will of God" (Acts 20:27).

The older translation, "the whole counsel of God," is better. The noun *boulē* as used by Luke and Paul does not mean "will" but "purpose" or plan. In Acts the word is used of God's plan of salvation (Acts 2:23; 4:28) and is also applied to human plans (27:12, 42).[9] That meaning is particularly clear when Paul says, "In him we were also chosen, having been predestined according to the plan of him who works out everything in conformity with the purpose *(boulē)* of his will" (Eph. 1:11). What Paul says he faithfully presented was the plan of God, his saving purpose in Christ. He kept back nothing of that full gospel message.

As his epistles show, the apostle Paul not only preached Christ crucified as the object of saving faith; he also expounded the sovereignty of God's plan as the basis for our growth in grace. All his exhortations are grounded in affirmations. His grand doctrine of our union with Christ shines through all his teaching about the Christian life. Because we died with Christ (were united to him in his death), we are to put to death sin in our members (Col. 3:3, 5). Because we rose with Christ (were united to him in his resurrection), we are to seek the things that are above, where Christ is seated at the right hand of God (Col. 3:1). The indicative, as has often been noted, is always the basis of the imperative. As we were brought to Christ, so do we live in Christ: by grace. Those who were joined to Christ in the plan and purpose of God, were joined to him in the saving work that he accomplished. Something has happened: "You died, and your life is now hidden with Christ in God" (Col. 3:3). Christ did not die merely to make their salvation possible, but to save those who had been given him by the Father. The good Shepherd gives his life for the sheep: "I am the good shepherd; I know my sheep and my sheep know me—just as the Father knows me, and I know the Father—and I lay down my life for the sheep" (John 10:14).

Far from pandering to pride, Paul's doctrine of salvation by grace sweeps away all excuse for pride. It is the religion of human works that clings to some shreds of merit as an excuse for pride. Those who know grace know that they were chosen, not because they were deserving, but because of the mystery of God's electing love and through the power of his life-giving word. No redeemed sinner may boast before God. "It is because of him that you are in Christ Jesus, who has become for us wisdom from God—that is, our righteousness, holiness and redemption. Therefore, as it is written: 'Let him who boasts, boast in the Lord'" (1 Cor. 1:30–31).

What, then, is the place of the sovereignty of God in relation to preaching? It is the gospel of the sovereign plan of God that is the message of preaching, for the message of Christ crucified can be nothing else. It is the sovereignty

---

9. David is said to have served the *boulē* of God in his generation (Acts 13:36). In this context too, the meaning is not simply that David obeyed God's commandments, but that he fulfilled the divine purpose or calling. A *bouleutēs* is a member of council (Luke 23:50).

of the word of God that empowers preaching, for the preacher does not declare human opinions, but the word that is a hammer to smash the rock in pieces, and a fire to burn away all pride and kindle the flame of faith (Jer. 23:29). It is in the sovereignty of God that the preacher is called:

> The word of the LORD came to me, saying,
> "Before I formed you in the womb I knew you,
>   before you were born I set you apart;
>   I appointed you as a prophet to the nations." (Jer. 1:4–5)

Preachers today are not prophets bearing the promise of the coming of the Lord, or apostles laying the foundation of the new covenant church. They do not give us the Scriptures; that has been done. But by the unction of the Holy Spirit they do give us Christ from the Scriptures, and for that task they are chosen instruments in the hand of God. Paul reminds Timothy of the purpose and grace of God, given us in Christ Jesus before the beginning of time, but now revealed through the appearing of our Savior (2 Tim. 1:9–10). This is the gospel of which Paul was appointed a herald and an apostle and a teacher (v. 11). It is the "good deposit" that Paul has committed to Timothy (2 Tim. 1:14). Paul urges Timothy to "fan into flame the gift of God, which is in you through the laying on of my hands" (2 Tim. 1:6). The ministry of the gospel is not a mere leadership role or speaking assignment. It is part of the eternal plan of God to accomplish his purposes. Undershepherds are called by the good Shepherd who gathers his sheep, calling them to himself (1 Pet. 5:2–4). The word of God is still the power of God to salvation. To be in awe of God's work is the privilege and joy of every true preacher of the gospel. One plants, another sows, but God gives the increase (1 Cor. 3:7).

I once asked Dr. Martyn Lloyd-Jones, "Isn't it hard to tell whether you have preached in the power of the Spirit or the energy of the flesh?"

To my chagrin, he answered: "Not at all. When you preach in the energy of the flesh, you feel exalted, lifted up. When you preach in the power of the Spirit, you feel humbled, filled with awe at the work of God."

Soon after that interview, the Lord showed me the truth of the doctor's remark. In a stuffy tower room in a castle in Mittersill, Austria, I spoke late one afternoon to a group of weary students just back from hiking in the mountains. A roaring fire had made the room too warm and had burned up most of the oxygen. More sleepy than exalted in spirit, I began to speak. But I did present Christ, and learned again to be in awe at the work of a sovereign God. Not any eloquence or suggestion of mine, but the power of his word reduced that group to tears and earnest prayer. When the dinner bell sounded I hesitated, then descended the stairs to an empty dining hall, where I waited until at last students came straggling down. Clearly I needed that lesson! So do we all.

Index of Persons

Index of Subjects

345

Index of Scripture